THE ECCLESIASTICAL ARCHITECTURE

OF SCOTLAND

FROM THE EARLIEST CHRISTIAN TIMES TO THE
SEVENTEENTH CENTURY.

THE

ECCLESIASTICAL

ARCHITECTURE

OF SCOTLAND

FROM THE EARLIEST CHRISTIAN TIMES TO THE
SEVENTEENTH CENTURY

BY

DAVID MACGIBBON AND THOMAS ROSS

VOLUME III

JAMES THIN

1991

THE MERCAT PRESS : EDINBURGH

This is a facsimile of the edition published by
David Douglas in 1896

Published by
JAMES THIN, SOUTH BRIDGE
EDINBURGH

ISBN   1873644000

THE

ECCLESIASTICAL
ARCHITECTURE
OF SCOTLAND

FROM THE EARLIEST CHRISTIAN TIMES TO THE
SEVENTEENTH CENTURY

BY

DAVID MACGIBBON AND THOMAS ROSS

AUTHORS OF "THE CASTELLATED AND DOMESTIC ARCHITECTURE OF SCOTLAND"

VOLUME THREE

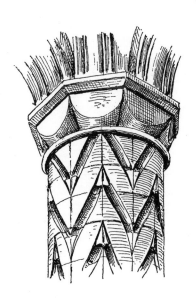

EDINBURGH: DAVID DOUGLAS

MDCCCXCVII

PREFACE.

In issuing the concluding Volume of this work, we take the opportunity to notice some points in the previous portions which have given rise to discussion.

In Vol. I. p. 297 we express disagreement with Mr. W. Galloway's opinion regarding the age of the chancel walls of St. Blane's, Bute. Mr. Galloway having asked for an opportunity of defending his views, we have pleasure in publishing his observations in the Appendix to this Volume.

Reference is made in Vol. II. p. 172 to Mr. T. L. Watson's theory regarding the vaulting of the lower church in St. Mungo's Cathedral, Glasgow. Having recently had the privilege, on the invitation of Mr. P. Macgregor Chalmers, of attending a meeting on the spot, when the usually obscure edifice was well lit up, and when it was shown by Mr. Chalmers that the points on which Mr. Watson based his opinion were untenable, we see no reason to believe that the beautiful design of the vaulting and the plan of the shrine were ever intended to be carried out in a mode different from that in which they are executed.

When treating of Melrose Abbey (Vol. II. p. 378) we ventured to criticise the views expressed by Mr. Chalmers in his work, *A Scots Mediæval Architect*. As Mr. Chalmers has been kind enough to approach us directly, taking exception to our remarks, we are glad to afford him, in an Appendix to this Volume, the opportunity he desires of stating his defence of his views.

Mr. Chalmers has done good service in drawing attention to some examples of Scottish mediæval architecture of a late date, which show a remarkable revival in point of design when compared with the general architecture of the country at the time.

From the series of examples given in this Volume there can scarcely be any question as to the gradual deterioration of ecclesiastical architecture which occurred generally throughout Scotland during the latter half of the fifteenth and the first half of the sixteenth centuries, and it is certainly surprising to find some exceptionally good work in a few structures of that period. Amongst these is the aisle of Car Fergus, in Glasgow Cathedral, the vaulting of which building is of about the date of 1500, as is evident from its containing several specimens of Archbishop Blacader's arms. The work is not all equal, but the vaulting has the groining (a rare kind of construction in Scotland at the period) well executed, and the bosses show a wonderful amount and variety of design. Some of the latter (such as that in the illustration kindly supplied by Mr. Chalmers in the Appendix) are admirable.

Mr. Chalmers has brought forward a considerable amount of evidence regarding the rood screen in St. Mungo's, which point to its being an exceptionally fine specimen of late pointed work. The vaulting and some other portions of the presbytery of Melrose Abbey are also classed by Mr. Chalmers in the same category.

The subject is an interesting one, and all students of Scottish architecture must feel indebted to Mr. Chalmers for drawing special attention to it. We trust the point will be further investigated.

There is one consideration connected with this revival to which we would draw attention, viz., that mentioned in the text (Vol. III. pp. 6 and 7) that a certain excellence in the carving and the design of the smaller features of the architecture observable in the later work may have been due to the foreign artists introduced at the time. We might, in view of the above circumstances, have given this remark a wider scope, so as to apply to such works as those above referred to and similar examples.

There is abundant evidence in the Exchequer Rolls that French master-masons were employed by James IV. and V. Thus the Merliouns,* a distinguished family of French master-masons, were in the royal service at Stirling in 1496, and members of the family are found at Linlithgow, Dunbar, Ravenscraig, Perth Church, &c. Latterly the king's *French master-mason* became a regular court appointment, and the office was held by several Frenchmen.†

This importation of foreign artists may perhaps account for some of the exceptionally good examples, especially in connection with places favoured by royalty; but a good deal of time would necessarily elapse before such work could become general. Hence the revival was limited, while the architecture generally gradually deteriorated or changed to Renaissance.

The monument of Bishop Kennedy, in St. Salvator's, St. Andrews (a design undoubtedly superior to the general Scottish work of the period), is probably a French example, both in design and execution.‡

Mr. Chalmers lays stress on the influence of Queen Margaret's marriage to James IV. as probably having produced some of the imitations of English perpendicular work found at Melrose and Linlithgow, and this may possibly have been the case.

In a review of Vol. II. in the *Glasgow Herald* attention

---

* See *The Castellated and Domestic Architecture of Scotland*, Vol. v. p. 530.

† *Ibid.* Vol. v. pp. 536, 538.

‡ See Mr. Chalmers' remarks in his work, p. 37.

was drawn to an error in the description of St. Andrews Cathedral (p. 31), where the restored illustration (Fig. 453) shows a single central shaft in the windows of the chapter house, instead of two coupled shafts. The shafts are gone, but the two bases are still traceable.

We have to thank the numerous clergymen, proprietors, custodians, and others, to whom it has been necessary to apply for permission to visit the various churches, for their assistance, which was always freely given. Our acknowledgments are also due to those gentlemen who have kindly continued their contributions to our work in the form of drawings and descriptions of churches, especially to Mr. T. S. Robertson, Dundee, and Mr William Galloway, Whithorn. Mr. R. Weir Schultz, London; Mr. John W. Small, Stirling; Mr. F. R. Coles, Edinburgh, and others have also been good enough to furnish us with several drawings and descriptions for this Volume, as is noted in the text.

To the Librarians of the Advocates' Library and the University Library of Edinburgh, and the Keeper of the National Museum of the Antiquaries of Scotland, we are greatly indebted for their valuable assistance.

We desire, further, to express our obligation to Mr. Alexander Ross, architect, Inverness, and Mr. R. Bruce Armstrong, for permission to use illustrations from their published works; and to Mr. W. Rae Macdonald, Edinburgh, and Mr. R. C. Walker, Dundee, for their aid in connection with the heraldry of the buildings and monuments.

EDINBURGH, *October* 1897.

CONTENTS.

Third or Late Pointed Period—Gradual transition from Middle
Pointed Style—Inferior, but peculiarly Scottish—Middle
Pointed buildings large and complete—Large Late Pointed
examples, chiefly restorations and collegiate, and designed
as single chambers without aisles—Some designed as cross
churches, but often unfinished—Characteristic features—
Eastern three-sided apse and pointed barrel vault, with
stone roof—Groins avoided, and contrivances in lieu thereof
—Windows low—Surface vaulting instead of ribs generally
used, but ribs sometimes applied to surface—Examples—
Stone roofs carefully wrought—Independent invention—
Examples of groined vaults—Decorated barrel vault, and
straight arches at Rosslyn—Forms of buttresses, pinnacles,
windows, tracery, &c.—Influences of Late English and
French Gothic—Doorways, porches, arms, central towers—
Monuments—Figure carving—Sacrament houses and smaller
features well executed, perhaps the work of French artists—
Collegiate churches spread over the whole country—Parish
churches converted into collegiate churches, ...   1–7

DESCRIPTIONS OF BUILDINGS.

Paisley Abbey (*Cluniac*), ... Renfrewshire, . 7
Dunkeld Cathedral (St. Columba's), . . Perthshire, . . 28
Iona Cathedral (*Cluniac* Abbey), . . Argyleshire, . . 47
St. Machar's Cathedral, ... Old Aberdeen, . 75
Trinity College Church, Edinburgh, . . Mid-Lothian, . . 89
Parish Church of St. John the Baptist, Perth, Perthshire, . . 104
    Do.   Dundee, ... Forfarshire, . . 123
Glenluce Abbey (*Cistercian*), .   .   . Wigtonshire, . . 132
Parish Church of Torphichen, .   .   . Linlithgowshire, . 139
St. Anthony's Chapel, Edinburgh, .   . Mid-Lothian, . . 145
Collegiate Church of St. Matthew, Rosslyn, Do. . . 149
    Do.   St. Mary, Dunglass, . Haddingtonshire, . 179
Parish Church of St. Marnan, Foulis Easter, Perthshire, . . 189
Collegiate Church of St. Salvator, St. Andrews, Fifeshire, . . 199
    Do.   St. Nicholas, Dalkeith, . Mid-Lothian, . . 205
Parish Church of St. Mungo, Borthwick, . Do. . . 214
    Do.   Our Lady, Ladykirk, . Berwickshire, . . 218

Collegiate Church of St. Mary and Holy
    Cross, Seton, ... Haddingtonshire, . 223
Collegiate Church of Arbuthnott, . . Kincardineshire, . 235
    Do.   Saints Mary and Ken-
    tigern, Crichton, ... Mid-Lothian, . . 243
Collegiate Church of St. John the Baptist,
    Corstorphine, ... Do. . . 250
Collegiate Church of St. Macrubha, Crail, . Fifeshire, . . 263
Parish Church of St. Mary, Whitekirk, . Haddingtonshire, . 269
    Do.   Mid-Calder, . . . Mid-Lothian, . . 279
King's College Chapel, ... Old Aberdeen, . 287
Church of the Carmelite Friars (St. Mary's),
    South Queensferry, ... Linlithgowshire, . 296
Collegiate Church of St. Bothan, Yester, . Haddingtonshire, . 309
Parish Church of the Holy Rood, Stirling, . Stirlingshire, . . 315
Collegiate Church of St. Saviour, Tullibardine, Perthshire, . . 330
    Do.   St. Mary, Maybole, . Ayrshire, . . 338
    Do.   St. Mary, Biggar, . Lanarkshire, . . 343
    Do.   Carnwath, . . . Do. . . 349
    Do.   St. Mary, Castle Semple, Renfrewshire, . 351
Church of the Franciscans or Greyfriars, Elgin, Morayshire, . . 356
    Do.   do.   do. Aberdeen, Aberdeenshire, . 358
Church of the Priory of St. Clement, Rowdil,
    Harris, ... Inverness-shire, . 363
Church of the Priory of St. Oran or St.
    Columba, Oronsay, ... Argyleshire, . . 372
Font of Church of St. Maelrubba, Skye, . Inverness-shire, . 381

EXAMPLES ARRANGED ALPHABETICALLY
BY COUNTIES.

ABERDEENSHIRE.
    Church of Kinkell, ... 383
    Do. Kintore, ... 386
    Chapel of St. Adamnan, Leask, ... 387

ARGYLESHIRE.
    Church of St. John the Baptist, Ardchattan, . . . 389
    Collegiate Church of St. Mund, Kilmun, . . . 390

AYRSHIRE.
    Alloway Kirk, ... 393
    Parish Church of Old Dailly, ... 394
    Do. Straiton, ... 396

PAGE

BANFFSHIRE.
Collegiate Church of St. Mary, Cullen, ... 398
Parish Church of St. John Evangelist, Deskford, . . . 406
Do. St. Bean, Mortlach, ... 408

BERWICKSHIRE.
Church of Abbey St. Bathans (Cistercian Nuns), . . . 410
Parish Church of Our Lady, Bassendean, ... 412
Do. Cockburnspath, ... 413
Do. Preston, ... 416

BUTESHIRE.
Church of St. Mary's Abbey, Rothesay, ... 418

DUMBARTONSHIRE.
Parish Church and Collegiate Church of St. Mary, Dumbarton, 423
Chapel at Kirkton of Kilmahew (St. Mahew), . . . 426

DUMFRIESSHIRE.
Canonby Priory (Austin Canons), Fragment of, . . . 431
Parish Church of Kirkbryde, ... 431
Church of St. Cuthbert, Moffat, ... 433
Do. Sanquhar, ... 435

FIFESHIRE.
Parish Church of Carnock, ... 436
Do. St. Serf, Dysart, ... 437
Do. St. Monan, Kilconquhar, ... 441
Do. St. Irenaeus, Kilrenny, ... 442
Do. Rosyth, ... 444
Church of the Dominicans or Blackfriars, St. Andrews, . 445
Do. St. Leonard's College, St. Andrews, . . . 448
Do. the Holy Trinity, St. Andrews, ... 451

FORFARSHIRE.
Parish Church of Airlie, ... 452
Do. Invergowrie, ... 454
Do. Mains, ... 455
Do. Maryton, ... 456
Do. Pert, ... 458
Do. St. Vigean's, ... 459

HADDINGTONSHIRE.
Church of the Red or Trinity Friars, Dunbar, . . . 462
Parish Church of St. Maelrubba, Keith, ... 465

KINCARDINESHIRE.
Church of St. Palladius, Fordoun, ... 468

PAGE

KIRKCUDBRIGHTSHIRE.
Church of Old Girthon, ... 469

LANARKSHIRE.
Priory of Blantyre (Austin Canons), ... 470
Parish Church of St. Michael, Covington, ... 472

LINLITHGOWSHIRE.
Parish Church of Auldcathie, ... 474

MID-LOTHIAN.
Collegiate Church of St. Triduan, Restalrig, ... 475

PEEBLESSHIRE.
Parish Church of Newlands, ... 479
Holy Cross Church, Peebles, ... 482
Church of St. Andrew, Peebles, ... 485

PERTHSHIRE.
Parish Church of St. Cathan, Aberuthven, ... 485
Church of St. Moloc, Alyth, ... 487
Do. St. Mechessoc, Auchterarder, ... 488
Do. Cambusmichael, ... 489
Abbey of Coupar (*Cistercian*), ... 491
Parish Church of Dron, ... 497
Church of Ecclesiamagirdle or Exmagirdle, or Glenearn, . 499
Parish Church of Forgandenny, ... 500
Abbey of Inchaffray (Austin Canons), ... 502
Collegiate Church of Innerpeffray, ... 507
Parish Church of Kinfauns, ... 513
Do. Meigle, Font of, ... 517
Collegiate Church of Methven, ... 519
Chapel of Moncrieff, ... 521
Parish Church of Wast-town, ... 522

RENFREWSHIRE.
Parish Church of Renfrew (Monument), ... 525
Parish Churches of Houston, St. Fillan's, and Kilmalcolm, . 527

SELKIRKSHIRE.
Parish Church of Selkirk, ... 529

WIGTONSHIRE.
Parish Church of St. Machutus, Wigton, ... 533

CHURCHES OF THE SIXTEENTH AND SEVENTEENTH CENTURIES.

PAGE

Mediæval Architecture terminated with the Reformation, 1560— Under James I. and Charles I. and II. a revival attempted— Two styles practised, one plain, the other somewhat ornate —Specimens of each—Influence of Domestic Architecture on Ecclesiastical—Picturesque examples, ... 534

The following churches of this period are arranged in alphabetical order :—

Parish Church of St. Drostan, Aberdour, .	Aberdeenshire,	.	535
Parish Churches of Anstruther, Easter and Wester, ...	Fifeshire,	. .	536
Parish Church of St. Mary, Auchterhouse, .	Forfarshire, .	.	541
Do. Aytoun, ...	Berwickshire,	.	543
Do. Balingry, . . .	Fifeshire,	.	543
Do. Blair, Blair-Atholl, .	Perthshire, .	.	544
Do. St. Brandan, Boyndie,	Banffshire, .	.	545
Do. St. Michael, Cupar, .	Fifeshire, .	.	547
Do. St. Bridget, Dalgety, . .	Do. .	.	549
Do. St. John, Dalry, .	Kirkcudbrightshire,		551
Do. Drainie and Michael Kirk,	Morayshire, .	.	553
Do. Durness, ...	Sutherlandshire,	.	557
Do. St. Cuthbert, East Calder,	Mid-Lothian, .	.	559
Parish Churches of Eassie and Nevay (St. Neveth), ...	Forfarshire, .	.	560
Pulpit from St. Cuthbert's Church, Edinburgh,	Mid-Lothian, .	.	562
Parish Church of St. Cavan, Feteresso, .	Kincardineshire,	.	562
Chapel of Fordel, ...	Fifeshire, .	.	565
Parish Church of Garvald, . . .	Haddingtonshire,	.	567
Do. St. John, Gamrie, .	Banffshire, .	.	567
Do. Gladsmuir, . .	Haddingtonshire,	.	569
Steeple of the Tron Church, Glasgow, .	Lanarkshire, .	.	571
Chapel of St. Mary, &c., Grandtully, .	Perthshire, .	.	571
Parish Church of Greenlaw, . .	Berwickshire,	.	574
Do. Insch, . . .	Aberdeenshire,	.	575
Do. Kemback, . .	Fifeshire, .	.	576
Do. Kilmaurs, Glencairn Monument at, . . .	Ayrshire, .	.	577
Do. Kinneil, . . .	Linlithgowshire,	.	578
Do. St. Bean's, Kinkell, .	Perthshire, .	.	579
Do. Kinnoull, Monument in, .	Do. .	.	580

			PAGE
Parish Church of Kirkoswald, . . .	Ayrshire,	. .	582
Do. Lauder, ...	Berwickshire,	.	582
Do. Leswalt, ...	Wigtonshire, .	.	585
Do. St. Colm, Lonmay, .	Aberdeenshire,	.	587
Do. Loudoun, Galston, .	Ayrshire,	. .	587
Do. Lyne, ...	Peeblesshire, .	.	589
Do. Morham, ...	Haddingtonshire,	.	591
Do. St. Fiacre or Fittack, Nigg,	Kincardineshire,	.	592
Do. Oldhamstocks, . . .	Berwickshire,	.	594
Do. St. Giles', Ormiston, .	Haddingtonshire,	.	596
Church of the Priory of Pittenweem, .	Fifeshire,	. .	599
Parish Church of Polwarth, . . .	Berwickshire,	.	601
Do. Prestonpans, Heraldic Panel from, . .	Haddingtonshire,	.	602
Do. St. Ethernan or Eddran, Rathan, . . .	Aberdeenshire,	.	604
Chapel and Castle of Southannan, West Kilbride, ...	Ayrshire,	. .	607
Parish Church of Stenton, ...	Haddingtonshire,	.	609
Do. Stow, ...	Mid-Lothian, .	.	611
Church at Terregles, ...	Kirkcudbrightshire,		615
Parish Church of St. Congan, Turriff, .	Aberdeenshire,	.	615
Do. Walston, ...	Lanarkshire, .	.	617
Do. Weem, ...	Perthshire,	. .	619
Do. Yester, ...	Haddingtonshire,	.	622
Specimen of Early Sculpture from Forteviot,	Perthshire,	. .	623
APPENDIX, ...			625

THE ECCLESIASTICAL ARCHITECTURE
OF SCOTLAND

FROM THE EARLIEST CHRISTIAN TIMES TO THE
SEVENTEENTH CENTURY.

VOLUME III.

THIRD OR LATE POINTED PERIOD.

In passing from the Middle Pointed to the Late Pointed periods in Scotland, we do not find any distinct break in the style of architecture such as exists between the First and Second Pointed periods. The middle pointed style passes by gentle gradation into the late pointed style, and there is some difficulty in fixing the period when the one ceases and the other begins. When buildings such as Melrose Abbey and Lincluden College are compared with Dunglass, Corstorphine, and other collegiate churches of the late period, the difference of style is very apparent, and it is at once seen that these edifices belong to different categories. But between such examples as Haddington Church and Paisley Abbey the distinction of style is not at first sight so striking. It is only when the whole character of the architecture is considered that it can be determined to which category each structure belongs. Although the line of division is thus to a certain extent arbitrary, there are some characteristics of the third pointed period which are peculiar to it, and render it a distinct and well marked epoch. This period, although inferior in many respects to those which preceded it, yet comprises more than any other certain elements which give it a claim to be considered peculiarly Scottish and national.

Many of the structures described in Vol. II. as belonging (in part at least) to the decorated period bear some resemblance to those of the same style in England. These edifices are mostly of considerable size, and contain all the usual divisions of choir, nave, and transept, nearly always with aisles. They are also generally vaulted with groined vaults, having wooden roofs above the vaults. The details of the buildings are likewise of similar character in both localities.

As in the preceding period, the large churches of the third pointed period in Scotland are nearly all restorations. No new churches of great size were undertaken. Some of the older large churches which had been damaged were reconstructed, but the new churches erected were almost

III.   A

entirely confined to parish or collegiate structures. The largest new church is that of Trinity College in Edinburgh, founded by the widowed queen of James II. Only a few of the larger of these churches have aisles, and are roofed with groined vaulting.

Most of the new edifices of the late pointed style in Scotland differ from those in England in many particulars. The Scottish churches are, as already stated, usually smaller in size, and consist of single compartments without aisles. Although frequently designed as cross churches, with choir, nave, and transepts, they are rarely finished, the choir or the choir and transepts being often the only portions carried out. The east end frequently terminates with a three-sided apse. This feature is almost entirely characteristic of the late pointed period. It undoubtedly owes its origin to the Scottish alliance and intercourse with France. But the leading and distinguishing feature of our late pointed style is the vaulting, the pointed barrel vault being almost universally employed. We have seen that a pointed barrel vault was used at Lincluden and Bothwell collegiate churches. It was, however, in the later edifices, after the middle of the fifteenth century, that that form of vault came into general use. This kind of arch was of simple construction, and was much employed in the castles of the period, being found convenient—first, because it was of easy construction; and second, because it could conveniently carry a roof composed of overlapping stones. This style of roof had the double advantage of being fireproof, and in the case of the castles, where it was often kept flat, of forming a platform from which the defenders could operate.

It has already been pointed out * that many features of domestic architecture were at this time imported into ecclesiastical architecture, and the above feature of the pointed barrel vault carrying a stone roof is the first and most important.

In carrying out this kind of vaulting in churches, several difficulties were encountered and had to be overcome. The most serious of these difficulties was the junction of the transepts, or side chapels, with the choir and nave. In the earlier Gothic churches this was managed by running the vault of the transepts or chapels into that of the nave, and forming a groin at the intersection. But the peculiarity of the late Scottish churches is that they carefully avoid all groins and intersections of arches. The junction of the vaults at the above intersections is, therefore, managed by a special contrivance, viz., by keeping the barrel vaults of the transepts or chapels quite apart from those of the central nave, the side vaults being stopped on gables carried up on arches in the line of the main side walls to receive them. The main nave vault is thus carried throughout the whole length of the central nave without a break, and where the opening into the transepts or chapels occurs, the main

* *The Castellated and Domestic Architecture of Scotland*, Vol. III. p. 25.

vault rests on an arch thrown across the side openings in the line of the main walls, and at a level below the springing of the main vault. The outer stone roofs of the transepts are also kept independent of that of the central nave, and do not mitre into it.

The windows of these churches, which have nearly always pointed arch-heads, are necessarily placed at a low level, so as to allow the point of the arch-head to come beneath the spring of the main vault. This is done so as to avoid even a small groin, such as would be required if the window arch-head were carried up into the main vault. The object is two-fold—first, to escape the difficulty of the intersection of the vaults ; and second, to avoid the small gablets over the windows and the small stone roofs and valleys which would be required at the junction of these with the main external stone roofs. The above features are all well exemplified at Ladykirk, Seton College, Corstorphine, and many other churches.

It should be borne in mind that the vaulting in England in the fifteenth and sixteenth centuries had also to some extent reverted to the plan of relying chiefly for strength on plain surface vaulting, and not on the ribs as in the earlier period. The example from Winchester Cathedral * helps to explain this. The intersection of the vaults is there very slight, and the numerous ribs introduced are almost all used ornamentally. This is also the case in the fan vaulting, so common in England in the fifteenth and sixteenth centuries, in which the ribs or tracery are applied as ornaments on the surface of the vaults.

Ornamental ribs are not uncommon in Scottish roofs. An early example, somewhat similar to that at Winchester, still exists over the presbytery of Melrose Abbey, where the intersection of the vaults is almost entirely abandoned, and numerous ornamental surface ribs are introduced. In later examples, however, the intersection of the vaults is completely given up, and any ribs employed are useless except as ornaments. Such are the roofs of St. Mirren's Chapel, Paisley, and the choir of Seton College.

An example of the shifts the builders were put to in order to escape intersecting vaults may be seen in the apse of Stirling Church. In other examples, such as Dunglass and Queensferry, the nave, choir, and transepts have walls carried up on the four sides of the crossing, against which the pointed barrel vaults are stopped, and access is furnished to the various arms of the church by small archways like doorways in the walls. At White-kirk the crossing is exceptional, having a groined vault ; but the choir, &c., have pointed barrel vaults, which stop upon walls at the crossing.

In the case of the apse of Linlithgow Church the difficulty of the intersection of the apse with the choir vault was avoided by sticking on the apse against the east end wall, like a large bow window. This

* See Vol. I. p. 61.

enabled the apse windows to be carried to a good height. Generally speaking the windows in the apse are very low, being kept down below the main arch, and admit little light, thus rendering the vault extremely dark, as, for instance, at Seton Church.

In most of the collegiate churches the barrel vaults supported a roof composed of carefully wrought flag-stones. These stones are arranged in courses, running from the eaves to the ridge, and every alternate course is higher than, and rests on, the edges of the intermediate courses. Each stone also overlaps the course which is below it in the slope of the roof. There is thus a considerable amount of cutting and fitting required, which is usually carefully executed. Sometimes each stone is hollowed in the centre, so as to carry the water away from the joints. The gutters are also wrought in stone on the same principle. Roofs of this description might evidently be made almost level, and in the case of many of the castles (as on the keep of Craigmillar Castle) that is done, and a platform for defence is thus created. In the churches, however, the stone roofs are usually pretty steep.

It is remarkable that this form of roof was a reproduction in Scotland, in the fifteenth century, of a fireproof form of construction which was much used in Provence in the eleventh and twelfth centuries. But in this country it was to all appearance an independent invention, as Provence in the fifteenth century was, architecturally speaking, very remote, and was cut off from Scotland by the intermediate styles of England and France.

It should be noted that the pointed barrel vault, although very general, was not universally employed in Scotland during the third period. One or two notable examples of well constructed groined vaults are to be found, such as the vaulting of Trinity College Church and that of "Blackader's Aisle" in Glasgow Cathedral. But these are exceptions to the general rule.

In Rosslyn College we have the finest example of the late Scottish forms of vaulting carried out to their fullest extent, together with some exceptional designs. This church differs from most of the other collegiate churches in having side aisles, and also in having groined vaults in the east end. The plan of the latter portion of the building, being copied from the arrangement at the east end of Glasgow Cathedral, has been carried out with groining, in imitation of the original; but in the other parts of the structure the vaulting conforms to that of the third pointed period in Scotland. The main central roof is covered with a continuous pointed barrel vault without a break, except an ornamental rib over each division of the bays. The soffits of each panel of the arch thus formed are carved with stars, fleur-de-lys, and other enrichments. The side aisles are also covered with a series of pointed barrel vaults. Each of these aisle vaults forms an extension of the main pier arch of the choir, carried across the aisle at right angles to the main choir. The Scottish plan of avoiding groins is thus adhered to. The above arrangement of the aisle vaults also enables the aisle windows to be carried up to a good height. The barrel vaults across the aisles rest on flat arches (made to resemble straight lintels), which run between the caps of the main piers and the responds against the walls. The whole construction recalls that of a castle with a large central hall roofed with a barrel vault, and having a series of side chambers entering off it, each covered with its separate barrel vault running at right angles to the main building. If the partitions between these side chambers were removed, and plain arches or lintels substituted, the construction would be exactly that of Rosslyn Church. Such a series of chambers, with barrel vaults running at right angles to a passage, is of common occurrence in the ground floors of the Scottish castles. An exceptional feature connected with the main vault of Rosslyn Church is that the same stones which form the interior arch also form the outside roof— the usual overlapping stone covering being omitted, possibly to avoid the extra weight. The exterior of the roof is thus curved like the interior.

During the late pointed period many varieties of details were indulged in. The buttresses are generally somewhat stunted. They are plain and solid, and have often rather elaborate canopies and corbels for statues placed on the front of the buttresses, without recessed niches. The buttresses have frequently numerous set-offs, and are generally finished with stunted square pinnacles having crocketed finials. The windows are almost always pointed, and contain simple tracery derived from the earlier styles. The copying of the forms of the older styles is specially noticeable in the windows and traceries.

At Ladykirk, the unusual form of elliptical windows is introduced, probably in order to admit as much light as possible at the haunches. As above explained, there are generally no aisles, and the windows, being kept down below the springing of the main arch, are, as usual, low, and here leave on the exterior a high space of blank wall above them.

The above form of construction does not require or admit of a triforium and clerestory. At Rosslyn, where there are side aisles, the side walls of the choir are carried up so as to permit of clerestory windows. The tracery is almost always set in the centre of the wall, and the same mouldings, usually double chamfers, are repeated in the reveal both on the inside and outside.

Where the choir, nave, and transepts have square ends, there is generally a large traceried window carried up in the gable under the barrel vault of the roof, by which the principal light in the church is obtained.

The details of the late pointed churches in Scotland have comparatively little connection with the late work either in England or France, but some signs exist of importations from both these countries.

At Melrose Abbey, Linlithgow Church and Palace, and a few other places, there are distinct indications of the influence of the perpendicular style of England; while the French influence is traceable in the apsidal terminations of the choir and occasionally of the transepts, and in some approaches to Flamboyant tracery. The latter influence may probably have also led to the crown-like terminations of some of the church towers. On the whole, however, it will be found that the details of the Scottish late pointed period are peculiar to itself, and are principally founded on survivals and revivals of details of the earlier styles.

The doorways, for instance, are generally of the old, round-headed form, with late foliage and enrichments. The common English perpendicular doorway, with four-centred arch enclosed in a square frame, is never met with; and although elliptical or three-centred arches occur over doorways and windows, the four-centred arch-head is never used. Fan tracery vaulting is also entirely absent in Scotland.

Porches to doorways are occasionally introduced, as at Aberdeen Cathedral and Whitekirk; and smaller porches are formed by arches thrown between buttresses, as at Rosslyn and Trinity College Churches.

Coats of arms are very commonly carved on shields at this period, and are often useful in determining the dates of portions of the buildings, monuments, &c.

A tower is generally erected, or intended, over the crossing, and is carried on the four walls, which, as we have seen, were generally built in this position, in order to stop the four barrel vaults of the different divisions of the church. The towers are somewhat stunted, and they are usually finished with short, stunted spires, having a number of lucarnes, or small dormer windows, inserted in them. The latter feature was probably imported from France or the Low Countries, where similar dormers abound in late work.

Monuments are of more common occurrence than in the earlier periods. They are frequently placed in arched and canopied recesses, which are ornamented with crocketed labels and finials. The carving of the crockets and other foliage is, doubtless, founded on the conventional perpendicular foliage of England. This, however, is mixed with a considerable revival of carving, copied from older work.

The introduction of numerous small figures of men and animals is a peculiarity of the period generally, and is found both at home and abroad. Much of the carving of Rosslyn Church is of this description, and similar carving may be seen at Melrose Abbey and Stirling Castle, and on the rood screens in Glasgow Cathedral and Lincluden College. Elaborate figure carving is common in other countries at this period, as at Henry VII.'s Chapel, Westminster, and in the churches of France and Spain.

Richly carved sacrament houses, such as are occasionally introduced, are a further indication of the taste for minute sculpture which prevailed at this time. It is not unusual to find in late buildings that some of the smaller features, such as sedilias, piscinas, and heraldic work, are well designed and carved with much spirit.   Perhaps some of this good carving may be due to the French masons who, we know, were numerous in Scotland during the reigns of James IV. and especially of James V.*

During the period now under consideration, the structures chiefly erected were, as already mentioned, either parish or collegiate churches. A considerable number of the latter were built and endowed by private founders during the fifteenth and sixteenth centuries.   A list of the collegiate churches existing in Scotland at the Reformation is given by Dr. David Laing in his preface to *The Collegiate Churches of Mid-Lothian.†*   They amounted, according to that list, to thirty-eight in number, and were spread over nearly every county in Scotland.   Only two of these had been founded in the fourteenth century, the remaining thirty-six being all founded during the fifteenth century and the first half of the sixteenth century.

The structures connected with a considerable number of these college churches are more or less perfectly preserved, and these, as well as several others not mentioned by Dr. Laing, are described in the following pages.

Many of these establishments had previously existed as parish churches or chapels before they were enlarged and made collegiate, and endowed by the munificence of the founders.

PAISLEY ABBEY, RENFREWSHIRE.

Paisley Abbey is fortunate in having found in the Very Rev. J. Cameron Lees, D.D., formerly one of the ministers of the parish, so able a historian.   We are largely indebted to his work, *The Abbey of Paisley, 1163-1878*, for the following historical notices.

The Abbey was founded by Walter, son of Alan, the High Steward of Scotland, who had accompanied David I. from Shropshire, and received lands from him in Renfrewshire.   Having resolved to follow the example of his patron, and found a monastery on his estate, Alan entered into an agreement with Humbold, prior of Wenlock Abbey, in the native county of his family, to establish at "Passelay" a house of the Cluniac Order of Benedictines, being the same order as the house at Wenlock.   Humbold therefore, in 1169, brought thirteen monks from the parent house, and, having settled them in Renfrewshire on an island of the Clyde called the King's Inch, returned to Wenlock.   There would at that time appear to have been a very ancient church in existence at Paisley, dedicated to St. Mirinus, an Irish saint of the sixth century, who had been a disciple of the great school of St. Comgal at Bangor. A new monastery was now to supersede the establishment of St. Mirin,

---

* *The Castellated and Domestic Architecture of Scotland*, Vol. v. p. 536.

† The Bannatyne Club, 1861.

but the name of the ancient saint was preserved in the dedication of the abbey.

It was dedicated to the Blessed Virgin; to St. James, the patron saint of the Stewarts; to St. Milburga, the patron of the monks of Wenlock; and to St. Mirinus, the Celtic missionary of the locality. The monastery was at first established as a priory; but, in 1245, it was raised to the rank of an abbey by Pope Honorius III.

The establishment was well endowed, and during the first half of the thirteenth century it was thoroughly consolidated under Abbot William, who presided from 1225 to 1248. During the prosperous reigns of Kings Alexander II. and III. the church was erected, but of the work of that period (the thirteenth century) there remain only a portion of the west front and part of the south wall of the nave, including the south-east doorway to the cloister, and three windows. The structure appears to have suffered severely during the War of Independence. It stood in the vicinity of Elderslie, the lands of Sir William Wallace, and doubtless met with a similar savage treatment to that allotted to the patriot leader. It is stated to have been burnt by the English in 1307, and the burning would appear to have led to a very complete destruction of the edifice, as the portions of the original work which survive are very small.

The connection of the Stewart family with the abbey continued till, through the marriage of Walter with Margery, daughter of Robert the Bruce, the Stewarts succeeded to the throne. The earlier Stewarts were all buried in the abbey, which also contains the tomb of Robert III.

In consequence of the destruction of the monastery, caused by the wars with England, the buildings long remained, like other structures in Scotland at that period, in a dismantled condition; but gifts having been received from the Bishops of Argyle and Glasgow to aid the monks in their distress, and to assist in restoring the fabric, operations were begun. Part of this work was apparently carried out by Bishop Lithgow (1384-1433), who was buried, by his own desire, in the north porch, where the inscription to his memory is still preserved. The chief part, however, of the rebuilding of the Abbey Church was carried out under Abbot Thomas de Tervas (1445-1459). This abbot obtained the privilege of having a tavern and selling wine within the gates of the monastery, and is believed to have raised money thereby for the reconstruction of the church. According to the ancient chronicle of Auchenleck, he found the place in ruin and the "kirk unbiggit." He carried up the triforium and clerestory, and finished the roof. He also erected a great portion of the steeple, and built a stately gatehouse. Having completed the building of the church, he proceeded to Rome, in order there to procure suitable furnishings, and brought back adornments of sumptuous character—jewels, cloths of gold and silver, precious books, the "statliest Tabernkle in al Scotland," and "ane lettren of brass."

During the fifteenth century many altars were erected and endowed by the burgesses, and the Chapel of St. Mirin, which occupies part of the site of the south transept, was erected in 1499, and endowed by James Crawford of Kylwynet, a burgess of Paisley, and his wife.

At the decease of Abbot Tervas, Pope Pius ii. decreed that the disposition of the office of abbot and of the whole revenues of the monastery should fall to the Pope. A commendator thus came to be appointed, and the rights of the abbey began to be invaded. However, Abbot George Shaw (1472-1498) endeavoured to guard the possessions of the monastery from encroachments. He also succeeded in having the village of the abbey erected into a burgh, with the usual privileges. Abbot Shaw likewise improved the buildings of the abbey. He erected a refectory and other structures, and reared a lofty tower over the principal gate, and enclosed the grounds and gardens of the convent with a wall of ashlar, about one mile in circuit, and adorned it with statues and shields.

Abbot Shaw placed his arms on several parts of this wall, and in the middle of the north portion he inserted three shields—the central one bearing the royal arms; that on the right the Stewart arms, for the founder; and that on the left the abbot's own arms. He also erected a tablet on the north-west angle, containing his name and the date of erection. Only a small portion of this wall remains, but the panels containing the royal arms and the inscription are preserved in the Coates Museum. The latter is as follows :—

> " Ya callit ye Abbot Georg of Schawe
> About yis Abbay gart make yis wav
> A thousande four hundereth zheyr
> Auchty ande fywe the date but veir
> [Pray for his saulis salvacioun]
> Yat made thys nobil fundacioun." *

Mr. Chalmers † is of opinion that this inscription was designed by John Morow, whose name appears on a tablet at Melrose Abbey.‡ "The character of the lettering in design and workmanship is the same as at Melrose. The references to the building operations, the poetical form of the compositions, the manner in which the names are introduced—'Callit was I,' and 'ye Callit'—and the devout expressions with which they close, make it clear that the inscriptions are the work of the same author." Whether that is so, or whether the inscriptions simply reflect the style, both literary and artistic, of the period is questionable. In any case, the idea is ingenious. Mr. Chalmers points out that the fifth line, which is erased, was probably cut out by the Reformers, as being out of keeping with their religious views, while the remainder indicates the care with which the historically valuable part was preserved.

* *St. Mirin*, David Semple, p. v.
† *A Scots Mediæval Architect*, p. 14 (P. M'Gregor Chalmers).
‡ See *ante*, Vol. ii. p. 378.

The days of Abbot John Hamilton (1525-1544), who became Bishop of Dunkeld, and was afterwards promoted to be Archbishop of St. Andrews, were evil for the monastery of Paisley, as for all other similar institutions in the country. When driven from St. Andrews, the archbishop sought safety at Paisley ; but that house being sacked and burnt by the Reformers, he had to take refuge at Dumbarton Castle, where he was made prisoner, and afterwards executed at Stirling.

The Master of Sempill had been appointed bailie of the monastery, and, at the dissolution, the whole of the church property was handed over to Lord Sempill. The property finally came into the possession of Lord Claud Hamilton, nephew of the archbishop, and the monastic buildings were converted into the "Place of Paisley," the residence of the Abercorn family. *

Before the Reformation the monastery consisted of the church, the cloister, and the conventual buildings. The church (Fig. 953) comprised a long aisleless choir, a nave with aisles, a north transept, a south transept, with St Mirin's Chapel attached to the south of it, and a tower and spire over the crossing.

The choir can still be traced, as the walls remain standing to the height of 9 feet, and contain an elegant sedilia and piscina. The choir measures, internally, about 124 feet in length by 22 feet in width. It may be questioned whether the choir was ever finished during the restoration. The walls present rather the appearance of having been abandoned at a certain stage in the progress of their erection than of a building which had fallen into ruin. They stand at a uniform level, marked by a string course all round, and have not the irregular heights generally found in ruins. The building is of fifteenth century work, and doubtless occupies the place of an earlier choir, which had been demolished.

The wall at the east end of the nave, which separates it from the transept, is of a substantial kind, and may have been erected when the structure was restored in the fifteenth century, with the intention of rendering the nave a complete church, until the transept and choir were restored. The latter seems never to have been carried into effect, but to have been in progress when all work was interrupted by the Reformation.

There are no indications at the junction of the choir and transept of the large piers which would naturally be built so as to correspond with those at the west side of the crossing (Fig. 954). The fine sedilia, although greatly mutilated (Fig. 955), is the principal feature in the eastern part of the edifice. It is 11 feet 2 inches long, and contains four seats, contrary to the usual practice, which is to have three seats. The design is elegant, and resembles that of the sedilia at St. Monan's, Fifeshire. Adjoining the

* The "place" is illustrated and described in *The Castellated and Domestic Architecture of Scotland*, Vol. v. p. 11.

sedilia is the piscina, the basin of which is broken, but the aperture is still visible. The recess, which has an angled head, slopes backwards.

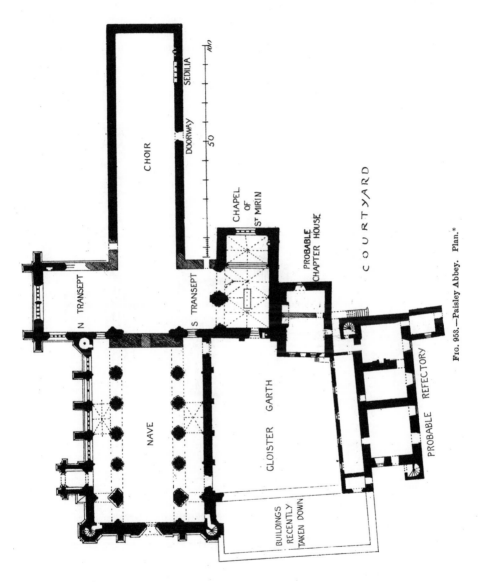

Fig. 953.—Paisley Abbey. Plan.*

In this respect it resembles one at Auchterarder. On each side are two small recesses, about 12 inches wide, for holding the sacred vessels.

* We are indebted to Mr. T. S. Robertson for assistance in connection with this Plan.

The north transept (see Fig. 954) is in ruins, but the north wall, with the remains of a fine traceried window (Fig. 956), still exists, as well as a traceried window in the west wall. These traceries were restored a few years ago. The mode in which the turrets at the angles above the buttresses are corbelled out recalls similar features at Dunkeld Cathedral. These turrets resemble the roofed bartizans of castellated structures.

Fig. 954.—Paisley Abbey. Junction of Nave with North Transept.

The south transept is also in ruins, and the tower and spire have disappeared. The Chapel of St. Mirin, however, is still well preserved, but the openings connecting it with the south transept have been built up.

The nave is the only part of the main divisions of the church which survives as a whole. It measures, internally, 92 feet in length by 60 feet in width, and contains six bays, divided by massive piers, all surmounted by a triforium and clerestory. There is a porch on the north side and two doorways from the cloister on the south side.

The oldest portion of the building is, undoubtedly, the eastern part of the south wall of the south aisle of the nave, where it adjoins the transept. This portion of wall consists of three bays (Fig. 957), containing the south-east doorway from the cloister to the nave, and three pointed windows in the upper part. The doorway is of the transition style, having a round arch-head, with numerous bold mouldings springing from carved and foliaged

Fig. 955.—Paisley Abbey. Sedilia in Choir.

caps with square abaci (Fig. 958). The windows above are very simple in style, and are apparently early first pointed work. This part of the building probably dates from the first half of the thirteenth century. The western portion of the south aisle of the nave (Fig. 959) and the whole of the south clerestory (see Figs. 957 and 959) are evidently portions of the restored church of the fifteenth century. The south aisle wall contains the south-west and south-east doors from the nave to the cloister. The windows of the south wall have the sills placed at a high level, so as to admit of the roof of the cloister walk being placed against it. The corbels which supported the roof still exist, and are shown in the sketches.

Fig. 956.—Paisley Abbey. Windows in North Transept.

FIG. 957.—Paisley Abbey.   East Part of South Side of Nave.

The west end of the nave (Fig. 960) is also in part amongst the ancient portions of the structure. The western entrance doorway is clearly, from the style of its architecture, a work of the thirteenth century. The door-

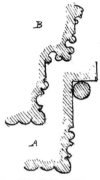

FIG. 958.—Paisley Abbey.
South-East Doorway in
Cloister.

A. Door Jamb.
B. Arch Moulding.

piece projects, and has a nook shaft on the projecting angles. The doorway is a single pointed opening, deeply recessed, with a series of free shafts in the jambs, having rounded and moulded caps, and the arch mouldings are arranged in square orders. The outer order contains a dog-tooth ornament. A sharply pointed arch flanks the doorway on each side, and has similar shafts and mouldings to those of the central opening. The aisle windows of the west front also belong to the first pointed period. The thin nook shafts, with moulded caps having round abaci and central bands, are all in the style of the thirteenth century.

The upper portion of the west front above the two large windows is undoubtedly of considerably later date. The design of the west front, which contains above the doorpiece two large windows, with pointed niches and small circles inserted between the arch-heads, is probably original, but the upper portion and gable, including the large traceried window, are doubtless part of the restoration of the fifteenth century. The tracery of the two central windows is peculiar, and may possibly be of the fourteenth century, but that of the large upper window is later, probably of the same period as the restoration of the interior of the nave. The tracery of the large upper window is a specimen of the late kind of design employed in Scotland in the fifteenth century. The change of style caused by the restoration of the fifteenth century is well marked in the interior at the west end of the nave. The first or western bay of the main arcade is original (Figs. 961 and 962), including the first arches (one on each side), the first pillars and the arches between them, and the aisle responds. These pillars and arches are of large dimensions and first pointed section (Fig. 963), and appear to have been designed to carry western towers, but a part of their thickness has been cut off next the choir. A portion of the triforium wall, a piece of the string course over the main arcade, and the corbelled vaulting shaft in the angle as high as the top of the triforium, are also parts of the original structure. The later work has been joined to the above old parts in a very awkward manner. The wall over the large pillars has been thinned on the side next the nave, and the different width and sections of the mouldings have not been properly adjusted, the result being that part of the older moulding is left at the springing of the second arch on the north side, and the mouldings of the later section are butted against it (see Fig. 961).

FIG. 959.—Paisley Abbey. West Part of South Side of Nave.

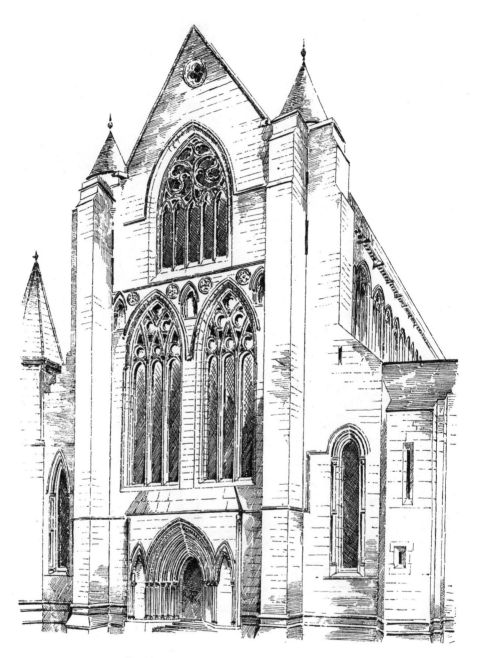

FIG. 960.—Paisley Abbey. West End of Nave: Exterior.

FIG. 961.—Paisley Abbey. West End of Nave and Part of North Side.

FIG. 962.— Paisley Abbey.   West End of Nave and Part of South Side.

There are signs of further alteration above the west arch. A clumsy new string course is introduced, which slightly changes its section after passing along half a bay. A second vaulting shaft is carried up in the angle beside the original one as high as the triforium arch and there stops. The first triforium arch, which is pointed (all the others being round), abuts against the wall in an awkward manner (see Fig. 961), the original design being changed.

FIG. 963.—Paisley Abbey.
West Piers and Respond in Nave.

The cap of the west pier on the north side belongs to the first pointed work, while the corresponding cap on the south side (see Fig. 962) and all the other caps belong to the restoration of the fifteenth century. The above cap and all the later caps in the nave have the upper mouldings run in a straight line without any break, while the lower mouldings break round the section of the piers (Fig. 964).* A moulded shaft, considerably off the perpendicular, rises from the top of the above cap to the string course at the junction of the old and the restored wall.

The piers of the nave, except the west piers, are of a clustered form not uncommon in late work in Scotland. The caps and main arches have good mouldings, and might be about the date of the restoration of St. Giles', Edinburgh (which they resemble), in the early part of the fifteenth century.

The design of the triforium is very remarkable (see Figs. 961 and 962), consisting of large segmental arches the same width as the main arches, springing from short clustered piers introduced between them. Each arch is filled in with two pointed arches resting on a smaller central shaft. These arches and the spandril between them are treated with bold cusping.

The triforium of the nave of Dunkeld Cathedral somewhat resembles that at Paisley Abbey. It contains a series of semicircular openings filled with similar pointed arches and cusping, but the work at Paisley is superior, and would appear to be the earlier of the two. In neither church is there any vaulting shaft to divide the bays.

The clerestory is probably designed in imitation of that of Glasgow Cathedral. It is divided into two pointed arches in each bay. These spring from a series of clustered shafts with round moulded caps, which have an early character, but are evidently late imitations of early work. The exterior views (see Figs. 957 and 959) show that each clerestory window contains a central shaft, with two cusped arches and quatrefoil in the arch-head.

* From a Sketch by Mr. T. S. Robertson.

The parapets of the nave and nave aisles are evidently, from the style of the mouldings and ornaments, of late date.

There seems to be no reason to doubt that, as above stated, the upper portions of the nave were carried out about the time of Bishop Tervas, in the middle of the fifteenth century. The earlier part of the restoration, including the main piers and arches, and perhaps the tracery of the two lower windows of the west front, were possibly executed by Bishop

FIG. 964.—Paisley Abbey. Pier of Nave.

Lithgow, who built the north porch, and the completion of the nave was carried out by Bishop Tervas. A striking peculiarity of the interior of the nave is a series of large corbels (see Figs. 961 and 962), which project from the spandrils of the triforium arcade. The object of these corbels appears to have been to enable a passage, which is formed in the interior of the clerestory windows, but does not run through the wall in a straight line from end to end as is usual, to be carried round the solid piers introduced between the windows. These projections recall, by the small corbels arranged in rows into which they are divided, the corbels generally used for the support of the bartizans of castles. Each of the large corbels springs at its lowest point from the sculptured grotesque figure of a man or animal. Dr. Lees states (p. 209) that these figures "were mostly the work of Thomas Hector, a sculptor who lived at Crossflat, and whom the abbot retained for his skill in his art." One of the corbels on the south side (near the west end) represents a man wearing the garb of Old Gaul. It may be mentioned that a somewhat similar gallery exists in Rouen Cathedral. It is carried round the piers of the nave on the side next the aisles, and is supported on shafts springing from corbels. This gallery has a light stone parapet resting on it. The design is of the thirteenth century, and is elegantly carried out; but it has, notwithstanding, a rather heavy appearance. It must be admitted that the projecting corbels at Paisley are clumsy, and considerably mar the effect of the interior. There appears to have been a parapet in front of the clerestory passage opposite the windows, and a similar parapet may have been carried round the large corbels, otherwise walking round them would have been dangerous. This would add still more to the heaviness of their appearance. Vaulting shafts are carried up between the windows of the clerestory, but the buttresses being very light, a vaulted roof has apparently not been contemplated. The present plaster vaulting is modern. The north wall of the nave aisle, except the doorway of the north porch, which is of first pointed work, has been rebuilt in the fifteenth century. The ingoing of the window jambs and arches consists, both on the inside and outside of the wall, of a great hollow, with the tracery set in the centre of the wall. The large north porch (shown in Billings' work) was taken down in 1863, in order to be erected anew, in what was considered a finer style. The porch contains the tomb of Bishop Lithgow, who selected this porch as his burial-place, and was interred there in 1433. Some of the tracery in the aisle windows is good for the period, like that in some of the windows of Dunkeld Cathedral, which building (as above mentioned) has considerable affinity with Paisley Abbey Church.

St. Mirin's Aisle (Fig. 965), as already pointed out, occupies the south end of the south transept, and was erected in 1499. It is a chapel 48 feet 3 inches long by 23 feet wide, having a vaulted roof about 32 feet 6 inches high. The main vault, like that of so many structures of the latter part of the fifteenth century, consists of a pointed barrel vault, the curve of which is drawn from a point lower than the springing of the arch, and thus forms an angle at the junction with the side walls. The surface of the vault is strengthened with a series of ribs, most of which spring from corbels in the side walls. The ribs are arranged so as to cross one another at the ridge, as if the roof were

Fig. 965.—Paisley Abbey. St. Mirin's Chapel, looking East.

groined; but they are almost entirely ornamental. The mouldings of the corbels are well designed, and show an imitation of first pointed work. The corbels being at a lower level than the top of the wall, the ribs project considerably in passing that point. The ridge has a bold rib enriched with carved bosses, and one of the transverse ribs is divided into two branches, so as to avoid descending on the top of the large arch in the north wall. There is a large pointed window in the east end, having jambs with single shafts (like the clerestory of the church). It has mullions dividing it into four lights, and the arch-head is filled with good simple tracery. Beneath this window runs a frieze 1 foot 8 inches broad, partly carved, with groups of figures showing, as discovered by Dr. Lees,* events in the life of St. Mirin. The east end of the chapel, where the altar stood, is raised four steps above the western part. The west wall contains an outer doorway from the cloister court, and there is a window with simple tracery above it; a curious large ambry adjoins the door in the outer wall. The chapel was connected with the south transept by two wide archways, now built up. There is a piscina near the east end (Fig. 966), with three-sided head, like that in the choir.

Above the vaulting of St. Mirin's Chapel, and in the angle formed by the sloping roof, there is introduced a chamber, with a pointed barrel vault, about 12 feet wide and nearly 10 feet high, to the apex of its sharply pointed vault. The three sides of this chamber thus nearly form an equilateral triangle. Like the chapel below, it is 48 feet in length. It is lighted by trefoil headed windows in the gables. Access to this chamber, which may have been occupied by one or more priests, is obtained from the adjoining buildings. It is to be regretted that the south and south-east sides of St. Mirin's Chapel are concealed from view by buildings of a poor description. It will be observed that the construction of the roof of St. Mirin's bears considerable analogy with that of Lincluden Abbey, although later in its features. There is a similar double vault over both these buildings, with a small chamber between them. At Lincluden the lower vault was (if it ever was completed) of a genuine groined construction, while at St. Mirin's the ribs were only imitative. The roof of St. Mirin's Chapel was clearly intended to be formed of stone slabs, resting on the pointed arch, but has never been carried out, the present roof being slated.

On the floor of this chapel there now stands an ornamental altar tomb (see Fig. 965), which was found lying in fragments near the abbey by Dr. Boog, one of the ministers of the parish, who, in 1817, had it brought here and put together again. It supports a recumbent female figure, believed to be the effigy of Margery, daughter of King Robert I., and mother of Robert II. The head of the figure is surmounted by a large cusped canopy, placed in a horizontal position, on the end of which is carved a

* Lees' *Paisley Abbey*, p. 211.

crucifixion. The pedestal is covered with a series of Gothic compartments, in each of which there is carved a shield, enriched with heraldic blazons and figures of ecclesiastics. The panels at the west end (Fig. 967) contain— the first the fess chequé of the Stewarts between three roses; the third the fess chequé, surmounted of a lion rampant, and the central one, two keys saltierwise, between two crosiers in pale.

Mr. Semple * is of opinion that the monument is made up of fragments from various quarters. On each side there are nine full compartments of

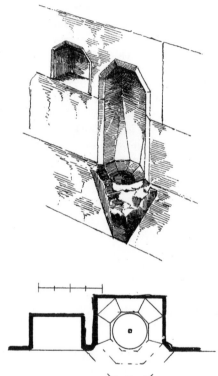

an oblong or oval form, and one half compartment at each end. At the foot the compartments are empty. On the right side the 1st compartment contains a bishop with crosier; the 4th, a bishop at prayer, and, on a scroll, the name Robert Wyshart (Bishop of Glasgow). On the left, the 1st compartment contains a bishop celebrating, with the name Johes D. Lychtgow (Abbot of Paisley); the 4th, an abbot at prayer, with the name of Abbot Lythgow repeated. Several compartments contain monks at prayer, and others are blank. Mr. Semple thinks that the left side may be part of Abbot Lithgow's monument, and the right side part of that of Bishop Wishart.

Of the cloisters and conventual buildings few traces remain; but the outline of the cloister court is preserved. It is surrounded (see Fig. 953)

FIG. 966.—Paisley Abbey.
Piscina in St. Mirin's Chapel.

with post-Reformation structures, occupying the site of the chapter house, refectory, &c. These were converted into the "place of Paisley," as the residence of the Abercorn family, which has been already fully described.†
These buildings probably contain portions of the walls of the refectory and other conventual structures erected by Abbot Shaw at the end of

* St. Mirin's, p. 23.
† See The Castellated and Domestic Architecture of Scotland, Vol. v. p. 11.

the fifteenth century. The western side of the cloister buildings was removed about twenty years ago, in order to widen the adjoining street. The wall, gatehouse, &c., erected by Abbot Shaw, have now almost entirely disappeared.

The cloistral buildings were much altered and added to in 1675 by the Earl of Dundonald, and fitted up as a mansion house, and they still bear traces of considerable splendour in panelled walls, with stone fireplaces and ornamental ceilings. One of the latter on the upper floor is a fine example of the plaster and painted decoration of the period.

Turning to the ground Plan, it seems highly probable that the walls are, in part at least, of pre-Reformation date, and that we have here

Fig. 967.—Paisley Abbey. End of Altar Tomb in St. Mirin's Chapel.

part of the work of Abbot Shaw, who erected a refectory and other buildings at the end of the fifteenth century. It will be observed that the main wall of the south range, running east and west, is very thick (4 feet to 5 feet), while the outside wall, forming the south side of the cloister, is only about 2 feet thick. The latter was probably erected when the place became a mansion house, in order to form a passage, and thus obviate the necessity of passing through the rooms, while the thick wall was the original outside wall of the refectory or of cellars below it. The south wall of this building also probably consists in part of the south wall of the refectory, but the large windows in it are, doubtless, insertions.

The building marked as chapter house on the Plan occupies the position in which that chamber would likely be. It is now divided into two, and has lost all traces of its ecclesiastical purpose—one side being used as a bottling store and the other as a stable. There is a large fireplace in the north wall, of distinctly Gothic design. That is not a usual feature in a chapter house; but in the sacristy over the chapter house of Glasgow Cathedral there is a large fireplace. At Paisley, the arrangement may have been reversed. The vestry may have been on the ground floor and the chapter house above. This building is at present some five stories in height, the upper floors being reached by the wheel stair shown on the Plan. It is from this high building that the chamber over St. Mirin's is reached, which is a fair indication that this chapter house tower, as it may be called, is as old as St. Mirin's. The same stair also accommodates the refectory range of buildings on the south side of the cloister, which are three stories in height, and have another stair at the west end.

It is thought by some that the first central tower erected over the crossing was of inferior workmanship and gave way. Another central tower is believed to have been erected by Abbot Tervas. This tower probably fell during the siege by Lennox and Glencairn, no doubt destroying much of the choir and transept in its fall. It has been mentioned above that western towers appear to have been contemplated. Possibly it may be one of these to which Martine, when speaking of John Hamilton, Archbishop of St. Andrews, refers when he says, "At which church [Paisley] he built a prettie handsome steeple, which fell before it was well finished." *

It is thought that the body of Archbishop Hamilton was buried in the abbey, and a tablet in the church looks as if it marked his grave. It contains his arms and initials, J. H., and "the motto he assumed, which contrasts strangely with his troubled life, 'Misericordia et pax.'"

Several monuments with inscriptions of sixteenth century date exist in the building. On the west buttress of the north transept, at 21 feet in height, is the shield of the Stewarts, with a pastoral staff and the word "Stewart."

One of the south piers of the nave is called the Cathcart pillar, having carved upon it a shield with the Cathcart arms (see Fig. 964). This is believed to be a memorial of Sir Allan Cathcart, one of the knights who sailed for the Holy Land with Bruce's heart. The heart was brought back by Sir Allan, and buried at Melrose.

DUNKELD CATHEDRAL, Perthshire.

Situated in the beautiful, though rugged, glen which forms the pass to the Highlands from the fertile lowlands of Perthshire, this grey and

* Martine's *Reliquiæ Divi Andreæ.*

venerable ruin adds an unexpected and charming interest to the lovely scenery of the locality. The mountain range through which the pass penetrates long formed a barrier to the access of the Scottish kings to the Celtic provinces further north, and the nearness of the Highland clans was a constant source of menace to the Church. For that reason the bishop's palace had to be constructed as a fortified stronghold ; hence, perhaps, the name of Dunkeld, the fort of the Keledei or Culdees.

After the destruction of Iona by the Norsemen in the beginning of the ninth century, Dunkeld was selected by the King of the Picts as a secure place, remote from the sea, and comparatively safe from the attacks of the Vikings, in which a mother church in lieu of Iona might be established. To this retreat a portion of the relics of Columba were brought by King Kenneth Macalpine in 850, and here he resolved to place the abbot of his new monastery as bishop over the Church in the territories of the Southern Picts, with a view to the ready reorganisation of the Scottish monasteries, so that they should form one diocese under one bishop.*

But the primacy of the Pictish Church did not remain long at Dunkeld, being transferred in the end of the ninth century to Abernethy, on the south side of the Frith of Tay.

The abbots in those days had become great lay proprietors, having lawful wives, and succeeding to the benefices of their abbacies by hereditary descent. One of these lay abbots of Dunkeld married a daughter of Malcolm II., and it is remarkable that it was by their descendants that the religious order in Scotland was changed. The new order of things, which had been initiated by St. Margaret, was continued by her son, Alexander I., who, in 1107, created two new bishoprics in the more remote and Celtic portion of his kingdom, the first being that of Moray, and the second that of Dunkeld. Alexander I. also brought, in 1115, a body of canons regular to Scone Abbey, and a few years later he established the same order in the diocese of Dunkeld. He also, in 1122, introduced canons regular to a monastery he had built on an island in Loch Tay, and, in 1123, founded the monastery of Inchcolm, and introduced the same order there.†

The Cathedral of Dunkeld has been the see of several distinguished bishops. Bruce's friend and supporter, Bishop Sinclair, held this see ; and Gavin Douglas, the well-known scholar and translator of the *Æneid of Virgil*, was Bishop of Dunkeld.

The buildings which now exist are of much more recent date than the days of Queen Margaret's sons. Alexander Myln, a canon of Dunkeld in 1505, and afterwards Abbot of Cambuskenneth and first President of the College of Justice, has fortunately left a history of the lives of the Bishops of Dunkeld, which professes to give a more minute account of the

* *Celtic Scotland*, Vol. II. p. 307.   † *Ibid.* p. 374.

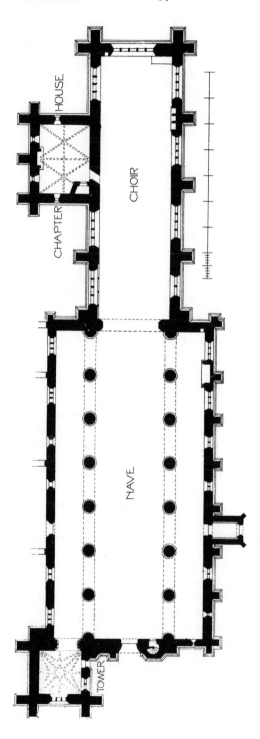

Fig. 968.—Dunkeld Cathedral. Plan.

dates of the different parts of the structure of the cathedral than we have of any similar building in the country. From this account it would appear that the existing structure is chiefly of the fifteenth century.

The edifice (Fig. 968) consists of an aisleless choir, a nave with two aisles, a north-west tower, and a chapter house to the north of the choir. The choir measures 103 feet long by 29 feet wide internally, and the rectangular chapter house attached to the north side is 27 feet long and 20 feet wide. Some portions of the choir indicate the style of the thirteenth

Fig. 969.—Dunkeld Cathedral. Wall Arcade at North-West Angle of Choir

century ; but this part of the structure was almost entirely rebuilt in the beginning of the present century. An original fragment may, however, still be observed in damaged portions of a first pointed arcade (Fig. 969) in the interior of the north wall near the west end. The arcade is below the level of the window sill, and extends to six arches of trefoil form, springing from the carved caps of single shafts. All the details (Fig. 970) are pure and good. A post to support a modern gallery cuts into the arcade, as shown in Fig. 969. From the floor to the top of the caps measures 5 feet 9 inches. The choir is now fitted up and used as the parish church.

The chapter house, on the north side of the choir, is now converted into a mausoleum for the families of the Dukes of Atholl, and contains several Renaissance monuments. It is two stories high (Fig. 971), the

Fɪɢ. 970.—Dunkeld Cathedral. Details of Wall Arcade in North-West Angle of Choir.

lower story being vaulted and of considerable height (Fig. 972), and is lighted by tall lancet windows cusped at the arch head. The buttresses are simple, and the whole character of the work is early, but it has been altered. The vaulting (Fig. 972) is round arched, but the wall ribs are pointed ; the roof has thus a flat appearance, and there are no horizontal ridge ribs. The chapter house structure has been added after the erection of the choir, as is evident from the portion of the original exterior base of the choir which still exists in the south-west angle of the interior of the chapter house adjoining the door (see Fig. 972). From the style of the design, this structure was probably an early addition. The upper

Fig. 971.—Dunkeld Cathedral. Chapter House from North-West.

chamber over the chapter house is doubtless later. The staircase leading to the upper floor is inserted in the south-west angle and projects into the chamber,* and cuts through the groined ceiling (see Fig. 972).

The heightening of the chapter house was apparently carried out by

* The steps of the wheel stair, which exist, have been accidentally omitted in the Plan.

Bishop Lauder, whose arms, a griffin segreant (Fig. 973), are carved near the top on the face of the north buttress on the east side. The upper

FIG. 972.—Dunkeld Cathedral. Interior of Chapter House.

chamber has been lighted by small windows, which are now partly built up. The windows of the lower story have been fitted with wooden shutters on the inside, some of which are still in position (see Fig. 972). At the doorway leading into the choir there is a curious small stoup cut on the base (see Fig. 972).

Against the centre of the north wall there is a recessed tomb (Fig. 974), which exhibits that peculiar kind of design, having mixed Gothic and Renaissance features, frequently found in the seventeenth century. It contains in the pediment a shield bearing—1st and 4th, a fess chequé for Stewart; 2nd and 3rd, three pallets for Athole, a pelican at top, and

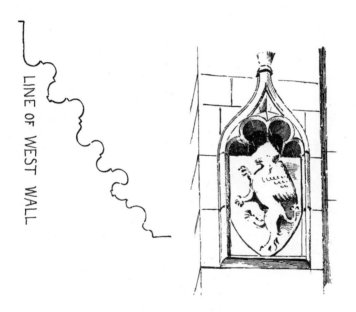

FIG. 973.—Dunkeld Cathedral. Section of Jamb of West Doorway, and Arms of Bishop Lauder on Chapter House.

the motto, *Furth Fortovn et fil ye Feteris.* The recess for the figure is 4 feet 11 inches wide by 3 feet 11 inches high, but it contains no effigy.

On the south wall there is a large eighteenth century monument with inscription (see Fig. 972), and, at the sides, thirty-two coats of arms, arranged in two rows of eight on each side, besides other arms.

Resting on the floor, and against the walls of the chapter house, there are numerous carved stones, several having arms, which appear to have come from some sixteenth or seventeenth century buildings; and in the room over the chapter house the remains of a rich Renaissance monument, carved in oak, lie scattered on the floor.

Fig. 974.—Dunkeld Cathedral. Monument in Chapter House.

Abbot Myln relates* that in 1312 Bishop William de St. Clare (Bruce's "own bishop") brought Magistrum Robertum Cementarium to the work of the choir and church, which he built from the foundation. This clearly refers to a restoration, as part of the thirteenth century walls is still in existence. Bishop Sinclair died in 1337, and was buried in the choir built by him, having filled the see for twenty-five years.

To the west of the choir is the nave, which measures, internally, 120 feet in length by 60 feet wide, and consists of a central compartment of seven bays, separated from the side aisles by arcades, which rest on plain round pillars. We are informed by Abbot Mylne that this part of the cathedral was founded by Bishop Cardeny on the 27th day of April 1406, and that he carried it up to the second arches, "vulgariter le blynd storijs." This bishop conferred great benefits on the see by acquiring lands for it and otherwise. He also founded and adorned the altar of St. Ninian in Dunkeld, and decorated all the windows of the choir with glass. Having on one occasion made a narrow escape during an attack on his house, he constructed a strong tower for the bishop's residence. He died in 1436,† and his fine monument (Fig. 975) is still preserved in the south wall of the nave.

In 1447 the king's secretary, John of Ralstoun, was made bishop, but he lived for only three years after his appointment.‡ He made provision of hewn stones from the quarry of Burnbane for continuing the building of the nave begun by Bishop Cardeny. Bishop Ralston died in 1450, and was succeeded by Bishop Lauder, who completed the nave and decorated all the windows with glass, and finished the roof. He also constructed a handsome portico to the church before the southern doorway, and placed figures of sculptured art therein. With his own hands Bishop Lauder dedicated the church in 1464. But still untired of his sacred work, he founded the campanile (Fig. 976) on 5th March 1469, and continued the building on high. The chapter house was also founded by him in 1457. This, no doubt, refers to the erection of the upper floor of the two story building on the north side of the choir above described. Perhaps this edifice contained the sacristy on the ground floor, on the level of the choir, and the upper story added by Bishop Lauder may have been the chapter house. At Glasgow Cathedral, the similar two story building contained the sacristy on the upper floor, on the level of the choir, and the chapter house on the lower story. This "Great and worthy High Priest" likewise, in 1461, constructed a bridge over the Tay, near his own palace, partly of stone and partly of wood. He likewise presented the church with numerous splendid vestments and silver vessels, including a silver cross containing part of the true Cross. He also had paintings executed at the high altar, representing the twenty-four miracles of St. Columba, and he constructed the bishop's throne and stalls in the choir.

* Myln's *Vitæ Dunkeldensis Ecclesiæ Episcoporum*, p. 13.
† *Ibid.* pp. 16, 17.   ‡ *Ibid.* p. 20.

In 1481 this prelate died full of years and of good works. By Bishop Lauder's influence the cathedral lands north of the Forth were raised into

Fig. 975.—Dunkeld Cathedral. Monument of Bishop Cardeny in Nave.*

* Inscription on tomb of Bishop Cardeny :—" Hic jacet Dns. Robertus de Cardony Eppis Dunkeldenni qui . . . ad incarnationem Dne MCCCCXX."—*Monuments and Monumental Inscriptions in Scotland*, by Rev. Charles Rogers, LL.D., &c., for Grampian Club, 2 vols., 1871 and 1872.

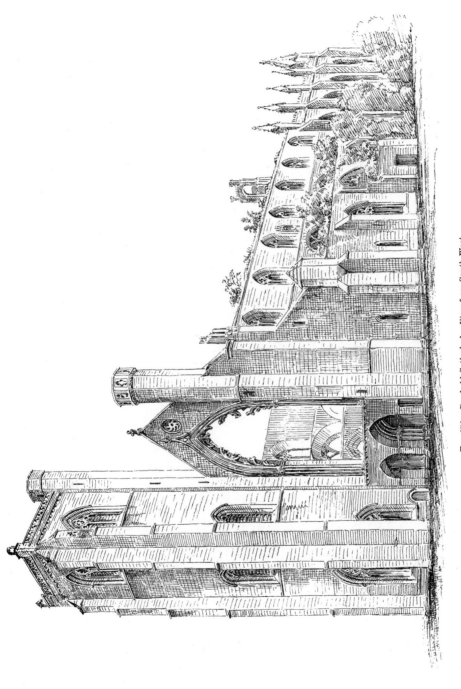

Fig. 976.—Dunkeld Cathedral. View from South-West.

the barony of Dunkeld, and those south of the Forth into the barony of Aberlathy.*

The bishops of Dunkeld, in addition to their palace or tower at Dunkeld, had also a country seat at Loch Cluny (where their house still exists on an island in the loch) and a residence at Cramond, in Mid-Lothian.†

The successors of Bishop Lauder are not stated to have added any buildings to the cathedral; but it is mentioned that some of them, especially Bishop Brown, adorned the interior with images and paintings, and added to the store of rich vestments and ornaments.

The Reformation came not long after the completion of the internal decorations and fittings. In 1560 two of the neighbouring lairds were commissioned to take down the images and burn them in the churchyard, and also to cast down the altars and purge the church of all kinds of monuments of idolatry. They were enjoined to see that the desks, windows, and doors were unharmed, nor the glass or iron work broken. But the spirit of destruction once let loose was not easily restrained, and the church was completely destroyed and the roof burnt.

The architectural style of the different portions of the edifice corresponds generally with the above dates fixed by Abbot Myln. The massive round pillars of the nave, 4 feet 6 inches in diameter (Fig. 977), and the heavy semicircular arches of the triforium have been supposed to indicate Norman work; but the details prove that here, as frequently occurs in Scotland, the ancient forms are repeated in later times. The caps and bases of the piers show that they belong to an advanced period, while the mouldings of the triforium arches and the trefoiled filling in clearly indicate work of the latter half of the fifteenth century. These features are, undoubtedly, peculiar; but other examples show that they are not singular. Thus at Aberdour Church ‡ and Aberdeen Cathedral (late works), the pillars of the piers are circular, and have similar caps to those at Dunkeld; and at Paisley the triforium arches are segmental, and are divided with cusped arches somewhat similar in style to those of Dunkeld Cathedral. The clerestory is very plain, and the windows are small. From the number of holes in the wall, used for the support of rafters and other woodwork, it seems likely that this portion of the wall was partly concealed by the timbers of the open wooden roof, and perhaps partly covered with panelling.

The great window in the western gable (see Fig. 976) is evidently a late feature, and seems to have been added sometime after the west wall had been erected. This is apparent not only from the style and the peculiar unsymmetrical position of the window, but also from the construction of the exterior (Fig. 978), where it will be observed that the original west door has had a portion of wall somewhat rudely added in front of the original

---

* Myln's *Vitæ Dunkeldensis Ecclesiæ Episcoporum*, p. 22.
† *The Castellated and Domestic Architecture of Scotland*, Vol. III. pp. 432 and 589.
‡ *Ibid.* Vol. II. p. 478.

wall, in order to support a balcony or gallery carried across at the base of the window. The older moulded doorway (the jamb of which is shown in

Fig. 977.—Dunkeld Cathedral. Nave, looking West.

Fig. 973) is thus overlapped and buried by two square piers, carrying plain arches above, stuck on in front of the original wall; while in a similar opening or recess, between the south pier and the tower at the

Fig. 978.—Dunkeld Cathedral. West End.

south side, the space is lintelled over between the square pier and the stair turret. As the stair turret probably existed (at least for part of its height) before this alteration, the large window, which occupies the full available width, had to be squeezed in as best it could, and thus came to stand in the unsymmetrical position it occupies (see Fig. 977). This supposed alteration may also, perhaps, explain the peculiar way in which the ogee canopy of the window is twisted to one side at the top (see Fig. 976), which Mr. Billings has difficulty in accounting for. The small circle in the gable being right over the entrance door (as the original window in the west end doubtless also was), it was found, when the window came to be enlarged, that there was no room to carry the canopy and its fleur-de-lys finial straight up without removing the small circular opening, and so the canopy and finial had to be pushed to one side.

The side aisles are 12 feet in width, and the south one has been vaulted. The tracery in many of the windows still survives, and is varied and generally good in design. A restoration of the tracery in the west window may be seen in Mr. Billings' work. The tracery is of the kind common in the Scottish architecture of the fifteenth century.

Attention has already been drawn to the peculiar flat-headed windows· at the west end of the north aisle of Dunblane Cathedral. At Dunkeld, the corresponding window is flat arched (Fig. 979), and at St. John's Church, in Perth, the window in the same position is either flat arched or has a lintel. It is singular and interesting to find this similarity of treatment, as regards the north-west window, in these three churches, which are all situated in one part of the country. Over the north-west window at Dunkeld are the arms of Bishop Brown (a chevron between three fleur-de-lys), surmounted by a mitre. There is an inscription on a ribbon round the arms, but it would require a very minute inspection to make it out. George Brown was consecrated Bishop of Dunkeld by Pope Sixtus iv. in 1484, and died 14th January 1514-1515, aged seventy-six years.

The ruins of a large porch still exist on the south side of the nave (see Fig. 976). From the forms of the finials and other details it has evidently been a somewhat late addition. This was, doubtless, the portico which Canon Myln states was erected by Bishop Lauder at the south entrance to the church.

The upper part of the stair turret of the west front, the broken angle pinnacle at the base of the gable, and the corbelled octagonal finial on the south-west angle of the south aisle are all late additions. The corbelled turret at the angle resembles the angle turrets of the castles. A similar turret exists at the angle of the north transept of Paisley Abbey.

The north-west tower is simple and good in design. According to Abbot Myln's account, it was not founded till 1469, and in style is good for the period. The windows of the ground floor and top story are well designed, and quite equal to the rest of the church. The ground floor is vaulted, and has been painted in a handsome manner, part of the painting being still preserved.

The monument of Bishop Cardeny in the south aisle of the nave, with

Fig. 979.—Dunkeld Cathedral.   North-West Angle of Nave and Tower.

its recumbent statue (see Fig. 975), its carved sarcophagus and arched canopy, is a good example of Scottish work of the fifteenth century. It is now much damaged, but the fine carving of the crockets and ornaments, and the sculptured figures of the angels bearing shields, are still fairly preserved. The arms on the shields are now so far decayed as to be with difficulty legible.*

A very fine altar tomb (Fig. 980) still remains in the south side of the eastern part of the choir, now used as a vestibule to the parish church. This is the monument of the famous "Wolf of Badenoch," son of Robert II., at one time a great enemy to the Church, and the destroyer of Elgin Cathedral. Having been compelled by the king to do penance, he received absolution at the hands of the Archbishop of St. Andrews, in the

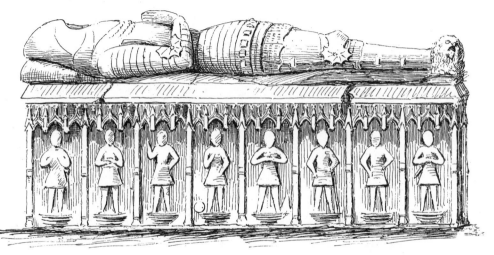

Fig. 980.—Dunkeld Cathedral. Monument of the "Wolf of Badenoch."

* The following reading of the arms on this monument is kindly supplied by Mr. W. Rae MacDonald:—On the recessed tomb of Bishop Cardeny in the nave there are several coats of arms. These, so far as they are legible, are—In centre of arch a small shield, quarterly 1st and 4th, a fess chequé (of two rows of panes only) between three open crowns, for Stewart and the Lordship of Garrioch; 2nd and 3rd, a bend between six crosses potent fitchée, for Mar; the 3rd quarter is defaced, but no doubt was the same as the 2nd. These arms appear on the seal of Alexander Stewart, Earl of Mar in right of his wife, Isabell Douglas (see Laing's *Seals*, Vol. I., No. 796). There is a shield at each end of the arch label; that on the east side is defaced; the west one bears two chevronells engrailed, and has a mitre above it, for Bishop Cardeny. On the pedestal there are four shields, supported by angels under arched canopies, the shields being separated by five figures of ecclesiastics with folded hands, and standing on pedestals. These four shields bear—(1) Three pallets, for Atholl; (2) two chevronells, for Strathearn (?); (3) defaced, but probably same as first; (4) faint traces of two chevronells.

Blackfriars Church, at Perth. The monument dates from about 1394. It contains a massive figure of the "Wolf" in complete armour, with his feet resting on a lion. On the sarcophagus are carved a number of figures in armour, in different attitudes.* There is a mutilated headless figure, supposed to represent Bishop Sinclair, lying beside the "Wolf of Badenoch's" monument; and other memorials of him are the engrailed crosses on the east and west gables. These are cut out of the solid stone, and have probably been renewed.

Nearly opposite Bishop Cardeny's monument, against the north wall of the nave, there is one of those grave slabs (Fig. 981) of which several

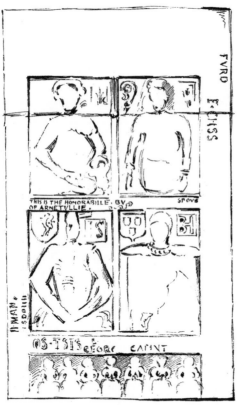

FIG. 981.—Dunkeld Cathedral.
Grave Slab.

examples have been illustrated, and unfortunately, like most others, it is in a very wasted condition from exposure to the weather. It is also broken, as shown on the sketch. The slab is of red sandstone, and measures 5 ft. 8 in. long by 3 ft. 4 in. wide. It is divided into four sunk panels, with a three-quarter size figure in each panel, and the figures are flush with the general surface. It cannot be determined what the costumes of the figures are. No. 2 has, on the dexter side, a bishop's crozier, and, on the sinister side, what may have been a shield. No. 1 was probably distinguished in the same way, there being something visible on the sinister side. No. 3 has, on dexter side, a shield with a lion rampant; on sinister side, a square with initials only,

* Inscription on tomb of the "Wolf of Badenoch" :—" Hic jacet Alexander Seneschalus, filius Roberti Regis Scotorum et Elizabeth More, Dominus de Buchan et Dns *de Badenoch, qui obit vigessimo quarto die Julii.*" The words in italics have been restored, and there is a mistake in the date, as Alexander Stewart died 20th February 1394.—*Monuments and Monumental Inscriptions in Scotland,* by Rev. Charles Rogers, LL. D., &c., for Grampian Club, 2 vols., 1871 and 1872.

the last of which (S) is legible. No. 4 is certainly the figure of a woman, with large epaulets and a necklace; on her dexter side is a shield with three innescutcheons, probably for Hay, and, on the sinister side, the initials B. H. Beneath each pair of figures there has been an inscription —the upper one, as far as legible, being, "This is the honorabille Bv . . . Spovs of Arnetvllie." Of the other marginal inscriptions nothing legible can be made out. Along the base of the stone there are sculptured seven small figures.

The dates of the different parts of the cathedral, as given by Abbot Myln, would, if thoroughly reliable, be invaluable in connection with the history of Scottish architecture. Few, if any, of our ecclesiastical edifices have the periods of their erection so distinctly recorded. The peculiarity of the design, however, renders it somewhat difficult to make any general application of the above dates to the architecture of other buildings. It seems likely that the different parts of the structure were begun at the dates given by Abbot Myln, but not completed for some time thereafter. From the analogy with other Scottish structures, especially with Paisley Abbey, which it in some respects closely resembles, the nave of Dunkeld Cathedral must undoubtedly be classed as belonging to the third pointed period.

IONA CATHEDRAL, ARGYLESHIRE.

The original settlement of St. Columba in Iona took place A.D. 563.[*] Dr Skene has shown[†] that the place where the monastery was first situated lay a short distance to the north of the existing ruins. The vallum which enclosed the establishment can still be traced, as well as the burying-ground, the site of the mill, and other features; but the principal erections, being constructed of wood and wattle, have necessarily disappeared. Owing to the destruction of the buildings by fire in 802 and the slaughter of the monks, it was thought desirable, in 818, to rebuild the monastery in stone for greater security, and also to remove it to the present site, which is better protected by nature. But the buildings were again destroyed by the Northmen, and seem to have remained in a ruinous state till 1074, when some attempt to restore the monastery was made by Queen Margaret.

In 1099 the last of the old order of abbots died, and for more than fifty years there is an unbroken silence regarding Iona. All the Western Islands had at this time passed under the rule of the Norwegian King of the Isles, by whom nothing was done to maintain the religious establishments, and Iona fell into a state of decay. The rule of the Norwegian Kings of the Isles having become oppressive, Somerled, King of Argyll, was applied to for protection, and after a great naval battle, fought between him and Godred, King of the Isles, in 1156, all the islands south

[*] Introduction, Vol. I. p. 10.   [†] *Celtic Scotland*, Vol. II. p. 96.

of Ardnamurchan Point were ceded to Somerled. Amongst these was Iona, where Reginald, the son of Somerled, undertook the rebuilding of the monastery on a larger scale. He adopted the policy of the Scottish kings, and introduced one of the religious orders of the Roman Church.

"Macvurich tells us that 'three monasteries were formed by him—the monastery of Black Monks in I or Iona, in honour of God and Saint Columchelle; a monastery of Black Nuns in the same place; and a monastery of Gray friars in Sagadul, or Saddle, in Kintyre;' and he appears to have established the Benedictines or Black Monks in Iona in the year 1203."

"The deed of confirmation of the Benedictine Monastery still exists in the Vatican. It is dated the 9th December 1203, and is addressed to Celestinus, abbot of Saint Columba, of the island of Hy, and his brethren professing a religious life; and the pope takes the monastery of Saint Columba under the protection of Saint Peter and the pope, in order that the monastic order which has been instituted in that place, according to the rule of Saint Benedict, may be preserved inviolate in all time to come; and he confirms to them the place itself in which the said monastery is situated, with its pertinents, consisting of churches, islands, and lands in the Western Isles." *

Celestine, the abbot of this monastery, appears to have attempted to thrust out the prior Celtic community; but the latter, with the support of the clergy of the north of Ireland, resisted and vindicated their right to remain in the monastery. The Celtic community, however, appear to have ultimately adopted the Benedictine rule, "while the functionary formerly known as the Head of the Culdees was represented by the prior of Iona, whom we afterwards find in the monastery."

About 1200 the districts to the west of the great range of Drumalban, which formerly belonged to the diocese of Dunkeld, were separated from it and formed into a new bishopric, first called of Argyle and afterwards of Lismore.

During the fourteenth and fifteenth centuries Iona was under the Bishop of Dunkeld, but in 1507 John, Bishop of the Isles, obtained the annexation of Iona to his see, and the Abbey Church became the cathedral of the diocese, and so continued till the Reformation.

In 1561 the abbey suffered from the Act anent "demolishing all the abbeys of monks and friars, and for suppressing whatsoever monuments of idolatrie were remaining in the realm." The carrying out of this Act was remitted to Argyll and Glencairn, and much has been written with regard to the great damage caused by the mob to the buildings and monuments and the valuable library.

The island passed into the hands of M'Lean of Duart, but from 1567 onwards the Protestant bishops of the Isles seem to have had the abbey in their possession. The buildings, however, appear to have been neglected,

* *Celtic Scotland*, Vol. II. p. 416.

and Charles I., in 1635, directed £400 to be spent in repairing them. But that does not appear to have been done, and by the end of the seventeenth century the edifices had fallen into ruin. In 1693 the island came into the hands of the House of Argyll, and within recent years the ancient buildings have been put in a good state of preservation by the present Duke.

The edifices which still survive in the island, although ruinous, exhibit probably the completest and most interesting group of ancient ecclesiastical structures in Scotland.

There is first the Chapel of St. Oran, a small twelfth century structure, surrounded by the very ancient churchyard, which contains so many beautiful specimens of Highland carved tombstones,* admirably illustrated by the late James Drummond, R.S.A., in his work on Highland monuments. Then there are the remains of the Benedictine Monastery, and those of the Benedictine Nunnery, at a short distance on each side of St. Oran's, both of which, though sadly mutilated, still show the general plan of the church and domestic edifices of these monastic establishments more completely than any other Scottish examples.

The Church of St. Oran has already been described.†

The nunnery is also described among the Norman structures.‡

The abbey or cathedral, which is now to be described, is classed along with the buildings of the third pointed period, as the greater part of the work connected with it belongs to a late date.

When the great distance of the Island of Iona from the centre of operations of mediæval architecture is considered, it is not unnatural to find those deviations from the rules and practice of the art which are so frequent in Scottish architecture even more accentuated here than is usual. The connection of the locality with the Celtic art of Ireland and the west of Scotland has also had considerable influence in moulding the style of the carving and decoration of the Cathedral of the Isles. §

These facts, although rendering the building somewhat difficult to class along with the general architecture of the recognised periods of Gothic in Scotland, yet add much to the interest of this isolated and unique structure.

It should also be noticed that the cathedral shows signs in all directions of having been much altered and added to ; but as the style of the masonry of the walls is much the same throughout, whatever its date, it is somewhat difficult to trace the points of junction of the work of the various periods. This masonry of all dates consists of large blocks of red granite of irregular shape, set with flat untooled face to the outside, and with filling-in of smaller pieces of granite and slaty stones between the larger blocks.

The monastery (Fig. 982) consists of the church, which contains a

* Vol. I. p. 20.   † *Ibid.* p. 220.   ‡ *Ibid.* p. 421.   § *Ibid.* p. 20.

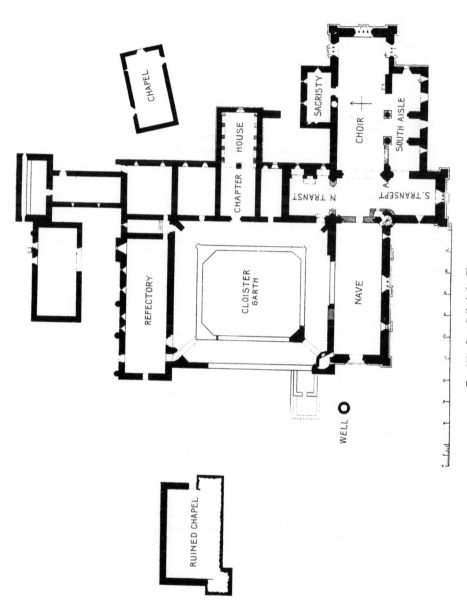

FIG. 982.—Iona Cathedral. Plan.

choir, 62 feet 6 inches long by 23 feet wide, with a south aisle ; a nave, 60 feet 9 inches long by 22 feet 6 inches wide ; north and south transepts,

Fig. 983.—Iona Cathedral. The Choir, looking East.

and a tower over the crossing. The eastern part of the choir (Fig. 983) forms the presbytery, which, like that of most Scottish churches, is without aisles, and is lighted by a large central and two side windows, all containing late tracery. On the south side of the choir, west of the presbytery, is an aisle, separated from it by two circular piers and three arches. From above the caps of the piers two bold arches are thrown across the south aisle, after the manner of flying buttresses (Fig. 984). It will be observed from this view that there is a peculiarity of construction in the upper part of the choir walls, the clerestory windows being placed over the piers and not over the arches, as is usual. This arrangement has had the effect of preventing the flying arches or buttresses from being carried as high as they might have been (Fig. 985) had the windows been placed over the arches in the ordinary manner. The flying arches or buttresses are thus very low, and interfere with the space in the aisle (see Plan). There are a sedilia, with three divisions, and a piscina (Fig. 986) near the east end of the south wall of the choir. Part of the pavement there still exists, and two steps are observable in the floor.

On the north side of the choir is the sacristy, which occupies the place of the north aisle. The door to the sacristy (Fig. 987) is of fine design, and the ornament of the caps of the shafts (Fig. 988), together with the caps of the piers between the choir and the south aisle and the arches of the crossing (Figs. 989 and 990), exhibit fine examples of Celtic carving, mixed with grotesque figures. Carving of an identical description is shown in Figs. 991 and 992 on slabs in St. Oran's Chapel, one of which, dated 1489, also exhibits late Gothic ornaments on the edge. This stone bears the following inscription, from which it would appear to be in memory of the father of Abbot Macfingone, and of the abbot himself (whose tomb and monument are preserved in the choir, as will be pointed out further on) :—" Hec : est : Crux : Laeclanni : Meic : fingone : et : ejus : fil—Ohannis : Abbatis : de : Hy : facta : Anno : domini : M⁰· CCCCLXXX : IX⁰· Numerous examples of carving of a very similar description occur throughout the West Highlands, and, where dated, are all of about the above period. The undated specimens are also distinctly in the same style and of the same epoch. There can, therefore, be no hesitation in assigning the sculpture in the cathedral, which is of a similar character (such as the caps in Figs. 988 and 990), to about the same date. The dog-tooth ornaments in Fig. 993 and other similar examples, which are not rare at Iona and throughout the Western Islands, are thus clearly a revival, at a late date, of ancient forms.

Close to the sacristy door, but raised to a considerable height above the choir floor, stands a round column (see Fig. 983), which supports two pointed arches. These arches appear to have opened into an upper aisle or chapel. They are carved with rows of dog-tooth or nail-head ornaments, which have the appearance of thirteenth century work ; but as they are

FIG. 984.—Iona Cathedral. View from South-East.

much decayed, they are probably of the late date to which, as we have seen, many examples of imitation dog-tooth enrichments at Iona and elsewhere belong.

The parapet of the choir (see Fig. 984) is simple, and is supported on massive corbels, like those common in the castles of Scotland. The water of the gutters escapes by small apertures through the parapet.

FIG. 985.—Iona Cathedral. Choir Pier and Arch of South Aisle.

The nave contains a good western doorway of late design (Fig. 994), with three orders of mouldings in the jambs, which have no caps, but have the jamb mouldings carried round the pointed arch. The nave and transepts have no aisles. The windows of the nave (Fig. 995) are much damaged. At each end of the south wall is a small single pointed light,

Fig. 986.—Iona Cathedral. Sedilia and Piscina in Choir.

and there has been a triple light window, with tracery, in the centre. The single light window at the east end of the nave has a carved head, with a water table over it, inserted above the window. Part of the north

Fig. 987.—Iona Cathedral. Door to Sacristy.

wall of the nave is demolished (see Fig. 994), and a door to the cloister near the west end has been built up (see Plan).

The north transept has two deeply-arched recesses in the east wall, containing small windows and a central arched recess, which seems to have contained a statue. This is apparently the oldest part of the whole edifice, the arches, shafts, and caps in the east wall (Fig. 996) having very much the character of transition work. A small window in the west wall, raised so as to be above the cloister roof (see Fig. 994), throws light on the point where the altar stood.

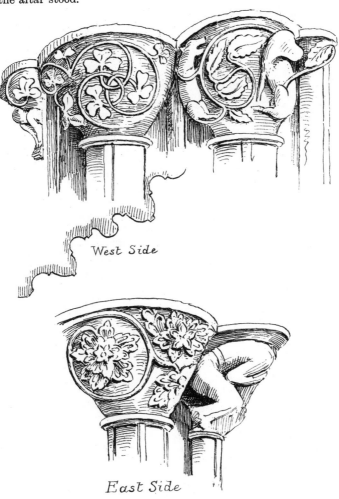

West Side

East Side

Fig. 988.—Iona Cathedral. Caps of Doorway to Sacristy.

The south transept is 22 feet by 17 feet, and is lighted by a three light traceried window in the south gable wall (see Fig. 984), and a small window placed at a considerable height in the west wall (see Fig. 995). The parapet and corbel table are the same as those of the choir.

The crossing has four arches opening into the choir, nave, and transepts, which carry a tower, 29 feet by 25 feet, over the walls, rising to two stories in height above the eaves, and crowned with a plain parapet, supported on simple corbels (see Figs. 984 and 994). The upper story has rectangular windows on each face, three of them filled with tracery of late patterns, and the one on the north with a window containing simple tracery

Fig. 989.—Iona Cathedral. Caps of Piers of Choir and Crossing.

(Fig. 997). The lintels are composed of straight arches, supported by a remarkable shaft on the inside, which recalls the turned shafts of pre-Norman work. The access to the tower is by a small wheel staircase at the south-west angle of the crossing. The original doorway of the staircase entered from the nave, but, after the Reformation, the adjoining

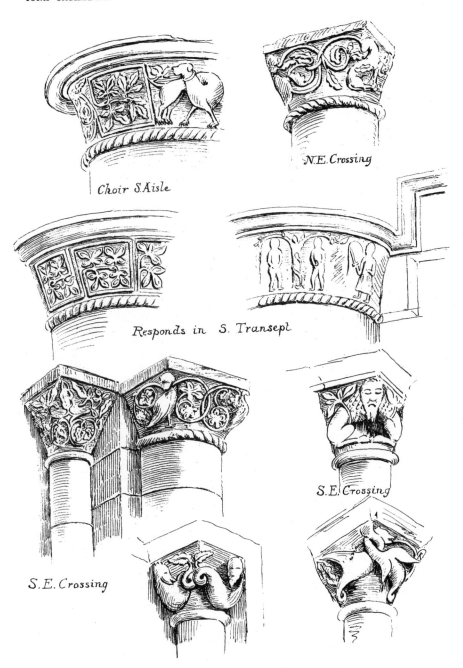

Choir S. Aisle

N.E. Crossing

Responds in S. Transept.

S.E. Crossing

S.E. Crossing

Fig. 990.—Iona Cathedral. Caps of Crossing, &c.

west arch of the crossing was built up, and a new door, with a small enclosing wall, was formed from the crossing into the wheel stair (as shown in the Plan). In the upper part of the tower are built recesses, as if meant for pigeons' nests; and the upper floor in the roof of the

FIG. 991.—Iona Cathedral.
Carved Slab in St. Oran's.

FIG. 992.—Iona Cathedral.
Macfingone's Slab in St. Oran's.

tower is lighted with slits in the wall near the corners, except on the south side, where a larger opening is introduced and filled with tracery (see Fig. 984).

The whole of the church has been roofed with timber, but is now quite open to the weather. The stone corbels intended to carry the principals of the roof still remain where the walls are complete (see Fig. 983).

Externally, the most prominent features are the buttresses and base course (see Figs. 984 and 995). These exist round most of the south wall of the nave, part of the south transept, and the east end of the choir. The angle buttresses have the general form, with bead on angle and sloping table on top, of thirteenth century work, and the broad, sloping base has also a similar character. Several small intermediate buttresses are introduced, which are in many cases awkwardly situated as regards the windows, being kept below the window sills. The base course on the south side of the nave is set at a level several feet above that of the south transept (see Fig. 995). It is stopped suddenly before reaching the eastmost bay of the nave. The base also stops equally suddenly on the west wall of the south transept, a few feet from the southwest angle buttress. The base course and buttresses would thus seem, where they exist, to indicate a rebuilding of those portions of the walls, the portions left without a base course being possibly older. Although the forms of the base course and buttresses are of early design, there is no doubt but that they are late erections, and that the forms and design are revivals or imitations of older features. Their association with the late doorway of the nave and the late traceries of the choir and south transept sufficiently proves their comparatively recent construction.

Fig. 993.—Iona Cathedral. Dog-tooth Ornaments on Slab.

In the above general description of the cathedral, the probable dates of the various parts have been casually referred to. It is now proposed to explain more fully the dates we would assign to the different portions of the structure and the reasons for doing so.

Dr Skene has the following footnote *—

" One of the columns which supports the great tower of the Abbey Church has on the upper portion the inscription, ' Donaldus O'Brolchan fecit hoc opus,' and seems to think that that inscription fixes the name of the builder of the church. Messrs Buckler, in their description of the architecture of the cathedral,† give the above inscription as reading, ' Donaldus ornatum fecit hoc opus.' "

The inscription is not now legible, but even if it were, it could give little clue to the date of the edifice.

* *Celtic Scotland*, Vol. II. p. 415.   † In *Iona*, by the Bishop of Argyll and the Isles (1866).

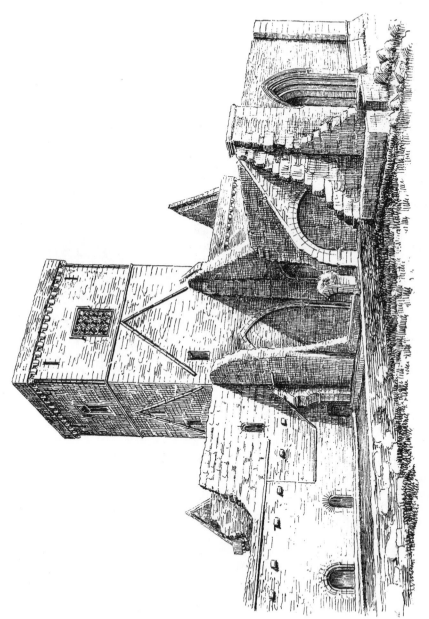

Fig. 994.—Iona Cathedral. View from North-West, showing Cloister Garth, Central Tower, &c.

Fig. 995.—Iona Cathedral. General View of Cathedral and St. Oran's Chapel, from South-West.

There will probably be little difference of opinion regarding the antiquity of the east wall of the north transept (see Fig. 996). The character of the arches, shafts, and caps, even worn away as they are, is distinctly late Norman or transition. The small round headed windows in the recesses of the wide internal bays are also quite in keeping with that

FIG. 996.—Iona Cathedral. East Side of North Transept.

style. The depth of the recesses on each side of the central arch, with its figure, which form a special feature, was rendered necessary by the extra width of the wall required (as will be pointed out further on) to admit of a passage in the thickness of the wall above. Almost all the rest of the church appears to be of a much later date, and to belong, with small exceptions, to the late fifteenth or early part of the sixteenth century.

Part of the crossing, however, is probably older ; but the other portions of the crossing seem to have been rebuilt at a late date, as the following indications show. The original arches of the north and west sides have no mouldings, but are only chamfered, and the caps, so far as visible, have an ancient character. The north arch has, at some period, been strengthened by the insertion of additional piers, and an additional arch within the then existing piers and arch (see Plan). The old arch is distinctly visible in the wall, and portions of the old piers are also exposed to view.

Fig. 997.—Iona Cathedral. North Side of Refectory.

The arches of the east and south sides of the crossing are of a different character from the above, the arches being fully moulded. The piers (Fig. 998) do not differ much from those of the older sides, and are all of an early form of design. The same character is kept up in the inserted piers of the north arch, although these must undoubtedly be later than the original piers. The mouldings seem all to have been imitated from early forms (such as we find in the choir arch of the nunnery).* The changes in the plans of the piers and mouldings, common in the central districts of the mainland, would be long in reaching this distant spot, and the old forms appear to have been, therefore, adhered to. Such continuations or imitations of early forms are very common in Scotland. It

* Vol. I. (Fig. 382.)

should be observed that the outer or central shaft of each pier has a fillet on its central line, which indicates (especially here) a somewhat advanced date (see Fig. 996). The bases are of a very late type, as also the caps, both of which differ from those of the earlier piers. From these facts we infer that the south and east sides of the crossing have been rebuilt at a late period, possibly at the time when the tower was erected. That part of the edifice is always justly regarded as being very late, and the rectangular windows and their tracery clearly support that view. If the above supposition is correct, then the insertion of the additional piers and arch under the north tower arch is explained. That addition would be made at the time the tower was built, in order to make sure that the support was sufficient to carry it. Similar extra strengthening was not necessary in the case of the west arch, as it already had sufficient piers and supports; and the additions to the piers of the north arch, which

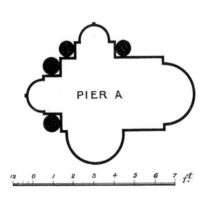

FIG. 998.—Iona Cathedral.
South-East Pier of Crossing.

previously were small, simply made them of similar strength to those of the west arch.

We therefore conclude that the original north and west arches and piers of the crossing are old, perhaps of the thirteenth century; while the east and south arches and piers have been rebuilt, and the additional piers and arch added to the north opening, probably when the tower was erected.

Let us now turn to the choir. When we consider the forms of the tracery of the three windows of the presbytery (see Figs. 983 and 984, and the north window in Fig. 999), the thickness of the mullions, and the number and smallness of their mouldings, there cannot be much difficulty in assigning these windows to a late date. The forms and decorations of the arches of the sedilia (see Fig. 986) also clearly indicate a late period. These are exceedingly good of their kind, and it is a misfortune that the Celtic ornament with which they are covered is now so far decayed as to be scarcely legible; but there can be no question as to the lateness of their date.

On turning to the south aisle the same impression is received. The circular and stunted form of the piers, with their remarkable bases and the peculiar form of their enriched capitals (see Figs. 989 and 990), strike one at once with the idea that they belong to a late and rather debased epoch. The insertion of the clerestory windows over the piers (an arrangement which is also met with at the nunnery) is bad construction, and led to the adoption of the low and poor flying buttresses (which are evidently an afterthought) as a means of steadying the main structure.

N. Side of Choir

E. End of S. Aisle
Exterior

piscina
S. Aisle

E. End of S. Aisle
Interior

FIG. 999.—Iona Cathedral. Window in North Side of Choir, East End of South Aisle, &c.

The north side of the choir is so peculiar in its arrangements that little can be gathered from it with regard to dates. If the pillar and arches of the high chapel over the sacristy (see Fig. 983) are of thirteenth century work, as their ornamentation would at first sight lead one to suppose, they might possibly have been re-erected in their present position; but they are more likely to have been made in imitation of thirteenth century work, and built here at a late period. The section of the

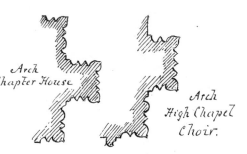

Arch
Chapter House

Arch
High Chapel
Choir.

FIG. 1000.—Iona Cathedral.
Section of Arch Mouldings.

arch mouldings (Fig. 1000) is almost identical with that of the chapter house arches, which (as will be afterwards explained) are almost undoubtedly of very late date.

These arches gave a view of the altar from a high chapel, which, as will be pointed out, was perhaps connected with the library or dormitory. The chapel has been added to the church, and the walls are not bonded into the choir. The decoration of the upper portion, with its imitation dog-tooth or nail-head ornament round a straight sided arch (Fig. 1001), shows that it is of very late date.

Fig. 1001.—Iona Cathedral. Interior of Sacristy and Chapel above.

This structure appears to occupy the position of the original north aisle, which at one time extended (or was contemplated) the full length from the presbytery to the north transept. The water table over the old aisle roof runs the whole length, and has a sloping water table where the roof abutted against the north transept. The old corbels to receive the timbers of the aisle roof also still exist. The aisle would no doubt block one of the Norman transept windows, but that could not be avoided.

The doorway from the choir to the sacristy (see Fig. 987) is a very fine feature, and one would be inclined to consider it somewhat earlier than the other parts of the sacristy and upper chapel. Possibly it may have formed an access to the aisle before the upper chapel was raised to its present position.

The above examination of the choir, south aisle, and sacristy leads to the belief that they are all of a late period, probably about 1500. The entire building bears evidence of having been in whole or part re-erected about the end of the fifteenth century or the beginning of the sixteenth century, possibly when it became the Cathedral of the Isles in 1506. Some portions, such as the north transept, the north and west sides of the crossing, the wheel stair to the tower and parts of the walling connected therewith, are older; but all the rest, including the east and south arches of the crossing, is of a much later date. Besides the points to which attention has been drawn above, it may be noted that the buttresses of the choir, which from their form may have been raised from ancient bases, have on each angle a single bead on their lower part and a triple bead on the upper part (see Fig. 984). The upper story of the tower, which is admittedly very late, has also a triple bead on the angles of the top story. May it not have happened that the building suffered from some cause, or was intentionally taken down and reconstructed about the end of the fifteenth or beginning of the sixteenth century? Such an event might account for the antique form of the buttresses, which may have been raised from existing portions of old buttresses; while the triple bead on their upper story would show the change of style introduced at the time of the reconstruction. It would also explain the preservation of the old doorway to the sacristy, while the upper parts of the walls were rebuilt. The very irregular appearance of the lower part of the north wall of the choir might also be thus accounted for. The interior string course on the north side, which rises in large steps from the sacristy door, is composed of stones partly enriched and partly plain, as if it formed part of a reconstruction in which old materials had been reused. The clerestory windows, with their ancient forms, are doubtless reproductions of the outlines which formerly existed.

The section of the south-east pier of the crossing (see Fig. 998) shows that the south transept is of about the same period as the choir, the round responds in each corresponding with the circular piers of the choir, and the carved caps being very similar in both (see Figs. 989 and 990); and the south wall of the transept, with its late traceried window and buttresses and base course, is evidently of the same period as the presbytery. The mouldings of the mullions are in both cases returned along the sills, an unusual and late arrangement.

The rebuilt part of the crossing has arch moulds which correspond in style with those of the south aisle arches, and the sculpture of the caps

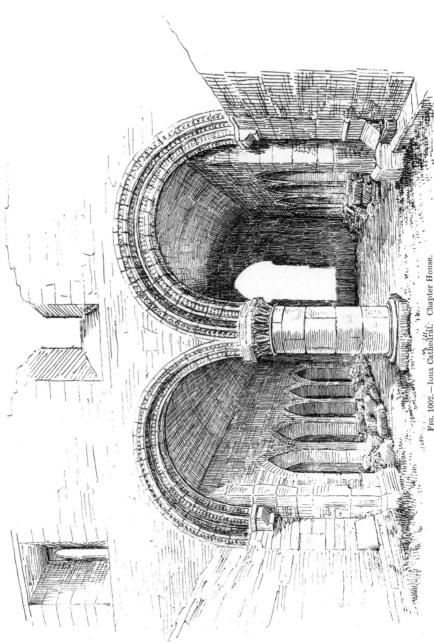

FIG. 1002.—Iona Cathedral: Chapter House.

also corresponds with that of the aisle piers, both containing, as above mentioned, fine examples of Celtic foliage and figures. The peculiar traceried windows at the east end of the south aisle of choir and the adjoining piscina (see Fig. 999) are also clearly of late date.

The cloister lies to the north of the nave; it measures 73 feet from north to south by 66 feet from east.to west. The cloister walk has had a wooden roof all round, resting on corbels (see Fig. 994) in the main wall, and on an arcade on the side next the cloister garth. Some fragments of the shafts and arches of the arcade are preserved in the chapter house, and the bases of a twin column, socketed for the shafts, stand on the wall at the north-west angle. The arcade would thus appear to have rested on coupled shafts, and, so far as can be ascertained by examination of the only surviving portion at the south-west angle and the fragments in the chapter house, the arches were pointed and carved with Celtic ornament somewhat similarly to the arches of the sedilia in the choir (see Fig. 986). In each angle of the cloister walk an arch has been thrown across the walk diagonally, so as to strengthen and steady the walls. Only one of these arches, that at the south-west angle (see Fig. 994), remains entire, those in the other angles being reduced to fragments. This arch is the only one which is moulded on the edge, the others being splayed. These arches have evidently been built after the walls adjoining, as they fit awkwardly against previously existing doorways at the north-east and north-west angles. That at the south-west angle butts against a structure which seems to have formed a turret adjoining the north-west angle of the nave. This turret contains a small chamber, at about 7 feet to 8 feet above the floor of the nave, which enters by a small door from the nave, and is said to be the porter's lodge. It has a curiously cusped loophole opening in the direction of the church door.

The cloister is surrounded by buildings on the east and north. The north transept has a door to the cloister, and a benitier is placed near the entrance. Next to the transept on the north is a chamber, 10 feet wide, entering from the cloister (see Fig. 982), and lighted by a window to the east. There is a fireplace in the east wall of this room, being the only fireplace in the monastery. It seems doubtful whether this chamber was not originally the slype or passage from the cloister towards the east, as there is no other passage.

Next to this, on the north, is the chapter house, which projects beyond the general line of the buildings, the portion next the cloister having the appearance of a vestibule. The inner cloister enters from the vestibule by two arches (Fig. 1002), which rest on a central round pillar and corbels at the sides. This pillar is sometimes stated to be of Norman work, and the chapter house is, consequently, regarded as of Norman date. But a careful examination of the pillar and its capital leads to the conclusion that it is comparatively a late structure. The carving of the cap

(Fig. 1003) is very peculiar. On the outer or west side, the ornament, which is somewhat decayed, resembles that of the caps of the adjoining nunnery church, and may easily be mistaken for ancient. But the ornament of the inner or east side of the cap (see Fig. 1003) is quite different, and is undoubtedly of very late design, being similar to that on the carved tomb-stones of the fifteenth or sixteenth centuries, such as that in Figs. 991 and 992. The dog-tooth or nail-head ornament of the arches, although at first sight like first pointed work, is found, on closer inspection, to consist of late imitations—showing three small nail-heads placed close together, so as to form an enrichment in a manner not at all transition like. The same remark applies to the enrichments of the high chapel in the choir (see Fig. 1000).

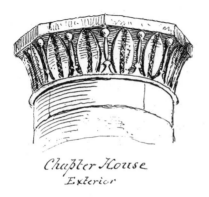

Chapter House
Exterior

Chapter House
Interior

Fig. 1003.—Iona Cathedral. Details of Central Pillar in Chapter House.

The walls of the eastern part of the cloister are not over 2 feet 6 inches in thickness (which would be very unusual in Norman work), and they have been strengthened by interior piers when the present flat barrel arch was erected over the chapter house. This probably took place when the upper part of this portion of the building was raised a story in height, possibly in order to form the library on the upper floor. It is evident, from an examination of the junction of the walls on the exterior, that the upper floor of this part of the building was added at a late period. Both vestibule and chapter house appear to have had a stone seat running along the walls, and the whole may possibly have formed the place of assembly of the monks. Probably, like the chapter house at St. Andrews, the western portion, or vestibule, was the original chapter house, and the inner division was added at a later period.

From the chapter house a passage is visible in the upper part of the east wall of the north transept. In order to admit of this, the wall of the transept (as above pointed out) has required to be made of great thickness, and this explains the depth of the two recesses under it in the transept previously referred to. As already mentioned, there was an upper floor over the chapter house and the adjoining portions of the east range of the cloister buildings. Part of this upper floor is believed to have been the library—the literary treasures of which were famous—and part would, no doubt, be the dormitory of the monks.

It seems not improbable that the passage in the transept wall may have led from the library or dormitory to the chapel in the upper aisle of the choir over the sacristy, and the use of that chapel would thus be explained. The chapel, as already mentioned, is a structure of late erection, as is apparent from the imitation dog-tooth running round the straight-sided arch of the east window (see Fig. 1002). The passage in the transept wall may be much older, but was possibly utilised in connection with the late reconstruction of the monastery, as above suggested.

To the north of the chapter house are two chambers of good size, over which an upper story has extended, as the remains of the windows show.

The north side of the cloister has been occupied by the refectory, a building 63 feet long by 20 feet wide. It is situated on the first or upper floor, and is of late work; but seems to occupy the position of a previous refectory, which formerly stood on the site, and of which some portions of the walls remain. The first refectory appears to have been on the ground floor, as the remains of what must have been a handsome doorway in the south wall near the west end of this range prove. This doorway has had three orders of mouldings with shafts and caps, about 7 feet high, apparently of thirteenth century work, of which some fragments remain, partly built into the adjoining angle structure. The latter is evidently a late erection, as it encloses part of the west jamb of the above doorway. The pier of the diagonal arch of the cloister walk at the east end of the refectory also encroaches on the door beside it. At a somewhat late period the refectory has been raised to the upper floor, and an entrance made to it by a wide staircase at the east end (which would also probably form the day staircase to the dormitory). The ground floor is low, and has loop-holes for windows. It has apparently been used for cellars or storages. There is a wide pointed doorway leading into it at the north-west angle (see Fig. 997). The north elevation of the structure is fairly preserved.

The buttresses seem to be reconstructions on the lines of the original ones, but the windows, both in the north elevation and towards the cloister, are of later date.

The eastern range of buildings is continued northwards beyond the refectory by a chamber 33 feet long by 12 feet 6 inches wide, which seems to have been connected on the upper floor with a lavatory and latrine. The latter has a built channel, evidently intended, from the low aperture at each end, for the passage of a stream of water, which could be

easily led into it from the neighbouring burn.   To the west of this stand
the walls, 3 feet high, of a nearly detached edifice, with a separate outer
doorway, which may perhaps have been an infirmary.   To the north-east,
the low walls are observable of a detached structure 58 feet 9 inches long
by 21 feet 6 inches wide.   The only wall opening traceable is the doorway, which has been of simple design.   This is supposed by some to have
been the kitchen, but it seems doubtful.   There is no appearance of a
fireplace.

A small detached chapel, 38 feet in length by 20 feet 9 inches in
width over the walls, lies to the north-east of the chapter house.   It has
had a doorway in the north wall, a small centre window in the east
wall, and a similar window in each of the side walls near the east end.
The windows are trefoil headed and cusped, and appear to be late.   The
doorway had two orders, with a bead on each.   The orientation of this
building is different from that of the cathedral.

Adjoining the south-west angle of the cloister, and built out from it, is
a small enclosure containing stone coffins (see Fig. 994).   Immediately
beyond this are the remains of another enclosure, connected with a Celtic
cross (called St. Martin's) near the west end of the cathedral (see Fig.
995).   The inner of these chambers, which encloses the stone coffins, is
called "St. Columba's Tomb."   Dr. Skene is of opinion that it is actually
the structure which contained the body of St. Columba, the coffin of that
Saint being placed on the right or south side, and that of St. Blathmac
(a martyr who died in defending the abbey against the Northmen in 825)
being placed on the left or north side.   This view is, however, controverted
by Sir Henry Dryden in a MS. of 1879, deposited in the Antiquarian
Museum in Edinburgh.

There is also a well in the same locality as the above enclosures.

The ruins of a chapel of some size (48 feet long by 30 feet wide over
the walls) lie at a short distance to the west of the cloister.   The walls
are reduced to a few feet in height, and are partly rebuilt in a rough
manner.   There seems to have been a doorway in the east end, but this is
doubtless not original.   A turret can be traced at the south-east angle and
another at the south-west angle.

To the north-east of the cloister lie the total ruins of what is called
the Abbot's House, and at some distance to the south-east of the church
may be observed the greatly demolished remains of a chapel.

In the choir are preserved several monuments.   On the south side,
close to the sedilia (see Fig. 986), lies the well sculptured effigy of Abbot
Kenneth; and on the north side, near the door of the sacristy, is the effigy
of Abbot M'Kinnon, the last abbot of Iona (the head being visible in
Fig. 987), around which is legible the following inscription, "Hic jacet
Johannes MacFingone, Abbas de Hy qui obiit anno Domini Millessimo
Quingentessimo cujus animae propitietur Deus Altissimus.   Amen."

In the floor of the choir a large slab shows the remains of brass work, and against the east wall rests the carved figure of a knight, with shield and spear, said to be the monument of a M'Lean (see Fig. 983).

ST. MACHAR'S CATHEDRAL, OLD ABERDEEN.

Old Aberdeen is situated on the river Don, about two miles north from the town of Aberdeen on the Dee. The cathedral, which is dedicated to St. Machar, is built in granite, and is now considerably reduced in size from its original dimensions. The nave (Fig. 1004) is entire and is used as the parish church. The walls of the transepts exist only to the height of about 10 feet. The choir has been entirely destroyed. The bishop's palace, which stood at the east end of the cathedral, has also disappeared. It was a large building, and "had a fine court, having a high tower at each of its four corners; an outer and inner gate; with a deep well in the middle of the court; and an iron gate by which the bishop passed from his palace into the choir." *

The cathedral stands on the north side of an extensive churchyard, and the situation is pleasant, having the houses of the chanonry—some of them quaint-looking and interesting—approaching it on the south. On the north it is skirted by high trees, which grow on a steep bank sloping down from the cathedral towards the Don.

The seat of the bishop was translated from Murthlack or Mortlack, in Banffshire, to Aberdeen by King David I. in the year 1136, St. Nectan being the last bishop of Mortlack and the first of Aberdeen. The third bishop, Matthew Kinninmond, began to build a cathedral between 1183 and 1199 to supersede the primitive church then existing, "which [new building], because it was not glorious enough, Bishop Cheyne threw down." †

A second edifice was begun by Bishop Cheyne shortly after 1282, and the work went on till the time when the country was involved in the war with Edward I. After Bruce was seated on the throne, Cheyne was temporarily banished, and " during his absence the king, seeing the new cathedral he had begun, made the church to be built with the revenues of the bishoprick." ‡

The cathedral thus erected was in its turn thrown down by Bishop Alexander Kinninmond, who succeeded in 1355, and he began a new building on a still larger scale about the year 1370. Of his operations there remain two large piers for the support of the central tower, which form the earliest portion of the structure of St. Machar's now remaining. These piers are built of red freestone, and are much more graceful and

* *View of the Diocese of Aberdeen:* Spalding Club, p. 151.
† *Ibid.* p. 148.   ‡ *Ibid.* p. 163.

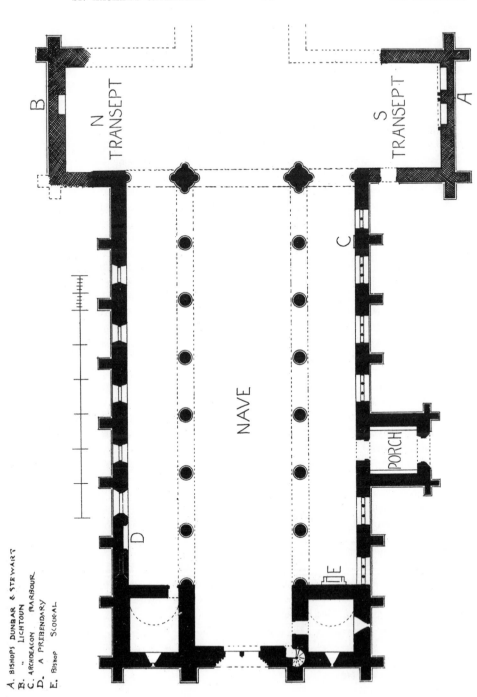

A. BISHOPS DUNBAR & STEWART
B. " LICHTOUN
C. ARCHDEACON BARBOUR
D. A PREBENDARY
E. BISHOP SCOUGAL

N TRANSEPT

S TRANSEPT

NAVE

PORCH

Fig. 1004.—St. Machar's Cathedral. Plan.

refined in character than the succeeding work, most of which is con-structed in granite. Bishop Kinninmond may possibly have built the bay of the nave adjoining for a buttress to the central tower. Freestone mouldings similar to those of the tower still remain at the springing, as if they had continued across to the first pillar; but the arch must have been taken down, as the existing bays are all of granite, and the granite mouldings—which are of quite a different section—are seen to butt against those of Kinninmond's time.

The nave may be said to be all of one period, and appears to have been principally built, including the two western towers, by Bishop Henry Leighton between 1422 and 1440. It was roofed in by his successor, Bishop Lindsay, and in the *View of the Diocese* it is said to have been leaded over by the Bishops Elphinston and Dunbar, and " ceiled by this last," A.D. 1518-1531. The flat ceiling of oak erected by Bishop Dunbar still remains (Fig. 1005), having been constructed by him at his own "pains and expenses." "James Winter, an Angus man, was architect of the timber work and ceiling of said church; which was well done, and may make his name famous to after ages." * It is ornamented with heraldic decorations, containing the arms of various European kings, Pope Leo x., the Scottish nobility, and Churchmen. These have been drawn and illustrated in colour by the New Spalding Club. Bishop Dunbar also finished Leighton's towers by adding the spires (Fig. 1006) in grey freestone. The general colour of the granite work is of a reddish yellow tint.

The edifice as it now stands measures on the outside as follows, viz.—length of nave about 143 feet, width 77 feet. The transept is about 121 feet long by 37 feet 6 inches wide. The centre alley of the nave is 30 feet 6 inches wide. The towers are about 23 feet 6 inches square, and about 111 feet high.

The west front of St. Machar's (see Fig. 1006) is entirely built with granite, except the spires, and is one of the most impressive and imposing structures in Scotland. It is extremely plain, not a single scrap of carving being visible anywhere, and most of the openings are of the simplest kind. This front is a veritable piece of Doric work, depending for its effect on its just proportion and the mass of its granite masonry. The towers and spires are of equal height, and almost identical in design. The great corbels and machicolations of the parapet are clearly derived from castellated forms, and the embrasured bands round the spires and their numerous lucarnes are distinct signs of the late date of their construction. The entrance doorway (Fig. 1007) is remarkable, the jambs being mere rounds and hollows, with a flat stone laid along at the springing of the round arch, marking where the capitals usually stand, while the arch mouldings are of the most elementary kind, all being designed to suit the

* Orme's *Description of Old Aberdeen*, p. 61.

hard granite of which they are constructed. Above this doorway is one of the most striking features of the composition, viz.—the seven lofty narrow windows (see Fig. 1006), about 26 feet in height, and each crowned

MOULDINGS OF ARCHES

BASE

CAP

FIG 1005.—St. Machar's Cathedral. The Nave, looking West.

FIG. 1006.—St. Machar's Cathedral. West Front.

FIG. 1007.—St. Machar's Cathedral. West Doorway.

with a round and cusped arch (Fig. 1009). The ground story of both towers is barrel vaulted; the apartment in the south tower has had a rude door knocked through the front wall, and is now used as a place for keeping spades and shovels in.

The south elevation (Fig. 1008) is marked by the same simplicity as the west front, being designed to suit the intractable material of which it is built. The clerestory is an absolutely plain wall, pierced by narrow round arched windows, without a moulding of any kind, while the windows of the side aisles are filled with the simplest tracery. The effect of this part of the building is much marred by the removal of the parapet which formerly ran along the top of the wall. The south

Fig. 1008.—St. Machar's Cathedral. View from South-West.

porch is a dignified structure. It was evidently meant to have a room over the entrance, for which a window is provided; but there is no indication

III.   F

of there ever having been an upper floor or an access stair, and the considerable height, as viewed from the inside, has an unmeaning appearance. The resemblance between this porch and the south porch of St. Michael's, Linlithgow, is striking, both having the inner crow-stepped gable built on the aisle wall. In the latter porch the upper room has been completed.

FIG. 1009.
St. Machar's Cathedral.
Top of West Windows.

The north aisle wall of the cathedral, which is fortunately not so well seen as the south wall, is quite modern, and has a mean and paltry appearance.

The pillars in the nave (see Fig. 1005) are all round on Plan, with round moulded caps and very simple bases. These are shown in section in Fig. 1005, and also on a larger scale in Fig. 1010, which contains Scougal's monument (afterwards referred to), and where there is also a view of part of the interior of the large west window. Beside the sketch of this monument will be seen a stone containing the arms, surmounted by a mitre, probably of Bishop Stewart, who died in 1565 (a fesse chequé debruised by a bend engrailed).

In the view of the interior (see Fig. 1005) it may be observed that the full thickness of the clerestory walls does not come down to the caps of the pillars, but stops short a few feet above. This arrangement has an unpleasing effect in perspective, leaving a portion of the cap projecting and bearing nothing. The two piers at the crossing, as already mentioned, are of freestone and are of clustered form, and have richly carved capitals. These capitals are necessarily concealed by the building up of the arches, which lead from the nave to the crossing. Fig. 1011 shows a part of one of these capitals, which can be seen from the transept.

Regarding the choir nothing can be now said from observation, as it was destroyed in 1560, and the ruins have since been entirely removed. Alluding to this, Orme says (p. 104)—"The glorious structure of said Cathedral Church being near nine score years in building, did not remain twenty entire, when it was almost ruined by a crew of sacrilegious church robbers."

There was an old choir standing in Bishop Elphinston's time, early in the sixteenth century, which, as Boece tells us in his life of that prelate,* was considered by the bishop to be in a style unworthy such a church, and he began to rebuild it on a plan corresponding with the western part of the building; "but lest he should die before it was completed, he would not take down the old choir till everything was in readiness to begin the new one, so that a considerable part was finished before his death." The work was continued by his successors, but it seems doubtful if it ever was entirely completed before the Reformation burst on the country.

The building of the central steeple, which had been partly carried out

* See Orme, p. 28.

by Bishop Leighton, was finally completed by Bishop Elphinston about 1511. The tower was supported by the four pillars of the crossing. "It

FIG. 1010.—St. Machar's Cathedral. Monument of Bishop Scougal in South-West Angle of Aisle.

was four storey high, and square, and had two battlements, and seems to have been about 150 foot high." *

* View of the Diocese, p. 150.

Bishop Leighton also built, in 1424, the north transept, or, as it was called, St. John's Aisle, where the beautiful sculpture of that bishop's effigy now lies inglorious beneath a rough brick arch (Fig. 1012). His tomb appears to have been entire when Orme (who died about 1725) wrote his description of the cathedral.* He describes it as an effigy *in pontificalibus*, on an altar tomb with a canopy, under which is this inscription : " *Hic jacet bone memorie Henricus de Lichtoun*," &c. Huddled in behind the figure there is a large stone slab with an inscription, which can hardly be seen on account of the rubbish and ivy.

The south transept was built by Bishop Dunbar in 1522. And so recently as the time of Orme large portions of it, which have now disap-

Fig. 1011.—St. Machar's Cathedral.   Part of East Pier from Transept.

peared, were standing, if, indeed, it was not almost entire at that date. Orme speaks of the "top of this aisle" as having then been taken down for the miserable purpose of furnishing stones for new buildings at the college; and he also mentions large windows as then existing, all of which have vanished. Indeed, almost nothing of this transept now remains except the tomb of the founder, Bishop Gavin Dunbar (Fig. 1013), and an empty tomb to the left of it, which were complete when Orme wrote. The latter contained the effigy of a bishop, "a lion at his feet, and under his head a pointed helmet for a cushion; arms, a lion rampant *queue fourche* debruised by a bend charged with three escallops." † This was

* Orme, pp. 42 and 62.   † *Ibid.* p. 43.

probably a tomb of the end of the sixteenth century. The foliage round the arch, modelled from seaweed, is carved with great spirit. Dunbar's tomb is perhaps the finest of the minor pieces of work now remaining here. It is remarkable how it escaped destruction on various occasions, and especially in 1693, when a gang of religious fanatics broke his effigy in pieces, defaced the inscription, smashed the hanging cusped tracery round

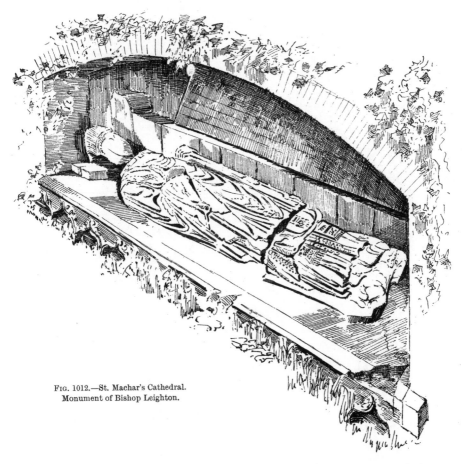

Fig. 1012.—St. Machar's Cathedral. Monument of Bishop Leighton.

the arch (apparently firing guns at it), and threw down the top of the monument. The existing cornice, with its two rows of corbels, was erected afterwards; and it must be allowed that it harmonises well with the earlier work, although it has more of the spirit of domestic than of ecclesiastical architecture. A similar kind of battlement is introduced over the centre panel of the Amond Monument, at Ellon, in the same county (see

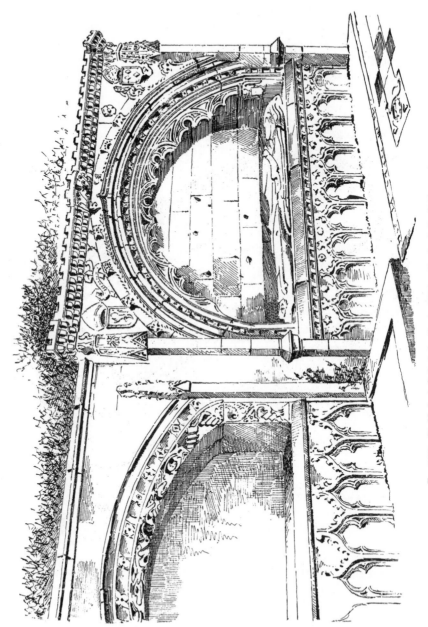

FIG. 1013.—St. Machar's Cathedral. Tomb of Bishop Dunbar in South Transept.

Fig. 1014), erected just about the time that this monument was repaired. In the spandrils of the arch of the bishop's tomb are the royal arms of Scotland and those of Dunbar (three cushions pendant at the corners in a bordure). The label terminals near the head and feet of the effigy are designed as angels bearing shields. Orme states that, in 1640, under the direction of the Earl of Seaforth and others, "A mason struck out

FIG. 1014.—Monument at Ellon, Aberdeenshire.

Christ's arms in hewn work, on each end of Bishop Dunbar's tomb," "and likewise chesel'd out the name of Jesus" from another part of the building.* Both of the above tombs are of freestone.

A very interesting monument, also in freestone, is built into the south wall of the nave (Fig. 1015). It is in bas relief, the depth of the recess above the effigy being only two inches from the projection of the arch

* Orme, p. 132.

moulding, yet within this slight recess the sculptor has obtained a wonderful effect in the beautiful figure, supposed to represent Archdeacon Barbour, the poet, who died in 1396. If this is Barbour's monument, it must have been erected a considerable time after his death, as the nave was not built till after that event. There is a long inscription beneath the monument, which, so far as we know, has never been decyphered. The length of the recess in which the figure lies is 3 feet 11½ inches.

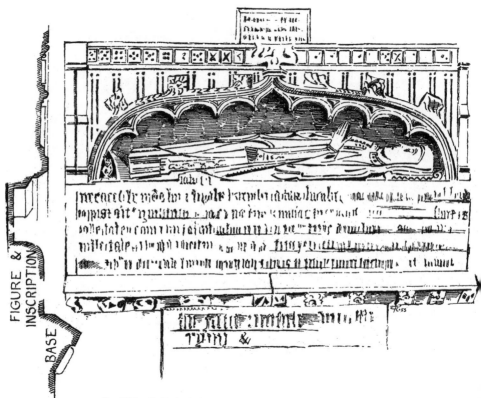

FIG. 1015.—St. Machar's Cathedral. Monument in South Wall of Nave.

The whole breadth of the monument is 4 feet 4 inches, and the height, including the inscription and base course (exclusive of the lower inscription), to the top of the horizontal cornice is 2 feet 6 inches. It stands at a height of 6 feet 6 inches from the floor to the bed of the figure.

At the west end of the south aisle is the monument (see Fig. 1010) of Bishop Patrick Scougal, who, as his epitaph says, "enriched the Cathedral of St. Machar," and other places in Aberdeen, "with considerable tokens of his great bounty." The monument was erected in 1685, the year of his death.

TRINITY COLLEGE CHURCH, EDINBURGH.

This church stood in the hollow between the Old and New Towns of Edinburgh, on the west side of Leith Wynd. It was founded by Mary of Gueldres, Queen of James II., shortly after that king's death in 1460, the charter of erection being dated 1462. The edifice was dedicated to the "honour and praise of the Holy Trinity, to the ever blessed and glorious Virgin Mary, to Saint Ninian the Confessor, and to all the saints and elect people of God." *

The foundation was established for a provost, eight prebendaries, and two clerks, and in 1502 there were added a dean and sub-dean. Lands and benefices sufficient were bestowed on the establishment for its maintenance.

Connected with the college was "Trinity Hospital," also founded by Queen Mary of Gueldres. After the Reformation the endowments passed into the hands of the Town Council, who maintained the Hospital as a city charity for decayed burgesses and their families.

The church became the place of worship of a new parochial division called "Trinity College Parish," and so continued till 1848, when it was removed to make way for the station of the North British Railway Company.

Trinity College Church was a very fine specimen of the Scottish Gothic architecture of the fifteenth century. It showed (as has been pointed out in the Introduction) that much of the middle pointed or decorated style continued to be used in this country long after it had been given up in England. This view is supported by Richman, who says of this church: "The interior is a very beautiful decorated composition, with the capitals of the piers enriched with foliage, not exceeded in design or execution in any English cathedral"; and he also adds, "This building is all of good decorated character, and deserving of minute examination and study." During the erection of the church "the master of works" was John Halkerston, who, in recent books, is frequently referred to as the architect; but, as has been pointed out elsewhere,† he seems to have acted as paymaster, not as designer.

The church (Fig. 1016)‡ consisted of a choir, with north and south aisles, and a five-sided eastern apse, north and south transepts, with the

* Wilson's *Memorials of Edinburgh*, Vol. II. p. 133.

† *The Castellated and Domestic Architecture of Scotland*, Vol. v. p. 532.

‡ This Plan is copied from that in the *Collegiate Churches of Midlothian*, by D. Laing.

commencement of a tower over the crossing, and a north sacristy. The nave was never erected, the arch leading to the west from the transept being built up, and having a circular window inserted therein. It is supposed that the progress of the structure was arrested by the death of the foundress, which occurred in 1463. The choir, including the apse, was 69 feet in length by 25 feet in width internally. The north and south aisles extended along the three bays of the choir, the north aisle

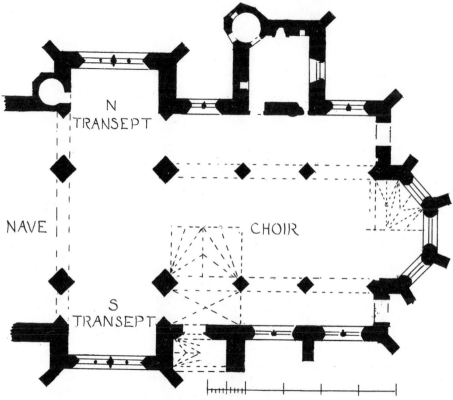

Fig. 1016.—Trinity College Church. Plan.

being 13 feet wide and the south aisle 9 feet wide. The apse was the full width and height of the central choir, and had a lofty window in each of its three central divisions. The transepts had small projections; the whole internal length of the transept, including the crossing, being 74 feet and the width 24 feet.

The choir and aisles were roofed with fine groined vaulting. That of the side aisles was simple, but the vault of the choir was ornamented with ridge ribs and several intermediate ribs, or tiercerons, springing from vaulting shafts, supported on corbels and provided with carved caps, and all the vaults were studded with carved bosses. The effect of the vaulting of the apse was specially beautiful. Each bay of the choir had clustered piers (Fig. 1017), with finely carved capitals. Above these was a string course, then a piece of plain wall in the space usually occupied by the triforium, and the whole was crowned with the traceried clerestory windows. A good general view of the interior, taken a short time before its destruction, is given by Billings.*

Owing to the removal of the building, it has been impossible to make original illustrations for this work, but we are fortunate in being able to publish copies of a series of sketches made by the late James Drummond, R.S.A., in 1845.

These picturesque sketches give a good idea of the nature of the structure, both internally and externally. Fig. 1018 is a view of the exterior of the south side of the choir, showing the three bays into which the aisle

FIG. 1017.—Trinity College Church.
Piers of Choir.

was divided by buttresses, from which flying arches extended to the upper part of the choir. The buttresses had simple set-offs, and were crowned with pinnacles, which, for the most part, seem to have been greatly decayed. In the depth of the buttresses next the south transept a porch was formed, which was roofed with fine groined vaulting. This porch is also well shown in Fig. 1018. The arch is moulded, and dies against the buttresses, and is crowned with a reversed curve and a flowered finial. There were carefully carved canopies and corbels for statues on the face of the buttresses on each side of the porch, and the other buttresses seem to have had similar niches. A round-headed doorway in the porch gave access to the choir, and had a square-headed window over it.

The aisle windows had double splayed jambs and arches (Fig. 1019) both in the exterior and interior of the wall openings, but the original tracery had been broken, and its place was supplied with one upright mullion in the centre and a transome (Fig. 1020). This sketch also shows the south end of the south transept, which preserved its four mullions, of varied thickness, and its tracery. The latter is of a kind not uncommon in late Scottish churches.

Fig. 1021 shows the exterior of the north transept, and the north side of the choir and the sacristy. The north end wall of the transept corre-

* Vol. II.

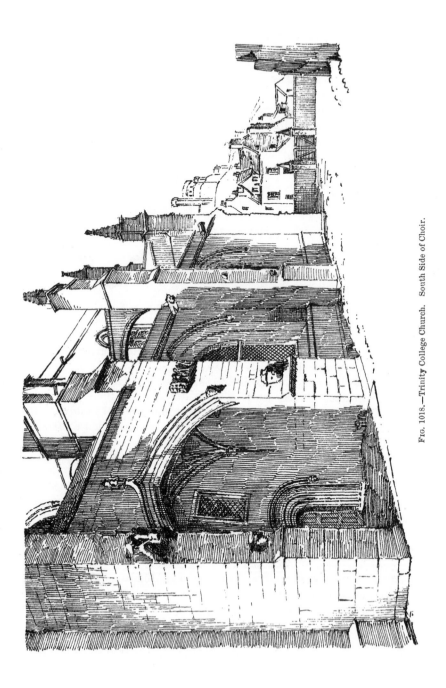

Fig. 1018.—Trinity College Church. South Side of Choir.

sponds with that of the south transept—the great window having double splays on the outer ingoing, and tracery, mullions, and transome similar to those of the south window. The angle buttresses and pinnacles, and parapet with corbel course, enriched with rosettes and gargoyles, all correspond at both ends of the transepts.

The upper part of the north side of the choir is also seen in this sketch. It had a plain parapet with bold gargoyles, and in each bay a moulded window in which the original tracery was preserved. This showed a central mullion with quatrefoil in the arch-head, and the smaller arches foiled or cusped. The buttress at the sacristy was well pre-served. The pinnacle was apparently original and of good design. On the front of the but-tress a small additional pinnacle was intro-duced, which would give considerable charac-ter to the design. Fig. 1018 shows that the same arrangement was evidently adopted in the corresponding buttress on the south side. The arches of the flying buttresses are also visible in the sketches of both sides of the church. The roof of the north aisle seems to have been covered with stone slabs.*

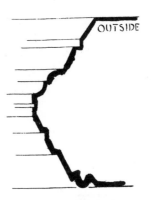

Fig. 1019.—Trinity College Church. Window Jamb.

A building 17 feet in length by 16 feet in width internally projected from the north wall. It is sometimes called the chapter house, but was more likely the sacristy, It had a round-headed doorway opening into the north aisle (Fig. 1022), a good window to the east, and a smaller square-headed window to the west. There are two ambries in the west and north walls, a fireplace in the north wall, and a squint window in the south-east angle commanding a view of the high altar. At the north-east angle there was a buttress with a pinnacle, and at the north-west angle (see Fig. 1021) an octagonal projection, which, doubtless, contained a wheel stair to an upper floor, the window of which is seen in the sketch. The roof was covered with stone slabs, and a chimney with battlement ornament crowned the north gable. The fireplace of the sacristy is said to have comprised a fine specimen of a Gothic chimney.

Fig. 1023 shows the interior of the south transept. The transept had no aisles or chapels. The main arches of the crossing spring from clustered responds against the walls with carved caps, and the groined vaulting of the transept—which was similar to that of the choir—with its numerous moulded ribs enriched with bosses, is seen springing from wall shafts and corbels. The south window, with its mullions and

* Sir D. Wilson states that the whole church was roofed with stone till 1814, when slates were substituted.—*Memorials of Edinburgh*, Vol. II. p. 174.

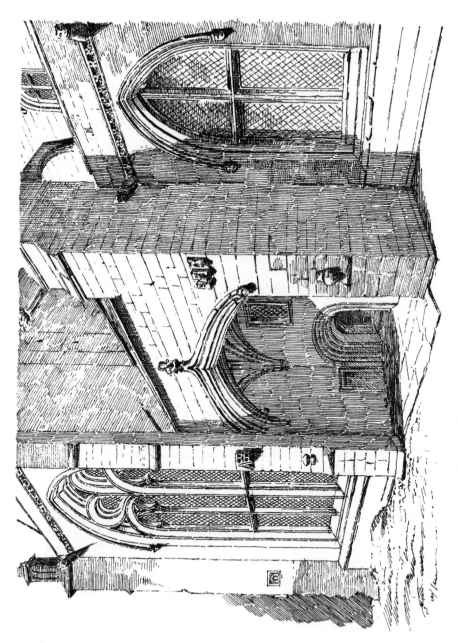

Fig. 1020.—Trinity College Church. South Porch and South Transept.

Fig. 1021.—Trinity College Church. North Transept and North Side of Choir.

tracery, is also well shown. A small circular window, with eight bold cusps, was inserted within the western wall arch.

Fig. 1024 is taken from the parapet walk of the south transept, and shows the upper part of the south side of the choir, the top of the stair turret, and the angle pinnacle of the transept. Of the choir there are

Fig. 1022.—Trinity College Church. North Aisle.

visible the parapet, with enriched corbel course, and the bold gargoyles and pinnacles of the east end buttresses. The south clerestory windows had lost their tracery, and a plain mullion and transome had been substituted. The cape house of the stair turret is plain, but picturesque, and the pinnacle of the angle buttress is of good, though late, design. Those of the apse are evidently similar.

FIG. 1023.—Trinity College Church. South Transept.

Fig. 1024.—Trinity College Church.   Choir, from Parapet of South Transept.

Fig. 1025 shows a view from the parapet of the choir looking south across the south transept. We here see the construction of the parapet and its corbel course, and an example of one of the gargoyles carved in the form of an animal. The monkey was a favourite subject of the carvers in this church, and it as well as other figures were used in great profusion. The cape house and angle pinnacle are also again visible.

FIG. 1025.—Trinity College Church. Looking South from Parapet of Choir.

To the right is the roof of the south transept, terminated with a foliated cross. A small ridge ornament of stone may also be observed on the top of the stone ridge of the roof.

In Fig. 1022 a small credence table or piscina is visible, which is illustrated on a larger scale in Fig. 1026. Fig. 1027 is a piscina which was probably in the choir. The carving has apparently been of a good style, but late. Fig. 1022 further shows that there was a doorway at the east end of the north aisle, which appears to have nearly blocked up the traceried window, the head of which is visible above. The Plan shows that there was a similar doorway at the east end of the south aisle.

FIG. 1026.—Trinity College Church. Credence Table in North Aisle.

FIG. 1027.—Trinity College Church. Piscina.

Fig. 1028 shows the interior of the south aisle looking westwards. These sketches in the north and south aisles show that the central aisle was shut off from the side aisles by solid partitions at the time the sketches were made.

In Figs. 1029 and 1030 are shown a great variety of the picturesque carvings with which the corbels, caps, &c. were enriched. These sculptures are all of a very grotesque and some of a debased character, and point to the late style of much of the work.

In Fig. 1031 is preserved a view of part of the exterior of the apse and of some old-fashioned structures adjoining. Although the building of Trinity Hospital is removed, the charity still exists and adds to the comfort of a number of old men and women.

When the church was demolished, a careful search was made to discover the remains of the royal foundress; and a skeleton, in an antique-shaped leaden coffin, was found in the apse, near the place where the high altar must have stood. This was probably the remains of the queen dowager.*

A very interesting memorial of Trinity College Church has been pre-served in a painting, which is believed to have been the altar-piece. It is

Fig. 1028.—Trinity College Church. South Aisle, looking West.

a Diptych, painted on both sides, and contains portraits of King James III. and his queen, Margaret of Denmark. It was executed in 1484, and has

* *The Collegiate Churches of Mid-Lothian*, p. xxxi.

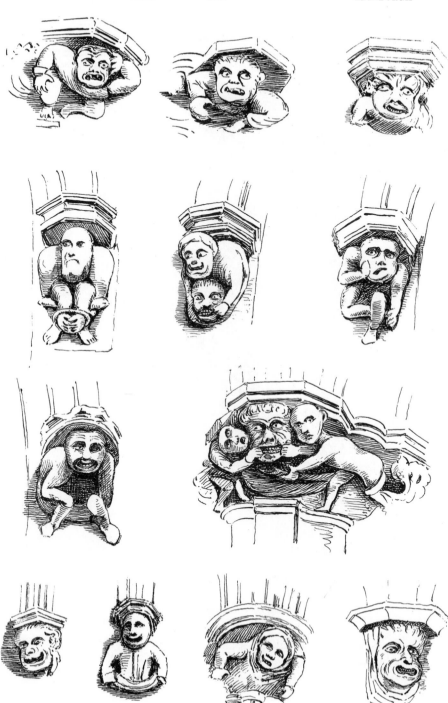

Fig. 1029.—Trinity College Church.   Carved Corbels, &c.

been restored to this country from Hampton Court by the gracious permission of Her Majesty, and is now exhibited in the Picture Gallery of

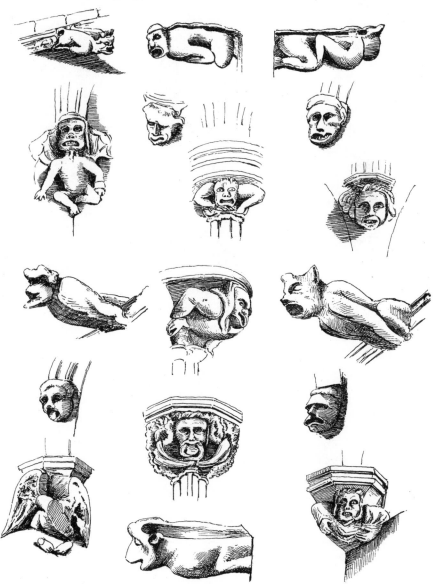

FIG. 1030.—Trinity College Church.   Corbels, Gargoyles, &c.

Holyrood House.   Dr Laing has endeavoured to prove its original purpose by identifying the portraits of Edward Bonkill, the queen's confessor, and

FIG. 1031.—Trinity College Church. Hospital and Part of Apse, from North-East.
(From a Drawing by William Douglas, 1845.)

probably that of Mary of Gueldres herself, in the character of an angel seated at the organ of the church, which forms the reverse of one of the panels.*

THE PARISH CHURCH OF ST. JOHN THE BAPTIST, PERTH.

The ancient City of Perth, one of the favourite residences of the kings of Scotland, formerly possessed, as might be expected, many well endowed religious establishments. The principal of these was the Dominican or Blackfriars' Monastery, founded by Alexander II. in 1231. The buildings were extensive, and formed the residence of the Scottish kings when in the Fair City. It was here that James I. was staying at the time of his assassination. The Carmelites or Whitefriars had also a convent close to Perth, founded in the reign of Alexander III. The Charter House or Carthusian Monastery in Perth was the only house of that order in Scotland. It was founded by James I. and his queen in 1429. The Franciscans' or Greyfriars' Monastery was founded by Lord Oliphant in 1460. There were also numerous nunneries and chapels, some of very ancient date; but all these religious establishments have now entirely disappeared, the only ancient ecclesiastical structure still remaining (and it has been greatly changed) being the Parish Church of St. John the

* *The Collegiate Churches of Mid-Lothian*, p. xxii.

Baptist, from which the city derived the title of "St. John's Town." This edifice still serves its original purpose of the parish church of the town, but it has in modern times been divided by walls so as to form three places of worship.

So far as we have been able to discover, no complete history of this church has ever been written, and the circumstances connected with its original erection and subsequent reconstruction do not appear to have been definitely ascertained and described. It is certain that a church existed here in the twelfth century, and it is obvious, from an inspection of the structure, that not a single stone of that early building remains to enable its size and appearance to be determined. All knowledge in regard to the existing fabric must, therefore, be derived from the internal evidence of the building itself, with such slight aid as can be got from written records. The following are some scattered notices of St. John's Church gathered from various sources.

The earliest mention of the church occurs in the *Registrum de Dunfermelyn* * under the years 1124-1127, when it was granted by David I., with its property and tithes, to the Abbey of Dunfermline.

Between the years 1189 and 1199 William the Lion granted a charter to Henry Bald of "that land which is in the front of the street, which leads from the Church of St. John Baptist to the Castle of Perth, on the east side opposite to the house of Andrew, the son of Simon." The same Henry Bald granted, about the year 1225, to the Abbey of Scone "these two booths which are in the front of the street which leads from the Church of St. John Baptist towards the Castle of Perth, on the east side opposite to the house of Andrew, the son of Simon; those two booths, to wit, which are towards the north." †

The Church of St. John the Baptist was consecrated by David de Bernham, Bishop of St. Andrews, in 1242. ‡ In Hay's *Sacra Scotia* (p. 323) it is stated that the heart of Alexander III. was buried in the Church of St. John.

In course of time the abbots of Dunfermline allowed the building to become ruinous, and endeavoured to lay on the citizens of Perth the burden of upholding the fabric. It is probable that early in the thirteenth century the Dominican Monastery was built in Perth, and about the middle of the century the Carmelite or Whitefriars' Monastery was erected, and the interests of the citizens may thereby have been diverted somewhat from the parish church. It was perhaps in connection with the repairs required at the time that Robert the Bruce, in 1328, granted that stones might be taken from the quarries of Kyncarachi and Balcormac, belonging to the Abbey of Scone, "for the edification of the Church of Perth." §

* Bannatyne Club, 1842.　　† *Memorabilia of Perth*, pp. 63-66 : Perth, 1806.
‡ *The Church of Scotland in the Thirteenth Century*, by William Lockhart, A.M.
§ *Memorabilia*, p. 23.

In 1335 King Edward III. was in Perth and slew his brother, John of Eltham, Earl of Cornwall, before the high altar of the Church of St. John, for his excesses and ravages in the western districts of Scotland.

In 1379 the tomb of Robert II. was brought from Leith to Perth, and temporarily deposited in St. John's Church before being taken to the Abbey of Scone and set up in it.*

In 1393-4, after the holding of a Parliament at Scone, Walter Trail, Bishop of St. Andrews, performed divine service in St. John's Church.†

From 1401 till 1553-6 there is a continuous record ‡ of the founding of altars in the parish church, and of endowments to already existing altars. In one of these, founded in 1402, it is stipulated that if the stipend of the chaplain of St. James the Apostle should exceed a certain sum, the excess of the endowment meant for that altar should be applied by the Provost and Town Council "for the maintenance and reparation of the windows and ornaments of the parish church."

The chapel in which St. James's altar was situated stood on the south side of the church, and having fallen into a state of ruin, it had been rebuilt about the year 1400, chiefly with the assistance which the magistrates received from William Whitson, a wealthy burgess of Perth.

By a notarial instrument made in 1410, containing certain obligations and confirmations, Euphame, Countess of Stratherne, "gave her bodily oath on the gospels to observe the same. Done in the Parish Church of the Burgh of Perth on St. Martin's altar." §

The foundation charter of the altar of St. John the Evangelist, founded in 1448 by Sir John de Bute, states that the altar was situated "in the new choir of the Parish Church."

The accounts of the Lord High Treasurer contain a payment under the year 1489—"To the Kirk werk of Pertht, xviijs." ‖   And again in 1496— "Item, the xij day of March, in Sanct Johnstoun, giffin to the kirk werk on the bred (altar) xjs. vjd." ¶   Along with other offerings at this time in St. John's there occurs the following—"Item, that samyn day giffin to Walter Merlioune, masoune, for his fee quhill Witsonday nixt tocum, quhilk is the Mertymes fee bipast, xxlib."

This church has the unenviable notoriety of having been the centre whence issued, in 1559, the unruly mob who in a short time demolished the splendid monasteries and other numerous religious houses of Perth and the neighbourhood, and whose example was only too readily followed by other communities throughout the whole country. Such was the effect of a sermon preached here by John Knox. • The fabric of St. John's was

* *Exchequer Rolls*, Vol. II. p. cxii. ; Vol. III. p. lxxii.
† *Book of Perth*, p. xxvi., by John Lawson : Edinburgh, 1847.
‡ *Perth : Its Annals and Archives*, by David Peacock, 1849, p. 589.
§ *Historical Manuscripts Commission*, 14th Report, Appendix, Part III. p. 26.
‖ *Accounts of the Lord High Treasurer*, Vol. I. p. 121.
¶ *Ibid.* p. 323.

spared after being purged of all monuments of idolatry. Nothing was left but the bare walls and roofs, which were retained for use as the Parish Church. Before the end of the century, the building was fitted up with galleries, and in course of time it was divided into three separate places of worship by thick walls, which still exist.

In 1585 the kirk-session declared the church to be in a "ruinous, pitiful, and lamentable state," and the minister was requested to preach a sermon and obtain a collection for the repair of the fabric,* but apparently not till 1598 did "the town begin to repair the new kirk in wallis and wandows." † The next item in the *Chronicle* regarding St. John's shows that the existing lead-covered spire on the central tower is of a considerable age, for in March 1607, "Thair rais ane great extaordinarire winde, that blew the lead of the steipill, to Mr John Malcolme's back yett." ‡ This was evidently a formidable mishap, as ten years elapsed before the session, in 1617, "appointed David Sibbald to be master of work to the reparation of the decayed parts of the steeple, and to recieve furth of an chest, containing the Hospital's writts, the sum of £20 (Scots), left over the last collection lifted for reparation of the kirk, and help to repair the said seeple with." §

As already mentioned, nothing now remains of the church of the twelfth century, referred to in the earlier of the above notes, no part of the present structure being older than the beginning of the fifteenth century. The rebuilding of the Chapel of St. James in 1400 is spoken of above, but that chapel no longer exists. In 1448 the east end of the church is referred to as the "New Choir," and we shall see as we proceed that the other portions of the edifice are of still more recent origin.

The church (Fig. 1032) ‖ consists of a choir and nave, with north and south aisles, and a north and south transept without aisles. The total length of the main building within the walls is about 191 feet by about 58 feet 9 inches wide. The nave and choir are of almost equal length. The transept measures about 91 feet in length from north to south, by about 23 feet 6 inches in width. There was a chapel on the west side of the north transept, which no longer exists, but the wide arch of the opening into it is partly visible in the transept. A view of this chapel is given in the *Memorabilia of Perth*, of which Fig. 1033 is a copy. It is represented as a lean-to of two stories in height, adjoining the north transept, the upper story being evidently reached by a stair in the erection on the west side.

It will be remembered that, in 1448, the east end of the church is referred to as the "New Choir," and it is quite evident from its style

* *Book of Perth*, p. 168. ‡ *Ibid.* p. 11.
† *Chronicle*, p. 7. § *Book of Perth*, p. 275.
‖ We are indebted to Mr. Ramsay Traquair, architect, Edinburgh, for assistance in connection with the Plan of this church.

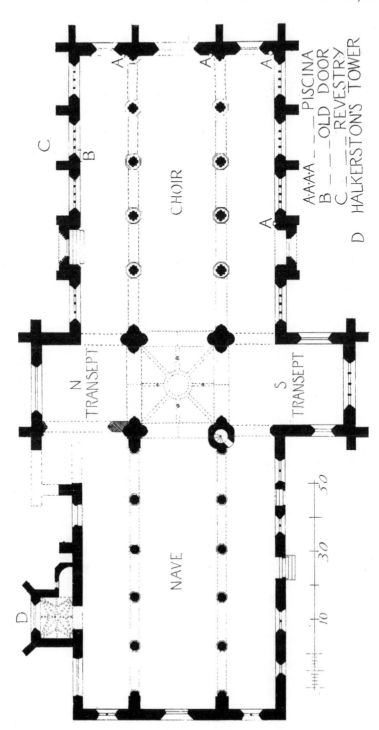

A·A·A — PISCINA
B — OLD DOOR
C — REVESTRY
D HALKERSTON'S TOWER

Fig. 1082.—St. John the Baptist's, Perth. Plan.

that the choir and crossing beneath the central tower are of about that period. The transepts may be later, and, judging from the details of the wide arch which exists in the west wall of the north transept, that arch

FIG. 1033.—St. John the Baptist's, Perth. View from North-west, from the *Memorabilia.*

must undoubtedly be later, one of the arch-jambs being patched on to the great pillar of the tower. The north gable of this transept was rebuilt in 1823.

The south transept is probably of the same period as the north transept.

A view of the church dated 1775, given in the *Chronicle of Perth,** and of which Fig. 1034 is a copy, shows the south side of the whole church, and the transept is drawn very much as it still remains. Another view of the south transept, made in 1765, and published in the papers referring to the Blackfriars' Monastery (where it is by mistake called the "north" front), shows the south transept nearly the same as the above.

A curious row of corbels is partly seen in the interior, projecting through the plaster along the top of the east wall of this transept. They were probably meant for supporting the upright pieces of timber which secured the feet of the rafters.

The two eastern bays of the main arcade of the choir are more elaborately moulded than the others, and round the eastmost pillar on the south side there is finely cut the following inscription (Fig. 1035), which is carved on a band running round the shafts of the pier, as shown in Fig. 1036 :—

Iohañes : fullar : et : uxor : ejus : mariota : foullar.

FIG. 1035.—St. John the Baptist's, Perth. Inscription on East Pillar of Choir.

It will be observed that the husband and wife mentioned in the inscription have the same name, with a slightly different spelling. The two shields

FIG. 1036.—St. John the Baptist's, Perth. Inscription on East Pillar of Choir.

* *Chronicle of Perth,* Maitland Club.

contain the same charges—viz., a key with a mullet—while on one are also carved the last letters of the lady's first name.

It has been recently pointed out by the Rev. John Ferguson, of Aberdalgie,* Perthshire, that John Fullar was one of the bailies of Perth, and that his name occurs as a witness in more than one of the charters belonging to the Charter House, Perth, of the year 1441. His identity is placed beyond doubt by the fact that the charges on the seal attached to the charter are the same as those on the two shields on the pillar, viz., a key in pale and a spur in fess. Mr Ferguson further states :—" We know from the *Registrum de Dunfermline* that an arrangement was made between the monastery and the magistrates of Perth, by which the latter received

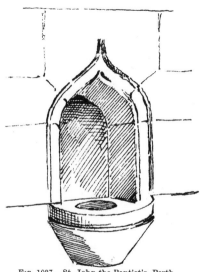

FIG. 1037.—St. John the Baptist's, Perth. Piscina in Choir.

the tithes of Perth for six years, subject to paying the vicar and a certain sum to the monastery, along with the fees for the right of burial in the choir, for the purpose of building 'Chorum, et vestibulum ecclesie parochiale dicti burgi de Perth, prout eis placencius et honestius videatur, ac eadem postquam fuerint edificata perpetuis temporibus sustentabunt in omnibus et singulis reparacionibus choro et vestibulo pertinentibus tectura,' &c. This agreement was made in 1440, the year before John Fullar was made a bailie. It is possible that the tithes and fees did not suffice for the execution of the work laid upon the magistrates, and that John Fullar and his wife volunteered to pay for a part, certainly for the pillar on which their names are inscribed." From this it is evident, as Mr. Ferguson remarks, that the work of renewing the building was to be begun after 1440. It is somewhat singular that the above two persons, who were evidently great benefactors to this church, should have been so completely forgotten that their good work at St. John's required to be rediscovered and brought to notice again here.

In the second bay of the choir from the east, on the north side (at B on Plan), there is a round arched doorway, now built up. It led to the sacristy or revestry, as it was sometimes called. After the Reformation the sacristy was used for meetings of the kirk-session, but it was taken down about the beginning of this century, and the meetings were

* *Scottish Antiquary*, January 1897, p. 137.

FIG. 1038.—St. John the Baptist's, Perth.   North Side of Choir.

afterwards held in the building, shown in Fig. 1034, on the south side of the nave near the west end, which has also since been in its turn removed.

The existing north and south doorways in the choir are modern, although the south one is in the position of the old doorway, as the print from the *Chronicle* shows (see Fig. 1034).

The four piscinas marked **A** on Plan and shown by Fig. 1037 all resemble each other.

The choir (Fig. 1038) has no triforium, but good plain masonry instead, undivided by wall shafts. The clerestory windows are small and round arched, and are divided into two lights by a central mullion, and have plain tracery in the arch-head. The whole details of the choir are very simple and refined for their period, and contrast favourably with most of our late Scottish churches. The section (Fig. 1039) shows that the pillars are simply and beautifully moulded. They are surmounted with good caps, and rest on plain bases (Fig. 1040). The mouldings of the arches (Fig. 1041) are distinctly marked, and rest well on the caps above the shafts or mouldings of the pillars. Some of these details resemble first pointed work, especially the section of the piers which is almost identical with that of the choir piers of St. An-

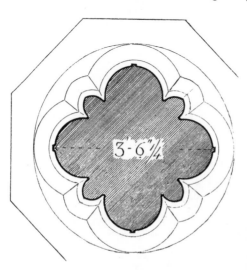

FIG. 1039.—St. John the Baptist's, Perth.
Section of Pier of Choir.

drews Cathedral, from which it is probably copied. The details of the crossing (Fig. 1042) are simple and effective, even as seen under the very unfavourable circumstances that a partition wall blocks up the east arch, and that there are galleries beneath the others. There is a west gallery, but it is omitted in the sketch. The massive piers, with their rounded shafts and very broad fillets, have a striking effect. The groining is of the usual kind found in this position in Scotland. It will be observed that in the ridge ribs, holes for bell ropes are most carefully wrought through the ribs, which are strengthened at those parts. The holes are not all equidistant from the centre. On the two great western piers of the crossing there are projecting corbels to carry the beams on which the rood was placed. Strong iron hooks are fixed in the tower arch above, which were doubtless used for the support of the rood, or to steady it.

Of the rood itself, as a matter of course, nothing remains. The south-west pier is built hollow to contain the stair to the tower. Since the Plan (Fig. 1032) was made the original doorway to this stair has been discovered, as shown in the view. The door shown on the Plan has been cut out at some later time.

As already stated, the nave is almost of the same length as the choir

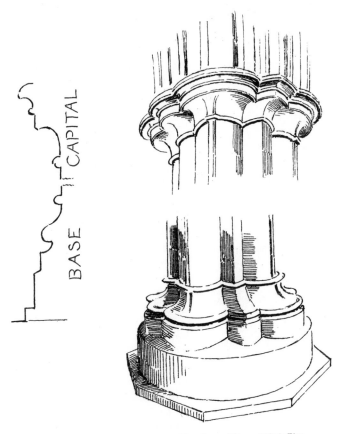

Fig. 1040.—St. John the Baptist's, Perth. Cap and Base of Choir Pier.

(being only about 12 inches less), but each of the arches of the arcade is of rather smaller span than those of the choir, owing to the internal projecting responds at the west end, which may be regarded as fulfilling the purpose of buttresses, and also to the enlargement of the two great piers on the west side of the crossing. Like the choir, the nave is divided into five bays. It has no triforium nor clerestory, but owing to the comparative lowness of the arcade arches (see Fig. 1042), while the ridge of the roof throughout is kept at about the same level as in the choir, there is a deep blank wall above the arcade arches. This wall is of rough masonry compared to that in the choir, and the whole of this part of the church is of a much coarser and ruder description, betokening a later age. The capitals of the piers are of the very rudest kind, and are a perfect contrast to the delicate work of the choir. In the meagre descriptions of St. John's to be found in the books on Perth, this rudeness is pointed to as a sign of great antiquity, but the reverse is unquestionably the case. This nave is undoubtedly "the New Kirk of Perth" referred to in the *Chronicle*, in which "ane Synodall assemblie" was held in April 1606.

It will be seen from the views (Figs. 1043 and 1044) that the top of the wall over the piers of the nave just shows itself and no more on the

FIG. 1041.
St. John the Baptist's, Perth.
Section of Arch Mouldings in Choir
and Nave.

outside, rising above the lean-to roof of the aisles. It has been contemplated, early in this century, to raise this wall and erect a clerestory, and two of the windows adjoining the tower on the north side (see Fig. 1043) have actually been built as part of a pretentious design, with massive buttresses surmounted by high finials, but the work has never been carried further, and indeed could not be carried further to the west, as there is no proper support for such massive building. Below the new clerestory (but not shown on the Plan) a new wall has been brought up to support it.

Fig. 1044 shows a peculiarity in the west wall, which seems to indicate that there has been some change of design here, the gable being thinned above the western doorway. There is a tradition that the church extended further west at one time, and it seems not improbable that a western tower in the centre of the front may have been contemplated and even begun. This tower, like those at Stirling, Linlithgow, and Dundee, may have been intended to open towards the church, with a wide arch, of which the jambs still remain; but this idea having been abandoned, and any part of the tower which then had been built having been taken down, the present makeshift gable was put up instead to fill up the gap, which, in these circumstances, would be left for the supposed opening into the church.

There is a large porch on the north side of the nave (see Fig. 1043), called Halkerston's Tower, the structure having been at one time much higher than it is now. It was a two storied building, the upper story having evidently been of great height and vaulted, as well as the lower one (see Fig. 1033). Two-storied porches are met with at Aberdeen Cathedral and Linlithgow Church, but they are not so rich in architectural

FIG. 1042.—St. John the Baptist's, Perth. Crossing, looking South.

adornment as this one seems to have been. This sketch is copied from a drawing in the *Memorabilia*, a book seldom to be seen, so that this

FIG. 1043.—St. John the Baptist's, Perth.   View from North-West showing New Clerestory, &c.

view is not well known. The circular part of the stair which formerly led to the upper floor, and now leads to a gallery over the north aisle,

Fig. 1044.—St. John the Baptist's, Perth. View, showing West End, &c.

FIG. 1045.—St. John the Baptist's, Perth.   Lower Story of Halkerston's Tower.

was finished with a conical spirelet like the corresponding feature at Linlithgow, and the top of it is seen in the view. The lower part of the tower, which forms the porch, is very effectively vaulted (Fig. 1045). The round arched doorway leading from the porch to the church partakes of the rudeness already referred to as characteristic of the whole western part of the church. A curious coincidence between a part of this church and of the Cathedrals of Dunblane and Dunkeld, all in the county of Perth, may be referred to. The north-west window of the nave aisle in the three buildings is treated in very much the same way in each edifice, and these windows have all a very decided resemblance to each other, and are quite unlike the other windows in their respective structures. They are all three light windows, and have square heads at Perth and Dunkeld, while at Dunblane the head is practically square, having a very flat segmental arch. The south aisle wall of the nave (Fig. 1046) is a curious medley (which we hope will not be restored). The round arched doorway near the east end is, we presume, original; but it is not easy to tell the new work from the old, as the mouldings of all windows and doors on the outside have received a great amount of patching with cement and paint, owing to the crumbling nature of the stone.

The erection of the west end of the church is clearly referable to about the time (1489) when, according to the *Lord High Treasurer's Accounts* (already cited) small payments were made "to the kirk werk of Pertht." It will be remembered that on the same day the payments were made to Walter Merlioune, the mason, and the conjunction of the two payments suggests the idea that Merlioune was the builder of the church. We have already partly traced his career * and found that in all probability he built the palace in Stirling Castle. The resemblance between the fretted work over the panels containing statues at Stirling Castle and that over the upper window in Halkerston's Tower is certainly very remarkable. There is also a resemblance in this feature of Halkerston's Tower to the large fretted panel over the outside of the east entrance to Linlithgow Palace. At Linlithgow the panel is filled with heraldic emblems, while at Perth it appears to have been intended to fill it with statues, as indications of brackets for supporting them are shown in three rows. There was a John Halkerston, "master of the work" to Mary of Gueldres at the building of Trinity College Church, Edinburgh, between 1461 and 1469. It is quite possible that he may in some way have been connected with the erection of the nave of St. John's, and so his name became attached to this tower as it was to a steep wynd in Edinburgh. However this may be, all the details of the western part of this church obviously belong to a late period, corresponding with above date.

The central tower (see Fig. 1046), which is about 31 feet square, could only have been built after the adjoining part of the nave was reared. It

* See *The Castellated and Domestic Architecture of Scotland*, Vol. v. pp. 529, 530.

is a very simple structure, with one window in each face. The parapet
and corbelling were renewed about forty years ago, following in the main

FIG. 1046.—St. John the Baptist's, Perth. The Nave, from South-West.

the old details, which were, however, much obliterated. A good deal of the stone facing was renewed at the same time.

The exterior of the church has been considerably altered and *improved* at various times. An open parapet has been carried along the top of the walls of the choir over the clerestory windows, and also along the walls of the aisles and up the sloping gables of the east end. Dormer windows to light the presbyterian galleries break in on this parapet on the aisle walls, and windows for the same purpose, constructed of wood, are seen on the roofs of the nave (see Fig. 1046). These dormer windows are all shown on the print in the *Chronicle of Perth* (see Fig. 1034), but not the parapets. This print shows a large and very elaborate porch, with a round arched doorway of many orders richly ornamented, as occupying the east-most bay of the choir. This was originally the gateway or porch of the Carthusian Monastery of Perth, which, after the demolition of the abbey in 1559, was set up in this position, where it remained till about the end of the eighteenth century, "when it was demolished by an edict of the Magistrates." *

The effect of the interior of St. John's is greatly marred by the cross partitions already referred to. This is much to be regretted, as the interior is exceedingly interesting, and, being in a comparatively fair state of pre-servation, exhibits more of its original features than the exterior does. When the church was complete, the effect of the gloomy nave, with its lofty unpierced wall above the main arcade, and the noble centre crossing, with the light refined choir beyond, must have been very striking and grand.

A peculiarity of the church and another resemblance to the nave of Dunblane and the north nave aisle of Dunkeld is the absence of vaulting in the aisles which many of our Scottish churches have. The aisles in St. John's never were vaulted, the only parts so constructed being the cross-ing and the north porch; the latter, it will be remembered, having also an upper vaulted story. This want of vaulting is a great defect of the church.

DUNDEE CHURCH TOWER.

The earliest notice in history of Dundee occurs in the first charter of Lindores Abbey, executed before 1198, in which the Church of Dundee is bestowed on the abbey. The church then existing is stated to have been erected by Earl David of Huntingdon, as a thankoffering for his escape from a great tempest. The Church of Dundee thus belonged to the Abbey of Lindores, which stood on the opposite side of the Frith of Tay, and a little further up the river.

In the time of Abbot James of Rossy (1442), an agreement was entered into between the abbot and the Provost and Burgesses of Dundee, by which the latter took on themselves the construction and maintenance

* *Book of Perth*, p. 109.

Fig. 1047.—Dundee Church Tower. View from North-West.

of the choir of the Parish Church of Dundee.* The only portion of the ancient parish church which now remains is the western tower (Fig. 1047). Although this structure had no immediate connection with the choir, it has evidently, as its style shows, been erected about the middle of the fifteenth century, probably about the time when the choir was built by the Provost and Burgesses in terms of the above agreement.

Three parish churches in connection with the tower were gradually developed from the original chapel. They comprised a large cruciform

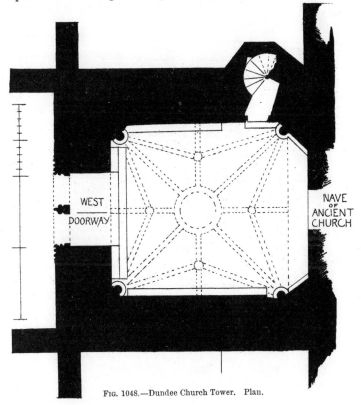

WEST
DOORWAY

NAVE
OF
ANCIENT
CHURCH

Fig. 1048.—Dundee Church Tower. Plan.

structure, the various portions of which were called St. Mary's, or the East Church; St. Paul's, or the South Church; and St. Clement's, or the West Church. The structure was greatly damaged by the English before the Union, and St. Clement's had suffered so much that it required to be rebuilt in 1789. The three churches were almost totally destroyed by fire in 1841, and in consequence the choir and transepts were thereafter rebuilt, St. Mary's still occupying the choir, St. Paul's the transept, and St. Clement's the nave.

* *Lindores Abbey*, by A. Laing, pp. 55, 107.

The ancient tower has escaped these various destructions and restorations, and is now the only representative of the church erected in the fifteenth century. It is a large and massive structure, measuring about 40 feet square over the walls (Fig. 1048), which are about 8 feet thick. Its total height is about 165 feet. The tower forms a prominent object in all views of the town. It contains in the lower stage the western

FIG. 1049.—Dundee Church Tower. West Doorway.

doorway to St. Clement's Church, or the nave (Fig. 1049), consisting of two round arched doorways, 8 feet 11 inches high, comprised within a larger circular or elliptical arch, which again is enclosed by a square moulding. The arch mouldings are enriched with foliage. The jambs and central pillar are moulded (Fig. 1050) with alternate rounds and hollows. The carved capitals have a continuous abacus, enriched either with rosettes or flowing foliage. In the spandril over the centre shaft there is a circular panel, enclosing the Virgin and Child ; and below, on a shield, are the arms of the Diocese of Brechin. "The late Bishop Forbes blazoned them *Argent*, three piles in point gules ; but Dr. Woodward thinks they should be *Or*, three piles in point gules." * This doorway, as well as much else about the tower, was greatly restored by Sir Gilbert Scott, and probably only certain of the carvings are genuine. One of these, which has not been touched, represents, on the ingoing of the northern capital, a boar eating acorns from a branch. It is quite in the spirit of such scenes as occur on the ancient sculptured stones which are so abundant in the neighbourhood of Dundee. The base is peculiar (see Fig. 1050). It projects but little beyond the outer member of the jamb, and the face is upright ; but considerable effect is obtained by the curved termina-tions of the various members. Above the doorway rises a lofty traceried

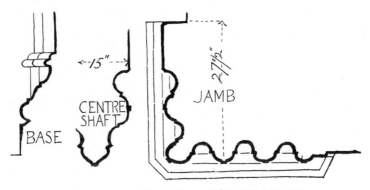

Fig. 1050.—Dundee Church Tower. Details of West Doorway.

window (Fig. 1051) divided, in the late Scottish mode, by a large central mullion having two arched branches which form two principal openings, each filled with late tracery of the ordinary kind. Above this window the tower is vaulted. In connection with this vaulting and what appears to have been an apartment below it there are some peculiarities. The floor of the tower is about 12 inches lower than the ground at the entrance, and the height from the floor to the groined ceiling is about 47 feet. It will be observed from the Plan and Fig. 1051 that at each of the four corners there is a large circular shaft, measuring about 13¼ inches diameter. Each individual shaft is fitted into its position in a manner different from the others. These differences are not of a slight or accidental kind, but appear to have been purposely made, there not having been any "restoration" on this part of the building. At the inner or eastern shafts (Fig. 1052) the walls are considerably bevelled towards

* Mr. R. C. Walker, Dundee.

FIG. 1051.—Dundee Church Tower.   Interior, looking West.

Fig. 1052.—Dundee Church Tower. Interior, looking East.

III.   I

the opening into the nave, and form parts of the piers of the great archway from the tower into the church. This opening, which is now blocked up, was about 17 feet 10 inches wide, and was arched beneath the vaulting (see Fig. 1052). The tall angle shafts have bases and caps, the mouldings of the latter being continued along the bevelled walls.

The vaulting ribs do not spring directly from the four angle shafts, as there appears to have been an intermediate floor of timber (or a gallery along the sides), which rested on the angle shafts and on large corbels visible in the side walls. Over each of the main shafts there rises, for about three feet or so, a group of very delicate shafting, having carved caps, from which spring the ribs of the groining. These delicate shafts are quite a contrast to the massive lower shafts, and, at first sight, suggest the idea of a great change having been effected in the vaulting at some later period. The mouldings above the small upper shafts are carried along the west wall and ingoing of the large window (see Fig. 1051). There is a considerable resemblance between the treatment here and that at the large west window in Paisley Abbey. There are stone benches round three sides of the tower.

Over the large west window there is another window (see Fig. 1047), with round arch-head, entirely filled with tracery, composed of small cusped circles, and above it a two-light pointed window. The tracery in the first of these windows recalls that in the tower windows of Iona Cathedral.

The tower is divided into two principal stages by an enriched parapet and outside passage, which surround it above the last mentioned window, at a height to the walk of about 96 feet. The parapet is pierced with quatrefoils and ornamented with crocketed pinnacles. The lower stage of the tower has boldly projected buttresses, which are just carried as high as is necessary for resisting the pressure of the vaulting, and each is crowned with a crocketed pinnacle, having a small flying buttress attached. Above these buttresses the tower is carried up with square angles, like most of the Scottish towers of the period. The upper stage has the wall set back, so as to allow of the passage round, and is divided into two stories. The lower story is the belfry and has triple pointed and cusped openings in the various sides, except the north side, where, owing to the space occupied by the staircase, there are only two openings. There is a bead on the angles of this story. The upper story appears to project slightly over the lower story, and contains two pointed and cusped windows over the solids, between the windows beneath them. The north side has only one such window. The tower is crowned with a cornice and an elaborate pierced parapet, having corbelled pinnacles at intervals, the ornamental upper parts of which are unfortunately wanting. The ornamentation of the parapet strongly resembles that of the tower of St. Giles', Edinburgh. The roof of the tower is of the saddle-back kind,

FIG. 1053.—Dundee Church Tower. View from North-East.

having gables towards the east and west, a form of roof with which ancient Scottish towers were often crowned.

Although the tower is thus finished, a careful examination shows that it was undoubtedly meant to have an open crown termination, but for what reason the idea was abandoned we cannot tell. The preparations exist for the springing of the angle arches. When the tower lately underwent renovation, it was proposed to remove the present cape house and put up a crown ; and a design for this was prepared, and is engraved in Lamb's *Book of Old Dundee.* Very fortunately the design was not carried out.

Attached to the north-east angle is a boldly projected stair turret, which ascends from the foundation to the summit. Figs. 1047 and 1053 illustrate this feature. The pierced parapet at the top returns round it, and the turret is finished with a pointed roof. A great many loopholes in the turret show the number of the winding spirals of the staircase. In the view (Fig. 1053) there is seen on the east side of the tower a plain, square-headed window, having four brackets arranged around it. We presume these were for supporting figures. Beneath them, and near the ridge of the church roof, there is a panel with a coat of arms, which is too far off to be made out.

This tower is undoubtedly the boldest and most striking edifice of its kind and date in Scotland.

GLENLUCE ABBEY, Wigtonshire.

This abbey, like so many others, stands in a fertile holm or flat ground in the quiet valley of the Water of Luce, about one mile and a half from the town of Glenluce. Although sometimes called *Vallis Lucis,* the name is probably the same as Luss in Dumbartonshire, meaning a place of herbs. The abbey was founded in 1190 by Roland, Lord of Galloway, and colonised by Cistercians from Melrose.

The buildings were at one time "extensive and magnificent," but the ruins are now very scanty. Of the church (Fig. 1054) there remain only parts of the south wall of the choir and the south wall of the south transept. The cloister enclosure is still marked by a good wall, but of the conventual buildings which formerly surrounded it, only the chapter house and some vaulted cellars on the east side survive.

The existing ruins cover about an acre of ground, but formerly the enclosure of the garden and orchard extended to twelve Scotch acres.

Little is known of the annals of the monastery. Its earliest charter is by Robert I., granting the property of the abbey to be held as a free barony, and this was confirmed by David II. At the Reformation the lands were leased at a low rate to the Earl of Cassilis, who was created

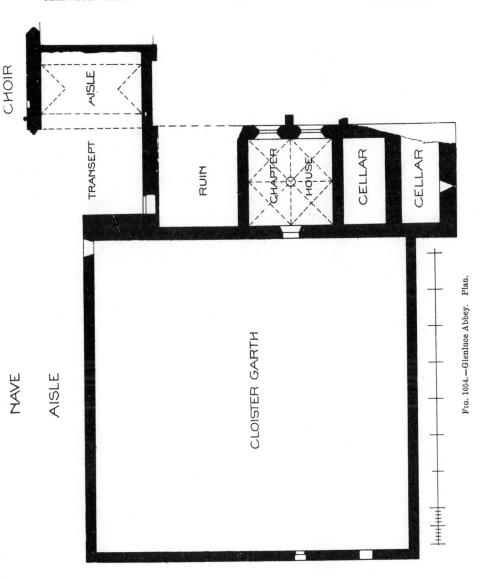

FIG. 1054.—Glenluce Abbey. Plan.

FIG. 1055.—Glenluce Abbey. Chapter House.

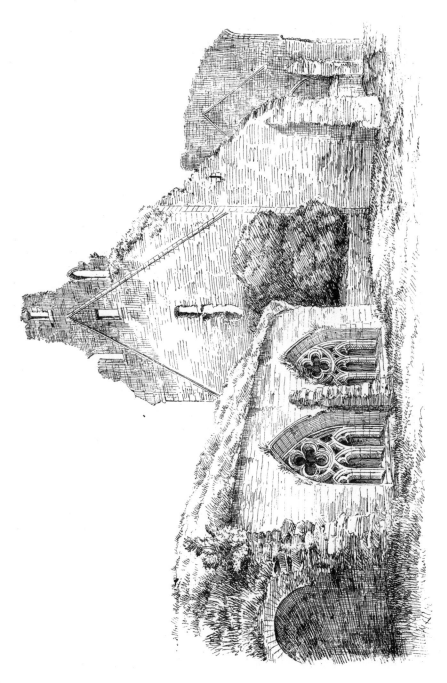

Fig. 1056.—Glenluce Abbey.   View from South-East.

bailie of the abbey. In 1587 the estates were annexed to the Crown. James VI. erected them into a temporal barony in favour of Laurence Gordon, commendator at the time. The lordship of Glenluce afterwards passed to the Stair family, and the lands to the Hays of Park.*

FIG. 1057.—Glenluce Abbey. Doorway to Chapter House: Exterior.

In this remote region the buildings remained long undisturbed, and as late as 1646 the abbey is referred to in the Records of the Presbytery of Stranraer as having received little injury. † "The steeple," says Symson,

* M'Kerlie's *Galloway*, Vol. I. p. 172.   † *New Statistical Account*.

who wrote in 1684, "and part of the walls of the church, together with the chapter house, the walls of the cloyster, the gatehouse with the walls of the large precincts, are for the most part yet standing."

So far as can now be ascertained from the ruins, the church (see Fig. 1054) seems to have comprised a nave with aisles about 90 feet in length,

Fig. 1058.—Glenluce Abbey. Doorway to Chapter House: Interior.

now entirely destroyed; a transept, of which part of the southern arm with its eastern aisle or chapels remains; and an aisleless choir, of which only a fragment of the south wall survives. From Symson's statement, above quoted, there was also a steeple, but whether over the crossing or not does not now appear. To the south of the nave lay the cloisters, the walls of which (partly old and partly reconstructed) now subsist, and enclose a space measuring 89 feet from north to south by 86 feet from east to west. The north, west, and south sides are enclosed with a stone wall, and on the east side there is a row of structures comprising the chapter house in the centre, a ruined heap on the north side of the chapter house, and two cellars with plain barrel vaults on the south side.

The chapter house (Fig. 1055) is the only portion of the abbey in good preservation. It consists of an apartment about 24 feet square, with a central pillar, from which spring the ribs of the groined vaulting. At the side walls the ribs rest on corbels. The apartment is lighted with two traceried windows (Fig. 1056), the tracery of which has been renewed within recent years, after the pattern of the old tracery. The door enters from the cloister on the west. It is of semicircular form (Fig. 1057), and exhibits in its capitals some peculiar and striking sculpture. The leaves of the foliage are large and the design is remarkable, some of the leaves, which are probably intended to represent sun flowers, having very much the appearance of starfish. The interior of the chapter house door-way (Fig. 1058) has also some peculiar sculpture, and the manner in which the ribs of the vaults descend on the round arch-head is well managed.

FIG. 1059.—Glenluce Abbey. Corbel in Chapter House.

The stone benches which surrounded the chapter house, including the abbot's chair between the two windows (see Fig. 1055), are much destroyed, but the central pillar and the vaulting are well preserved. The capital of the pillar is carved with foliage of a late character, and the corbels supporting the ribs of the vaults at the wall show similar work. One of these corbels is quaintly carved, in imitation of a figure clothed in the costume of the fifteenth or sixteenth centuries (Fig. 1059), thus giving an indication of the date of the building. From this and the work on the doorway above referred to, as well as the character of the work generally, we have no hesitation in fixing the date of this part of the abbey about the end of the fifteenth century. The bosses of the vaults are carved with various devices, one of them bearing a lion rampant, which is probably meant to represent the arms of the founder, the Lord of Galloway.

The design of the tracery in the windows (see Fig. 1056) is good for the period. It is remarkably like that of the chapter house at Crosraguel Abbey, which was also fifteenth century work.

This sketch likewise shows the small portions of the church which still remain. The lofty south gable of the transept is visible with the sloping water table of the roof of the building, which stood on the south of it.

This building has apparently been at least two stories in height. It no doubt extended over the chapter house wing, and contained the dormitory, &c. (as at Crosraguel). A small lancet window on each side of the water table near its apex and another small window over it seem to indicate that there was an apartment in the roof of the transept. The wall seen in the distance is part of the south wall of the choir. It contains the water table of the roof of the east aisle of the transept, and is broken off at the jamb of a high window, which lighted the choir or presbytery, thus showing that the latter must have extended further eastward than the existing ruin.

TORPHICHEN CHURCH, LINLITHGOWSHIRE.

This church, from the circumstance of its castle-like appearance and its possessing a complete dwelling-house over the transepts, was included in *The Castellated and Domestic Architecture of Scotland,* Vol. II. p. 131, in which a full description of it is given, illustrated with numerous drawings. The building is here introduced with the view of more fully explaining some features formerly omitted, and also to form a complete record of such an important example.

The new features introduced in the Plan (Fig. 1060) are the choir, the nave, and an outbuilding to the north. The width and height of the choir and the arch leading into it are clearly seen against the central tower (Fig. 1061), while the lower part of the east wall and part of the north wall of the choir are still standing, as shown in the Plan, although reduced to only a few feet in height.

The present parish church (Fig. 1062) occupies the site of the nave, the ancient splayed base being utilised in the north wall, where it is visible along the whole length. It is also probable that the west end of the present church corresponds with the position of the old west end. In that case the dimensions were as follow, viz. :—The choir was about 63 feet 6 inches long by 25 feet 6 inches wide, and the nave was about 65 feet 6 inches long by 25 feet wide. The total length of the church was 158 feet 3 inches outside measure. The total length of the transept was about 68 feet. There was apparently an aisle along the south side of the nave, the beginning of the wall of which is visible on the Plan. A row of buildings existed as a continuation northwards of the north transept, and at a distance of about 31 yards northwards a portion of these buildings still remains, measuring about 40 feet in length. The first erection to the north of the transept had a window with stone seats looking into the church, and it had also a communication with the house over the church. There may thus have been a row of dormitories on the upper floor extendng northwards.

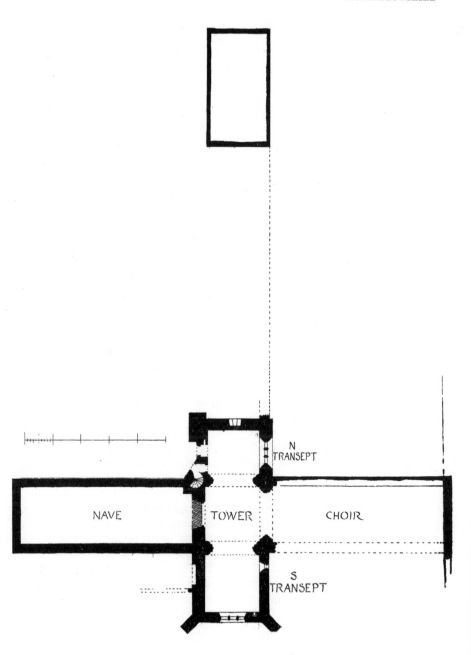

FIG. 1060.—Torphichen Church. Plan.

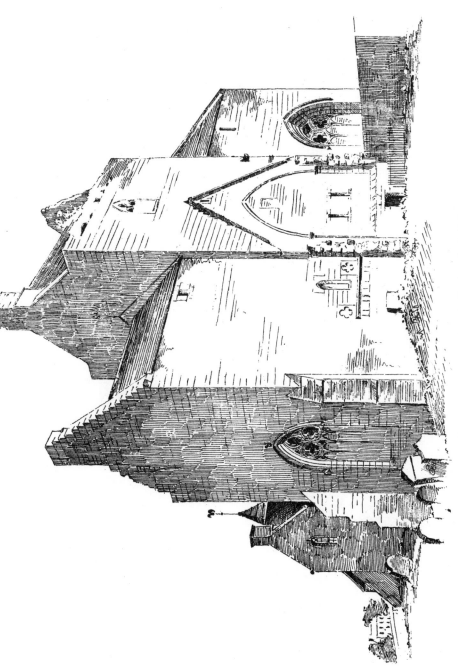

Fig. 1061.—Torphichen Church. View from South-East.

Fig. 1062.—Torphichen Church. View from South-West.

FIG. 1063.—Torphichen Church.   Transept, looking South

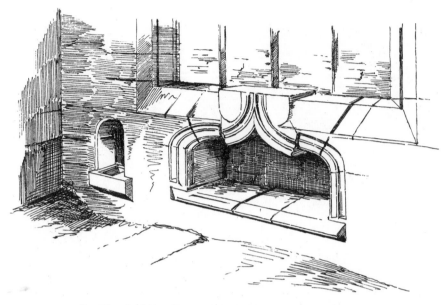

FIG. 1064.—Torphichen Church.   Recess for Monument in North Transept.

Fig. 1063 is a general view of the transept looking towards the south, and shows the recess for a tomb under the south window.   Fig. 1064 is

FIG. 1065.—Torphichen Church.   Doorway at North-West Angle of Transept.

an enlarged view of this tomb recess ; the centre stone of the ogee arch has dropped slightly, owing to a failure in the walls at the south-east corner. The piscina alongside has a neatly constructed square basin.

Fig. 1065 shows the outside of an angular headed doorway near the north-west corner of the transept. The doorway with the projecting hood, seen alongside, leads into the staircase giving access to the house.

Measured drawings of these two last subjects were given in the account already referred to.

ST. ANTHONY'S CHAPEL, EDINBURGH.

This edifice occupies a very picturesque situation on the summit of a crag in the bosom of Arthur's Seat, not far above the base of the hill. Immediately to the north and west of the walls the ground descends in an abrupt and precipitous manner, and to the south the surface, which gradually rises, is rough and rocky (Fig. 1066); while on the east a huge wall of rock towers high above the building, completely hemming it in on that side.

Only the north wall of the chapel and the returns of the west and east walls remain, together with the foundations of the south wall, enough, however, to enable it to be determined fairly well what the completed building was like. In the drawings (Fig. 1067) the indications existing are completed and restored, so as to give a better idea of what the structure was like than can be done by description alone. The present condition of the edifice is shown in the ground Plan, section from east to west and north elevation (Fig. 1068), and in the general view from south-east (Fig. 1069). The building measures on the outside 43 feet in length by 18 feet 3 inches in width, but the internal dimensions of the chapel proper (see Plan) are only 32 feet 9 inches by 12 feet.

The chapel (see Fig. 1068) was divided into three bays by a vaulted and groined ceiling, portions of the ribs of which, with their corbel supports, still exist in the north wall. The height of the vaulting at the wall is about 14 feet.

There was a window in the central and eastern bay of the north wall, and a doorway in the west bay, and, according to Maitland,[*] the same arrangement existed on the south side. There is a locker in the usual place at the east end of the north wall. Maitland further says that in the "southern wall near the altar is a small arched niche, wherein was put the holy water." This, however, does not now exist. There was a priest's house over the western bay, the size of which can still be determined by the existing return of its east wall, as seen in the north elevation, and the longitudinal section. Part of the building, at the west end, on the

[*] *Maitland's History of Edinburgh*, p. 152.

ground floor, was screened off from the chapel by a partition wall, of which the indications exist. On the ground floor this was vaulted, as shown by

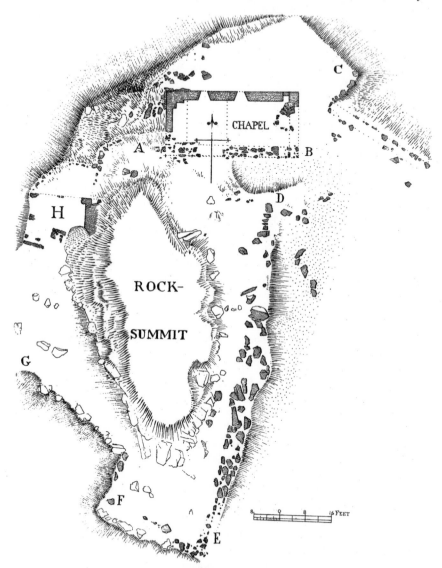

Fig. 1066.—St. Anthony's Chapel. Plan of Site.

section at tower, and contained a locker. Within this space at the south-west corner there was, doubtless, a wheel stair, which by the first revolution led to an entresol over the arched space just referred to. This entresol was probably a garderobe, and was lighted by a small window, shown on the Plans and Section. The stair, continuing upwards, would land at the first floor over the chapel, which consisted of a room about 15 feet by 13 feet, lighted by a north window. Adjoining this window a portion of the north wall is thinned by about 15 inches at the floor level so as to form a recess, which contains a window. Over this the wall is carried at its usual thickness by a half arch, as shown by the longitudinal section. Probably this recess was screened off from the room to form a small closet. There was a fireplace in the west gable ; part of its flue still remains, with one of its corbels for supporting the lintel and chimney breast. In the restored drawing (see Fig. 1067) it is supposed that there was an upper room. Assuming that the

SECTION of CHURCH

ENTRESOL WEST END SECTION at TOWER

SOUTH ELEVATION

Fig. 1067.—St. Anthony's Chapel. Suggested Restoration.

first floor room was 10 feet high in the ceiling—and it is not likely to have been higher—the height of the existing wall at the north-west corner warrants this assumption, as above the 10 feet level it rises 3 feet more in its present broken down condition. That it rose to a higher level than it does now is almost certain, in which case an upper room would be obtained, as shown by section at tower (see Fig. 1067). This corresponds with Maitland, who says that the tower was perhaps upwards of 40 feet in height. The second floor room would, of course, be reached by a continuation of the stair. At the staircase landing a small outside bartizan is introduced in the restored drawing, such as is frequently found in the pele towers. This arrangement of the two upper rooms is similar to what is found in the church of the Carmelite Friars at South Queensferry and at Torphichen, both of the same period as St. Anthony's. There is also, but on a more elaborate scale, something of the same arrangement at Stobhall in Perthshire, already illustrated.*

To the south and west of the chapel there are remains of walls, and particularly of what is called the hermitage (see Fig. 1066); but these are very fragmentary, and so intermixed with the natural rock, which crops up everywhere, that not much can be made out in connection with them.

Of the origin of the chapel nothing appears to be known, and almost the same may be said of its history. One of the earliest notices of it—if not the earliest—occurs in the *Treasurer's Accounts* of 1473, as follows— "Item, vj^{to} Februarij, to offir in Sanct Antonis in the crag, to the King, xijs." In the same accounts it is again referred to in 1491 and 1496

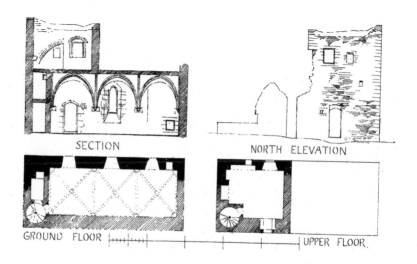

FIG. 1068.—St. Anthony's Chapel. Plans, Section, and North Elevation of Existing Structure.

—"Item, at he laid down for the King, on Sanct Anthonis day in Sanct Anthonis chapel, besid Edinburgh, to the Kings offerand ixs." Again in 1498, the King (James IV.) made an offering in "Sanct Anthonis of the crag of xjs. viijd."

An exhaustive review of the present condition of the chapel and hermitage, and an account of the various references to them by different writers, has been prepared by Mr. Fred. R. Coles. † Mr Coles gives reproductions of various old views, with notes on all the earlier known drawings, as also observations on St. Anthony and churches dedicated to

* *The Castellated and Domestic Architecture of Scotland*, Vol. II. p. 358.

† *Proceedings of the Society of Antiquaries, Scotland, 1896.* We are indebted to Mr. Coles for the Plan of the site (see Fig. 1066).

him, and for further information on this subject we beg to refer readers to this valuable paper.

Grose states that hermitages were frequently erected on the sea coast, and at dangerous places, and that the patron or tutelary saint of these hermitages was St. Anthony the hermit, and suggests that the situation of St. Anthony's on the crag which stands conspicuous from the Firth of Forth

FIG. 1069.—St. Anthony's Chapel.   View from South-East.

was perhaps chosen with the intention of attracting the notice of seamen coming up the Firth, who, in cases of danger, might be induced to make vows to its tutelar saint. There is a fine spring of clear water close to the site, which may have led to the establishment of the hermitage there. The building contains almost no features by which its date can be ascertained, but it is here classed along with the buildings of the third period, to some of which it bears in certain respects an analogy.

THE COLLEGIATE CHURCH OF ROSSLYN, MID-LOTHIAN.

The village of Rosslyn is picturesquely situated on the high north bank of the river North Esk, about seven miles south from Edinburgh; and the ancient castle of the St. Clairs* stands on an isolated promontory called the College Hill, which, adjoining the village of Rosslyn, juts out

* See *The Castellated and Domestic Architecture of Scotland*, Vol. I. p. 366.

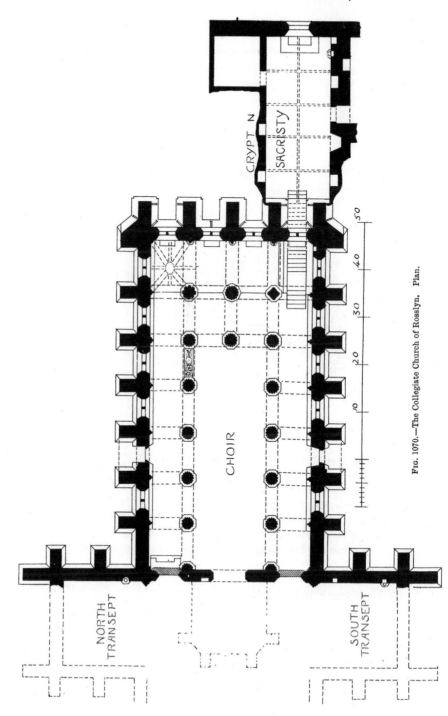

FIG. 1070.—The Collegiate Church of Rosslyn. Plan.

into the deep valley of the Esk. The celebrated Church of Rosslyn, erected by the proprietors of the castle, stands on the brow of the steep bank of the river above the castle, and commands a splendid view of the valley. The church, so far as erected, is in perfect preservation, and is a charming portion of an incomplete design. It is, in some respects, the most remarkable piece of architecture in Scotland; and had the church been finished in the same spirit as that in which it has been so far carried out, it would have gone far to have realised a poet's dream in stone. When looked at from a strictly architectural point of view, the design may be considered faulty in many respects, much of the detail being extremely rude and debased, while as regards construction many of the principles wrought out during the development of Gothic architecture are ignored. But notwithstanding these faults, the profusion of design so abundantly shown everywhere, and the exuberant fancy of the architect, strike the visitor who sees Rosslyn for the first time with an astonishment which no familiarity ever effaces.

The principal authority regarding the history of the church and the family of the St. Clairs of Rosslyn is Father Richard Augustin Hay, prior of St. Pieremont, whose mother, by a second marriage, became wife of Sir James St. Clair of Rosslyn. About the year 1700, Father Hay made copious extracts from the family documents, which have been since lost, and these extracts, together with his comments, have been published under the title of the *Genealogie of the Sainteclaires of Rosslyn, including the chartulary of Rosslyn*.

The edifice was erected by Sir William St. Clair, third Earl of Orkney, who succeeded to the estates about 1417. About thirty years afterwards he founded the Collegiate Church of Rosslyn. Certain letters which occur on shields along the cornice of the north wall have been ingeniously deciphered by Dr. Thomas Dickson, of the Register House, Edinburgh, as the initial letters of the following words,* viz. :—WILZAME · LORDE · SINCLARE · FUNDIT · YIS · COLLEGE · YE · ZEIR · OF · GOD · MJJJJL. The structure appears, however, to have been begun a few years earlier, about 1446, as in the year 1447 †'ⱬ continuator of the *Scotichronicon* says, "Dominus Willelmus de Sancto Claro Comes Orcadiæ *est in fabricando sumptuosam structuram apud Roslyn;*"† and probably the foregoing inscription refers to some ceremonial event connected with the building. Sir William died in 1484, and he appears to have left the building very much in the condition in which we now find it. In that case its erection would be the labour of about forty years.

The church was a collegiate foundation, for a provost, six prebendaries, and two singing boys or choristers, and was dedicated to St. Matthew. It consists (Fig. 1070) of a choir with north and south aisles, connected

---

* *Proceedings of the Society of Antiquaries, Scotland*, Vol. XII. p. 223.
† *The Collegiate Churches of Mid-Lothian* (Bannatyne Club), p. xciv.

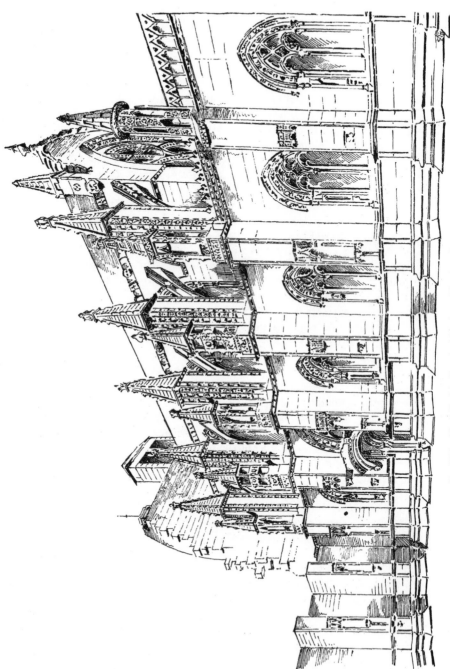

FIG. 1071.—The Collegiate Church of Rosslyn. View from South-East.

by an aisle which runs across the east end, and gives access to a series of four chapels beyond it to the east. The dimensions of the building are as follow, viz. :—interior—length of choir, 48 feet 4 inches ; width of central aisle, 17 feet 10½ inches ; width over aisles, 35 feet ; total exterior length, 69 feet 8 inches ; height to the apex of the roof, 41 feet 9 inches. The original intention was to have completed the building as a cross church, with choir, nave, and transepts, but the choir only has been completed. The transepts have been partly erected, the east wall being carried up to a considerable height, but the nave has not been erected. The length across the transepts, as founded, is about 72 feet. Mr Thomson, the custodier of the chapel, who saw the west walls of the transept exposed, states that the transepts were intended to be 18 feet wide, as drawn on Plan. The Rev. Mr. Thompson, Rosslyn, in his guide to the chapel, says that the foundations for the entire building had been laid, and that those of the nave, which extended to about 91 feet to the west, were dug up and exposed at the beginning of the present century. This exactly corresponds with the length which the nature of the ground would permit.

The choir, both internally and externally, is remarkably symmetrical, the bays being all of the same dimensions, with only slight differences in the carving, which do not affect the general design. Thus (Fig. 1071) all the buttresses rise unbroken by set-offs to the wall head of the aisles, where the cornice continues round them, and they have all on the face canopies of the same size and style. Above the cornice on the ten buttresses on the north and south sides of the choir there rise on each two massive pinnacles, connected by a small flying buttress between them (Fig. 1072). The outer pinnacles, which are flush with the face of the buttresses, are square on Plan, and are decorated according to two alternate patterns (Fig. 1073), viz., canopied niches in the one, and large rosettes set in hollows in the other. The inner pinnacles (Fig. 1074), which rest on the thickness of the wall, are all practically alike. They are oblong on Plan, and are so placed as to offer most resistance to the flying buttresses, which are thrown across the aisles and rest upon them. The pinnacles are ornamented with rosettes on the angles, and crockets on the sloping top. The back of these pinnacles and the lower parts, where not seen from below, are left plain, without any ornament. The flying arches abutting against the pinnacles are carved with a revived Norman-like chevron.

The pinnacles (Fig. 1075) on the buttresses of the east chapels are naturally somewhat different, as they have no thrusts from flying buttresses to counteract. There is only one pinnacle on each of these buttresses, and although they are all of different design, their effect corresponds with that of the outer pinnacles of the aisles of the choir. The back of these pinnacles is left unfinished (Fig. 1076), like those at the sides, but the portions visible are very elaborately carved.

The windows of the aisles (see Fig. 1072) are all of two lights, and

Fig. 1072.—The Collegiate Church of Rosslyn. North Doorway and Buttresses, &c.

FIG. 1073.—The Collegiate Church of Rosslyn. South Side of Choir, looking East.

have the same mouldings and orders of decoration both in the inside and outside of the wall, each jamb having two beaded shafts with carved caps. These beads are continued round the arches, and a large hollow

FIG. 1074.—The Collegiate Church of Rosslyn. Pinnacles on Buttresses, from Roof of Aisle.

FIG. 1075.—The Collegiate Church of Rosslyn. Pinnacles at East End.

Fig. 1076.—The Collegiate Church of Rosslyn. Pinnacles over East Chapels, from Roof of Aisle.

moulding connects them, which in the arches is always filled with carving. In the jambs there are two different patterns in the alternate windows, the one being a simple niche with canopy and bracket for a figure, and the other the same, but with a moulded block instead of the figure. There is very little variety in the tracery. The windows on each side correspond with those on the opposite side. In the eastern chapels four of the windows have the engrailed cross of the St. Clairs wrought into the tracery.

The clerestory windows (see Fig. 1072) are all after one design, the shafts, mouldings, and arches on the outside being repeated in the interior (Fig. 1078). These are similar to those of the aisle windows just described. Their decoration consists of large rosettes, occurring at regular intervals in the hollow moulding between the shafts of the jambs. All the clerestory windows are single lights. The tracery of the large window in the east end (Fig. 1077) is modern. Its design is probably founded on ancient remains, but whether or not it accords well with the rest of the building.

The north and south doorways, which are opposite each other, are recessed in quasi porches (see Figs. 1072 and 1073), formed by round arches thrown between the buttresses, and the minor differences of the doorways are shown in the sketches. The upper part of a window appears over each, as in the south doorway of Glasgow Cathedral. The aisle roofs being flat, there is no triforium or blind story, and the clerestory windows are carried down to the string course over the main arches (see Fig. 1078).

Turning now to the interior, it will be observed that the main piers are composed of a series of round mouldings, separated by slight square fillets, and that the corresponding wall shafts or responds (Fig. 1079) are of trefoil form, with good caps and carved bases, which rest on the side bench. The arch mouldings of the main arcade (see Fig. 1078) are shallow, with regularly recurring orders of decoration, each arch having an enriched hood moulding. The upper part of the wall slightly overhangs on a bold carved and moulded string course. The wall space between the clerestory windows is ornamented with two canopies and massive brackets placed one over the other.

The choir roof, which consists of a pointed barrel vault (see Fig. 1080), is divided by strengthening ribs into compartments corresponding with the bays, and each compartment is decorated differently (see Fig. 1078). The dividing ribs are moulded, and have large projecting cusps in the form of fleurs-de-lys, &c., on the soffit. The compartments of the roof are entirely "powdered with stars" or rosettes, set square or diagonally. The construction of the aisle roofs is peculiar, although something similar is frequent in castles, as will be afterwards alluded to. A regularly constructed straight arch with proper radiating joints, concealed behind upright joints, spans each aisle (see Fig. 1079) from pillar to wall shaft. These horizontal arches or lintels have flat relieving arches over them, which in some instances are visible. The aisles are roofed with a series of

Fig. 1077.—The Collegiate Church of Rosslyn. East End of Choir, above Roof of Aisles.

pointed barrel vaults thrown between the above straight arches, and
running at right angles to the axis of the building (Fig. 1081).   This is

FIG. 1078.—The Collegiate Church of Rosslyn.   Interior of Choir, looking East.

one of the most unusual features of construction in the edifice. The
straight arches or lintels, as they may be called, are all most profusely

FIG. 1079.—The Collegiate Church of Rosslyn. Interior of West End of North Aisle.

carved with foliage or figure carving (Fig. 1082), the amount of decoration on each being, as usual, of corresponding artistic value.

On the arched roofs of the north and south aisles, to the east of the

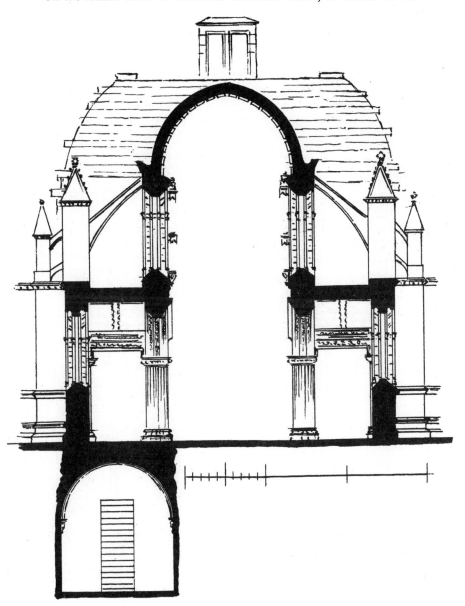

Fig. 1080.—The Collegiate Church of Rosslyn.   Transverse Section.

Fig. 1081.—The Collegiate Church of Rosslyn.   East Aisle and 'Prentice Pillar.

doorways and of the east aisle, there is carved in each bay an engrailed cross, the one limb running along the crown of each arch, and the other downwards from this on each side. But in the north and south aisles, in the three bays west from the doorways, the engrailed band is only continued along the crown of the arch, the other limb being omitted, which may possibly be meant to distinguish the more sacred part of the edifice.

The eastern chapels are the only part of the building in which there is groined vaulting. The compartments are oblong, and have pointed cross arches (Fig. 1083), the diagonals meeting at the apex. Elaborately carved pendants, about 4 feet long, occupy the place of the usual boss ; while at the springing of the arches, against the east wall, great projecting horns, resting on curved corbellings or cones above the caps of the wall shafts, radiate outwards and downwards, one horn to each rib, so that they are in groups of three.

Fig. 1082.—The Collegiate Church of Rosslyn. Details of Carving of Straight Arches.

The object of these curved cones, with their projecting horns, may be explained as follows :—It will be seen on referring to the Plan (see Fig. 1070) that the centre line of the east chapels is not in the centre of the space between the two eastmost buttresses, and consequently not in line with the centre of the north and south windows between those buttresses. In order to make the centre line of the vaulting coincide with the centre of the windows, it was necessary to introduce some kind of support for the foot of the east arches, at a distance of about 2 or 3 feet from the east wall. The above cones and horns were introduced for this purpose, and from them the vaulting on the east side springs. In connection with this arrangement, the late David Roberts, R.A., contended that the "east wall of Rosslyn had been pulled down and set further back, to give 3 feet more room." * But this supposition finds no warrant whatever from an

* *Transactions of the Royal Institute of British Architects, 1846.*

examination of the building. A more likely explanation is that the above cones may have been introduced as a kind of imitation of the springing of

FIG. 1083.—The Collegiate Church of Rosslyn. Eastern Chapels.

the fan vaulting common in England in the fifteenth century. The heavy pendants were also probably derived from the same source.

Against the east wall of the choir were the remains of four altars, which have been restored (see Fig. 1083), one of them being situated over the stair leading to the lower chapel. Beside it there is a square headed piscina, and on the south side of the other altars there are ogee headed recesses in the wall. On the east side of the south doorway there is a richly carved stoup.

In the transepts (Fig. 1084) there are remains of three canopied piscinas, two in the south transept and one in the north transept. They bear a general resemblance in their details to the sacrament houses in some of the churches in the north, and to the piscinas in Melrose Abbey. Between the two in the south transept there is a recess in the wall, showing where an altar has been intended, and a similar indication in the north transept on the north side of the piscina shows the same intention. Over each of these altars there are three moulded and carved brackets, probably meant for statues. On the south side of the centre opening into the choir there is a recess for another altar, and on the north side there is an arched piscina; both have carved brackets above them. A bracket in a similar position, relative to the altar and piscina, exists at Dunglass Church.

A singular feature of the church, which would have been more apparent had it been finished, is that the choir is almost cut off by a solid wall from what would have been the other divisions of the structure. Fig. 1084 shows the wall as seen from the outside. The openings into the side aisles are about 4 feet 3 inches wide and about 11 feet high, and the opening on the ground level into the central aisle is about 7 feet wide. These three openings are all covered with straight arches. Above the central opening there is a lofty aperture like a window covered with a pointed arch, probably meant to contain the rood. Above the caps of the jambs of the side openings there are two carved figures (Fig. 1085), that on the north being St. Sebastian, and that on the south St. Christopher.

Beyond the east end of the church and on a lower level, so as to suit the slope of the ground (Fig. 1086), a chapel has been erected, which is reached from the south aisle by a straight stair of twenty-five steps. This chapel measures 36 feet in length from east to west by 14 feet wide. It is barrel vaulted (Fig. 1087), and is lighted by one window only, at the east end. The window is a simple pointed one, without tracery. There are several ambries in the walls, and an eastern altar with a piscina. There are also a fireplace and a small closet about 11 feet square on the north side. A door leads out on the south to what has been an open court, where there are indications of other buildings having existed or been intended. It would thus appear that in all probability

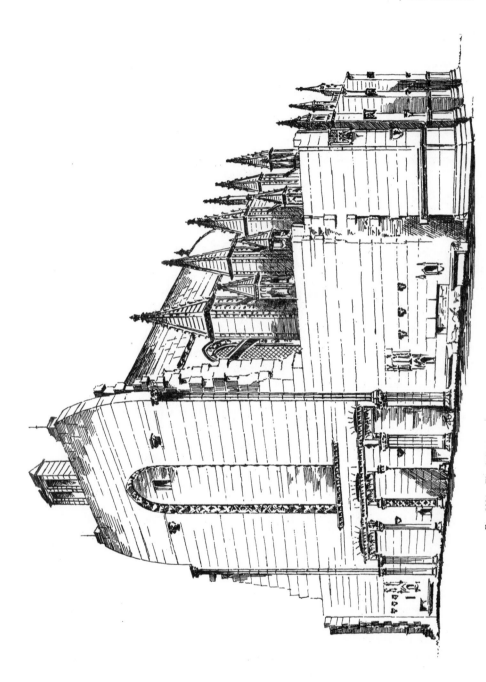

Fig. 1084.—The Collegiate Church of Rosslyn. West End of Choir and East Wall of Transepts.

there was a residence here, and the chapel may have served both as sacristy and private chapel.

This chapel or sacristy is supposed to have been built in the lifetime of Sir William St. Clair's first wife, Lady Elizabeth or Margaret Douglas, daughter of Archibald, fourth Earl of Douglass, and first Duke of Touraine, from the circumstance that her arms (Fig. 1088) are sculptured on the east wall. The shield has two coats impaled: *Dexter*, a coat quarterly, dimidiated, viz.—First a galley within a double tressure, flory counter

South.   North.

FIG. 1085.—The Collegiate Church of Rosslyn. Caps of Openings to Choir.

flory, for Orkney; 3rd a cross engrailed for St. Clair, being the 1st and 3rd quarters of the arms of the Earl of Orkney; *Sinister*, in base a heart, and on a chief three mullets, for Douglas, the shield being surmounted of a fess charged with three fleurs-de-lys (2 and 1) for Touraine. Lady Elizabeth died in 1452.

The barrel vault of the sacristy (see Fig. 1087) is semicircular, and supports a flat roof formed with overlapping stones. The vault is strengthened with transverse ribs carved with the engrailed cross, which spring from corbels sculptured with figures of angels and saints (Fig. 1089).

In considering the history of Rosslyn Church many of the statements of Father Hay regarding the St. Clairs and Rosslyn require to be received with considerable caution. He was a hero worshipper, and Sir William was his hero. The latter is represented by the Father as living in more than royal magnificence at Rosslyn, with many of the nobles of Scotland waiting upon him as servants. That is a very incredible statement, as is also the assertion that under the fostering care of Sir William, Rosslyn became the "chiefest town in all Lothian, except

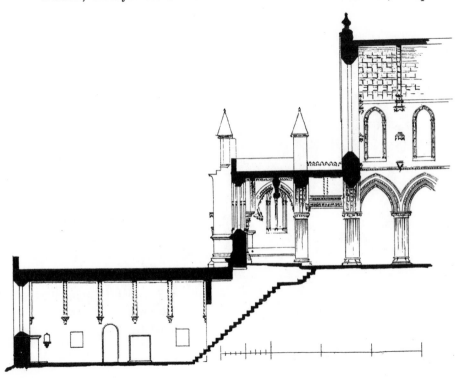

FIG. 1086.—The Collegiate Church of Rosslyn. Section through East End of Church and Lower Chapel.

Edinburgh and Haddington." But few who visit this chapel will be inclined seriously to quarrel with the Father on account of his enthusiasm for the Rosslyn family. To the purest in Gothic architecture Rosslyn may seem barbarous and debased, but it must be allowed to be splendid barbarism, meted out with the most liberal hand. Sir William is further represented by Father Hay as bringing artificers from foreign lands, and setting them to work on Rosslyn College, and on this unsupported statement many writers have found the prototype of this building abroad, some in France and some in Spain, and even Rome is hinted at in the well known story of the 'Prentice Pillar. The unusual richness of the ornamentation of the edifice, so different from most of the structures

FIG. 1087.—The Collegiate Church of Rosslyn. Lower Chapel or Sacristy, looking West.

erected in this country at the time, has doubtless led to these attempts to attribute the design to a foreign architect or a foreign country, where richly decorated structures exist.

FIG. 1088.
The Collegiate Church of Rosslyn.
Arms of Sir W. Sinclair's First Wife.

But this amount of decoration, being so exceptional in Scottish edifices, seems to have proved misleading. No parallel to Rosslyn has, so far as we know, been discovered abroad, and it is unnecessary to go so far afield in search of a model. The leading principles of the design are really Scottish, and it will be found, on careful analysis, that Rosslyn Church presents a rich and finished epitome, both as regards constructive and decorative elements, of the Scottish ecclesiastical architecture of the third or late pointed period. The plan of the east end of Rosslyn Church so closely resembles that of the choir of Glasgow Cathedral, that there is hardly room to doubt that the latter was the model after which the former was designed. The disposition of the pillars in the two buildings agrees exactly, the side aisles in both being connected by an eastern aisle, which in each case has a central pillar in the east arcade, and in each edifice a series of chapels beyond this aisle forms the east end. The details are, as is natural, seeing that the buildings are about two centuries apart in date, entirely different, but it is curious to observe how in both cases even the minute parts of the design are remarkably alike. Thus the triple niche over the central pillar of the east arcade at Glasgow finds a counterpart in the same position at Rosslyn (see Fig. 1078). The east wall and gable of both choirs occupy the same relative position, rising above the eastern aisle and chapels. Churches with an eastern aisle are not unknown in England, such as Abbey Dore, Herefordshire, and Romsey Abbey, Hampshire; but the

FIG. 1089.
The Collegiate Church of Rosslyn.
Corbels in Lower Chapel.

former has three openings in the east end, thus showing an arch in the centre; while Romsey Church, Glasgow Cathedral, and Rosslyn Church have the peculiarity of having a pillar in the centre of the east arcade.

Much has been made of the resemblance between the barrel vaults of

Rosslyn and those of the south of France, but there does not appear to be any connection between them. The pointed barrel vault was the form commonly practised in Scotland in the fifteenth century, both in churches and castles. Mr Fergusson says that this kind of vault is "foreign and unlike the usual form of vaults found in Scotland," but the examples given in this book show that he is mistaken. Pointed barrel vaults are to be found in the churches at Seton, Queensferry, Ladykirk, Whitekirk, Borthwick, Crichton, Corstorphine, Dunglass, and many others, and numerous examples might be given from the castles. There can, therefore, be no doubt that the masons of Scotland were at this period quite familiar with that system of vaulting, some of which, such as the vaults of Borthwick Castle, in the same district and built a little earlier than Rosslyn, are of considerably larger dimensions. The pointed barrel vaults of castle halls and churches are generally covered with sloping stone roofs, as at Bothwell, Borthwick, &c., but at Rosslyn the curved form of the roof has been adhered to, externally as well as internally. The coping of the east gable has been finished to this curve (see Fig. 1077), and there is no indication of any straight roof having been intended. It is possible, however, that it had been originally contemplated to cover the extrados of the choir vault, which still remains unprotected, with an outer stone roof, in accordance with the usual practice; but, owing to the slightness of the clerestory walls, the outer stone roof was omitted in consequence of its great additional weight, which, it may have been believed, would be too great for the side walls to sustain. The roofs of the aisles and east chapels, which are almost flat, are covered with overlapping flags. Until the building was restored some thirty years ago, these parts of the building were covered with a temporary slated roof, which cut off one half of the clerestory windows. The mark of this roof is still visible in the walls.

When we examine smaller details, we find the same methods adopted by the Rosslyn builders as were familiar to the other builders of the country, thus all the lintels or straight arches connecting the main pillars with the side walls, which are such striking features at Rosslyn, are composed of small stones, having radiating joints in the same manner as is frequent in the lintels of the wide fireplaces in the halls of the castles. It may also be noted that the jambs of these fireplaces often terminate in curious moulded caps, often very clumsy, and not unlike the caps of the responds at the east wall of Rosslyn. The plans of the castles sometimes show a series of small parallel apartments, with barrel vaults abutting at right angles upon a passage or wider hall, which may have suggested the parallel barrel vaults of the aisles of Rosslyn. But, indeed, the form of the main arcade itself suggests such an arrangement. The carved canopies and corbels placed on the face of the buttresses and window jambs (see Fig. 1090) are thoroughly characteristic of the Scottish churches of this period, and when their general design is considered, these features at Rosslyn will be found not to differ materially from those of the churches of Melrose, Linlithgow, Seton, Trinity College, and other buildings. Compare the disposition of small canopied niches round some central feature, such as the buttress niche (Fig. 778) at Melrose, and the pinnacles (see Figs. 1075 and 1076) at Rosslyn.

On the sides of each buttress at Rosslyn (see Figs. 1072, 1073, and 1091) there is a splayed moulding, a kind of set-off which runs from the front of the buttress back to the wall, on the top of the base string course. A somewhat similar set-off occurs on some of the buttresses of the chapter house of Glasgow Cathedral, built a few years before Rosslyn.

A large number of details from Melrose have a very decided resemblance to those found at Rosslyn. Thus the staircase turret (Fig. 773)

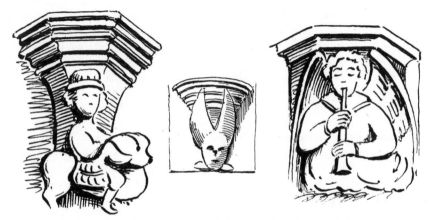

Fig. 1090.—The Collegiate Church of Rosslyn. Corbels on Window Jambs and Buttresses.

at the west side of the south transept of Melrose is in spirit so very like the work at Rosslyn that, had it been included in the illustrations of the latter, only those who have local knowledge would have detected it. The same remark applies to the south doorway from Dalkeith Church, given further on. A striking resemblance also occurs between the mouldings of the sacristy doors at Lincluden and Bothwell and the details of the clerestory windows at Rosslyn. In all these examples the mouldings consist of an outer and inner shaft, separated by a large hollow, containing carved work; and the shafts have, in every case, caps and bases treated in a similar manner.

The soffit cusping so common in the arches at Rosslyn is a decoration of the most frequent occurrence throughout Scotland; at this period, indeed, there is hardly an arched tomb recess in the country which is not so decorated. Carved rosettes set in hollows, which abound everywhere at Rosslyn, are likewise the common decoration of the period, both in churches and castles. Similar decorative enrichments are also very common in Tudor buildings in England, as, for example, in Henry VII.'s Chapel at Westminster, where also the small figures so frequent at Rosslyn above the caps and on buttresses, &c., find their counterpart, thus showing an association of ideas with English rather than foreign work.

The doorways at Rosslyn, with the porches formed in front of them by arches thrown between the buttresses, are paralleled by the doorways at Glasgow Cathedral; Trinity College, Edinburgh; and St. Salvator's, St. Andrews. The engrailed cross which enters so largely into the decoration of Rosslyn, being employed all along the arched roof of the aisles and of the lower chapel, and forming the motive for the tracery of some of the windows at the east end, is peculiarly local, being the distinctive feature of the St. Clair arms, while the loop tracery in many of the windows is of common occurrence in Scotland. A number of details illustrated in Fig. 1092, being chiefly the corbels of niches, have a very marked resemblance to the similar carvings at Trinity College, Edinburgh. Those containing the fox preaching to the geese and the dromedary are specially interesting. Other examples (such as Fig. 1093) show that the character of the foliage is the same as that of many of our Scottish churches. Much of the carving at Rosslyn has considerable affinity with the late wood work in English churches (see Fig. 1082).

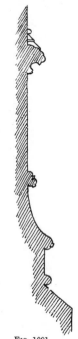

Fig. 1091.
The Collegiate Church of Rosslyn.
Base Mouldings and Lower String Course, with Peculiar Moulding above the latter.

These comparisons are probably enough to prove that Rosslyn Church was built after the manner and style of its age and country, and only differs from other Scottish churches of the same period in possessing a superabundance of rich detail and carving in excess of what is usually found.*

The transepts, which project two bays to the north and south, were obviously intended to be two stories high, and probably of the same height as the clerestory walls of the choir. Indeed, a part of the east wall of the north transept exists of this height. The walls of the transept are well buttressed, as if to maintain a vault, and there are no windows in the existing lower part of the transepts, the intention probably being to light them with large traceried windows at each end, as in Trinity College.

* In this connection George Gilbert Scott, in his *Essay on the History of English Church Architecture*, p. III., says that it is an "exceedingly able example of the style of the Scottish architecture of the fifteenth century."

The portions of the transepts and crossing which have been completed are too small to enable it to be clearly determined how these parts of the structure were intended to be carried out and vaulted. The west gable

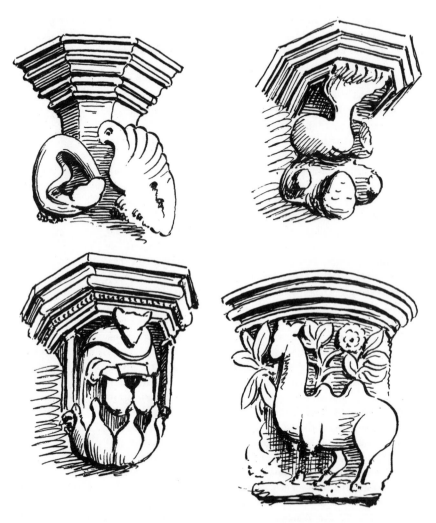

FIG. 1092.—The Collegiate Church of Rosslyn. Details of Corbels.

of the choir (see Fig. 1084) is built with a curved outline on top, which seems to indicate the form of an intended barrel vault. The gable has been left unfinished, and the existing belfry is obviously a late addition. The above curve, if completed, would comprise the full width of the chapel, embracing both the centre aisle and the side aisles, and would rise considerably above the apex of the roof. The space included between the curves is about 36 feet wide, which is a wider span than would likely be undertaken at this period. The curved form of the top of the west wall of the choir may, therefore, be dismissed as an indication of a probable vault.

Attention has already been drawn to the usual mode of finishing the barrel vaults of churches at this period (see *ante*, page 3), viz., by the introduction of four solid walls (with small apertures) at the four sides of the crossing on which the barrel vaults of the various arms of the churches were stopped. This system has, so far as the structure is completed, been adopted at Rosslyn, the wall on the east side of the crossing

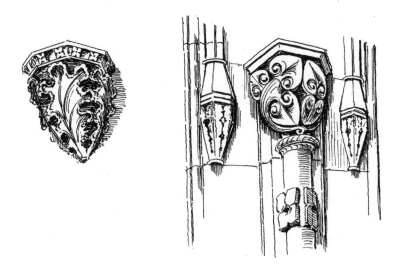

Fig. 1093.—The Collegiate Church of Rosslyn. Details.

being built so as to receive the barrel vault of the choir. There seems to be no reason why the same plan should not have been intended to be used for the completion of the other sides of the crossing. The edifice would then be in harmony with the other collegiate churches of the period, and may have been intended to be completed with a central tower.

The building shown by dotted lines at the west end is a vestry and organ chamber erected a few years ago.

The sculpture with which the chapel is so profusely adorned generally represents Scriptural scenes, and has been very minutely described by the Rev. Mr. Thompson in his *Guide to Rosslyn Chapel*.

One of the most unique examples amongst the remarkable decorations of the edifice is the ornamentation of the south pillar of the east aisle,

FIG. 1094.—The Collegiate Church of Rosslyn. Carved Slab over Entrance to Vault.

generally known as the "'Prentice Pillar" (see Fig. 1081). It consists of a series of wreaths twisted round the shaft, each wreath curving from base to capital round one quarter of the pillar. The ornamentation of the wreaths corresponds in character with the other carving of the church; and the grotesque animals on the base find a counterpart in those of the chapter house pillar at Glasgow Cathedral.

Beneath the choir are the vaults in which many of the St. Clairs are buried. The entrance is under a slab on which the incised outline of a knight in armour is carved (Fig. 1094), with a dog at his feet, and a small shield at his head, bearing a lion rampant contourné.

FIG. 1095.—The Collegiate Church of Rosslyn. Monument to George, Fourth Earl of Caithness.

The monument to George, fourth Earl of Caithness, who died in 1582, originally stood against the wall of the north aisle. It was removed in 1736, and placed against the wall at the west end of the north aisle (see Fig. 1079). This monument (Fig. 1095) contains the family motto, "Commit thy work to God," and the arms of the St. Clairs.

THE COLLEGIATE CHURCH OF DUNGLASS,*
HADDINGTONSHIRE.

This deserted but very complete edifice is situated within one mile of Cockburnspath Railway Station. It is in a good state of preservation, and its masonry may be described as almost entire, with the exception of the damages done to it during last century, when it was fitted up for

* See *The Castellated and Domestic Architecture of Scotland*, Vol. III. p. 26.

stabling and other farm purposes ; or, as stated in the Hutton Collection,*
made in the eighteenth century, "It is at present employed in a great
variety of domestic uses." The structure now stands a neglected ruin,
and is put to no purpose whatever, except that the south transept is used
as the burial-place of the family of the Halls of Dunglass.

The building (Fig. 1096) is cruciform, and consists of a nave 40 feet
long by 20 feet wide internally, a choir 33 feet 3 inches long by 17 feet
9 inches wide, and north and south transepts, each 21 feet 7 inches long
by 13 feet 9 inches wide. The total internal length of the church is
90 feet 8 inches, and the total length of the transept from north to south

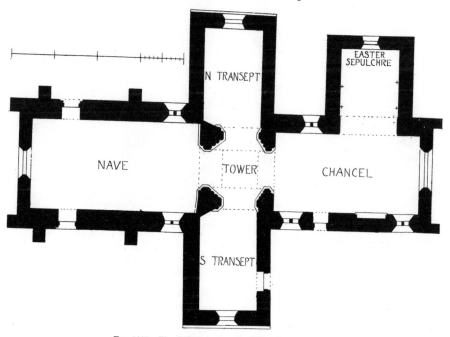

FIG. 1096.—The Collegiate Church of Dunglass. Plan.

is 63 feet. There is a sacristy 19 feet 3 inches in length by 13 feet 7 inches
in width internally on the north side of the choir, from which it enters by
a low centred arch, pointed and splayed.

The edifice (Fig. 1097) is roofed throughout, with the exception of the
tower over the crossing, with a continuous pointed barrel vault over each
arm of the cross, having a roof of heavy overlapping stone slabs resting
on the outside of the arch. There is thus no timber used in the construction of the walls and roof.

The tower has been divided, internally, into three stages, and the

* In the Advocates' Library, Edinburgh.

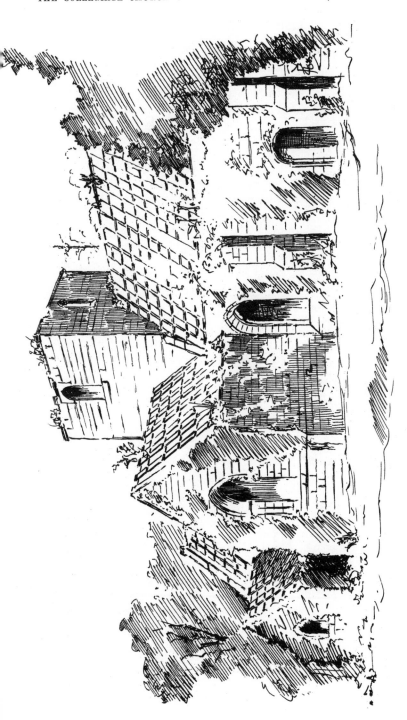

Fig. 1097.—The Collegiate Church of Dunglass. View from North-West.

FIG. 1098.—The Collegiate Church of Dunglass. Interior of Nave, looking Eastward.

FIG. 1099.—The Collegiate Church of Dunglass. Interior of Crossing from the Choir, looking West.

corbels for supporting the floor beams still remain. The lower set of corbels are set immediately above the apex of the tower arches, one of them being seen in the sketches of the interior of the crossing (Figs. 1098 and 1099). In the north side of the west wall of the tower (see Fig. 1098) a door opens into the nave at a high level, which probably was reached by wooden steps, there being no stone stair of access to the tower chambers.

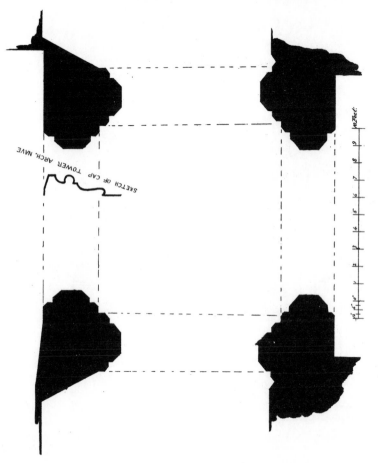

FIG. 1100.—The Collegiate Church of Dunglass. Plan of Piers of Tower.

It will be seen from the drawing (Fig. 1100) that the plan of the tower piers is peculiar. The two western piers stand out from the angle of the walls of the nave and transept, to which they are attached by a strip of masonry, only some 9 or 10 inches thick. The tower is thus considerably off the centre of the transept, and is much less in breadth

than the limbs of the cross.   The two eastern piers project from the angle
into the choir, but not so as to diminish the width of the transept.   It is
difficult to account for the extremely unusual and eccentric position of the
tower supports.   Possibly the choir and tower were first built, and when
the nave and transepts were erected, it was thought desirable to make
them wider than at first intended.   The piers of the crossing are simply
splayed and notched on the inner diagonal faces, and they are all alike;
but the arch faces or mouldings vary, those of the nave and transepts
corresponding with the piers, while the choir arch is moulded on both
faces with shallow mouldings.   The former arches spring from moulded
caps (see section Fig. 1100) and the latter from caps carved and moulded
(Fig. 1101).   The splayed base of the
piers is omitted on the chancel side.

The windows in the end walls of the
nave, choir, and transepts are all pointed,
and were filled with tracery; but the
tracery in every case is gone, and the
west wall under the window sill has been
cut out to allow of the passage of carts
and horses.   Below the end windows of
the transept and sacristy are sepulchral
recesses, which were probably enriched

FIG. 1101.
The Collegiate Church of Dunglass.
Cap of Tower Arch, Choir.

with cusping, which is now cut away.   The ornamental brackets for
supporting these enrichments have label terminations of angels.   One
of these, playing on a stringed instrument, is shown in Fig. 1102.   The
side windows of the church have segmental sconsion arches and double
lights, with massive tracery (see Figs. 1099 and 1103).   The north and
south doorways of the nave are round arched, with moulded jambs (see
Fig. 1097).   The other doorways are plain, with lintels.

The sedilia in the south wall near the east end (Figs.
1103 and 1104) is a very beautiful one, and is fairly
well preserved.   It contains the usual three seats indicated by three ogee crocketed arch-heads.   These arches
rest on carved capitals at each end (Fig. 1105), and the
intermediate ones on corbels supported by angels, one
holding a shield, and the other playing on a voil.   The
sedilia is recessed about 13 inches, and is 6 feet 6¾ inches
long (see Fig. 1103) by about 5 feet 3 inches high from
the seat to the springing of the arches.   Between the
sedilia and the east wall and below the sill of the window

FIG. 1102.
The Collegiate Church
of Dunglass.
Corbel in Sacristy.

there has been a piscina, which has been cut away, and its position is
merely indicated against the wall, as shown in Fig. 1103.   It appears
to have been supported by a shaft from the floor.   Adjoining this, in the
east wall, is seen (see Fig. 1104) a projecting corbel with a shield on the

face. This was probably meant either to support a light or a figure in connection with the altar.

Fig. 1103.—The Collegiate Church of Dunglass.   Sedilia and South Window in Choir.

In the sacristy there are on the side walls four consecration crosses at the points marked on the Plan.

There is a diversity of opinion as to the name of the founder and the date of the founding of the Church of Dunglass. According to Nisbet * it was founded by "Sir Thomas Home, in the reign of Robert III." (1390-1406). He married Nicola or Nicolas Pepdie, who brought him the

Fig. 1104.—The Collegiate Church of Dunglass. Sedilia and South Window of Choir.

lordship of Dunglass, and their arms (Fig. 1106), which adjoin the north transept window, Nisbet says are impaled, viz., the lion for Home, and
* *Heraldry*, Vol. I. p. 274, and Vol. II. pp. 21 and 151.

the "three birds called papingoes, relative to the name of Pepdie." In Keith's *Catalogue* and by Spottiswoode we are told that the Collegiate Church of Dunglass was founded in the year 1450 by Sir Alexander Home of that Ilk. Chalmers, in the *Caledonia*, Vol. II. p. 512, says it was founded by Sir Alexander Home of Home in 1403. He was the son of Sir Thomas and Nicolas Pepdie. Sir James Hall, in a letter written in 1789 (see Hutton Collection), finds from examination, evidently of original documents in his possession, that it was founded by Sir Alexander in 1403. Dr. Laing also adopts this date as correct.* Perhaps, as above suggested, the choir and tower may have been built in 1403, while the nave was not erected till after 1450.

FIG. 1105.
The Collegiate Church of Dunglass.
Details of Sedilia.

FIG. 1106.
The Collegiate Church of Dunglass.
Arms of Sir Thomas Home and his Wife
in North Transept.

Dunglass Church is generally regarded as having been Collegiate. In the appendix to the *Scotichronicon*, it is stated that in the reign of James II. the buildings of Douglas (probably a mistake for Dunglass) were in progress,† and in the *Originales Parochiales*, Vol. I. p. 153, the following note occurs :—"About the middle of the fifteenth century a petition regarding the erection of the Parish Church of Douglas (evidently mistaken for Dunglass) into a Collegiate Church was presented to the Apostolic See, but though the Pope's consent seems to have been obtained, the purpose never was fulfilled."

* *Preface to Churches of Mid-Lothian*, Bannatyne Club, p. III.
† *Collegiate Churches of Mid-Lothian*, by David Laing. Bannatyne Club, p. II.

FOWLIS EASTER CHURCH, Perthshire.*

This edifice, which is one of the best preserved and most interesting of the minor churches of its date in Scotland, is situated about six miles north-west from Dundee.

The lands of Fowlis came into the possession of the family of Gray by marriage about the year 1397, when the only daughter of the last Mortimer of Fowlis and Aberdour married Sir Andrew Gray of Broxmouth. He was the first Lord Gray, and was succeeded by his son Andrew, the second Lord Gray, and it was doubtless by this Andrew Gray that the church was built. He died in 1469, and, judging from the style and various features of the architecture, the building seems to have been erected in his lifetime. Spottiswoode states that it was built by Sir Andrew Gray of Fowlis during the reign of James II. (1437-1460), and there is still

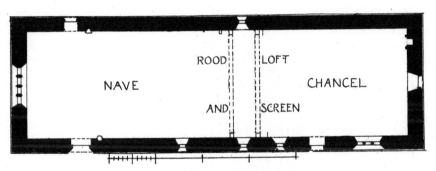

FIG. 1107.—Fowlis Easter Church. Plan.

more conclusive evidence that the church was built by Sir Andrew. He married Elizabeth, eldest daughter of Sir John Wemyss of Rires and Kincaldrum, and the arms of Gray and Wemyss are carved on the skew stones of the church. Further, in the *Old Statistical Account* it is stated that the "beam which supported the organ loft" bore the inscription:—
" Hoc Templum Structum fuit Anno Millesimo Centesimo Quadragesimo Secundo ab A. Gray."

The church (Fig. 1107) is a simple oblong structure without buttresses or projections of any kind. It measures about 88 feet long by 28 feet wide outside the walls. It is built of fine ashlar in large courses of stone, obtained from the den of Fowlis in the immediate neighbourhood. The stone is of a bluish-grey colour, and has well stood the test of time. There are north and south doors (Fig. 1108) nearly opposite each other near

* We are indebted to Mr. T. S. Robertson, architect, Dundee, for assistance with the drawings and description of this church.

FIG. 1108.—Fowlis Easter Church. View from South-East.

the west end, and a priest's door near the east end, all round arched. The edifice was divided into a nave and chancel by a rood screen and loft.

FIG. 1109. – Fowlis Easter Church. Corbels, &c., at Rood Screen.

The corbels for supporting the loft still exist, as shown on the Plan and in Fig. 1109. The nave is lighted by a large four light window in the west gable (see Fig. 1110), and one narrow lofty pointed window in the south wall (see Fig. 1108). There are one upper and one lower window in the south wall at the rood loft, the lower window pointed and the other square headed, and immediately to the east, in the south wall, another narrow and tall pointed window. Between the priest's door and the east gable the chancel is emphasised by a large three light traceried window in the south wall (see Fig. 1110), and also by a slight rise in the base, which runs all round the church. There is a small round window in the east wall fitted with a piece of cast iron tracery, put in about the beginning of this century. Only one window occurs in the north wall, viz., at the rood loft, which corresponds to the lower window on the south side, and is furnished with similar corbels

at each side, for the support of the rood loft.　There is in addition a
lower corbel a few feet west from the window, which was probably the
wall rest of the upper step of the stair leading to the loft.　The south-
west doorway (Fig. 1111) has a very impressive appearance.　The jambs
and arch are moulded with two deep and wide hollows, having a filleted
round between, which terminates, like many late Gothic mouldings, on a
splayed base.　The round arch is surmounted by a richly carved ogee
shaped label, resting at each side on figures bearing shields, and terminating with a heraldic display at the top, where on a shield couché are
carved the arms of Lord Gray, namely, a lion rampant, within a bordure

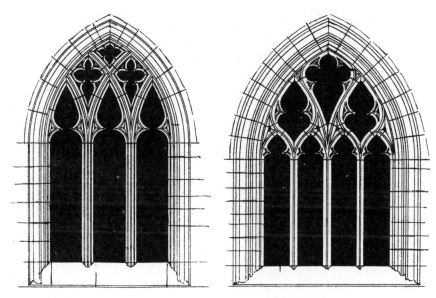

Window in South Wall of Chancel.   Window in West End Wall.

FIG. 1110.—Fowlis Easter Church.

engrailed, above which is a helmet supported by two lions, and bearing
a swan's head and neck, with wings elevated for crest.　The carving is,
unfortunately, a good deal decayed.

Adjoining the interior of each of the west doorways is a stoup ; that on
the north side is shown in Fig. 1112.

The ambry or sacrament house stands in the east wall on the north
side of the altar.　It is one of the most elaborately carved and sculptured
examples now remaining in Scotland.　The sacrament house is well shown
in the drawing by Mr. Robertson (Fig. 1113).　It is 5 feet 6 inches high
by 3 feet wide across the cope and base.　The opening, which is checked

DOOR JAMB

FIG. 1111 —Fowlis Easter Church.   South-West Doorway.

for a door, has an ogee arch with richly carved buttresses on each side. Above the recess is sculptured a remarkable group (Fig. 1114). In the centre is the bust of the Saviour, on a larger scale than the other figures, holding in His left hand the globe, surmounted by a small cross—the attribute of sovereignty. On each side is an angel—that on the right holding the cross, and that on the left the pillar of the scourging. Both have a nimbus, but are without wings. Above the cornice which runs along the top of the ambry and in the hollow of the roof or cope the Annunciation is sculptured. The Blessed Virgin stands on one side and the angel on the other, holding the scroll with the salutation. Between them is the pot of lilies, and behind the Virgin an open book, symbolising the prophecies regarding her.

FIG. 1112.
Fowlis Easter Church.
Stoup in North Wall.

Above the ambry are seen indications of broken work, as if there had been something more sculptured above, and in the village, built into one of the cottages, there is a series of figures (Fig. 1115), which have clearly been taken from the church, and which possibly stood over this ambry. These carvings are just the length required to fit the space, the panel containing them being 3 feet 1½ inch wide. Mr. Robertson, however, thinks that these figures formed part of a tomb, and that the broken remains on the top of the ambry indicate the former existence of some kind of parapet; but in any view, to bring these figures back to the church would be a fitting conclusion to the admirable work which has lately been carried out by the minister, the Rev. Dr. Burr, with the assistance of Mr. T. S. Robertson, architect.

The alterations lately effected consisted in removing a partition wall, which, along with the rood screen, separated the east end of the building from the part used as the Parish Church, and in removing the plaster ceiling, which cut across the tracery of the west window, preparatory to putting on a new open timber roof. The belfry replaces a nondescript erection of last century. The bell (Fig. 1116), which is old, is 14 inches high by 17¼ inches in diameter at the lip, and is attached to the stock by three canons. The stock is of oak, and, although bound with iron, is much rent. The bell is very heavy and of simple but beautiful form. The letters of the inscription seem to have been formed separately, and fitted round the mould in which the bell was cast.

The font (Fig. 1117) is richly sculptured, but is much mutilated. It is octagonal in shape, and measures 3 feet high, with a round basin, 20½ inches wide. In the panels round the basin are sculptured scenes from

III.   N

Fig. 1113.—Fowlis Easter Church. Sacrament House.

the life of Christ, which are much broken and defaced. The Baptism occupies one space, and Christ bound with a figure on each side (Fig. 1118)

FIG. 1114.—Fowlis Easter Church. Sculpture on Ambry.

is carved on another. The panels also contain the arms of Gray and Wemyss, with others now obliterated.

FIG. 1115.—Fowlis Easter Church. Sculpture in Village.

The door of the rood screen is still preserved. It is of dark oak, and is one of the few examples of pieces of furniture of this description remaining in Scotland (Fig. 1119). It has open work in the upper part, occupying nearly half the height (see details in Fig. 1120) and four

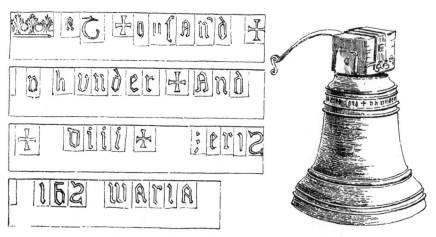

FIG. 1116.—Fowlis Easter Church. Bell.

panels below, the lower two having the linen pattern, and the two above (forming the centre of the door) being decorated with tracery work.

One of the most remarkable features of this church consists of four large pre-Reformation paintings on oak panels, two being at present hung on the east wall and two on the north

FIG. 1117.—Fowlis Easter Church. Font.

FIG. 1118.—Fowlis Easter Church. Carvings on Font.

Fig. 1119.—Fowlis Easter Church.   Half of Door of Rood Screen.

wall.* The two on the east wall are in much the better state of preservation. The upper picture represents our Saviour on the Cross, the soldier on horseback on his right thrusting the spear into his side, and numerous other figures on both right and left. The lower consists of eleven panels, each representing a saint, some male and some female. The tenth panel has near the foot the Gray shield in colours. On the north wall the upper painting has the middle part entirely rubbed off, and also, to a considerable extent, the central part of the upper division; but what remains shows a large head and shoulders, surrounded with a glory. Probably this part of the picture was a representation of the Trinity. To the right of this is a female saint with a sword piercing a king's head; at her feet and behind her there probably was another figure, now wanting, to balance the two figures on the left, namely, John the Baptist, holding the lamb in his arms, and behind him the Virgin and Child. The lower division has in the centre a representation of the entombment, with three figures on either side. The panels of the other picture are not in their correct places, but they represent some figures on horseback, and others on foot—subject uncertain.

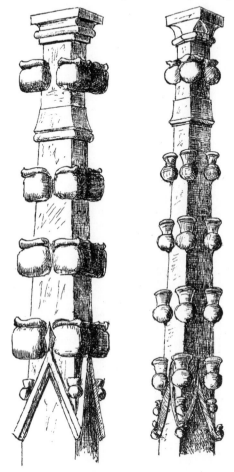

FIG. 1120.—Fowlis Easter Church.
Details of Upper Part of Rood Screen.

As already mentioned, the skew putts contain arms. These are as follow, viz. :—

* We have to thank Mr. W. R. Macdonald for descriptive notes of these pictures.

S.W. Wemyss of Reres 1st and 4th lion rampant, 2nd and 3rd a bend.
S.E. A lion rampant within a bordure engrailed for Gray, impaling the
       dexter half of the foregoing arms, namely, 1st a lion rampant,
       3rd a bend.
N.E. Scotland, lion rampant within a double tressure flory counter flory.
N.W. Lion rampant; for what family is uncertain.

COLLEGIATE CHURCH OF ST. SALVATOR, ST. ANDREWS,
FIFESHIRE.

The College of St. Salvator was founded and endowed by Bishop
Kennedy, in 1456, for a provost and prebendaries. This bishop was
distinguished for his liberality to the Church. He also founded and
endowed a Franciscan Monastery in St. Andrews, which has now entirely
disappeared.

The Church of St. Salvator is the only portion of the college buildings which still survives. It is now attached to the united colleges of
St. Leonard's and St. Salvator, which form the existing University of

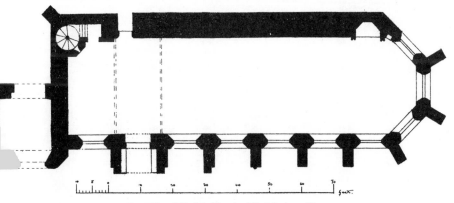

FIG. 1121.—Collegiate Church of St. Salvator. Plan.

St. Andrews, and the other buildings of which are modern. The church
bears the marks of the period when it was erected, the latter half of the
fifteenth century. It consists (Fig. 1121) of a single oblong chamber
about 107 feet long and 28 feet wide internally, with a three-sided apse
at the east end. There are now no windows in the north and west walls,
but the south wall is divided by buttresses into seven bays, with a large
pointed window in each, which, together with the three windows of the
eastern apse, sufficiently light the church. The central window of the apse
is larger than the others. The tracery in the windows is modern. The

buttresses between the bays are bold and effective (Fig. 1122), having a broad moulded base and being enriched with canopied niches for statues on their face.   The canopies on the buttresses next the apse are placed

FIG. 1122.—Collegiate Church of St. Salvator.   View from South-East.

facing one another on the angle of the buttress instead of on the face, an arrangement not easily explained.   The buttresses are now finished on top with gabled pinnacles, but these are a modern restoration.   The

original pinnacles were, doubtless, of the late and rather stunted character
usual at the period, of which one specimen survives, at the north-east

FIG. 1123.—Collegiate Church of St. Salvator. South-West Porch.

angle of St. Salvator's, where, however, it is little seen. Between two of the buttresses, near the south-west corner, a porch is introduced under the

Fig. 1124.—Collegiate Church of St. Salvator. View from South-West.

window (Fig. 1123), the buttresses being slightly extended beyond the others to receive it. The porch is roofed with groined vaulting, and has a stone bench on each side, and a canopied niche on each side of the wide entrance arch. A shield at the apex bore the arms and mitre of Bishop Kennedy. The doorway within the porch has a three-sided head or arch, and the north door opposite it has a similar top.

The tower at the south-west angle of the church is of the usual plain unbuttressed form (Fig. 1124) common at the period in Scotland. On the ground floor it contains the gateway to the college. Over the outer archway are the arms of Bishop Kennedy in a cusped panel (Fig. 1125), having a canopied niche on each side. Over this the tower rises to the string course under the belfry story, with no features but small loops in the wall. The belfry story has a lofty double window on each of its four sides. These windows are pointed and cusped, and a broad cusped transome divides them in their height. The angles of this story are splayed, and it is finished with a new plain parapet resting on a simple corbel course. The tower is surmounted by an octagonal spire of the stunted kind common at this time, and with a very marked entasis. It is divided by two string courses in the height, and has two tiers of lucarnes.

FIG. 1125.—Collegiate Church of St. Salvator. Bishop Kennedy's Arms in Tower.

In the interior of the north wall, close to the apse, stand the remains of the splendid monument erected by Bishop Kennedy (Fig. 1126). It forms in appearance the interior of an apse with five sides, elaborately carved with minute niches and recesses, and is covered with vaulting (now broken). This apse is spanned by a moulded and pointed arch carried on clustered shafts. Beside these, and over the arch, there is a succession of niches and figures, interspersed with tall much subdivided windows. Unfortunately this monument was greatly damaged by the fall of the roof, which occurred last century. According to tradition six splendid silver maces were found within the tomb, one of which is preserved in the college, and the others were distributed amongst the other Scottish universities. But it has been shown by Mr. Alex. J. S. Brooke, F.S.A. Scot., in a paper read before the Society of Antiquaries of Scotland (see *Proceedings*, 1892, in which these and other Scottish maces are fully illustrated), that this tradition is erroneous, and that the maces of Glasgow,

Fig. 1126.—Collegiate Church of St. Salvator. Monument of Bishop Kennedy.

Aberdeen, and Edinburgh Universities are of different dates, and were made expressly for these universities. The three maces belonging to St. Andrews are :—1, The mace of the Faculty of Arts ; 2, the mace of the Faculty of Canon Law, now the Theological Faculty ; and 3, the mace of St. Salvator's College—all of St. Andrews. No. 1 has a beautiful knop or head of tabernacle work, in three stages. It probably dates from early in the fifteenth century, and is of French workmanship. No. 2 is of a somewhat similar design, but is probably of Scottish manufacture. No. 3 is the most beautiful of the three St. Andrews maces. It bears the arms and initials of Bishop Kennedy, and the knop is of elaborate tabernacle work, containing allegorical and other figures. The style of workmanship of the mace of St. Leonard's, which is still preserved at the College, corresponds with that of the tomb. The inscription on the mace states that it was made in Paris, by John Maiel, in the year 1461. It seems not improbable that the tomb was also designed in France. To the right of the monument there is a very effectively designed sacrament house, having the royal arms, and those of Bishop Kennedy above it. The shield of the latter, with his mitre, is also seen to the left of the monument. This sacrament house is somewhat earlier in date than several others given below, and is of superior design. In this case the pyx, supported by two angels, is carved on the corbel beneath. Shafts, with cap and base on each side of the ambry, support a pointed arch above, ornamented with crockets and finial. A crocketed pinnacle encloses the composition on each side. The whole design is good and is well carried out.

THE COLLEGIATE CHURCH OF DALKEITH, Mid-Lothian.

The town of Dalkeith stands between the rivers North and South Esk, about six miles south from Edinburgh. A church dedicated to St. Nicholas existed here from an early period. It was raised into a collegiate church in the fifteenth century, and since the Reformation has been the church of the parish.

This church (Fig. 1127) consists of a nave of three bays with aisles, and a western tower, north and south transepts, and an aisleless choir of three bays, with an eastern apse. The western part of the church and a portion of the choir extending as far as the south doorway (at which point a wall has been erected across the building, as indicated by dotted lines) are used as the Parish Church. About 1854 this church underwent a thorough restoration. Much of the interest attached to it as an ancient building was thus effaced, but the original plan has not been greatly altered. The appearance of the building before the above date is shown by Fig. 1128, which is reproduced from a drawing in the Hutton Collection in the

Advocates' Library.* The steeple shown in this view is said to have been built in 1762.† It resembles somewhat the old steeple of Glasgow College, ‡ and is much more likely to have been built, as the latter was, in the seventeenth century than in the eighteenth. The tower was probably repaired at the latter date, when, as we are informed, the church itself was so treated. The walls of the tower, where they have been left unrestored, and the staircase turret adjoining are undoubtedly older than the eighteenth century.

The eastern portion of the choir (Fig. 1129) has stood for centuries in a roofless and ruinous condition. It has originally been vaulted, probably with a pointed barrel vault supporting a stone roof. As much

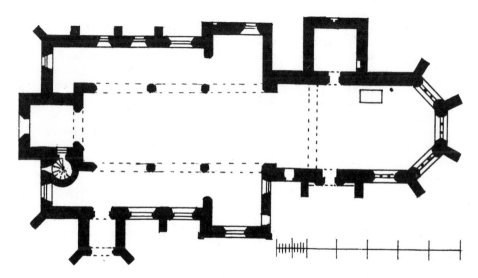

FIG. 1127.—The Collegiate Church of Dalkeith. Plan.

of the vault remains (Fig. 1130) as is self-supporting, and has on the surface and in the angles of the apse moulded ribs at intervals springing from corbels. The east end terminates in an apse of three bays, in each of which, and in the bays of the south wall, are windows of three lights, filled with plain looped tracery. The windows of the apse have been partially built up (see Fig. 1129). The apse windows are built at the same level as the other windows, thus leaving a great height of plain wall above them. This height of wall over the windows was

* We have to thank the Curators for permission to publish this illustration.
† *Collegiate Churches of Mid-Lothian*, Bannatyne Club, p. xci.
‡ See *The Castellated and Domestic Architecture of Scotland*, Vol. IV. p. 160.

Fig. 1128.—The Collegiate Church of Dalkeith.   View from South-East.   (From a Drawing by Charles Sanderson in the Hutton Collection in the Advocates' Library.)

rendered unavoidable by the barrel vault of the interior, which required the arches of the windows to be kept below the springing of the main vault, as may be observed at Ladykirk, Seton Church, and elsewhere. In the churches of Linlithgow and Stirling the central window of the apse is larger than the others, but in those cases the vaulting is different, and allows greater height for the windows. The parapet above the walls of the choir is plain and rests on a string course, which has been carved with foliage. The doorway in the south side (Fig. 1131) is round arched, and in the freedom of the treatment of its details very much resembles what is found in the neighbouring Church of Rosslyn.

Fig. 1129.—The Collegiate Church of Dalkeith. The Eastern Apse.

The buttresses (Fig. 1132), like those of Rosslyn, are massive, and although they have five or six stages, they do not recede at these stages till the wall head is nearly reached, where they are finished with a gablet beneath which a large gargoyle is projected. The buttresses were crowned with square pinnacles, finished with crockets and finials, only two of which now remain, in a very ruinous state. They have been carefully wrought on the inside, so as to adjust themselves to the sloping flanks of the stone roof, the water from which was conveyed through the buttresses by the projecting gargoyles to the ground. There is a canopied niche on the face of all the buttresses, as well as those on each side of the south doorway.

A monument in the choir (Fig. 1133) contains two recumbent figures, a husband and wife side by side. The effigies (Fig. 1134) are not recessed, as is frequently the case in an arched tomb in the wall, but lie in the open church where shown on the ground Plan, and they appear to be

Fig. 1130.—The Collegiate Church of Dalkeith. Interior of Apse.

in their original position.   From the heraldic coats on the monument
(see Fig. 1133) it is obvious that the knight was a Douglas, and that the
lady was of royal descent.   On a lozenge at the head of the knight are the

Fig. 1131.—The Collegiate Church of Dalkeith.   South Doorway.

arms of Douglas of Dalkeith, viz., two stars on a chief.   And on a similar lozenge at the head of the lady are the same arms impaled with those of Scotland (Fig. 1135).   The same arms are also repeated at the sides of

FIG. 1132.—The Collegiate Church of Dalkeith.   North-East Side of Apse.

the monument (see Fig. 1133), with what appear like coronets above them, from which Mr. James Drummond* gives it as his opinion that the persons represented are James, 4th Lord of Dalkeith, who was created Earl of Morton in 1457, and his wife Johan, third daughter of King James I. The former died about 1498. Mr. Drummond supposes the lady survived her husband, but the Lady Johanna must have died before the year 1490.† The facts on which that view is founded are the presence of the royal and Douglas arms impaled, and "the male figure being sculptured with an earl's coronet, to which none of the previous lords of Dalkeith had a right, although they were allied to royalty." ‡

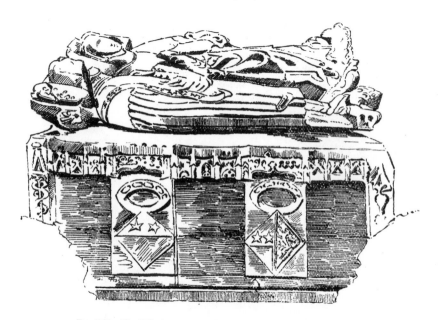

Fig. 1133.—The Collegiate Church of Dalkeith. Monument in Choir.

The monument is in a very dilapidated condition, the base and lower half of the pedestal being buried in earth and rubbish, the accumulation of centuries. The arms on the pedestal (see Fig. 1133) are the same as those already referred to as carved at the heads of the figures. They are repeated on the opposite side of the pedestal, but in inverse order. The canopied work along the top of the pedestal is similar to what is seen surmounting a fragment of royal arms at Dunfermline (see Fig. 218), which fragment may also have been part of a tomb.

* *Proceedings of the Society of Antiquaries of Scotland*, Session 1857-8, p. 25.
† *Ibid.* p. 94.   ‡ *Ibid.* p. 27.

The precise date of the founding of the Chapel of St. Nicholas does not appear to be known, but since 1372, when Robert II. granted a licence to James of Douglas to endow a chaplainry therein, frequent notices of it appear.*

In 1390 Sir James Douglas, first Lord of Dalkeith (already referred to), " bequeathed, besides a cup and a missal, a sum of money for the reparation and roofing of the Chapel of St. Nicholas at Dalkeith ; " and by another

FIG. 1134.—The Collegiate Church of Dalkeith. Effigies on Monument in Choir.

deed two years later, " he assigns the residue of his goods to the fabric and ornament of the said chapel," † and for other purposes.   Before his death, in 1420, he raised the chapel to the rank of a Collegiate Church, and is supposed to have finished the building, endowing it with " stipends and manses for a provest and five prebendaries, as perpetual chaplains." ‡

* See *Bannatyne Miscellany*, Vol. II. p. 101.
† *Collegiate Churches in Mid-Lothian*, Bannatyne Club, p. lxxxiv.   ‡ *Ibid.*

In 1467 St. Nicholas was disjoined from Lasswade, and Dalkeith was made a separate parish, and in 1477 the church was enlarged by the addition of three canonries, endowed by the Earl of Morton. At the Reformation, St. Nicholas' was settled as the Presbyterian church of the parish.

FIG. 1135.—The Collegiate Church of Dalkeith.
Shield at Head of Lady.

In 1686 the minister reported the church to be ruinous, and the Presbytery ordered it to be made wind and water tight.

On the north side of the church there is a vault occupied as the funeral vault of the Buccleuch family.

ST. MUNGO'S CHURCH, BORTHWICK, MID-LOTHIAN.

This church is situated near the well known castle of the same name in the south-east part of the county, and about nine miles from Edinburgh. With the exception of the south aisle or chapel, the church (Fig. 1136) was entirely rebuilt about forty years ago.* To judge from what of the old plan can now be made out, the structure has originally been a Norman one, with aisleless nave and choir, and a circular eastern apse. The reconstruction of the edifice included that of the apse and the south wall of the chancel, which, although not entirely new, are yet practically so, none of the ancient architectural features being left, but only, at most, some of the walling. The apse is about 16 feet wide by about 10 feet 6 inches deep, and was lighted by three narrow widely splayed windows. The chancel was about 16 feet 6 inches long by 22 feet wide. The south wall contained two windows, and apparently a piscina, but all these features have disappeared, as well as the more important arches which formed the entrance to the chancel and the apse.

A south aisle or chapel (see Fig. 1136) has been added to the church. It is entire and is a good example of Scottish Gothic of the latter half of the fifteenth century, having in all probability been built about the same

* A plan and view of the church before it was rebuilt and some notes regarding the building are given in the *Arniston Memoirs*, by G. W. T. Omond, p. 6.

time as the castle, the licence for the erection of which is dated 1430. William de Borthwick, a man of some eminence, was created Lord Borthwick shortly before that date, and the aisle is believed to have been erected by him. This aisle is vaulted with a pointed barrel vault, covered on the

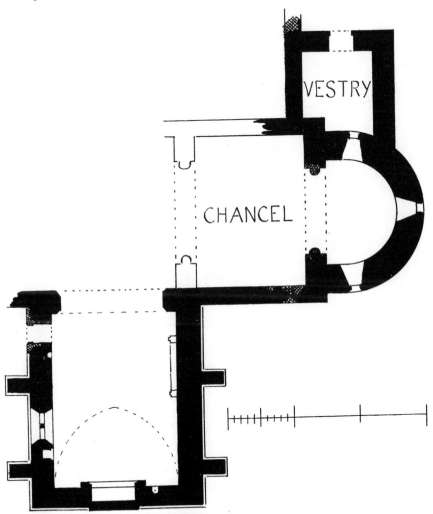

FIG. 1136.—St. Mungo's Church. Plan.

outside with a stone roof (Fig. 1137), to resist the thrusts of which massive buttresses are provided. The roof consists of overlapping stone flags, carefully wrought, and the cornice at the wall head (Fig. 1138) is ornamented with carved heads and leaves alternately. The chapel contains in the south wall a recess for a monument, and the remains of two piscinas and a locker in the south and west walls. There is a small pointed window in

FIG. 1137.—St. Mungo's Church. South Aisle, from South-West.

the west side, and a larger one in the south end. The tracery of the latter is probably modern, as is the west doorway. The wide arch which

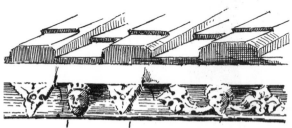

FIG. 1138.—St. Mungo's Church. Cornice of Aisle.

formerly opened into the church has been built up.

A stately monument (Fig. 1139), containing two recumbent figures, is built against the east wall of the aisle. The statues are supposed to be those of the founder of the castle and the aisle, the first Lord Borthwick and his wife, who was a Douglas. The monument is not now in its original position. Before the time of the rebuilding

it stood in the inside of the wall of the apse, and it was then removed
and placed in its present position, where it has apparently suffered from

FIG. 1139.—St. Mungo's Church.   Monument of Lord Borthwick and his Wife.

over restoration.   The effigies, which are remarkably well preserved,
have been entirely coloured, and considerable traces of the colour
still remain.   The length of the arched recess in which the figures lie

is 7 feet, and the depth of the recess 3 feet $8\frac{1}{2}$ inches. The height to the arched recess is about 3 feet $6\frac{1}{2}$ inches, and the total height of the monument is 10 feet 3 inches, and the width over the buttresses 8 feet 11 inches. The design is of a usual form, and the enrichments indicate a late date in the fifteenth century.

The Church of Borthwick was annexed by Chancellor Crichton to his newly erected College of Crichton. After the Reformation Borthwick was united to Heriot and Stow, and served by a reader, but in 1596 James VI. erected it into a separate parish. In 1606 the kirk-session complained that the church was falling into ruin for want of proper repair. Commissioners from the Presbytery met the complainers, and after deliberation they refused to "stent" themselves for the repair of the church, but offered instead to sell the vestry (see Plan) "as a family burial-place to any gentleman who would pay such a price as would enable them to repair the choir." * An offer of the building was made to Sir James Dundas of Arniston, who ultimately purchased it, and with the money thus raised the church appears to have been repaired in a rough fashion. The chancel arch was built up and a gable wall erected above it, which thus became the east end of the church, and the apse was left outside. A gallery was then placed against the east gable. The structure remained in this condition till 1780, when it was destroyed by fire. The walls which survived the fire are those shown on the Plan (see Fig. 1136). The vestry (now the Dundas burial vault) and south aisle, both having stone roofs, remain comparatively unscathed. The nave and the north wall of the chancel have entirely disappeared.

LADYKIRK CHURCH, BERWICKSHIRE.

This very complete and almost unaltered church stands on the high north bank of the river Tweed, nearly opposite Norham Castle. Before the Reformation the parish consisted of the two parishes of Upsetlington and Horndene. In 1296 the parson of the former swore fealty to Edward I., who, while endeavouring to arrange regarding the succession to the crown of Scotland, adjourned the Scottish Parliament from Brigham in England to an open field in Upsetlington. The existing church is said to have been built in 1500, and dedicated to the Blessed Virgin by James IV., in gratitude for his delivery from being drowned by a sudden flood of the river Tweed.

The structure (Fig. 1140) is a specially characteristic example of the Scottish church architecture of the period. It is a triapsidal cross church, without aisles, having an apsidal termination at the east end of the chancel and at the north and south ends of the transept. The body of

* *Arniston Memoirs.*

the church and the transepts are covered with pointed barrel vaults, with ribs at intervals, springing from small corbels (Fig. 1141); and the whole is roofed with overlapping stone flags (Fig. 1142). The nave and chancel are 94 feet 6 inches in length by 23 feet 3 inches in width internally, and the transepts, which are very short, each measures 12 feet in depth from north to south by 19 feet in width. The side windows are of considerable width, but being entirely below the springing of the vault, they are low compared with the height of the church. The side walls rise greatly above the windows on the exterior, and have a heavy appearance, while the lofty vaults of the interior render the building dark. The arches

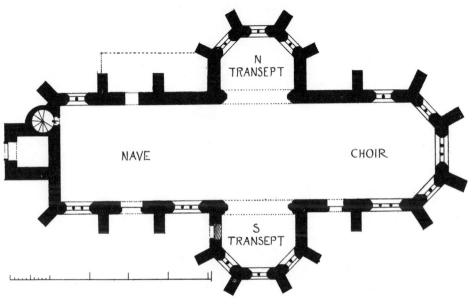

Fig. 1140.—Ladykirk Church. Plan.

which open from the main church into the transepts (see Fig. 1141) are also kept below the springing of the main vault, and are therefore low, but the windows in the transepts are kept well up. To resist the pressure of the heavy vaults and roof the walls are well buttressed, and the buttresses terminate with the somewhat stunted pinnacles in vogue at the time. It will be noticed that the overlapping stone roofs are constructed in three distinct portions, viz., one roof extending over the whole of the nave and chancel, and two separate roofs over each transept. The roofs and vaults of each of the transepts terminate against a gable raised on the side walls of the main part of the church, and the transepts are entered by low arches, on which these gables rest.

FIG. 1141.—Ladykirk Church.　Interior, looking East.

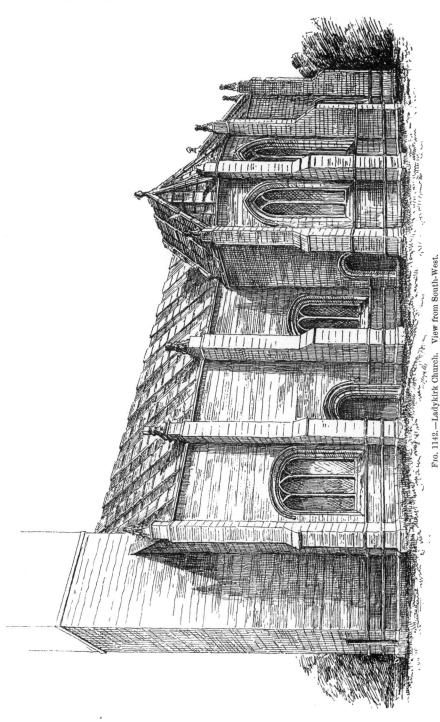

Fig. 1142.—Ladykirk Church. View from South-West.

Both the interior and exterior of the church are quite plain, especially the former, in which there is no attempt at ornament of any kind. As regards the exterior, the buttresses with their pinnacles, and the windows with their simple tracery, give a pleasing effect, especially as seen from the east (Fig. 1143).

Perhaps the most striking feature of the exterior is the elliptic form of the arches over the side windows of the nave and choir (see Fig. 1142). This peculiar form has evidently resulted from the desire to make these windows as wide as possible, so as to admit light. But as all the window

Fig. 1143.—Ladykirk Church. View from South-East.

arches required to be kept below the springing of the vaults, the interior is but imperfectly lighted. There are three doorways in the building—the south-west door in the nave, the priest's door in the chancel, and a door in the south transept. These are all semicircular in the arch-head, as is common in Scottish examples. That in the south transept is now built up.

The tower at the west end is 14 feet square externally. The lower part is of the same date as the church, and has the base courses returning round it. The upper part has been rebuilt. The doorway to the tower is from the outside.

SETON COLLEGIATE CHURCH, HADDINGTONSHIRE.

A disused edifice situated in the private grounds of Seton Castle, about two miles east from Prestonpans Railway Station. The parish of Seton having been joined to that of Tranent in 1580, service in the church has from that time been abandoned.

There was a church here from an early date. It is rated in the ancient Taxatio at 18 merks. In a MS. pedigree of the family of Seton, by Maitland of Lethington, quoted by Grose,* it is stated that Sir Alex. Seton, in the time of David II., was buried in the Parish Church of Seton. Also that Katherine Sinclair, wife of William, first Lord Seton, about 1390, "Biggit ane yle on the south side of the Paroch Kirk of Seton of fine estlar, pendit and theikit it with, stane, with ane sepulchar thairin quhair she lies." Her son John (died 1441) was buried in this aisle.

George, the second Lord Seton, in 1493, made the church collegiate. He built the sacristy and covered it with stone in the reign of James IV. He died in 1507, and was buried near the high altar.

George, the third Lord Seton, who was slain at Flodden, "Theickit the Queir of Seton with stane." Jane Hepburne, his widow, after his decease, "Biggit the forework of Seton above the zit, and also she biggit the northomoss yll of the College Kirk of Seton and took down the yll biggit be Dame Katherine Sinclair on the south side of it, the said college kirk, because the syde of it stood to the syde of the kirk, to mack it a parfecte and a proper cornet and a cross kirk and biggit up the steeple as ye see it now to ane grit hight swa that it wants little of compileiting." This lady also presented the church with many ornaments of silver and rich vestments.

From the above quotations it would appear that the parish church existed in the fourteenth century. This church was probably rebuilt towards the end of the fifteenth century, and was added to by the second Lord Seton when he made the church collegiate in 1493, and completed by the third Lord Seton. The transepts and tower and spire would appear to have been erected by the Dowager Lady Seton in the sixteenth century, after her husband's death at the Battle of Flodden.

The collegiate foundation consisted of a provost, six prebendaries, one clerk, and two singing boys. The edifice has undoubtedly been rebuilt or restored at the date of its being made collegiate. It corresponds in style with the numerous collegiate foundations established in the fifteenth and sixteenth centuries. The eastern apsidal termination, the stone roof supported on a pointed barrel vault, and other details point to its date

* Vol. I. p. 64.

and associate it with the other collegiate churches of Scotland erected in the fifteenth century.

In 1544 the structure suffered much at the hands of the English invaders, who carried off the organ and bells, and burnt the timber work.

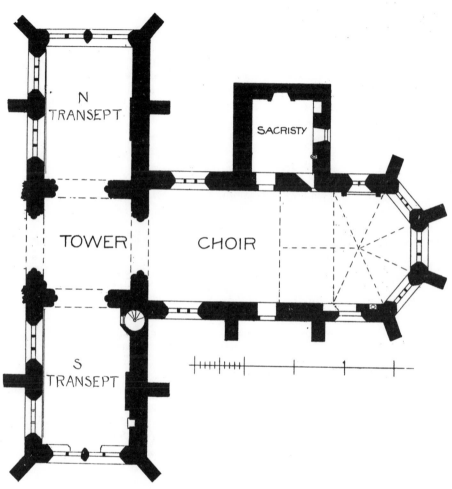

Fig. 1144.—Seton Collegiate Church.. Plan.

The stone roof of the choir was removed at some period. The masonry, however, survived, and the edifice has now been roofed in and properly defended from the weather by the late Lord Wemyss, who, along with his Countess, is buried in the choir. The broken tracery of the windows has been renewed by the present Lord Wemyss. The church was designed

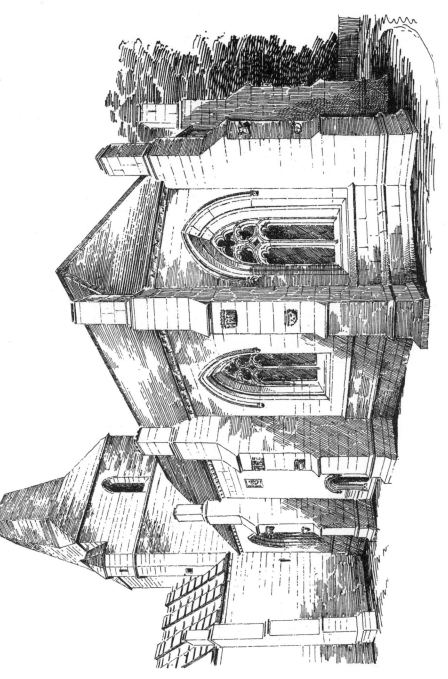

Fig. 1145.—Seton Collegiate Church. View from South-East.

as a complete cross without aisles, and with a central tower and spire over the intersection, but the nave has never been built. The portions erected (Fig. 1144) consist of the choir (with its three-sided apsidal east end), a north sacristy, a north and south transept, and a central tower and spire over the crossing. The choir is 53 feet in length by 22 feet in width internally. The exterior (Fig. 1145) is divided into three bays, separated by buttresses. There is a round-headed doorway in the central bay of the south wall, with a panel containing a coat of arms in the upper part of the wall, and mullioned windows in the other bays (including the apse), except that in the north wall at the part where the sacristy is built. The arched heads are all filled with tracery of a simple character and of

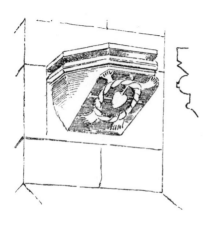

Fɪɢ. 1146.—Seton Collegiate Church.   Corbels on Buttresses.

a pattern common in third pointed work. The buttresses are of good substantial form, and each is crowned with a square, but rather stunted, pinnacle, the enriched pyramidal tops of nearly all of them being wanting. A carved corbel and canopy are placed on the face of each buttress to receive a statue, but they are now all empty. Fig. 1146 shows two of these corbels, one containing the Seton arms. The cornice of the choir is enriched with flower ornaments.

The interior of the choir (Fig. 1147) is extremely simple. It is roofed with a pointed barrel vault, the surface of which, towards the east end, is ornamented with moulded ribs. These ribs spring from corbels in each angle of the apse and in the side walls, and extend to nearly the centre of the choir, where they cease, leaving the remainder of the vault plain. The idea has apparently been, by the introduction of these ribs, to make the presbytery somewhat ornamental. The windows, being below the

Fig. 1147.—Seton Collegiate Church.   Choir, looking East.

springing of the vault, are necessarily low, and the vault is in consequence dark. There are a plain sedilia, with elliptic arch, and an ornate piscina (Fig. 1148) at the east end of the south wall. Opposite them in the north wall a monument (Fig. 1149) under the north-east window contains, in an arched recess, an effigy, probably that of the second Lord Seton, who erected the church into a college. The choir is now roofed with wood and slates above the vault, but it was no doubt originally covered with a roof of overlapping stone slabs. The door to the sacristy is opposite that in the south wall. The sacristy is about 14 feet by 12 feet. It has a plain barrel vault, which supports an upper story, of which the window is visible (Fig. 1150), but there is no apparent means of access to it. The building has a roof of overlapping stone flags. The sacristy has one small eastern window, with a piscina near it, and a fireplace. In the angle next the apse there is a squint commanding a view of the altar.

The tower is 25 feet square. On the ground level there are arched openings 9 feet 6 inches wide (Fig. 1151) towards the choir and each transept, and also in the west wall towards the intended nave, the latter being built up. The stair turret is placed at the south-east angle, and partly projects into the south transept (Fig. 1152). It is also visible on the exterior (see Fig. 1145). The tower is carried up over the crossing one story in height above the roof, and is crowned with a broach-spire, the top of which is unfinished. This is one of the very few examples of broach-spires in Scotland. The ground floor over the crossing is groin vaulted, and has a circular opening in the centre.

The transepts are each about 27 feet long by 18 feet wide, and each is divided into two bays, with buttresses, pinnacles, and traceried windows, similar to those of the choir. These traceries were all much damaged, but they have been repaired by Lord Wemyss. The vaulting (see Figs.

Fig. 1148.
Seton Collegiate Church.
Piscina in Choir.

Fig. 1149.—Seton Collegiate Church. Monument under North-East Window.

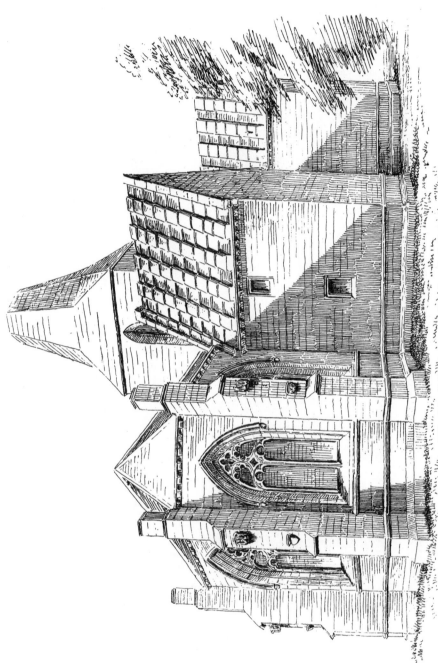

FIG. 1150.—Seton Collegiate Church. View from North-East.

1151 and 1152) is of the pointed barrel kind, similar to that of the choir, but without ribs, and supports a roof composed of overlapping stone flags

Fig. 1151.—Seton Collegiate Church. Transept, looking South.

Fig. 1152.—Seton Collegiate Church.   View from South Transept, looking North.

(see Figs. 1145 and 1150). The north and south end windows of the transepts (Fig. 1153) are peculiar. They are of considerable size, and

FIG. 1153.—Seton Collegiate Church. Transept, from South.

each is divided into two compartments by a large stone mullion built in courses, each compartment being filled with smaller tracery. Several examples of this mode of treating large windows about this period may be mentioned, such as King's College, Aberdeen ; Haddington Church, &c.   There is an arched recess under the two large end windows of the north and south transepts (see Figs. 1151 and 1152), which perhaps at one time contained monuments.   A piscina occurs in the east wall of the south transept (Fig. 1154), and another, supported on three heads, on the north-west pier of the tower.   Other monuments in the Renaissance

Fig. 1154.—Seton Collegiate Church.   Piscina in South Transept.

style have been erected against the east walls of the transepts (see Fig. 1151).   An octagonal font (Fig. 1155), carved with shields bearing the Seton and other arms, is placed in a temporary manner in the crossing.

From the history of the structure it would appear, as above mentioned, that the transept and tower were erected by Jane Hepburne (Lady Seton) in the sixteenth century.   The style of the transept is

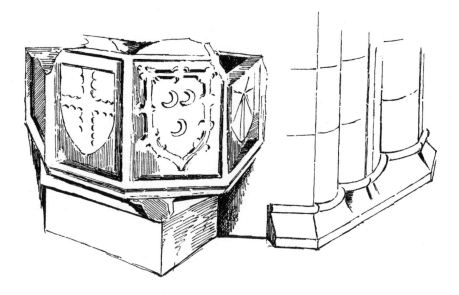

FIG. 1155.—Seton Collegiate Church. Font at Crossing.

evidently later than that of the choir, but the details of the buttresses have been copied in the later part of the structure from those of the earlier part.

THE COLLEGIATE CHURCH OF ARBUTHNOTT,
KINCARDINESHIRE.

This church, which is dedicated to St. Ternan, is situated about three or four miles from Bervie, and not far from the old mansion of Arbuthnott. It is an exceedingly interesting and picturesque structure, and contains work of three distinct periods, representing different phases of Scottish ecclesiastical architecture. There is first the chancel (Fig. 1156), dedicated by Bishop Bernham in 1242, and possibly the nave may also be in part of the same period. Then there is the very striking south wing or aisle, which is known, from the Arbuthnott Missal, to have been built by Sir Robert Arbuthnott in the end of the fifteenth century. This aisle (Fig. 1157), which is two stories in height, is a remarkable example of the style with which we are familiar in the collegiate and other churches of the period. In the third place, the quaint west end (Fig. 1158) represents an example of the application to an ecclesiastical structure of features of the domestic architecture of the country, of which there are so many examples throughout Scotland.   In February 1889 "the nave, then the only part in use, was burned, and the fire destroyed a partition which cut off the chancel."   None of the structural features of the church suffered any damage, and the chancel and the south aisle, having little or nothing in their construction of a combustible nature, escaped altogether.   The church has been well restored by Mr. A. M. Mackenzie, architect, Aberdeen,* a new roof having been placed on the nave and chancel, and suitable new fittings and furniture introduced.   The three windows in the east wall of the chancel have been renewed, exactly after the remains of the original ones.

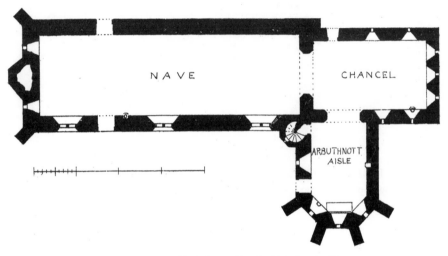

Fig. 1156.—The Collegiate Church of Arbuthnott.   Plan.

The nave, which measures internally about 60 feet 6 inches long by 18 feet wide, has a north and south round-arched doorway, with a bead moulding on the angles.   These doorways are, perhaps, of the sixteenth century.   The three windows on the south side have centre mullions, and are finished with straight lintels (see Fig. 1157); and, although renewed, they represent the original arrangement.   Besides these there are two small windows in the west gable (see Fig. 1158).   A stoup in the wall inside adjoins the south door.

The chancel arch is about 12 feet wide by 13 feet high.   It has a double splay on each side, and is acutely pointed.   The chancel is about 26 feet 5 inches long by 15 feet 6 inches wide.   The total internal

* In regard to this church we are indebted to an illustrated article by Mr. A. M. Mackenzie, in the *Transactions of the Aberdeen Ecclesiological Society, 1890*, and to Mr. T. S. Robertson and Mr. W. S. Walker of Dundee.

length of the church is 90 feet. There is a small north doorway in the chancel, which was evidently not meant to lead to the outside, but to a

Fig. 1157.—The Collegiate Church of Arbuthnott. South Aisle.

sacristy or some such apartment; and projecting tusk stones in the corner outside the door show that such a building was contemplated. The chancel (Fig. 1159) is lighted by small widely splayed windows on each side, and three lintelled windows in the east end (Fig. 1160).   Mr. Mackenzie shows reasons for believing that this gable has been reconstructed, and that it originally had only two windows in the lower part, with perhaps some kind of central window at a higher level, something like what is found at Mortlach.   The pointed piscina (Fig. 1161) beneath the eastmost south window (see Fig. 1160) has, as usual, been mutilated.

Fig. 1158.—The Collegiate Church of Arbuthnott.   View from South-West.

To connect the chancel with the Arbuthnott Aisle a round archway (see Fig. 1160), 7 feet 8 inches wide, has been cut through the chancel wall.   The details of this arch are shown in Fig. 1162.   This chapel or aisle, which has an apsidal south end, measures about 20 feet 3 inches long by 12 feet 11 inches wide, and has a vaulted stone roof (Fig. 1163) about 18 feet high, with a semi-octagonal dome over the apse.   This view gives an idea of the appearance of the interior of the chapel. In front of the apse windows stands a sarcophagus 6 feet 2 inches long by 2 feet 2 inches wide, having a rude recumbent figure on the top. It contains the following arms on the front, beginning at the head, viz., Douglas, Arbuthnott, Arbuthnott, Stewart; and there appear to be indications that there have been other shields, now cut away. There is a round arched entrance door to the aisle on the west side (see Fig. 1157), with a stoup beneath the adjoining window on the inside, and in the east wall are the remains of a credence. A turret staircase (see

FIG. 1159.—The Collegiate Church of Arbuthnott. View from North-East.

Fig. 1157) gives access from the aisle to a priest's chamber on the upper floor, which Bishop Forbes, believing it to have been the place where the Missal referred to below was written, describes at some length.* It had a strong door, which folded back into a recess. The room is of the same size and shape as the aisle below, and is lighted with three windows with square heads, two in the apse, and one (the largest) looking towards the west (see Fig. 1157). The latter is strongly guarded with an iron grating of the usual construction. The windows are fitted with seats like those commonly found in the castles. "There is a stoup for holy water at the

* Arbuthnott Missal, 1864, p. lxxxvii. The Pitsligo Press.

FIG. 1160.—The Collegiate Church of Arbuthnott. Interior of Chancel.

entrance, and a small ambry, ornamented with a single trefoil, probably for the reservation of the holy Eucharist." *

FIG. 1161.
The Collegiate Church
of Arbuthnott.
Piscina beneath
Eastmost
South Window.

The external appearance of this chapel is illustrated in Fig. 1157, where the fine angle buttresses of the apse, with their considerable projection and height (owing to the upper story) and their picturesque pinnacles, and the stair turret are fully shown. The buttresses have each an ornamental corbel and canopy for a statue placed on their face, but without any niche. Fig. 1164 shows one of them with its elaborate carved work. The very quaint aspect of the whole building looking from the west is seen in the drawing (see Fig. 1158). The height of the two turrets, as shown on Mr. Mackenzie's geometrical drawings, is the same, viz., 41 feet 6 inches.

The Arbuthnott Missal, already referred to, with its two companion volumes the Psalter and Office of the Blessed Virgin, have been well described by Mr. William MacGillivray. They were specially written for the use of this church by the vicar, James Sybbald. The Missal was finished in the year 1491, and was presented by the writer and the founder

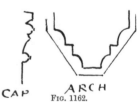

CAP FIG. 1162. ARCH
The Collegiate Church of Arbuthnott.
Details of Arch to South Aisle.

* *Proceedings of the Society of Antiquaries*, Session 1892. Vol. II. third Series, by William MacGillivray, W.S., F.S.A., Scot.

FIG. 1163.—The Collegiate Church of Arbuthnott.   Interior of Chancel.

III.   Q

of the aisle "to the high altar of the pious Bishop St. Ternan." The Psalter was finished in 1482, and from internal evidence the last of the three volumes was probably written a short time before the Psalter.

FIG. 1164.—The Collegiate Church of Arbuthnott. Corbel and Canopy on Buttress.

From the Register of the Great Seal of date 30th May 1505, it appears that the chapel was then endowed by Robert Arbuthnott, "James Sybbald, Vicar of Arbuthnott," being one of the witnesses. Sir Robert died in 1506, and the vicar in the year following.

The building adjoining the church, seen in Fig. 1158, is the old manse.

THE COLLEGIATE CHURCH OF CRICHTON, Mid-Lothian.

This edifice stands on the south side of the valley where the river Tyne takes its rise, about four miles from Tynehead Railway Station. It is seen from the railway, together with Crichton Castle, from which it is only about a quarter of a mile distant.

The building is still in use as the parish church. It consists (Fig. 1165) of a chancel, measuring internally about 44 feet from east to west by about 24 feet 10 inches in width, a central tower about 24 feet square,

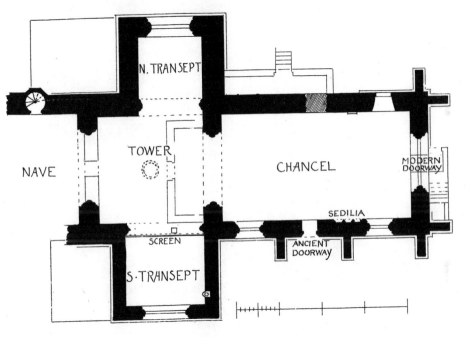

FIG. 1165.—The Collegiate Church of Crichton. Plan.

and north and south transepts, the total length of which, from north to south, is about 70 feet. The north wall of the nave is erected for a length of about 16 feet, but of the south wall only a few feet have been built.

To adapt the edifice to the Presbyterian system of worship, probably the very worst plan which could have been devised has been adopted, and is shown on the Plan by clear lines. The original fabric may be said to remain, but it is greatly deformed. As the tower opened into the unbuilt nave it had necessarily to be walled up, and has an entrance doorway left in the centre. This doorway, which is round arched, seems to be old,

Fig. 1166.—The Collegiate Church of Crichton. View from South-East.

and was probably brought from a building which appears to have formerly stood on the north side of the church. Across the interior of the tower a stone wall has been built to enclose the modern church. The portion of the tower outside this wall thus forms a vestibule, from which a stair

Fig. 1167.—The Collegiate Church of Crichton. Window on North Side.

leads to a west gallery fitted up in the enclosed portion of the tower. Another door has been slapped through the east wall to the outside, and an outer stair at the east end leads to an inserted gallery running across that end. One window and a sacristy or similar building on the north side have been done away with, to allow the erection of a passage for reaching another gallery, which runs along the north side of the chancel. The north transept has, perhaps, been worst used of all. A wall has been built between the moulded responds to a height of about 5 feet, and the whole area of the transept at this level is roofed over to form a burial vault. The south transept is not utilised in any way except as a sort of lumber place.

Instead of this unsuitable and costly arrangement, the area of the church as it stood would suffice to give more accommodation than is thus obtained, and that without sacrificing the dignity of the building, as has been done by the arrangements just described.

It would appear from a letter by the Rev. John Gourlay, the parish minister, to General Hutton, dated Crichton, 4th April 1789, that the

Fig. 1168.—The Collegiate Church of Crichton. Sedilia.

tower, with probably the transepts, then sufficed for the congregation. He says, "There is a high building upon the one end where the bell hangs, and where divine service was lately performed, but since considerable reparations were given, it is now again altered to what is called the quire."

The original entrance to the church was on the south side of the chancel (see Fig. 1165). It has been partly destroyed and is now built up, but portions of its moulded jambs can still be seen. The mouldings are of a common kind, consisting of two beads separated by a hollow. The doorway has been 3 feet 10 inches wide. Above the doorway a window has been roughly hacked through the wall, and on the inside of the sill there are rudely carved the initials P. L., with the date 1729. These are probably the initials of the worthy who contrived certain of the alterations above described. At the same time two small windows have been knocked through the side walls beneath the original windows on the north and south sides nearest the east end. One of these is shown in the view Fig. 1166, and the other on the north side is shown on the Plan. These windows have been referred to by Mr. Muir and in the Architectural Publication Societies Dictionary as examples of lychnoscope or offertory windows; but undoubtedly they were inserted to give light beneath the east gallery, and are of no older date than last century. Only one of the original windows, that on the north side, retains the original tracery (Fig. 1167). Indications of the tracery of the transept windows also still remain. The choir has been divided into three bays by buttresses, which have the numerous set-offs of the period, and are finished with the ordinary late pinnacles. The high blank wall over the windows, which generally accompanies the pointed barrel vaults, has been in this case lightened by the intro-

FIG. 1169.
The Collegiate Church of Crichton.
Arms in West Wall.

duction of a false parapet (see Fig. 1166), with enrichments of square shaped flowers, both in the main cornice and in the upper cornice, which represents the cope of the parapet. But here there is no parapet wall, the eaves of the roof being placed where the parapet cope would be in ordinary circumstances. This is a plan often adopted in domestic buildings, from which the idea was, no doubt, borrowed in this instance. The transepts are without buttresses and have a bare appearance. Adjoining the south entrance doorway there are what appear to be the remains of a sedilia (Fig. 1168). The lower portion is entirely concealed, and the eastern shaft and recess are almost blocked. In the north wall opposite the original entrance there can be seen on the inside the indications of a round arched doorway, now built up, which probably led to the sacristy or a chapel, now destroyed, as already mentioned. Five feet east from this blocked doorway there are slight remains of a sixteenth or seventeenth century monument (see Plan), now cut away to permit of the erection of the gallery over, and it seems probable that from this monument was taken the coat of arms (Fig. 1169) now built into the wall which closes up the west archway of the tower. The shield bears the Nicolson arms, and are probably those of Agnes Nicolson, third wife of Patrick, first Lord Elibank, who possessed the ecclesiastical lands of the Collegiate Church of Crichton about the beginning of the seventeenth century. Mr. Billings shows another coat of arms on the outside of the turret stair, but this part of the building is now a dense mass of ivy. The turret stair is in the north wall of the nave, and is placed at some distance from the tower. Fig. 1170 shows the piscina in the south transept. Across this transept, where shown on the Plan, there is a wooden screen (Fig. 1171) of late erection, but not without some character, near its centre, and beneath the south arch of the tower there stands up, a few inches from the pavement, a broken worn stone about 12 inches square, the purpose of which is not obvious.

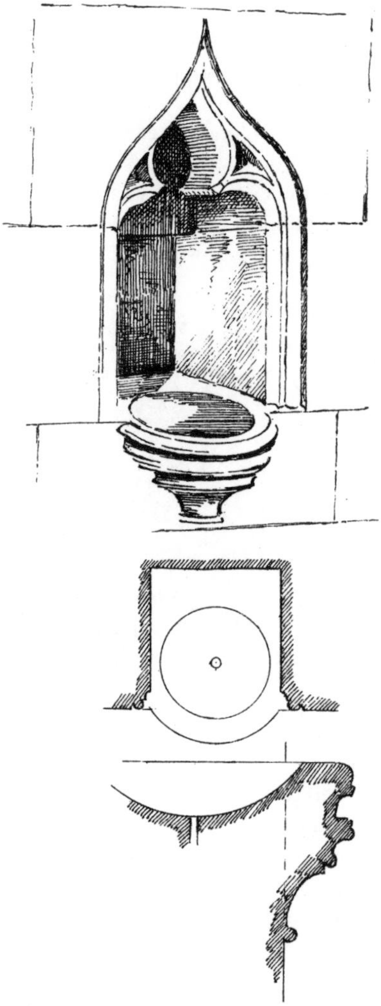

The church throughout is vaulted with a pointed barrel vault, but no provision has been made for the vaulting of the nave. Crichton Church was converted, in 1449, by Sir William Crichton, well known as Chancellor Crichton, into a collegiate establishment for a provost, nine prebendaries, and two singing boys, and was suitably endowed. The existing structure was probably erected at that time. Sir William also built an extensive addition to the Castle of Crichton, and doubtless the same builders were employed on church and castle, as many of the details closely resemble each other. From Mr. Gourlay's letter, already referred to, it appears that there was a provost's house about a mile distant. He mentions that it was then used as a farmhouse and called Rosehall, and that there was a place of worship beside it and a churchyard, but with the exception of the latter nothing now remains.

FIG. 1170.
The Collegiate Church of Crichton.
Piscina.

The tower is supported by pointed arches springing from responds in the four sides. The responds are of simple section, and the caps contain some good late foliaged carving (see Fig. 1171).

The walls are carried up with one low story above the set-off

FIG. 1171.—The Collegiate Church of Crichton.   Arch and Screen in South Transept.

immediately over the sloping water table of the roofs. This story contains, in each face, a two-light window with square lintel and central mullion. The story is surmounted by a plain parapet, supported by a corbel course, and the tower is finished with a gabled roof, having a simple belfry on the apex of the east gable.

THE COLLEGIATE CHURCH OF CORSTORPHINE, MID-LOTHIAN.

The village of Corstorphine is situated about three miles west of Edinburgh.

The church is intimately associated with the Forrester family. It was erected and endowed by them, and their tombs and monuments, emblazoned

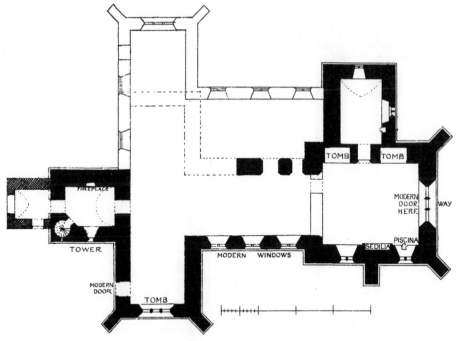

FIG. 1172.--The Collegiate Church of Corstorphine. Plan.

with heraldic emblems, are conspicuous on its walls. The manor was acquired by Adam Forrester, a burgess and provost of Edinburgh, in the year 1376, and the title of Lord Forrester of Corstorphine continued in the family till the year 1763.

There was a chapel at Corstorphine as early as the year 1128, which was granted to the new Abbey of Holyrood. This structure afterwards became the parish church, and continued to be so after the erection of the collegiate church, which still exists. Of this original chapel no trace now remains. It stood on the north side of the present building, on part of the ground now occupied by the existing north transept. This transept, which was built in the present century, is not the immediate successor of the old parish church, but takes the place of an aisle which was built in 1646, the erection of which caused the removal of what remained of the old parish church.

The existing church (Fig. 1172) consists of a chancel, a nave with north and south transepts situated at its west end, a western tower and spire, and a sacristy on the north side of the chancel. The whole building is small in size and of low proportions, the height of the tower and spire being only 50 feet, but although somewhat debased in style, it is very quaint and picturesque.

The structure suffered great alteration and damage from a restoration which took place about the beginning of this century. At that time the north transept, together with the seventeenth century aisle, above mentioned, and a part of the nave were taken down.* A new north transept was built, and a new additional nave was erected on the north side of the old nave. A doorway was knocked through the east wall of the chancel, which necessitated the shortening of the large east window above it by raising the sill. At the same time, the

FIG. 1173.
The Collegiate Church of
Corstorphine.
Stone Built into Wall of Field.

chancel was converted into a lumber chamber and porch, by the process of building up the chancel arch. As regards the sacristy, its floor has been dug out to a depth of about 7 feet, and it is now used as a heating chamber and coal cellar.

During this restoration a quantity of carved and moulded stones was removed from the church to Juniper Green, in the vicinity, where probably about fifty fragments, several containing the Forrester arms, were built into a wall on the road leading from the above village to Baberton House, but the wall has since been removed. Fig. 1173 is a sketch of one of these stones, bearing three hunting horns impaling a bend engrailed. At Hermiston House, also, several carved blocks

* Particulars regarding this church are to be found in *The Collegiate Churches of Mid-Lothian*, Bannatyne Club, edited by David Laing; and a paper by the same author in the *Proceedings of the Society of Antiquaries of Scotland*, Vol. XI. 1874-76, p. 353.

Fig. 1174.—The Collegiate Church of Corstorphine. View from South-East.

removed from Corstorphine Church have been preserved, some of which contain the Forrester arms.

The plan of the building (omitting the alterations above described) is remarkable. It seems to consist of two portions—(1) the transepts and division to the east of them, forming one church, and (2) the choir further

FIG. 1175.—The Collegiate Church of Corstorphine. Sedilia in the Chancel.

to the east, which seems to have formed an independent chapel. This view is supported by the history of the structure.

In the east wall of the chancel a stone is fixed, with an inscription in memory of the first provost of the college, the stone being "apparently transferred," says Mr. Laing, "from the place where the provost was buried." The inscription is in the following terms, viz. :—

Istud · collegiū · incepit · āno · dn̄i · M^{o},cccc^{o}xxix · et · eodē · āno magr̄ · nicholay^{q} · bānachtȳ · p^{r}posit^{q} · hic · subt^{q} · iacēs · qui · obiit · āno dn̄i · M^{o}cccc^{o}lxx . . . cui^{q} · āniu^{r}sare · simul · p̄risq · mr̄is celebrabitur · xiiii^{o} · die · mēsis · iunii · p · quo · ānuus · redditus · x s · in · villa · de · kyrk · cramuound · orate · pro · āib^{q} · eor$^{l.}$ [This collegiate church was begun in the year of our Lord 1429, and in the

FIG. 1176.—The Collegiate Church of Corstorphine. Piscina in Chancel.

same year Mr. Nicol Bannatyne was provost here, who, lying beneath, died in the year 1470. A commemoration of him and his successors in office will be celebrated on the 14th of June annually, for which an annual rent of £10 is set apart, out of the lands of Kirk Cramond—Pray for their souls.]

This inscription clearly fixes the date of the commencement of the collegiate church, but although it has been transferred to the chancel, there is nothing to show that the collegiate church it refers to is the chancel. It is quite as likely to have reference to the church to the west of the chancel, from which it was probably removed to its present position. Both from the arrangement of the Plan and the aspect of the eastern part of the building generally, it presents a distinct individuality. It is both

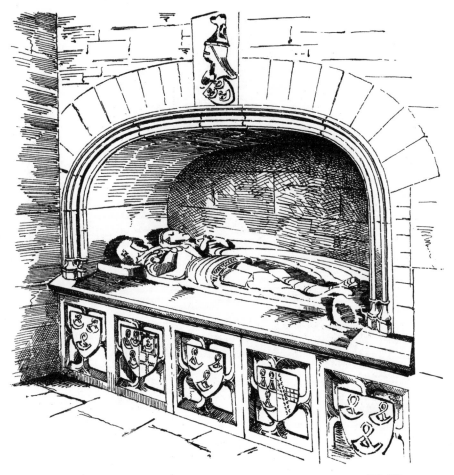

FIG. 1177.—The Collegiate Church of Corstorphine. Tomb of Sir John Forrester and his Wife.

higher and wider than the church to the west, and suggests the idea of having been built at a different time. Now it is matter of history that Adam Forrester, already mentioned, who died in 1405, built a chapel dedicated to St. John the Baptist adjoining the parish church, and it is not unlikely that this chancel was that chapel.

In 1425-6 a charter was granted by King James I. for the endowment of three chaplainries in the chapel contiguous to the Parish Church of Corstorphine,* and securing to it, amongst other things, the annual rents in Edinburgh bestowed by the late Sir Adam Forrester. That charter clearly shows that this chapel, wherever situated, was in existence before

FIG. 1178.—The Collegiate Church of Corstorphine.
Tomb of Sir John Forrester (younger) and his Wife.

the year mentioned in Provost Bannatyne's inscription. Further, in the Chamberlain Rolls of 1434,† reference is made to the three chaplains of the Chapel of St. John the Baptist—"contiguous to the Parish Church of Corstorphine," showing the independent existence of that chapel after the

* *The Collegiate Churches of Mid-Lothian*, p. lxvi.
† Chamberlain Rolls, Vol. III. p. 263.

date in the Bannatyne inscription.   It seems, therefore, most probable that this was the chapel erected by Sir Adam Forrester.

Sir Adam was succeeded by his son Sir John Forrester, who filled the office of Great Chamberlain of Scotland, and on the return of James I. from England was appointed Master of the Household in 1424.   The

FIG. 1179.—The Collegiate Church of Corstorphine.   Tomb in South Transept.

collegiate church was founded and endowed by Sir John.   Although the inscription to Bannatyne, the first provost, says that it was begun in 1429, the foundation was only completed by a Papal Bull in 1444, at which date Sir John was probably living.   The foundation consisted of a provost, four prebendaries, and two singing boys.

III.   R

From the above records, and also from the style of the architecture, there can scarcely be a doubt but that the church to the west was the collegiate church erected after 1444, and in designing it, the plan was so arranged as to incorporate the older Chapel of St. John the Baptist as the chancel of the new church. It is remarkable that, although the chancel

Fig. 1180.—The Collegiate Church of Corstorphine. Tomb in South Transept.

contains monuments to his successors, there is none to Sir Adam, the supposed founder of it. It may, however, be mentioned that Mr. Laing believes that an inscription on a stone, which has been built out of its proper place, in the small porch to the west of the tower, has been taken from a monument to Sir Adam.

Whether the above view of the history of the Church of Corstorphine is correct or not, the chancel or the Chapel of St. John the Baptist is the

Fig. 1181.—The Collegiate Church of Corstorphine. Window and Arms in South Transept.

most interesting part of the building. It measures internally 25 feet 6 inches in length by 21 feet in width, and is covered with a pointed barrel vault, having a roof of overlapping stone flags. It contains an

FIG. 1182.—The Collegiate Church of Corstorphine. View from South-West.

east window of three lights (Fig. 1174), having perpendicular tracery, the lower part of which has been altered, as above pointed out.

There are two small windows in the south side of the chancel, and between them, in the interior, is a fine sedilia, somewhat mutilated (Fig. 1175). Beside it is a piscina (Fig. 1176), with the basin, as usually happens, cut away. In the niche of the piscina there is a stone shelf used as a credence table, and over the niche a projecting round canopy. A very similar canopy exists over the upper small niche on the exterior of the east gable.

In the north wall of the chancel are two recessed tombs (Figs. 1177 and 1178). These monuments, judging from the disturbed appearance of the surrounding masonry and from the different character of the two designs, were apparently not original parts of the chapel, but were subsequently inserted as the occasion arose. The arch stones of the westmost tomb (see Fig. 1177), that of Sir John Forrester (the eldest son of Sir Adam) and his wife, are cut away or concealed by the west wall of the chapel, an arrangement not likely to have been adopted had the tomb been erected when the chapel was built. This monument is usually called the Founder's Tomb, from the circumstance that Sir John founded the collegiate church. He was twice married: first, to Jean Sinclair, daughter of Henry, first Earl of Orkney; and, second, to Dame Marion Stewart, Lady Dalswinton, widow of Sir John Stewart.* His effigy rests on the tomb, along with that of one of his wives. Sir John died after the year 1444.

The eastmost tomb (see Fig. 1178) is that of the son of the foregoing, also Sir John, who died before 1454. It contains his effigy and that of his wife. It does not appear to be known to what family the lady belonged; but from the heraldic blazons (to be afterwards described) she seems to have been a member of the Wigmer family.

There is another tomb situated in the south transept (Figs. 1179 and 1180). It is believed to be that of Sir Alexander Forrester, son of the last mentioned Sir John. The date of his death is not recorded, but he is known to have been alive in 1467. It contains his effigy only. There has been a finial on the tomb, which is now gone.

The amount of heraldic carving on the above tombs, on the gable of the south transept (Fig. 1181), and on the western porch (Fig. 1182) is considerable and is well preserved.†

The arms represented on the various shields throughout the whole series comprise, for the different members of the Forrester family above mentioned,

FORRESTER OF CORSTORPHINE, viz. :—

Argent, three hunting horns stringed sable.

These occur alone and conjoined with the arms of their wives, viz. :—

    I. Sinclair, Earl of Orkney.

        1st and 4th. Azure, a lymphad within a double tressure, flory counter flory, or (for Orkney).

        2nd and 3rd. Argent, a cross engrailed (for Sinclair).

* See Crawfurd's *Officers of State*, p. 311 ; and Crawfurd's *Peerage*, p. 148.

† We have to thank Mr. W. Rae Macdonald for assistance in connection with this heraldry.

II. Stewart of Dalswinton.

  Or, a fesse chequé azure and argent, surmounted of a bend engrailed gules.

III. Wigmer.

  Argent, on a bend sable a ribbon dancettée of the field.

IV. Forrester (differenced with Sinclair—probably an unauthorised coat).

  Argent, a cross engrailed and couped between three hunting horns sable.

The above arms are distributed as follow on the three tombs—

First Tomb, Sir John Forrester (see Fig. 1177).

1st shield. Forrester.

2nd shield. Forrester impaling Sinclair, Earl of Orkney. The dexter half only—viz., 1st and 3rd quarters of the complete 'arms—being given.

3rd shield. Forrester.

4th shield. Forrester impaling Stewart of Dalswinton.

5th shield. Forrester.

Second Tomb, Sir John Forrester, son of above—Eastmost (see Fig. 1178).

1st shield. Forrester.

2nd shield. Forrester impaling Wigmer.

3rd shield. Forrester.

Third Tomb, Sir Alexander Forrester (see Figs. 1179 and 1180).

1st shield. Sinclar of Orkney (1st and 3rd quarters only) impaling Forrester (the same arms as first tomb, 2nd shield, but reversed, in error).

2nd shield. Forrester.

3rd shield. Forrester differenced with Sinclair.

The shields on the gable of the south transept (see Figs. 1174 and 1181) are as follow—

1st. Central shield, Forrester.

2nd and 3rd. (Two shields, one on each side of the large window.) Forrester impaling Wigmer.

These shields are all reversed, so that the shield is couché the wrong way and the crest looks the wrong way. The impaled shields have Forrester on the sinister instead of the dexter, and the Wigmer arms make the bend and ribbon sinister instead of dexter.

South Transept.

The shields, both on the gable outside and on the tomb inside, seem to have been carelessly executed from an impression of the arms, thus placing everything in the reverse way ; so that what in the original is on the dexter side of the shield is here on the sinister, a bend is converted into a bend sinister, and so throughout.

The two shields on the porch are—1st, Forrester ; 2nd, Forrester impaling Wigmer.

The sacristy, on the north side of the chancel, enters by a plain lintelled door between the two tombs (see Fig. 1172). It has a rough pointed barrel vault, and looks, from there being windows at two levels, as if it had contained two stories. The sill of the east window projects about 11 inches ; and Mr. Muir considers it, without doubt, to have been an altar.* Adjoining this window is a piscina, with the orifice of its drain wrought on the base mouldings outside.

As regards the architecture of the church, it accords well with the other collegiate structures of the latter half of the fifteenth century. The perpendicular tracery in the east window of the chancel and the south window of the transept (see Figs. 1173 and 1181) is remarkable, such tracery being very uncommon in Scotland. These two large windows are recessed in the wall, the outer jambs having two or three broad splays. The side windows have the tracery flush with the outer face of the wall.

The buttresses have the usual numerous set-offs. They have now finials, consisting of cubic stones carved as sundials ; but, as Mr. T. S. Muir states, these are modern additions, the buttresses having doubtless been originally pinnacled above the eaves.

The tower to the west of the transept (Fig. 1182) is one of the most characteristic features of the structure. It measures externally about 18 feet 6 inches from north to south by 17 feet 3 inches from east to west. The tower has a door to the church, and also a west doorway. It thus formed an entrance porch to the building ; but another porch has been added to the west, which is vaulted and covered with a stone roof.

The tower is built with ashlar, and rises, without buttresses, to the eaves. A two-light window is introduced on each face under the cornice. Above the tower there is a stone spire of the stunted description usual at the period. Four pinnacles give some relief to the angles at the base of the spire. The latter is divided by battlemented string courses into three stories, and has lucarnes in the middle story.

After the Reformation the collegiate church became the church of the parish in 1593, and has so continued ever since.

THE COLLEGIATE CHURCH OF CRAIL, FIFESHIRE.

The quaint old seaport of Crail lies near the eastern point of the north side of the Frith of Forth. It is one of the earliest places in Scotland which are known to have carried on commerce with the

* *Ancient Parochial and Collegiate Churches of Scotland*, p. 53.

Continent, having had intercourse with the Netherlands in the ninth century, where its salt fish were sold, and the name of Crail occurs on a map of the twelfth century.

There was in ancient times a royal castle at Crail, in which David I. resided, and a number of names still exist in the locality, showing its connection with royalty. The earliest charter of the burgh was granted by Bruce in 1310, and confirmed by subsequent kings. It is believed that at one time Crail was the site of a priory dedicated to St. Rufus, the tradition of which is preserved in several local names, such as, the prior's croft, the prior's walls, the nun's peat field, and the house of the prioress, which in 1640 was in the hands of a neighbouring proprietor.

The Church of Crail belonged from an early date to the Cistercian Nuns of Haddington. In 1177 the stipend is mentioned. This church was made collegiate and well endowed by Sir William Myreton, vicar of Lathrick in 1509. He also established the altar of St. Michael the Archangel in 1512, and in 1514 he founded an altar to the praise and honour of God, the Virgin Mary, and all saints, which he placed in the presentation and donation of the bailies and community. Sir William Myreton also showed himself a benefactor of the town by founding schools there in 1525, one being for the teaching of grammar and the other of music. In 1515, besides the above chaplainries, there existed in the church chaplainries of St. James the apostle, St. Bartholomew, and St. Nicholas. An inventory has been preserved, from which it appears that the various altars were well furnished with plate and vestments. On account of the foundation of the new College in the parish church, a charter was issued by Andrew, Archbishop of St. Andrews, confirming letters by the Prioress of Haddington, by Sir William Myreton, by the bailies and community of Crail, and by the parishioners of the parish church, for the foundation of a provostry with ten prebendaries, to be in the gift of the Prioress. In 1520 another prebend was added, viz., that of St. John the Baptist. The priory of Haddington having been erected in 1621 into a temporal lordship in favour of John, Master of Lauderdale, the kirk lands of Crail fell to him.

But in 1587 James VI. had granted a charter to the town of everything belonging to the chaplainries, altarages, and prebends, or to the kirk or college, except what pertained to the Abbey of Haddington. This charter was granted on account of the prebendaries and others following the usual course as the Reformation approached, and alienating the lands of their benefices for their own private advantage. The old College Church thus passed into the hands of the burgh, and was confirmed to it in 1633 by Act of Parliament, and is still used as the parish church.*

Although the fabric has been subjected to a considerable amount of modern improvement, many of the original features still remain. The

* See *The East Neuk of Fife*, p. 405, and *sequ.*

main body of the church (Fig. 1183) consists, as it has always done, of an oblong main structure, divided by two rows of columns into a central nave, and two side aisles. The nave is 63 feet long, the central division being 27 feet 6 inches wide, and the side aisles 11 feet wide. The central columns carry pointed arches (Fig. 1184), and in the wall above them was originally a small window over each column (not over the arches as usual) with widely splayed jambs and trefoil head. The roof of the aisles, being below the sill of these clerestory windows, was necessarily low. This was found in recent times to be a disadvantage, and the walls of the aisles have been rebuilt and heightened, so as to allow the roof of the central nave to run down over them without a break (Fig. 1185). The old clerestory windows are thus roofed in, and are only visible in the inside

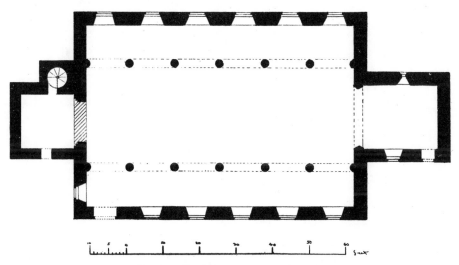

FIG. 1183.—The Collegiate Church of Crail. Plan.

of the nave. The windows of the aisles are all modern. The piers are round and bear simple caps (see Fig. 1184), and these and the clerestory windows are plainly of a very late date, although the cap mouldings (see Fig. 1184) have been copied from old forms.

To the east of the nave was the choir, now converted into a vestry 20 feet 6 inches long by 17 feet wide. The chancel arch springs from two responds, the shafts of which have an ancient appearance, but they have probably been reconstructed in imitation of ancient work. One of the small original windows is preserved in the north wall of the chancel. It is about 18 inches in width, and has a plain pointed arch with chamfer on edge.

There has been an arch at the west end of the church with similar shafts to those of the chancel arch. This arch opened into the tower which rises against the centre of the west wall of the church, and is divided into several floors, and provided with a newell stair leading to them.

The tower (see Fig. 1185) is a picturesque object, though perfectly plain. It rises with square angles, without buttresses or other breaks from the base to the parapet. Its short spire, together with the projection containing the turret stair, form a pleasing group. The whole presents a characteristic specimen of our simple Scottish church steeples.

Fig. 1184.—The Collegiate Church of Crail. Main Arcade and Clerestory Windows.

Although it has been thought that some of the features (above referred to) belong to the first pointed period, it is much more likely that the whole structure, except the recent work, dates from the beginning of the sixteenth century, when the collegiate establishment was instituted, and when the old parish church appears to have been reconstructed. Several similar towers of late date in the locality will be illustrated.

The church has apparently been renovated, internally, after the Reformation, when a good deal of carved oak work has been introduced. This oak work (Fig. 1186) is now employed as a lining of the walls along the south and east sides of the church, and is obscured by a number of pews which abut against it. It is excellent work of the period, and it is

Fig. 1185.—The Collegiate Church of Crail. View from North-West.

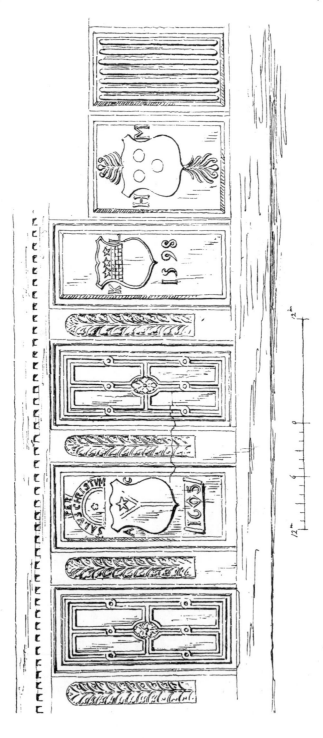

Fig. 1186.—The Collegiate Church of Crail. Carved Woodwork.

unfortunate that it should be so completely lost to sight. One of the panels contains a shield with a coat of arms, apparently that of Cunningham of Barns, with the initials A. C. and the date 1605. When the church was handed over to the town the rights of Cunningham of Barns were reserved. He had thus some interest in the church or lands. This carved work seems to have been the gift of Alexander Cunningham, who at the above date was Laird of Barns. The arms of his wife, Helen, daughter of Thomas Myrton of Cambo, are seen, with her initials, on the smaller panel to the right. Another shield bears the coat and initials of Katherine Lindsay, wife of Thomas Myrton of Cambo, with the date 1598. Other shields (not shown in the illustration) bear the arms of Learmonth of Balcomie (1594).

ST. MARY'S, WHITEKIRK, Haddingtonshire.

This charming old building is one of the few rural parish churches of mediæval times still used for divine service. The church seems to have had its origin in a neighbouring holy well. The following extract from documents in the Vatican gives some account of its origin and history:—*

"The great number of miracles performed at this well were so numerous that in 1309 John Abernethy, with the assistance of the monks of Melrose, procured a shrine to be erected, and dedicated it to the Holy Mother. In 1413 there were no less than 15,653 pilgrims of all nations, and the offerings were equal to 1422 merks. In 1430, James I., King of Scotland, being a good man who loved the Church, built the Abbey of the Holy Cross at Edinburgh, and took the Chapel of Fairknowe into his protection, added much to it by the building of houses for the reception of pilgrims, called it Whitechapel, where he often went and made it a dependant on his own abbey of the Holy Cross. In 1439, Adam Hepburn of Hailes built a choir all arched with stone, agreeable to the mode of Peter de Main, and so it continued in great prosperity as a place of sanctity until the year 1540, that the cup of vengeance was full, and heresy covered the North."

Whitekirk was a dependency of Holyrood, as mentioned in the above extract. It was a great place of pilgrimage, and was visited, amongst others, by Pope Pius II. (Æneas Sylvius), who came to render thanks to the Virgin for his safe landing in Scotland.

In the seventeenth century the east end was used as a church and the west end as a school. In 1760 the Parish of Tynningham was added to Whitekirk, and some of the fittings of the former were brought to the latter. Thus the Haddington gallery in the north transept was adorned with the front of the gallery from Tynningham. During this century some attempts have been made to improve the structure. In

* From *The Churches of St. Baldred*, by C. L. Ritchie, p. 31.

1832 a "pseudo south transept" was built, and the Seacliffe gallery (which resembles a large Dutch cabinet) was introduced.

This church, like many others erected in the fifteenth century, is on

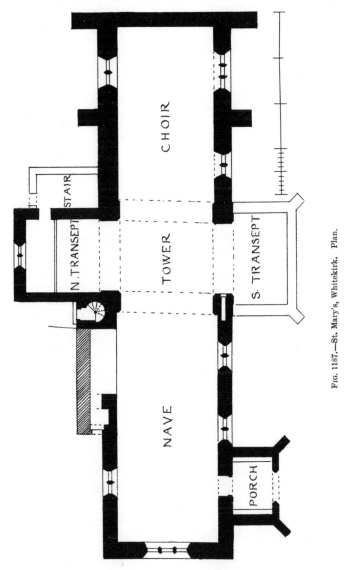

FIG. 1187.—St. Mary's, Whitekirk. Plan.

the plan of a cross without aisles (Fig. 1187). The choir is vaulted with a pointed barrel vault, and the outer roof is slated. Over the crossing (Fig. 1188) rises a square tower, finished with a plain parapet. The east

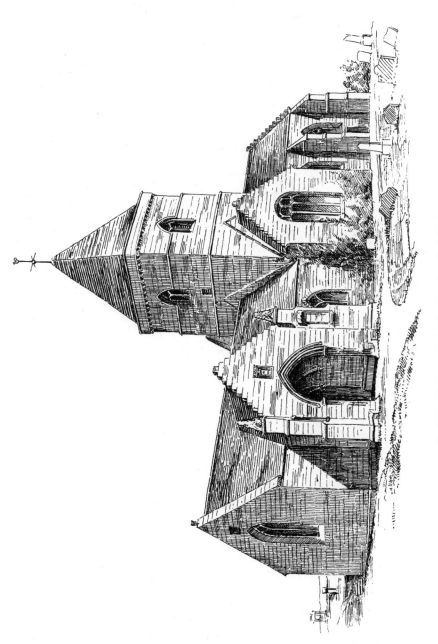

Fig. 1188.—St. Mary's, Whitekirk.   View from South-West.

end is square, and there is a fine entrance porch at the south-west angle. The church is built with red freestone, which is toned with age, and the whole building is one of the most picturesque and pleasing of our old parish churches.

The nave and choir measure internally 103 feet in length by about 22 feet in width. The choir is divided by bold buttresses into two bays,

in each of which is a traceried window, the cusping of which is peculiar. The forms of the buttresses and tracery are shown in Fig. 1189. The east end has a small circular quatrefoiled window set high in the wall (Fig. 1190), over which is a panel containing a shield bearing a fessé with a

FIG. 1189.—St. Mary's, Whitekirk. Buttress and Window in Choir.

crozier behind it, probably the arms of Abbot Crawford of Holyrood (1460-1483).

The west end (Fig. 1191) and the south transept have been rebuilt.

The south-west porch (Fig. 1192) is one of the most striking features of the structure. It measures 13 feet wide by 9 feet deep internally, and has a stone bench on each side. The entrance is by an open archway, with clustered shafts, having enriched caps from which spring the bold mouldings of the arch. At each of the outer angles of the porch is a diagonal buttress having a niche on the inner face, and finished on the top with crocketed pinnacles. Over the doorway there is a panel with small buttresses at the jambs, and canopied head with scroll ornament over.

FIG. 1190.—St. Mary's, Whitekirk. East Gable.

The interior of the porch is roofed with pointed barrel vaulting, having ribs springing from carved corbels. The door to the church is square headed and is surmounted by a niche, which formerly contained a statue of the Blessed Virgin.

The interior of the church (Fig. 1193) is very plain. The tower is supported on arches at the crossing, which spring from attached piers with moulded caps. The space over the crossing is vaulted with groins, having a circular boss in the centre. The tower (see Fig. 1188) is carried up with plain walls to two stories above the roof, and has in the upper

FIG. 1191.—St. Mary's, Whitekirk. View from North-West.

part or belfry a window on each side, with central mullion, now much decayed by the weather. A stair turret (Fig. 1194) is attached to the north-west angle of the tower, and enters from the exterior. The north wall of the nave has been altered at the point adjoining the tower.

At a distance of about 100 yards north from the church stands a plain

III.   S

FIG. 1192.—St. Mary's, Whitekirk. South-West Porch.

building (Fig. 1195), which is believed to have been the tithe barn of the parish. It is situated on the edge of a rocky ridge which slopes steeply

FIG. 1193.—St. Mary's, Whitekirk. Interior, looking East.

downwards on the north side. In the view (Fig. 1196) taken from the low ground on the north side the top of the church spire is seen. The barn measures about 65 feet 4 inches in length from east to west, by about 20 feet in breadth over the walls. It has been built at two periods. The western portion, measuring on the outside about 21 feet 3 inches by 20

FIG. 1194.—St. Mary's, Whitekirk. The Tower, from North-West.

feet, has originally been a pele tower, with walls about 5 feet in thickness, and was altered at a later period, when it was extended into a barn. The present entrance to the keep is in the south wall, which appears to have been rebuilt of the same reduced thickness (2 feet 4 inches) as the barn walls. This doorway leads into a vaulted ground floor, from which a door

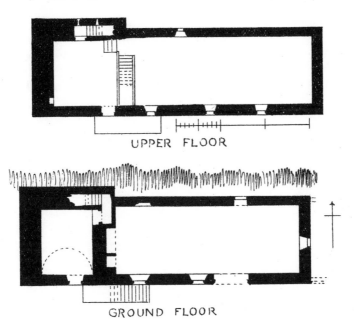

UPPER FLOOR

GROUND FLOOR

Fɪɢ. 1195.—St. Mary's, Whitekirk. Plans of Tithe Barn.

to a small lobby gives access to a narrow straight stair leading to the first floor, contained in the thickness of the north wall. The stair is lighted

Fɪɢ. 1196.—St. Mary's, Whitekirk. Tithe Barn, from North-East.

with narrow slits, and the door at the top leading into what was originally the hall is finished in the way usual in such structures, with well wrought splays round the stone jambs and lintel. On the first floor the east wall of the pele tower has been taken down. The junction of the tower with the barn is plainly visible from the rough face of the masonry in the interior of the north wall, where the east wall of the tower has been cut away. The upper part of the tower being thus thrown into the barn, a few steps, as shown on the Plan, lead up to the latter. There is an upper floor in

FIG. 1197. —St. Mary's, Whitekirk. Tithe Barn, from North-West.

the roof of the barn supported on the ties of the roof and reached by a wooden stair. The windows of this floor are shown in the gables. When the barn was built the upper part of the north wall of the keep (Fig. 1197) was lowered sufficiently to allow of the eaves of the roof of the new and narrower building being continued straight along over the wider building of the tower. The barn proper is entered from the south side by a doorway 7 feet 7 inches wide, and is lighted by two windows in the south side and one in the gable. There is also a narrow doorway on the north side, which can only have been for occasional use, the ground being steep on that side, with only a narrow footing along the wall, which is kept back from the line of the tower in order to obtain this footing. At the west

end of the barn and in the old wall of the keep there is a fireplace 8 feet 6 inches wide, with a stone division. The fireplace, which is 5 feet high, has an oaken lintel with a well wrought relieving arch over it. This fireplace must have been used before the wall above was taken down, and indicates that the tower had probably been first enlarged as a residence and the whole afterwards converted into a barn. In the north wall near the fireplace there is a flat recess with a pointed arch 13 inches deep, the sill being about 3 feet above the floor. There are indications (see Plan) that the barn walls once extended further eastwards.

Near the west corner of the south wall is a panel (Fig. 1198) with an effaced coat of arms.

FIG. 1198.—St. Mary's, Whitekirk.
Panel in South Wall of Tithe Barn.

MID-CALDER CHURCH, MID-LOTHIAN.

The town of Mid-Calder is situated in the western part of the County of Mid-Lothian.

The church was begun in the sixteenth century by Master Peter Sandilands, Rector of Mid-Calder, a younger son of the sixth Knight of Calder. Having raised the walls of the vestry or revestry and laid the foundations of the choir, and being then an old man, he provided the money for the entire completion of the church, including the nave, tower, &c., and paid a sum over to Sir James Sandilands of Calder (his nephew) and his son John, who bound themselves to complete the structure according to a bond engrossed in the public records. This bond is to the following effect :—*

After the usual preliminaries and having acknowledged the receipt of the sum of "xvj hundrethe merkis gude and vsuale money of the realme," they undertake "to big and compleit the revestrie of the paroche kirk of Caldor with

* See *Proceedings of the Society of Antiquaries of Scotland*, Session 1857 and 1860, p. 160, where the " bond " will be found transcribed, with other information regarding the church.

ane walter tabill at the heich that it is now vnder the thak inlikwise with ane
wthir walter tabill abone the thak on the est gauill of the queir weill pendit in
half round to the said queir vnder the said tabill inlikeuise weill thekit with
thak stane And sall rais abone the said tabill in the est gauill of the queir and
abone the turneqres and the tabill thairof tua lichtis als fair as thai may be had
efferand to the heicht of the queir And abone the walter tabill abone the thak
of the revestre and thre penis thairof to ryse cunteranis of buttreis vpoune
the said eist gauill thre penis thairof And the remanent of the said queir to be
endit of the lenthe and widenes as it is foundit and in heicht fra the sollis of the
said queir duris to the vuer pairt of the walter tabill vnder the thak thairof
xxxij futtis And the south thre lychtis in the sydevall of the said queir betuix
the foure buttreis to ryse as thai are foundit als heich as thai may be had in the
pend of the said queir efferand to the heich foirsaid And the saidis buttereis
tobe compleit endit as thai ar now foundit And the north turneqres in the
west pairt of the north sydevall thairof tobe tane avay And the said north
vall to ryse xvj futtis of heicht as it is foundit rouch werk with corbell and
walter tabill on the vther pairt thairof for ane closter and fra thine vp effeirand
to the heicht of the said queir aislar werk And the said queir tobe compleitlie
pendit with croce brace and rinruif conforme to Sanct Anthonis Yle in Sanct
Gelis Kirk And at the west end of the said queir forgane the south west
buttreis to rais ane substantious wall of rouch werk sevin fut of breid fra ilk
sydewall with ane brace to be raisit tharein als heych as it may be had to serue
the west gavil of the queir with hewin oggeruris And abone the said brace in
the forsaid west gavill sulyeis tobe laid and ane stepil tobe raisit tharepoun viij
futis of breid and lenth or vj futis braid and xij futis lenth within the sidwallis
of the said stepill quhilk sidwallis salbe of vj futis of heich abone the queir thak
at all partys with lychtis at all partis for the sound of the bellis in the said stepill
to be persit for the orlage hand and bell in place maist gagand and convenient
tharto And in the northe angell betuix the foresaid wall vnder the grete brace
and northe wall of the kirk syd to rais ane commodious turngreis to serue the rud
loft of the said kirk and stepill foresaid als esaly as it may be had Item to big
ane kirk on the west pair(t) of the said queir nixt the said brace contenand in
lenthe iiijxx of futis and xxviij futis braid within the wallis respectiue of
rouche werk And the wallis thairof to be foure futis thik and xxvj futis heych
fra the sole of the durris to the vuir part of the watter tabill of syd wallis with
foure buttreis one ilk syd of the said kirk eslar werk efferand to the queir and
four lycht to be biggit in the southsyd wall of the said kirk of x futis of wydnes
and als heych as thai may be had squair lintalit efferand to the said heicht And
in the southe wall of the said kirk betuix the twa buttreis to be biggit ane
honest dur with ane plain proche with sege stabill on ilk syd thikyt with thak
stane and ane honest dur in the west gavill of the said kirk with ane lycht abone
the samen in myd gavill xij futis of breid rysand of heich in poyntcast als heich
as it may be had efferand to the heycht of the gavill with sufficient mygallis in
all the lychtis of the said kirk and queir with plane substantious cornettis of
stane or irne quhilk salbe thocht maist gainand in the lychtis raisit of poyntcast
And to put in ilk lycht of the wyndois grete lokartis of irne for binding of glas
thareto And inlikuiss to put grete crukis in the said kirk durrys as efferis
And the said haill kirk to be pendyt and weill thekyt with thak stane and the
watter tabill of the sidwallis of the said kirk and queir to be larg of sulye betuix
buttreis and buttereis and in ane caisment hevin for leid to be lad thairin to

schout the watter by the wyndowis of the said kirk and queir to the angellis next the buttreis And ilk buttere of the foirsaid kirk and queir to haif ane honeste fiall And the alter of the queir tobe biggit of aislar werk and the haill queir tobe weill pathit with greis befoir the said alter and vther wayis as efferis with tua halie wattir fattis weill hewin to the said kirk and queir And the foirsaidis kirk and queir to be biggit and completit in maner foirsaid That is to say the said queir within the space of thre yeris nixt efter the dait herof And the said kirk within the space of vthair thre yeris nixt and immediatlie thairefter." Following on this, John Sandilands, already mentioned, binds himself to give a "Charter and infeftment," securing to the chaplain the sum "of xx merkis money" annually.

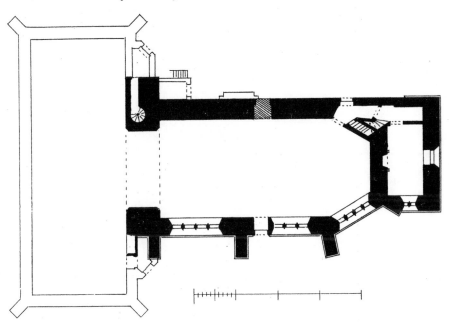

Fɪɢ. 1199.—Mid-Calder Church. Plan.

The actual building (Fig. 1199) consists of a choir with tripartite apse having a sacristy or vestry to the east, and it has been carried out, so far as completed, very much in terms of the foregoing bond.

The vestry, which projects from the east end of the choir, seems to have been erected before the bond was executed, and the foundations of the choir seem to have been laid at that time. The remainder of the choir was apparently carried out afterwards, but the nave, which was carefully specified in the bond, was never erected.

The vestry contains two stories, the lower one being a burial vault, which is "pendit" or vaulted, while the upper floor forms the vestry. The

Fig. 1200.—Mid-Calder Church. View from South-East.

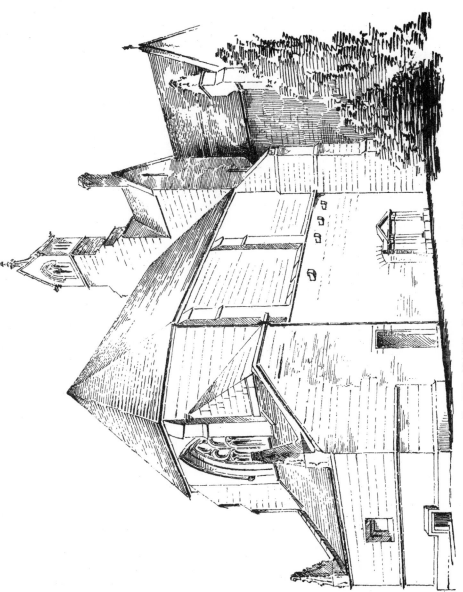

Fig. 1201.—Mid-Calder Church. View from North-East.

small stair leading to both floors is placed in the north-east angle of the apse. The east wall of the choir (Fig. 1200) is raised above the roof of the vestry, and is provided with a traceried window to the east; but there is no window in the north-east side of the apse, which is occupied by the wheel stair (Fig. 1201). The buttresses are erected as required by the

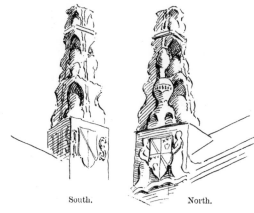

South.   North.

FIG. 1202.—Mid-Calder Church.
Pinnacles on Sacristy.

bond, and the three south windows are introduced between them. The north wall is carried up with rough masonry, and without any windows or openings, and has the water table and corbels prescribed as suitable for the roof of a cloister walk along that side (see Fig. 1201). The choir roof has been intended to be vaulted and the lower courses of the springing are built, but the vault was never completed. The springings show that the vault was intended to be groined. It is specified to have a "cross brace and rinruif," like a chapel in St. Giles' Church, but the meaning of these terms is not definite.

At the west end of the choir a very thick wall is built on each side, with a pointed arch between (described as a brace) to support the belfry,

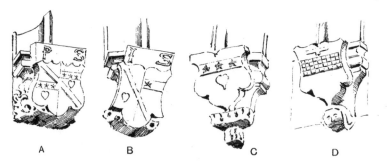

A   B   C   D

FIG. 1203.—Mid-Calder Church.   Terminations of Labels.

which is minutely specified. The latter, however, was not executed till recently. The lower part, however, above the roof was built, and the modern belfry has been carried up upon it. In the north pier is a "turngreis" or wheel stair described as leading to the rood loft, but in reality it now leads to the family gallery and to the lower part of the belfry (see Fig. 1201). A proposed nave is also minutely described. It was to be 80 feet in length and 28 feet in width, to have four buttresses on each side of ashlar work, and four windows in the south wall, 10 feet wide, and square lintels. Also an "honest dur," and a porch on the south side with stone seats and stone roof, and another "honest dur" in the west gable, with a large window over it. The windows were to be glazed and the roof provided with gargoyles.

The altar was to be built with ashlar, and the floor paved and steps placed before the altar.

The above instructions have, so far as the structure is executed, been carefully complied with, and the edifice presents a favourable example of the work of the early part of the sixteenth century. Ornament has not been spared, and is specially exhibited in the heraldic carving on the shields, with which the weather mouldings terminate. These shields gener-

FIG. 1204.
Mid-Calder Church.
Arms on Corbels
supporting Rood Loft.

ally contain the arms of the Sandilands family and their connections the Douglases, of which several examples are given below.

FIG. 1205.—Mid-Calder Church. Woodcarving.

The following is a short notice of the arms on the different parts of the building. On the angles of the projecting sacristy (the lower story of which contained the family burial vault) there are two pinnacles, with

very late crocketing, and finials (Fig. 1202). The south pinnacle contains
the Sandilands arms and the initials of J. Sandilands, and other lettering,

FIG. 1206.—Mid-Calder Church. Middle Bay in Choir.

much decayed. The north pinnacle exhibits the Sandilands arms quartered
with Douglas, and having two angels as supporters, the arms surmounted
by a helmet, with a lion's head for crest.

The arms on the label terminations are as follow :—

On the central apse window, north side, Douglas ; south side, Sandilands (a bend).

1st window west from central one.

Dexter side—Lion or Griffin rampant.

Sinister side—Cockburn—The family being allied to the Cockburns of Ormiston.

2nd window to west.

Dexter side—Lindsay (fesse chequé) (Fig. 1203, **D**).

Sinister side—Sandilands quartered with Douglas, and initials P. S. (Fig. 1203, **A**).

3rd window to west.

Dexter side—Douglas (Fig. 1203, **C**).

Sinister side—Sandilands and Douglas, with initials J. S. (Fig. 1203, **B**).

In the interior of the church the same arms occur on corbels as in the one supporting the rood loft, now the family gallery (Fig. 1204).

There is also a remarkable carved panel in oak (Fig. 1205), which combines the above arms *reversed*, with the initials J. S. and J. L., and the date 1595, together with certain Scripture texts.

The Douglas descent is throughout prominently displayed, and the heart and stars sometimes occupy the chief part of the shield. One coat, from centre window (see Fig. 1203, **D**), exhibits the bearings of a fess chequé of four tracts, with a St. George's cross in chief, being the arms of the distinguished predecessor of Sir James Sandilands, Lord of Torphichen, and St. John, viz., Sir Walter Lindsay, head of the Knights of St. John of Jerusalem in Scotland, the cross having reference to the badge of the order.

The tracery in the large windows is well preserved, and is of a kind usual in late work in Scotland, having curved bars without cusping (Figs. 1200 and 1206). The round-headed doorway to the choir is introduced in the central bay under the window, the lower part of which is stepped up to allow of its introduction.

KING'S COLLEGE CHAPEL, Aberdeen.

The west end of this fine chapel, with its extremely picturesque tower (Fig. 1207), fronts the main street of Old Aberdeen, and forms the north-west corner of the college quadrangle.

The chapel (Fig. 1208) is a long narrow building, with a three-sided apsidal east end, measuring inside the walls about 122 feet 6 inches in length by about 28 feet in width. It is divided into six bays by projecting buttresses, and has a large window filled with mullions and tracery in each bay on the north side, except the second one from the

FIG. 1207.—King's College Chapel. West End and Tower.

west, which contains a doorway. Similar large windows are continued round the apse (but the centre one is built up), and there is also one in the east bay of the south side. Over the west doorway there is a large west window (see Fig. 1207) of four lights, with solid built mullions and loop tracery enclosed within a round arch. All the other large windows just referred to have pointed arches (except the second from the east end on the north side), the tracery in those of the apse and in each adjoining window being modern. The other four north windows have, like the large west window, a solid built central mullion going right up to the apex of the arch, and having each half filled with the usual loop tracery. This mode of division of the tracery of a window by a large central built mullion into two distinct portions, each filled with its own tracery, is not uncommon in Scotland, as, for instance, at Seton College, where, however, the mullion divides into two arches and forms two pointed divisions in the arch-head. Besides the north doorway

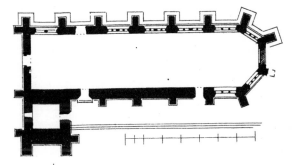

Fig. 1208.—King's College Chapel. Plan.

already mentioned, there are two to the quadrangle and one in the west end, all having elliptic arched tops. The mouldings of the west doorway have bases, but no caps. The south side of the chapel (Fig. 1209) forms a complete contrast to the north side. Instead of large windows occupying each bay, small clerestory windows, with flat arch-heads, occur at intervals along the top of the wall, while the lower part of the wall is left plain, being doubtless intended as a provision for a covered cloister walk. This, how-ever, was never carried out, but instead of it Bishop Stewart (1532-1545) erected a building against this side of the chapel, consisting of two floors, and containing a library, a jewel house, vestry, and class-rooms. These were taken down and re-erected on the same site about 1725, and about fifty years afterwards were destroyed by fire, when the south side of the chapel assumed its present appearance, being "cased and buttressed with granite as we now see it."* Dr. Macpherson further tells us that the coats

* *Archæologia Scotica*, Vol. v. Part iii. p. 436, by Norman Macpherson, LL.D.

of arms which now adorn this side of the chapel had been nearly all on the walls of the library, and, having escaped the fire, were, along with some others, inserted in the new granite work. These arms, along with many other coats throughout the building and the college, have been minutely described.* We need only mention here the arms of the founder of the college, Bishop William Elphinston, which occur at the west end of the south side of the chapel, viz., a chevron between three boars' heads

FIG. 1209.—King's College Chapel. South Side.

erased, surmounted by a mitre between the initials W. E. and "at sides O. B. A. D. MDXIV. Æ.S. LX (XX) IV." The royal arms occur on the north-most buttress of the west front of the tower, dated 1504, while those of Margaret Tudor, wife of James IV., appear on another shield in the west

* *Proceedings of the Society of Antiquaries of Scotland*, New Series, Vol. XI., by P. J. Anderson, M.A., LL.B.

front. Adjoining the west doorway an inscription informs us that the chapel was begun by James IV. in 1500. It apparently occupied about

Fig. 1210.—King's College Chapel. Rood Screen.

six years in building, as the contract for covering it with lead is dated 1506.

Fig. 1211.—King's College Chapel. Tower, from South-East.

FIG. 1212.—King's College Chapel. Upper Part of Tower.

The interior is divided by a wooden screen of very rich carved work, the central portion of which (Fig. 1210) is about 9 feet 7 inches wide, with

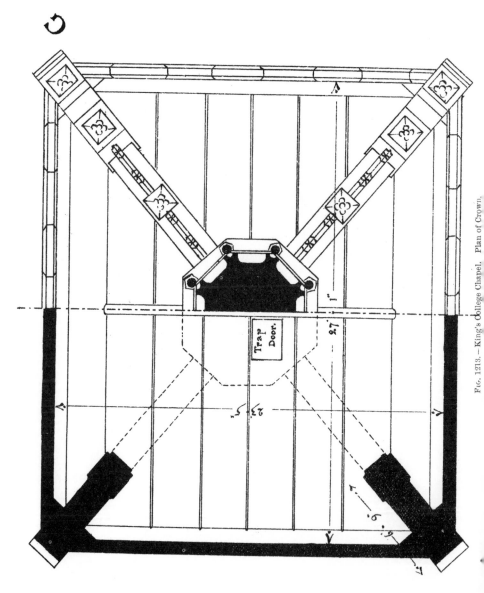

Trap Door.

FIG. 1213. — King's College Chapel. Plan of Crown.

double folding doors about 5 feet 9 inches wide by 7 feet 3 inches high. The side portions of the screen within the choir form a continuation of the canopied stalls occupying each side of the choir. Owing to the circumstance of the nave having been fitted up as a library, the ancient arrangement of the screen with its rood loft, ambone, and altars on the nave side were destroyed. Dr. Macpherson, in the paper already referred to, has by illustrations and description traced its original construction, and to this the reader is referred.

The tower at the south-west corner (Fig. 1211) is not quite square, measuring over the walls about 29 feet from north to south, and about 4 feet less from east to west. It has massive corner buttresses, with numerous stepped intakes towards the top, similar to the buttresses of the chapel, being a style of buttress of very frequent occurrence in Scottish late churches, as, for example, at Stirling Church. The tower is finished with one of the few crown steeples remaining in Scotland, being, with that of St. Giles', Edinburgh, and the Tolbooth, Glasgow, the only three surviving of those which we could at one time boast. The general style of the structure is very similar to that of St. Giles', but in this case there are only four arches thrown from the angles of the tower to the central lantern (Fig. 1213), while in the case of St. Giles' there are eight, which produce a fuller and richer effect. The tower (see Fig. 1211) is about 63 feet in height to the top of the battlements. From that point to the base of the lantern pillars (Fig. 1212) is about 15 feet 9 inches, from whence to the top of the cross is about 20 feet. The total height is thus about 99 feet.*

The upper part of the steeple was blown down in a violent storm on 7th February 1633. Spalding, under that date,† says :—" This hideous winds was marked to be such, as the like had never been seen here in these parts, for it would overturn countrymen's houses to the ground, and some persons suddenly smo'red within, without relief. It also threw down the stately crown bigged of curious eslar work, off the steeple of King's College of Old Aberdeen, whilk was thereafter re-edified and built up, little inferior to the first." The part blown down was probably only the lantern on the top of the four arches, the details of this part having a decidedly Renaissance character, and being different from the other parts of the tower. Doubtless the arches themselves would suffer in the crash, and would require repairing and rebuilding in part, which was evidently done, as the date 1634 is carved on the soffit of the crossing. This difference of detail is interesting, as showing how persistently these old designers wrought in the style of their time. Although it is evident that the present lantern is not quite the same as the original one, it must be admitted to be an extremely happy and picturesque composition.

* We are indebted for these dimensions and for Figs. 1208, 1212, and 1213 to Mr. J. C. Watt, architect, Aberdeen.

† The History of the Troubles and Memorable Transactions in Scotland, by John Spalding.

In connection with the rebuilding Spalding mentions two names. First, under the year 1640 he says :—" Dr. Gordon, medicinar, and one of the founded members of the College of Old Aberdeen, and common procurator thereof, departed this life upon the 10th of March, in his own house in Old Aberdeen ; a godly, grave, and learned man ; singular in publick works about the college, and putting up on the steeple thereof the stately and glorious crown, which you see thereon, which was thrown down by the wind." Second, under the year 1642 he says :—" Saturday the 10th September, George Thomson, Master Mason, new come frae Strathboggie to Aberdeen, suddenly fell over Thomas Thomson's stair, and with the fall became speechless and senseless, and departed this life upon the Thursday thereafter. An excellent mason, of singular device ; he builded sundry brave buildings ; among the rest, he re-edified the steeple of the College Kirk of Old Aberdeen." It has been supposed * that Dr. Gordon was the architect who designed the lantern, but the same claim might be put forward for the then Bishop, for in Gordon's description of Aberdeen (p. 23) we are told—" Bot the crown was quicklie afterwards restored in a better forme and condition, by the direction of Patrick Forbes of Corse, then Bishop of Aberdeen." It is quite as likely that Thomson was both the architect and builder, and that the bishop and Dr. Gordon were the men of affairs.

The old lantern, which had stood for upwards of a century, appears to have been neglected and to have fallen into a state of disrepair, as in 1620 the authorities ordained " that the heid of the gryt stepill sould be mendit in steane leid and tymer as the samen was abefoir;" † but evidently nothing was done, and so it yielded to the storm.

Most of the windows on the west front of the tower appear to be modern.

This tower, with its crown and most of the chapel, is built of sandstone.

THE CHURCH OF THE MONASTERY OF THE CARMELITE FRIARS, South Queensferry.

Queensferry is a town on the south side of the Frith of Forth, at the point where the water narrows and is spanned by the Forth Bridge.

At the time the drawings of this church were made, about thirty years ago, it was entire, as shown on the Plan (Fig. 1214), the nave only being roofless ; but a few years afterwards the nave was ruthlessly cast down, and the materials were entirely destroyed. The transept and

* *Early Scottish History*, by Innes, p. 314.   † *Fasti Aberdonenses*, p. 283.

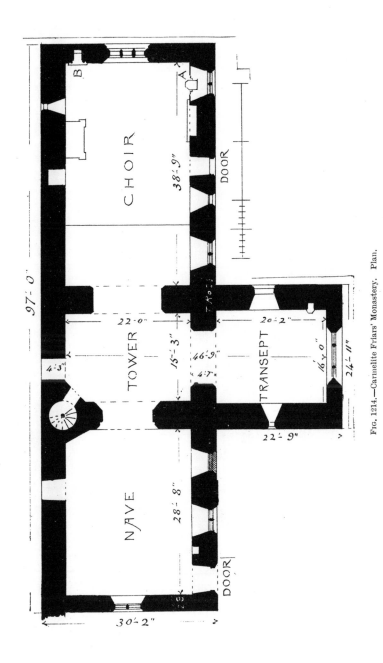

FIG. 1214.—Carmelite Friars' Monastery. Plan.

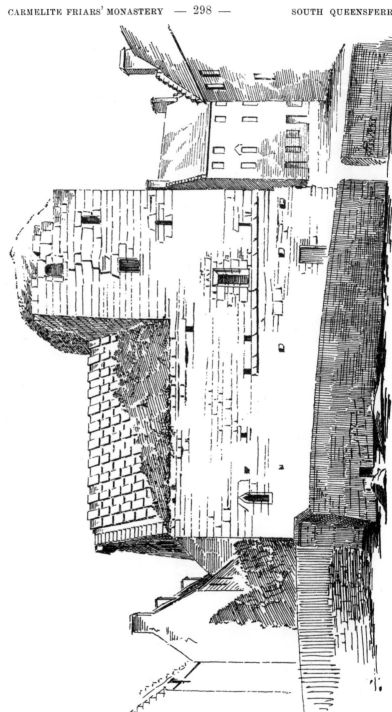

FIG. 1215.—Carmelite Friars' Monastery. View from North.

choir, with the stone roof of the latter, were almost entirely hidden from view beneath a dense mass of ivy; while the beautiful east end was quite unapproachable owing to the incongruous surroundings. The

FIG. 1216.—Carmelite Friars' Monastery. Crossing, from Transept.

tower, the arches of which originally opened into the church being built up, was used as a stable, while the transept was turned into a potato or coal store and a huckster's shop. The fortunes of the structure were at the lowest ebb when, at the end of 1889, its renovation as a place of worship was undertaken by the Dean and Chapter of St. Mary's Cathedral, Edinburgh, under the direction of Mr. J. Kinross, architect.

Fig. 1217.—Carmelite Friars' Monastery. Interior of Choir.

The church stands at the west end of Queensferry, on the north side of the street, and the description of its situation in the oldest extant charter relating to it, which is of the year 1457, is quite intelligible at this time. James Dundas of Dundas grants " to God and the Virgine Mary, and brethren of the Order of the Virgine Mary of Mount Carmel, and their successors, a piece of ground lying in the town of the Ferry, with the pertinents, with the yard and green adjacent to the church of the Virgine Mary, and whole houses builded in form of a monastrie, as also that other piece of ground lying betwixt the burn which runs near the cross of the said town on the east parts [this burn can still be identified where it comes down by the road immediately to the west of the town house] and the highway [the present main street of Queensferry] and ditch that goes towards Echline [a neighbouring farm, and still known by this name] on the south parts, and the rivolute [still to be seen] running from the town of Echline to the sea on the west, and the sea on the north parts." The "houses builded in form of

FIG. 1218.—Carmelite Friars' Monastery. Section through Choir.

a monastrie" have all disappeared, except a portion of the north wall, seen in shadow in the accompanying view from the north (Fig. 1215).

FIG. 1219.—Carmelite Friars' Monastery. View from South-West.

The monastic buildings were on the north side of the church, between it and the sea. The above wall, which stands on the shore of the Frith of Forth, at the distance of about forty paces northward from the church, determines the width of the monastery from north to south, while its length from east to west can also be fairly well ascertained. The eastern buildings of the monastery occupied the position seen on the left part of

FIG. 1220.—Carmelite Friars' Monastery.   Doorway in Nave (now destroyed).

the church in the north view, between the point where the water tabling ends and the small pointed window near the east end ; and perhaps also some of the old houses on the east occupy the sites of monastic buildings. In like manner the western buildings in all likelihood occupied the position of the old house seen on the right hand in the same view. A covered cloister ran along the north side of the church, the corbels for carrying its lean-to roof being still visible, as well as the stone tabling for protecting the same.

The church is an aisleless structure 97 feet long by 30 feet 2 inches in breadth over the

FIG. 1221.
Carmelite Friars' Monastery.
Door in Choir.

EAST WINDOW

SCALE FOR DETAILS

FIG. 1222.—Carmelite Friars' Monastery.
East Window.

walls (see Fig. 1214). It has a south transept projecting 22 feet 9 inches and 25 feet in width. The crossing is separated from the three limbs of the church by projecting piers (Fig. 1216) carrying round arches, above which rises the central tower. When the masonry which blocked up the archway leading into the choir was lately taken down, it was found that there had been a parapet about 3 feet high separating the crossing from the choir. The responds of the massive parapet coping were discovered wrought on the stones of the piers on either side. The choir and crossing only have stone vaults. These are barrel vaults, as shown in the view of the choir (Fig. 1217), where the vault is pointed, and in the crossing (see Fig. 1216), where it is round and at right angles to that of the choir, from which it is cut off and separated by the tower arch. The springing of the tower arches is kept below that of the vault over the crossing, as is usually done, in similar circumstances, in late structures, so as to avoid the difficulties of groined vaulting. The roof covering of the choir is of large overlapping stones, wrought after the manner so often found in the castles and churches of the fifteenth century. A wide gutter runs along the eaves (Fig. 1218), from which the water escapes by numerous gargoyles.

There was a pointed entrance door in the south wall (Figs. 1219 and 1220) at the west end of the nave, and leading into the choir there is a

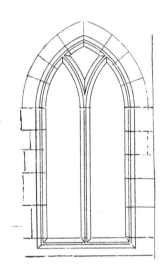

FIG. 1223.—Carmelite Friars' Monastery.
Window in Choir.

FIG. 1224.—Carmelite Friars' Monastery.
West Window of Nave (now destroyed).

round-arched door (Fig. 1221), which is, however, lintelled in the interior (see Fig. 1217). In the opposite wall a door leading to the cloisters has the reverse arrangement, being round-arched in the inside and lintelled on the exterior, where, on its west jamb, there is a Maltese cross. A similar cross is visible on the west side of the transept near the south end. There was a door into the cloisters from the crossing (see Fig. 1215) and another existed from the nave.

The windows of the choir (Figs. 1222 and 1223) are all pointed, and filled with the simplest tracery. Those of the nave and transept (Figs. 1224 and 1225) have square heads formed of straight arches, as shown in the detailed drawings. These windows have cusped tracery, which, in the nave, remained entire to the last, while that of the transept window

(Fig. 1226) was destroyed, the tracery having been cleared out to make a cart entrance ; but sufficient indications existed to permit of its restoration. There are various small cusped windows throughout the church, including the small one already referred to in the north wall of the choir, that window and a high straight headed one in the tower being the only church windows in the north side. The two upper windows in the east

FIG. 1225.—Carmelite Friars' Monastery. Window in Transept.

wall (Fig. 1227) serve, from their high position, to light the roof, and, as seen from the interior (see Fig. 1217), they recall similar features often found in the halls of castles, notably at Borthwick. On the outside of the east end between these two smaller windows over the large one there is a niche, which probably held a statue of the Virgin. It is surrounded with various shields, the charges of which are effaced. Above this, on the apex of the gable, there remains the corbelled base of a belfry. The

III.   U

window in the tower above referred to is peculiar, as will be seen from an enlarged sketch (Fig. 1228). It has a deeply-splayed sill and lintel, with moulded jambs butting against them at top and bottom. The piscina is shown in Fig. 1229, and the ambry and sedilia are seen in the view of the choir (see Fig. 1217) and in the enlarged drawings (Figs. 1230 and 1231). On either side of the choir there is a row of large splayed corbels at the springing of the arched roof, which seems to indicate that there was an upper room over the choir.

Over the tower vault at the crossing there is an upper vault containing two floors, the exposed ruinous arch of which is seen in the view from the

Fig. 1226.—Carmelite Friars' Monastery. Transept and Tower, from South.

south (see Fig. 1226). These floors are reached by the wheel stair shown on Plan. The intermediate floor, having been of timber, was supported on stone corbels. In each room there is a fireplace in the south wall; the one in the lower room is about 6 feet wide, and is suggestive of having been used for a kitchen; and there can be no doubt (as will be seen from the terms of a charter to be quoted) but that these rooms formed a residence. From the lower room there is a square window (now built up) looking into the choir. It is immediately under the vault, and measures about 3 feet wide by 4 feet high, and had probably some kind of closing shutter. The windows of these rooms are all square-headed, and overlooked the monastery.

FIG. 1227.—Carmelite Friars' Monastery, East End.

The upper part of the tower is gone, but it was doubtless finished with a cape-house and parapet walk, after the manner of termination so frequent in Scotland in the castles of the fifteenth century, which were contemporaneous with the monastery. The similar tower at Torphichen Church, about eight miles distant, that of Dysart on the opposite shore, and various other examples throughout the country are finished in the same way. In the rocks on the shore adjoining there has been cut out a haven for small boats, which is traditionally believed to have been the work of the friars.

FIG. 1228.—Carmelite Friars' Monastery.
North Window in Tower.

This monastery and church were founded and endowed by the family of Dundas of Dundas, it is believed, about the year 1330. The earliest notice of it is about a century later, in a charter of confirmation dated 1st October 1457, granted by Lord Seton, Baron of Winchburgh, of a charter granted by James Dundas of Dundas, dated 6th March 1440, the terms of which have already been quoted. The monastery existed for about two hundred and fifty years, and in 1585 James VI. disponed to Sir Walter Dundas the whole revenue of the establishment, "together with the kirk of the said place, and whole bounds, with the steeple and houses above the same." The place has ever since remained in the possession of the same family.

The present structure is evidently, from its style, of a late date. The construction of the vaulting, with its low arches at the crossing, and pointed vault covered with stone roof over the choir; the plain outline of the tower and walls, without buttress or break of any kind;

FIG. 1229.—Carmelite Friars Monastery.
Piscina.

and the square lintelled windows, are all indications of a date about the end of the fifteenth or beginning of the sixteenth century.

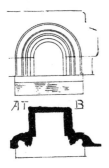

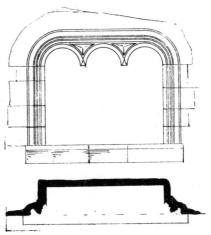

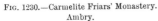

FIG. 1230.—Carmelite Friars' Monastery. Ambry.

FIG. 1231.—Carmelite Friars' Monastery. Sedilia in Choir.

ST. BOTHAN'S COLLEGIATE CHURCH, YESTER, HADDINGTONSHIRE.

A structure partly old and partly new, which stands beside the mansion house of Yester, the seat of the Marquis of Tweeddale. Its position is very fine, situated as it is by the side of a clear flowing stream, and surrounded by splendidly wooded braes.

The construction of the old part of the building, as seen in the interior, is very massive and, considering its small dimensions, imposing, and it remains in a good state of preservation.

The edifice (Fig. 1232) consists of a choir and transepts. Of the nave hardly anything exists, and there is nothing to indicate that it ever was built. The present west wall is modern, probably of this century. The choir measures, internally, 13 feet from east to west by 18 feet 6 inches wide. The total length across the transepts is about 53 feet 6 inches from north to south by 13 feet in width, all inside dimensions. It will be observed that the nave and choir are not quite in the same line.

The crossing (Fig. 1233) is covered with a pointed barrel vault in continuation of that of the choir, and is supported at the springing by very massive low round arches, which span the entrance to each transept. The choir vault is separated from the crossing by a late arch, supported on pillasters of a Renaissance form, and it has been emphasised by having ribs on the surface of the vault, as shown on the Plan by dotted lines, but these do not now exist. The transepts are also vaulted with plain pointed vaults carried to a considerable height, but cut off from the crossing, as at Ladykirk and Queensferry, by the arches introduced to carry the central vault of the crossing. As the church was without buttresses, the walls are of considerable thickness (not less than 4 feet) in order to resist the pressure of the arches. In the north wall of the south transept, near the apex of the roof (see Fig. 1233), there is a small door, now built up, which probably gave access to a small chamber in the haunch of the vault over the crossing.

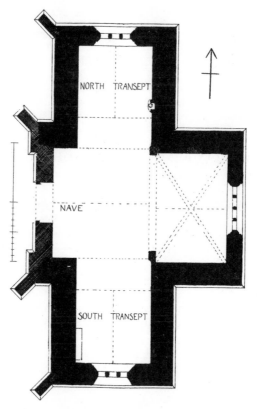

FIG. 1232.—St. Bothan's Collegiate Church. Plan.

In the east wall of the north transept there is a piscina (Fig. 1234), enriched with carved crockets round the ogee arch. The basin is, as usual, broken away. On one side of the arch is a shield, having a smaller shield on the dexter side, bearing three inescutcheons, and on the sinister side three cinquefoils, being the arms of Hay of Tweeddale.

The piscina is $22\frac{1}{2}$ inches wide, measuring over the enrichments, by

26 inches high, and 3 feet 3 inches from the floor up to the level of the basin.

Fig. 1233.—St. Bothan's Collegiate Church.   From South Transept.

FIG. 1234.—St. Bothan's Collegiate Church.   Piscina.

There is an end window in each of the three limbs of the cross, and none in the side walls. The windows in the transepts (Figs. 1235 and 1236), although not entirely alike in their details, have a general resemblance to each other. They are flat arched, and have mullions with a plain space above, occupying the centre of the thickness of the wall. The windows are of three lights, with circular tops fitted with cusping. The space above the lights, usually occupied by tracery, is filled with solid masonry. The window in the east end (Fig. 1237) is pointed, and is filled with tracery which has been re-newed, and is dated over the centre arch 1635. In the south transept there is a simple monument of Renaissance charac-ter (see Fig. 1236), which contains a fine shield with the Hay and Cockburn arms impaled—the first a mullet between three inescutcheons and the initials W. H., and the second a cres-cent between three

FIG. 1235.—St. Bothan's Collegiate Church. Transept Window (Exterior).

cocks with the initials H. C. This shield contains traces of colour, and
on the frieze there are five pateræ also in colour.

Fig. 1236.—St. Bothan's Collegiate Church. Monument in South Transept.

An earlier church than that just described existed here, and was dedicated to St. Bothan, after whom also the parish was named, until, on the erection of the present mansion house, the baronial name of the extensive domains of Yester superseded the old parochial name.

In the ancient *Taxatio* (1176) the Ecclesia de Bothani was rated at 30 marks, and it is again referred to in Bagimont's Roll (1275) as the

Fig. 1237.—St. Bothan's Collegiate Church.   East End.

Præpositura de Bothans, and is rated at £40. The territory of Yester was from the twelfth century in the possession of the family of Gifford, and in 1418 it passed, by marriage, into the possession of Sir William Hay of Locherwart, with whose descendants it still remains.*

In 1421 Sir William founded the Collegiate Church of St. Bothan for a provost, six prebendaries, and two singing boys. And he and his

* *Caledonia*, pp. 433, 512, 534.   Nisbet, *An Essay on Armories*, p. 98.

successors endowed it with sufficient revenues. After the Reformation it continued to be the parish church till 1708, when a new church was built in the neighbouring village of Gifford.

PARISH CHURCH, Stirling.*

This is one of the best preserved of the old churches of Scotland, and although it has suffered severely by various renovations and restorations, it is still a building of very considerable interest. The church occupies a high situation on the Castle Hill, and as approached up the steep streets, the lofty east end which first appears to view, with its prominent buttresses and tall windows, has a most imposing and picturesque effect.† The edifice consists of two divisions, the nave and choir, which were built at two different periods. The nave, which is the oldest part, is undoubtedly the church referred to in the Chamberlain's Accounts for the year from July 1413 to June 1414, in which he "discharges himself of the issues of ayre held at Stirling, because it was granted to the work of the parish church which had been burnt." Of the earlier church which had been burnt nothing now remains. The date of the east end or choir is known to be between 1507 and 1520.

The building (Fig. 1238) consists, from end to end, of a central nave with north and south aisles (the aisles being vaulted in stone), an eastern apse, and a western tower. The nave has five bays, the choir three bays, and they are separated by a wide bay, which may be termed the crossing. The crossing now serves as an entrance hall to the two churches which are located in the edifice, walls being built across each side of the crossing so as to enclose the choir as one church and the nave as the other. The total internal length of the building, exclusive of the apse and tower, is about 160 feet by about 55 feet in width; including apse and tower the internal length is about 200 feet.

The original entrance to the church was through the western tower, and as the ground rises considerably towards the west, there must have been steps down to the floor of the nave. The western doorway was destroyed in 1818, when the sill of the window above was lowered into the space occupied by the door arch, but the bases and lower part of the door jambs still remain (Fig. 1239). The tower, which is vaulted, opens into the nave (as at Linlithgow) through a lofty pointed arch, springing from moulded responds (Fig. 1240).

* A short account of this church, pointing out the relation which existed in the sixteenth century between the domestic and ecclesiastical architecture of Scotland, is given in *The Castellated and Domestic Architecture of Scotland*, Vol. v. p. 141, but the main features of the edifice are not there fully described.

† See Fig. 1258 in Vol. II. p. 142 of *The Castellated and Domestic Architecture of Scotland*.

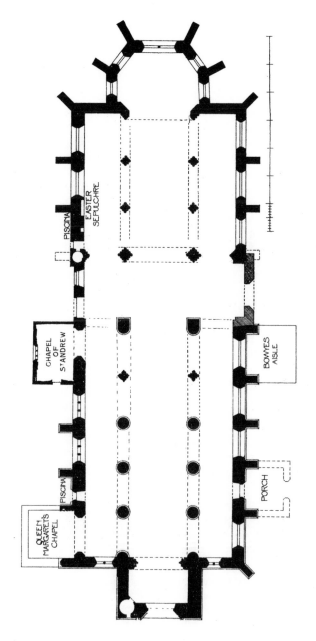

FIG. 1238.—Stirling Parish Church. Plan.

FIG. 1239.—Stirling Parish Church. Tower, from South-West.

FIG. 1240.
Stirling Parish Church.
Responds of Tower Arch.

The piers of the nave (with the exception of two) are round and massive cylinders, and the east and west responds (Fig. 1241) are semi-cylinders. The piers and responds have circular and delicately carved and moulded capitals (see Fig. 1241), with but slight projection or undercutting. The moulded bases, where not destroyed, are also round and of slight projection, those of the responds terminating on semi-octagonal plinths. The general appearance of these pillars illustrates what is so often found in Scotland (both in ecclesiastic and domestic work) during the fifteenth century and onwards, viz., a tendency to imitate Norman and early pointed details. This tendency is also seen in the nave piers of Dunkeld Cathedral, in the piers and arches of the naves of Aberdour Church and Dysart Church, in the imitation of first pointed work in the late cloisters of Melrose, and many other examples which might be cited. But the later counterfeit is never perfect, there being always some touch of contemporary design which reveals the imitation. The two exceptional piers, above referred to as not being cylindrical, are the fourth piers (Fig. 1242) from the west end (Fig. 1243). These piers are composed of clustered shafts with moulded capitals, the upper members of which do not follow the contour of the piers,

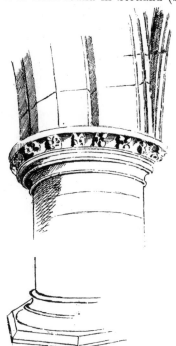

FIG. 1241.—Stirling Parish Church.
West Respond of Nave Arcade.

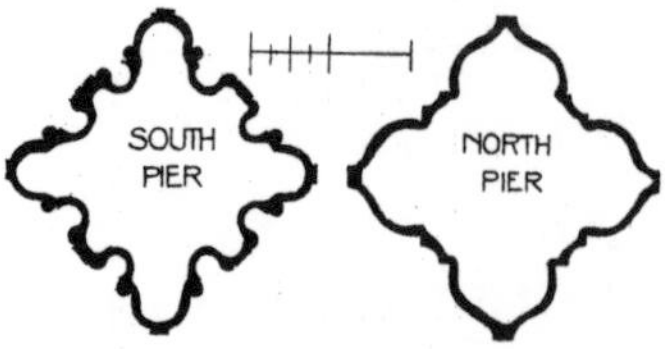

but sweep unbroken across the cap in the same manner as in the caps in the choir (Fig. 1244), and in those of the interior of the oriel windows in the great hall of Stirling Castle adjoining (Fig. 1245), at Torphichen, and other late churches; and in the capitals of the clustered jambs of the hall fireplaces in many castles throughout the country. It will be observed from

SOUTH
PIER

NORTH
PIER

FIG. 1242.—Stirling Parish Church.
Piers in Nave in Fourth Bay from West End.

Fig. 1243 that the nave aisles are vaulted with groined arches, while the central nave has a wooden roof.

The Plan (see Fig. 1238) shows that the two piers of the fifth bay from the west end of the nave consist of a semi-round attached to a square. These formed the west piers of the crossing. The next piers (the first in the choir) are, like the last, of large size, and suggest that a

FIG. 1243.—Stirling Parish Church. Interior of Nave from North Aisle, looking West.

central tower was contemplated, if not built. There was, over the crossing, an upper room known as the king's room, from which the service could be seen. It was destroyed about the middle of this century. The room was reached by a wheel staircase in the north wall, where the door leading to it is still to be seen. This staircase is now filled with the chimney flues of a heating apparatus. The bay between the tower piers

is arched with round arches, which are now almost concealed, this part
of the church being occupied with modern staircases, vestries, and gallery.
A round arch also spanned the church between the eastmost of the two
piers of the crossing. The latter arch was taken down about the year

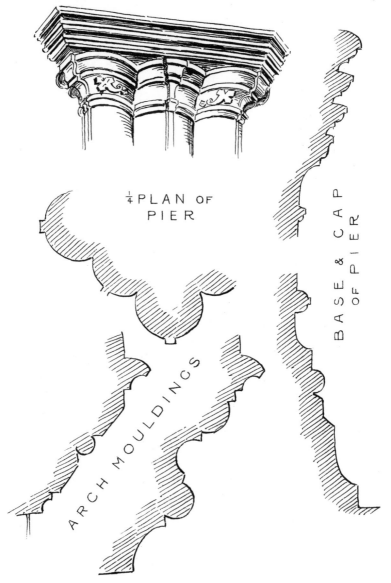

¼ PLAN OF
PIER

BASE & CAP
OF PIER

ARCH MOULDINGS

FIG. 1244.—Stirling Parish Church. Piers, Caps, and Arch Mouldings in Choir.

1869, thus destroying the room above, and the pier was enlarged. From the enlarged part a pointed arch was thrown across, thus sacrificing the beauty and fitness of the church, in order to introduce a small gallery. About the same time the interior stone work was, unfortunately, re-dressed.

Fig. 1247, together with the view from south-west, above referred to, gives some idea of the effect of the apse and the picturesque appearance of the church as seen from the north-east. The south side of the building

FIG. 1245.—Stirling Castle. Oriel in Great Hall.

has been lamentably injured by a kind of great porch or transept erected in the centre, which gives access to the two churches into which the edifice is now divided.

Of the building of the east end or choir interesting particulars are given in the Register of Dunfermline. In the year 1507 an agreement was entered into between James Beaton, Abbot of Dunfermline, and the Town Council and community of Stirling, wherein it is stated that the latter having "takin apon hand to big and compleitlie edifye, and end ane gud and sufficient queyr conformand to the body of the peroch kirk of

III.   X

the said burght," they were to deliver to the abbot the "body" of the parish church (that is the west end or nave) to be used by the Convent as a "queir ay and quhill the said queyr now to be biggit, be fully and compleitlie biggit and endit." Under this arrangement the Convent was to

FIG. 1246.—Stirling Parish Church. Interior of Choir.

pay £200 Scots, and to provide all the ornaments necessary for the high altar and for the upholding of the same, and promised infeftment yearly

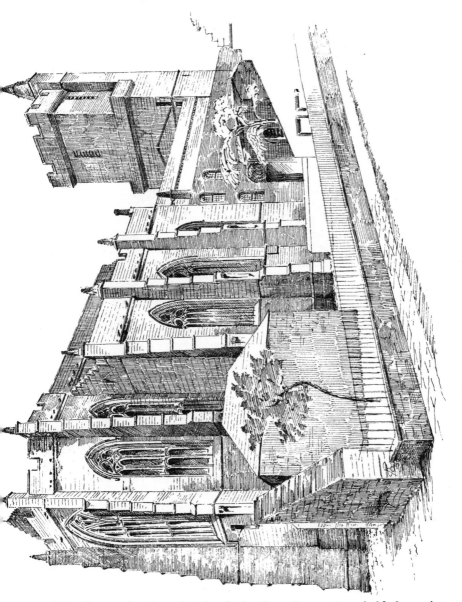

FIG. 1247.—Stirling Parish Church. View from North-East.

of 40s. Scots. On the other hand, the Council agree to uphold the queir perpetually in all things "swa that the hie alter thair sall be honestly and honourably uphalding in the said ornaments as thai resceve the samyn thairto fra the said abbot and Convent." By the year 1520 the work appears to have proceeded so far that a service, by order of the Provost and Bailies, was held in the choir, but it does not appear to have been then quite finished, as in 1523 Robart Arnot, "Maister of the kirk wark," is ordered to make payment for timber for the queir.* The choir (see Fig. 1247) consists of three bays with north and south aisles, and an eastern apse of five sides. The latter is applied like an oriel window to the east end of the church, somewhat in the same way as the apse of St. Michael's, Linlithgow. It is wider than the central division of the choir, and fits on awkwardly to it, causing the two side divisions of the apse to be lost to view when one looks from the west end (see Fig. 1246). The vaulting of the apse is managed in a peculiar manner, arches being intro-

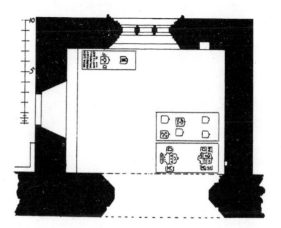

FIG. 1248.—Stirling Parish Church. Plan of Chapel of St. Andrew.

duced on each side in order to bring the central space into a form as nearly a parallelogram as possible, and thus enable it to be covered with a pointed barrel vault, strengthened with small ribs.† The mullions of the apse are treated somewhat like perpendicular work.

The side aisles are vaulted with stone, and the tracery is modern. The piers are of an ordinary late section (see Fig. 1244), and the details recall the later work of St. Giles', Edinburgh. The caps are of the character of many late Scottish buildings, such as St. Giles' and St. Michael's (choir), the abacus containing a number of straight members, while the bed moulding breaks round the mouldings of the piers. The small shreds

* The Story of the Parish Church of Stirling, by Treasurer Ronald, p. 12.
† See also Fig. 1259 in The Castellated and Domestic Architecture of Scotland, Vol. v. p. 143.

FIG. 1249.—Stirling Parish Church. Interior of Chapel of St. Andrew.

of foliage introduced are very peculiar. The bases also recall some of the above buildings. There is no triforium, and the clerestory windows, which are round-headed, are brought down to the string course immediately over the arches of the main arcade.

FIG. 1250.—Stirling Parish Church.
South-East Corner of St. Andrew's Chapel.

At the north-west corner of the church there was a small chapel (now removed), with a wide opening into the church. It had a vaulted roof, which abutted against the clerestory. Half buried in the ruins of this chapel is the recess of what appears to have been a piscina. The chapel is called Queen Margaret's, and is supposed to have been built by James IV. in honour of his queen.

Another chapel dedicated to St. Andrew, at the north-east end of the nave, is still entire. This chapel (Fig. 1248), which till within the last few months was private property, has been handed over to the keeping of the authorities of Stirling, and is now, for the first time for many years, if not centuries, made accessible to the public, so that drawings of the interior can now be made. The partition which closed the access to the chapel from the church still remains, and a door which was cut through the east wall at the time the partition was put up is still in use, but these alterations are not shown on the Plan (Fig. 1248).*

FIG. 1251.—Stirling Parish Church.
North Window of St. Andrew's Chapel.

The chapel measures about 15 feet 9 inches in length, and has a width of about 12 feet from

* We are indebted for this Plan and other details of the chapel to Mr. John W. Small, architect, Stirling.

the north wall. Its height from the original floor to the apex of the roof is about 15 feet 8 inches. It enters from the church by a round

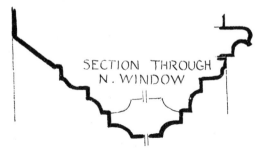

FIG. 1252.—Stirling Parish Church. Section of North Window of St. Andrew's Chapel.

arched opening about 10 feet wide (Fig. 1249), with splayed and notched jambs and arch, the jambs having a very simple moulded cap (Fig. 1250).

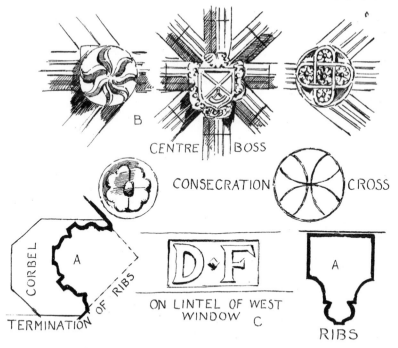

FIG. 1253.—Stirling Parish Church. Details of St. Andrew's Chapel.

This opening is not in the centre of the chapel. There are a north and a west window. The former (Fig. 1251) is pointed, and is divided by

mullions into three lights, and retains the original tracery.   Fig. 1252
shows the section of the mouldings of the arch and jambs.   The window

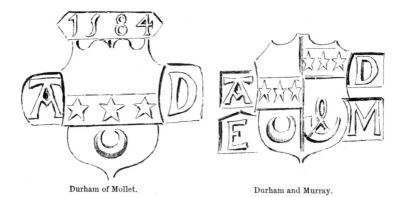

Durham of Mollet.   Durham and Murray.

Fig. 1254.—Stirling Parish Church.   Arms in St. Andrew's Chapel.

in the west wall is square lintelled, and has a straight sconsion arch
(see Fig. 1249).   This chapel exhibits, in small space, three methods of

Fig. 1255.—Stirling Parish Church.
Founder's Arms in St. Andrew's Chapel.

covering an opening, the architect
being apparently indifferent as to
which was used, so that it served
the purpose.

The chapel is groined in the ordinary manner, the masonry being, as
usual, very fine.   The ribs are all of
the same general section (Fig.
1253, A A), but each set is slightly
different in size, the diagonals being
the largest.   There are no wall ribs.   The details of the carved bosses
at the intersections are shown in Fig. 1253, B.   A stone bench runs
along the west side only.

There is a roughly formed square recess,
about 12 inches wide (see Fig. 1248), in the
north wall near the east end, and in the east
wall at the south-east corner (see Plan and
Fig. 1250) there is an ogee-headed recess,
about 7 inches high by 5 inches wide and $2\frac{1}{2}$
inches deep, at about 3 feet 6 inches from the
floor.   There are recesses somewhat similar to
the latter at Paisley Abbey.

St. Andrew's Chapel was erected by Duncan
Forrester of Garden, Knight, whose initials are

Fig. 1256.—Stirling Parish Church.
Arms and Initials
in St. Andrew's Chapel.

cut on the lintel of the west window (see Fig. 1253, **C**), and his arms, together with a saltier for St. Andrew, are carved on the centre boss (see Fig. 1253, **B**). The name of Duncan Forrester occurs in charters

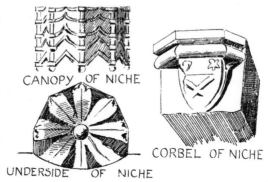

CANOPY OF NICHE

CORBEL OF NICHE

UNDERSIDE OF NICHE

FIG. 1257.—Stirling Parish Church.
Details of Niche in St. Andrew's Chapel.

relating to Stirling in 1479 and onwards for a period of forty years. He was provost of the town of Stirling, and appears to have been a liberal benefactor to this church. As shown on the Plan there are three interesting grave slabs in the chapel. One of these, of the date 1584, contains the arms of Durham of Grange (Fig. 1254); but as no member of that family had A. D. as initials at that period, the monument may probably have belonged to the Durhams of Mollet, one of whom, with the above initials, married Eliz. Murray. This would correspond with the initials and lower shield on the slab (see Fig. 1254) in which the Durham and Murray arms are impaled. The adjoining slab exhibits six shields. One of these contains the founder's arms (Fig. 1255), and another a curious figure arranged saltier-wise. Nothing can be determined as to the carving on the other shields. The remaining slab contains the arms and initials of Duncan Forrester (Fig. 1256), possibly the son of the founder, and the Erskine arms with the initials M. E. A consecration cross is shown (see Fig. 1253), which is carved on the north wall of the chapel.

In Fig. 1257 are shown detached portions of a niche, including the canopy and corbel, lying on the floor. The exterior base of the church, which is partly returned round the west side of this chapel, is shown in Fig. 1258.

There were north and south doorways to the nave, opposite each other, in the second bay from the west. The south one had a large porch, now destroyed.

The tower, which is oblong in plan, measures about 31 feet from north to south by about 22 feet from east to west, and, according to Mr. Ronalds, it is 85 feet high to the top of the parapet, and 15 feet more to the apex

BASE OUTSIDE

FIG. 1258.
Stirling
Parish Church.
Exterior Base.

of the spirelet. It is quite evident that it has been built at two periods. The lower part, judging from the window mouldings and what remains of the base of the west door, is contemporary with the church, or of early fifteenth century work. The upper part is contracted to nearly a square of about 25 feet on Plan, there being a balcony on the north and one on the south (see Fig. 1239). A turret stair in the north-west corner gives access from the church to the top. This tower, especially as seen from the west, is very picturesque, where the long unbroken line of the stair turret contrasts beautifully with recessed outlines of the other corner (see Fig. 1248).

This tower is amongst the best specimens of the Scottish architecture of the sixteenth century, as applied to ecclesiastical structures.

TULLIBARDINE CHURCH, Perthshire.

This edifice, which is unused, although in an almost perfect state of preservation, is situated about six miles south from Crieff. It "was founded in honour of our Blessed Saviour, for a provost and several prebendaries, by Sir David Murray of Tullibardine, ancestor of the Duke of Athol, in

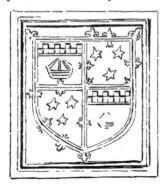

the year 1446." * Sir David died the same year and was buried in the church, where his arms (Fig. 1259) still remain on the interior of the north side of the choir, quartered with those of his wife Isobel, second daughter of Sir John Stewart of Innermeith and Lorn. The lady's arms, it will be observed, occupy the first and fourth quarters.

FIG. 1259.—Tullibardine Church.
Arms of Sir David Murray in Chancel.

This is one of the few collegiate churches in Scotland which were entirely finished and still remain unaltered. It is of a cruciform plan (Fig. 1260) and has a small western tower entering from the church by a narrow doorway. The building measures internally from east to west along the south side 62 feet 1½ inches, and along the north side 64 feet 6½ inches by 18 feet 5½ inches in breadth, and the walls are 14 feet 3 inches high from the floor to the wall head. The measurements over the transepts are 64 feet 5 inches from north to south, by 15 feet 10 inches in width (inside measure). The tower is a small apartment of 6 feet 11 inches by 4 feet 9 inches.

There are two entrances, one being at the west end of the south wall

* Spottiswoode.

(Fig. 1261). It is round-arched with a bead and hollow moulding and a rude string cap. The other is a plain lintelled doorway in the north transept.

In each of the north and south walls of the transept there is a traceried window, the one to the south (Fig. 1262) having three lights and the other (Fig. 1263) two lights. The walls are of considerable thickness, and the tracery is well recessed (Fig. 1264) and gives, in consequence,

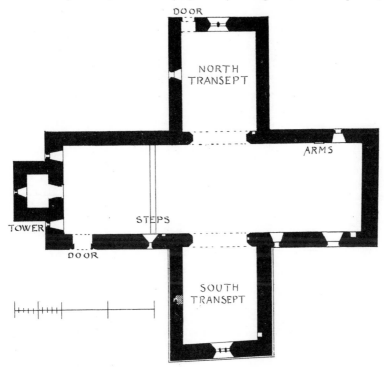

FIG. 1260.—Tullibardine Church. Plan.

a massive and substantial appearance to the otherwise well designed windows.

The other windows are simple and such as are found in castles and minor churches. That adjoining the entrance to the south transept is interesting from having its sconsion arch (Fig. 1265) neatly constructed so as to die away upon the splay. In the west gable there are two narrow windows. The lintels of these, instead of being level, lie at the same angle as the slope of the gable, and just a little below it (Fig. 1266). A similar kind of window may be observed at Dunblane at the east end of

the room over the north aisle of the choir. The transepts each open from
the church by a segmental arch (see Fig. 1265), springing from splayed

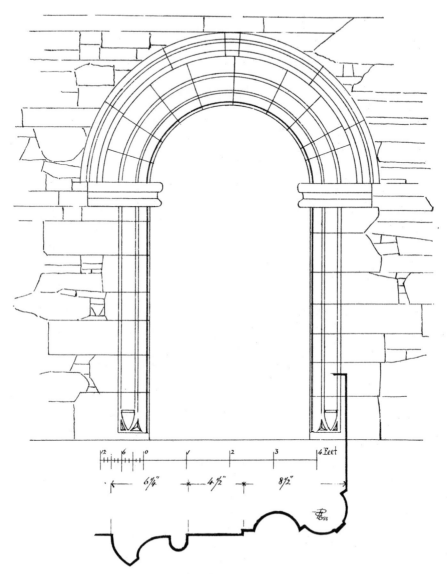

FIG. 1261.—Tullibardine Church. South Doorway.

responds, having moulded bases and caps (Fig. 1267). From the floor to
the top of the caps measures 8 feet 2 inches, and the arch has a rise of

2 feet 10 inches, in a width of 11 feet 9½ inches. It is difficult to say how the roof at this part was finished originally. The present roof at the east end is of considerable antiquity, having timbers about 6 inches square, but the part resting on the transept arch is comparatively modern. That it was not finished as it is now is almost certain, as there appears to have been a gable over the arch, separating the transept roofs from the main roof.

There are several ambries in the church. The one at the east end of the south wall is handsome (Fig. 1268), having a pointed ogee arched

Fig. 1262.—Tullibardine Church. View from South-East.

head, with bead and hollow mouldings and bases wrought in the hollows. In the east jamb of the south transept arch (see Plan and Fig. 1265) there is a narrow arched recess about 6½ inches wide by 3½ inches in depth.

The east end of the church appears to have been covered with tapestry, as the laths for attaching it to are still in position on the walls. At the west wall and the end walls of the transepts the pieces securing the feet of the rafters are brought down the walls flush with the face, and would also afford facilities for hanging tapestry.

A peculiar feature of the church is the rise of the floor at the west end by two steps. The steps appear to be original, and may possibly be in connection with a burial vault beneath.

In the exterior of the north wall of the transept (see Fig. 1263) are inserted two shields. The one over the doorway (Fig. 1269) contains the arms of Murray of Tullibardine—three stars within a double tressure,

FIG. 1263.—Tullibardine Church. North Transept.

flowered and counter-flowered. The other contains the arms of Sir William Murray of Tullibardine (son of Sir David, the founder of the College) impaled with those of his wife Margaret, daughter of Sir John Colquhoun of Luss. On the skew stones (Fig. 1270), which are peculiarly shaped, the star is frequently wrought.

In the west wall of the tower there is a niche (Fig. 1271) with a canopy and bracket. If it ever was adorned with a figure it is now empty, and the figure has disappeared. Beneath the niche there is a

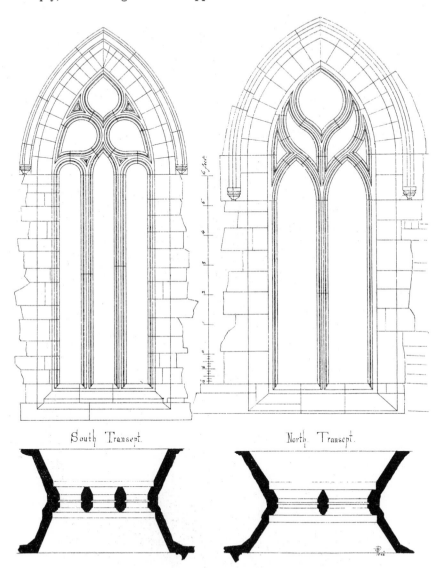

Fig. 1264.—Tullibardine Church. North and South Transepts.

small round opening, a kind of spy hole or shot hole from the tower, which was doubtless a place of security.

Fig. 1265.—Tullibardine Church. Interior, looking South-East.

We have to thank Mr. T. S. Robertson for assistance in connection with this Sketch.

Fig. 1270.—Tullibardine Church.
Skew Stone.

Fig. 1267.
Tullibardine Church.
Jamb of
Transept Arch.

Fig. 1268.—Tullibardine Church.
Ambry at East End of South Wall.

Fig. 1266.—Tullibardine Church.
Window in West Gable.

Fig. 1271.
Tullibardine Church.
Niche in Tower.

Fig. 1269.—Tullibardine Church.
Arms on Exterior of North Transept.

COLLEGIATE CHURCH, Maybole.

The ancient town of Maybole, which is situated on the side of a hill about nine miles south from Ayr, was formerly the capital of Carrick, and contained the castle of the Earl of Cassillis * and the town houses of the lairds of the district. Being within two miles of Crosraguel Abbey and having a collegiate establishment within the town, the ecclesiastical

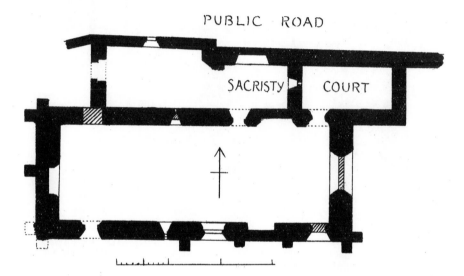

FIG. 1272.—Maybole Collegiate Church. Plan.

element would not be wanting in the society of the place. At the Reformation the house of the provost was the scene of a celebrated debate between John Knox and Quentin Kennedy, Abbot of Crosraguel, in September 1561.

The college stands on gently sloping ground near the base of the hill on which the town is situated, and is now enclosed within the streets.

In 1371 a chapel was founded in Maybole by Sir John Kennedy of Dunure, and endowed for one clerk and three chaplains. This was probably the earliest foundation of the kind established in Scotland, but it had many successors as collegiate churches in the following century.

* Illustrated in *The Castellated and Domestic Architecture of Scotland*, Vol. III. p. 498.

Fig. 1278.—Maybole Collegiate Church. View from South-West.

In Abercrummie's description of Carrick,* written in the end of the seventeenth century, the collegiate church is mentioned as being still entire, "being now used as the burial-place of the Earl of Cassillis, and other gentlemen who contributed to the putting of a roofe upon it, when it was decayed." It is further mentioned that the "Colledge consisted of a rector and three prebends, whose stalls are all of them yet extant, save the rector's."

The houses or "stalls" of the prebends are now all gone, and the church is again roofless. The freestone has been taken away from many of the buttresses, and the tracery of the windows is broken and most of the windows built up.

The church as it now stands (Fig. 1272) consists of a simple oblong 52 feet long by 18 feet wide internally, but there are evidences of its having been altered. There was a small sacristy on the north side, with a good pointed doorway leading into the church.

Tracery in East Window

Tracery in S.E. Window

FIG. 1274.—Maybole Collegiate Church. Tracery in Windows.

Both in the north and south walls (Fig. 1273) of the edifice there is a very narrow pointed and cusped window, which does not correspond with the other details of the building, and close to the narrow window in the south wall there is a dressed corner, now built against, which seems to indicate a complete change in the structure at this point. The east window and the two windows adjoining it in the north and south sides still retain part of their tracery (Fig. 1274), which is of a late character. A recess with pointed arch-head for a tomb or an Easter sepulchre in the north wall of the choir (Fig. 1275) contains mouldings enriched with imitations of the dog-tooth, and the arches of the south-west doorway (see Fig. 1273) have also similar dog-tooth ornaments. The church having been founded in 1371, when the first pointed period (to which the dog-tooth belongs) had long passed away, there can be no doubt of the above ornaments being very late revivals, even if the style of their execution did not make that apparent.

* *History of the Kennedies*, p. 167.

The south-west doorway is, however, a good late *adaptation* or imitation of a thirteenth century design, like other imitations of early work which were common during the third pointed period. The doorway is surmounted by a shield bearing the Kennedy arms.

The west end (see Fig. 1273) has a buttress in the centre, while in the inside opposite it the recess of a built up window is observable (see Plan), thus further indicating alteration. It seems probable that the church was originally small, and the narrow windows, above referred to, may possibly be remains of the original fabric. Then at a later date the

FIG. 1275.—Maybole Collegiate Church.   Interior of East End.

structure was probably enlarged and partly rebuilt, when the enlarged traceried windows, the recess in the choir, and the south-west doorway —all of which are undoubtedly late—were introduced. This may have occurred about A.D. 1500. The ruined sacristy still retains its barrel vault (Fig. 1276).

Abercrummie further says—"On the north syde of the kirk is the buriall place of the laird of Colaine within ane enclosure of new square-stone lately built." This enclosure remains, and its architecture corresponds with the date mentioned, viz., seventeenth century. The entrance doorway (see Fig. 1276) is elaborate, but considerably decayed, and over

Fig. 1276.—Maybole Collegiate Church.   Doorway to Burial Vault.

it a large shield bears the Kennedy arms, impaled with another. The church itself is now used as a burial ground by certain families of the name of Kennedy.

BIGGAR COLLEGIATE CHURCH, Lanarkshire.

The town of Biggar lies in a valley in the Upper Ward of Lanarkshire, through which communication is obtained between the upper reaches of the Clyde and the Tweed. From an early period Biggar was a rectory in the Deanery of Lanark. The parson of Biggar is mentioned in deeds of the twelfth century, and several of the rectors held important appointments at Court.

In 1545 the Church of St. Nicholas was founded and endowed by Malcolm, Lord Fleming, the Lord High Chancellor of Scotland. The charter of foundation still exists. It was addressed by Lord Fleming to Cardinal Beaton, and states that the church was to be erected in honour of the Holy Trinity, the Blessed Virgin Mary, St. Nicholas the patron of Biggar, and St. Ninian. The purpose of the foundation was to support a provost, eight canons or prebendaries, four singing boys, and six poor nuns, and the presentations and endowment of these officials were reserved to the Lord Fleming. The special duties of the prebendaries were as follow :—The first prebendary was to instruct the singing boys in music, the second was to be master of the grammar school, the third was to act as sacristan—to ring the bell, to light the tapers on the four altars, and to attend to the vestments and ornament thereof—and the fourth prebendary had charge of the poor nuns and gave them their allowances. A hospital was to be provided for the poor nuns, and suitable houses were to be erected for the provost and canons.

During the progress of the work, Malcolm, Lord Fleming, died. The building was carried on by his son, and scarcely completed before the Reformation supervened to interrupt the work.[*]

This church (Fig. 1277), like many of the collegiate edifices erected prior to this time, is cruciform in plan, consisting of chancel with apsidal east end, transept, and nave, with square tower over the crossing. There are no aisles in any part of the church.

It is supposed by Grose (who saw the building more than 100 years ago, before it was restored) that the nave, which is built with whinstone rubble work, was probably part of an original church which was enlarged by Lord Fleming, by the addition of a transept and chancel. This may have been the case, but the nave is now so completely altered and modernised that it is impossible to say. The chancel, transept, and tower

* *Biggar and the House of Fleming*, p. 164.

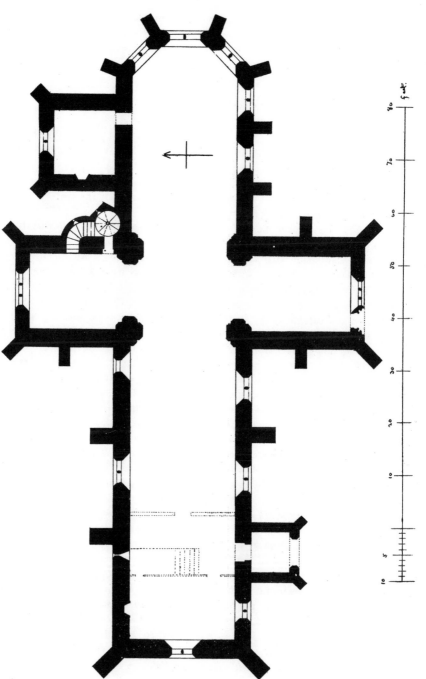

FIG. 1277.—Biggar Collegiate Church. Plan.

over the crossing are evidently of a different period from the nave, being all built with freestone ashlar.

The total length of the structure internally is 112 feet by 20 feet

Fig. 1278.—Biggar Collegiate Church.   South Transept and Tower.

4 inches in width, but about 24 feet have been cut off the west end of the nave so as to form a lobby and staircase to a gallery and a vestry at the west end.   A south-west porch gives access to these places.   Formerly the

FIG. 1279.—Biggar Collegiate Church.   View from South-East.

chapter house existed on the north side of the chancel, but it was removed, and a new vestry is now erected in its place.

The principal entrance into the collegiate church was by a round arched doorway in the south wall of the transept (Fig. 1278), and it is believed that there was also a door in the west end. A small wheel staircase in the south-east angle of the north transept leads to the roof and tower, and also to an organ gallery in the north transept. The top of the stair turret, as seen in the view, is modern.

The exterior, as viewed from the south-east (Fig. 1279), has a good effect, with the square battlemented tower rising boldly above the buttressed chancel and transept. The windows are all pointed and filled with simple tracery, and the buttresses are of simple but good design, having a broad water table on top, and no pinnacles.

The windows are each set in a rectangular recess, which, although a novelty, cannot be said to to be an improvement. It is in keeping with the square forms of the Renaissance then being introduced. The arches and jambs have triple splays. The doorway in the south transept is a little more ornamental. The arch is round, as very usual in Scotland, and there are

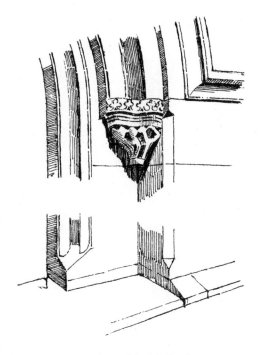

FIG. 1280.—Biggar Collegiate Church.
Details of Doorway in South Transept.

two recessed arches, the inner one moulded and the outer having enriched caps (Fig. 1280).

The tower contains a room on the first floor with a fireplace, and over it is the belfry.

It is understood that the ancient roof was of oak, and that the timbers in the chancel were gilt and emblazoned, doubtless with the arms of the Flemings, who were buried there.

The interior (Fig. 1281) has been greatly remodelled, but the principal arches at the crossing are preserved. The roof being of timber, the arches

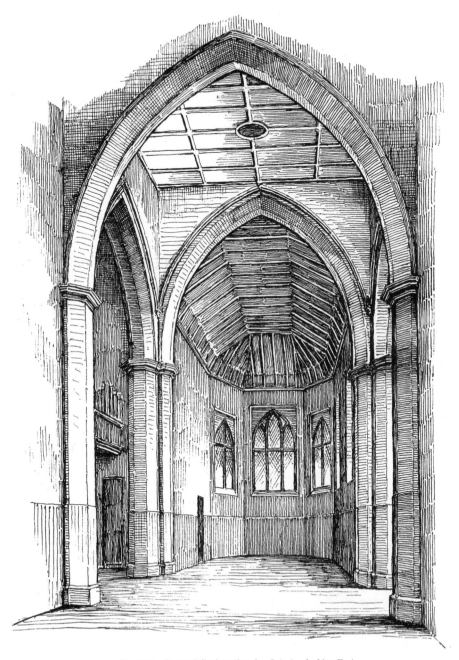

FIG. 1281.—Biggar Collegiate Church. Interior, looking East.

of the transepts are carried well up, and the windows are also of good size, so that the church is well lighted, and forms, in this respect, a striking contrast to Ladykirk and similar vaulted structures.

After the Reformation the offices and emoluments passed into the hands of laymen.

CARNWATH CHURCH, LANARKSHIRE.

Carnwath is situated about two miles west from Carstairs Junction.

The original foundation of this church dates from a very early time. In the middle of the twelfth century it was bestowed by William de Sumerville on Glasgow Cathedral, which grant was confirmed by Pope Alexander III. in 1170. The existing building is, however, of much more recent date. It formed the north wing of the parish church, and was added after a Collegiate foundation had been erected in 1425 by Thomas, first Lord Somerville, for a provost and six prebendaries, and is thus

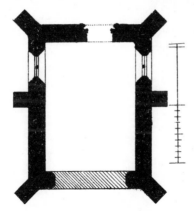

FIG. 1282.—Carnwath Church. Plan of North Transept.

described in the *Memoire of the Somervilles*, written about the end of the seventeenth century :—" The yle itself is but little, however neatly and conveniently built opposite the middle (on the North side) of the church ; all aisles, both within and without, haveing pinickles upon all the corners, wherein are engraven, besydes other imagerie the armes of the Somervills and Sinclaires (the family of the wife of the founder), very discernable to the occular aspectione, albeit it be two hundereth and fyfie-eight years since they were placed there." *

The parish church, which formerly consisted of chancel, nave, and transept, has been removed, and there now only remains a portion of the

* *The Upper Ward of Lanarkshire*, Vol. II. p. 483.

north transept, which has been used as the burial-place of the Lords Carnwath-Somerville till the latter half of the seventeenth century, and the Lockharts since then.

The building (Fig. 1282) stands north and south, and measures about 25 feet long by 22 feet 6 inches wide (externally). The style (Fig. 1283)

FIG. 1283.—Carnwath Church. View from North-West.

is generally like that of the contemporary churches of Scotland; but the large north window is remarkable from having a closer affinity than usual with the English perpendicular. In order to carry the heavy stone roof, shown in the sketch, the building is covered with a pointed barrel vault such as is generally employed for this purpose; and, as frequently happens, the vault is divided into bays, and is ornamented with decorative ribs springing from shafts attached to the wall. Some of the caps bear the arms of the founder and his spouse. The vaulting gives rise to the massive buttresses employed, and to the depressed form of the two-light square-headed side windows on each side, one of which is seen in the sketch.

The building having been restored, several new features have been added. Thus the belfry on the south gable and the cross on the north gable are modern. The north doorway under the large window is also an insertion, but is believed to have been formed with the stones of the old doorway of the church. The pinnacles referred to in the above quoted description still exist (although partly restored), but the coats of arms on the buttresses are no longer visible. The outline of the arch in the south gable, which formerly opened from the transept into the church, can still be traced (see Plan).

The interior contains a fine altar-tomb, bearing the recumbent figures of Hugh, Lord Somerville, who died in 1549, and his second wife, Janet, daughter of William Maitland of Ledington, who died about 1550. Lord Hugh was a great favourite of James v., who frequently visited him at his Castle of Cowthally.

In the churchyard of Carnwath there is another recumbent effigy, apparently of older date, but its history is unknown.

CASTLE SEMPLE COLLEGIATE CHURCH, Renfrewshire.

This somewhat remarkable structure stands in the midst of beautiful woodland scenery, on a gentle acclivity above Lochwinnoch, near the point at the north end where the Black Cart flows from the loch.

A collegiate church was founded on this site, and endowed in 1504

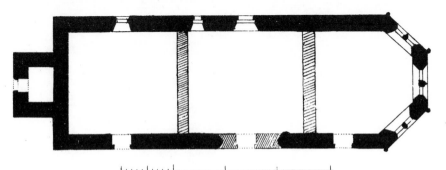

Fig. 1284.—Castle Semple Collegiate Church. Plan.

FIG. 1285.—Castle Semple Collegiate Church. View from South-East.

FIG. 1286.—Castle Semple Collegiate Church. View from North-West.

by John, first Lord Sempill, near his own residence of Castle Semple. The establishment consisted of a provost, six chaplains, two boys, and a sacristan. The church (Fig. 1284) measures within the walls 66 feet in length by 19 feet in width. The building is a simple oblong, terminating toward the east in a three-sided apse, and having a square tower projecting from the centre of the west wall.

Fig. 1287.—Castle Semple Collegiate Church. Monument to John, Lord Sempill.

The style of the east end (Fig. 1285) is very remarkable. The forms of the double windows indicate plainly that they are very late survivals of spurious Gothic work, and a close examination of the building tends to confirm this view. The other windows in the side walls have been greatly altered, but they do not present any features at all like those of the apse. Over the door to the chancel are two coats of arms with the letters R. L. S. and A. M. S., the dexter shield bearing the Sempill arms and the sinister the Montgomerie. The square tower at the west end (Fig. 1286) is extremely simple, and has no analogy with the work at the east end.

There can be little doubt that the tower and most of the side walls are of about the date of the original foundation, while the east apse has been added in the sixteenth century, to receive the monument of John, Lord Sempill, who fell at Flodden in 1513. A few remains of the original square-headed windows in the side walls are still traceable.

The interior has, within recent times, been divided by two solid walls into three compartments, so as to form separate private burial-places, and this operation seems to have caused the further altera-tion and building up of the side windows.

In the eastern compartment stands, against the north wall, the large monument to Lord Sempill (Fig. 1287), which bears the follow-ing inscription :—

· · · JOHN · LORD · SEMPIL ANDE · HIS · LAYDI · D · · · MAR-GARITA · · ·

It must have been erected after 1513, and shows the last expiring effort of the Gothic decorative spirit. The cusped half-arch half-lintel is a kind of compromise be-tween the Gothic and Renaissance, and the exuberant foliage of the upper portion shows late Gothic forms run wild.

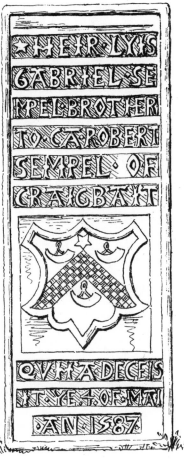

FIG. 1288.
Castle Semple Collegiate Church.
Slab to Gabriel Sempill.

The architecture of the apse windows corresponds in extravagance with that of the monument.

A monumental slab in the central compartment (Fig. 1288) is erected in memory of " Gabriel Sempel," who died in 1587. This shows the style

FIG. 1289.—Castle Semple Collegiate Church.
Carved Stone.

of lettering which was in use about that time, together with the Sempill arms.

A carved stone (Fig. 1289) (from a sketch by Mr. William Galloway), which seems to have been the socket of a cross, stands in the building, and was perhaps used at one time as a font. It is octagonal in form, and has an oblong sinking in the centre.

GREYFRIARS' CHURCH,* ELGIN.

The mendicant orders were introduced into Scotland by Alexander II. (1214-49), who is stated to have founded eight convents for Dominicans, but only two for Franciscans. From an old undated charter it is believed that the latter order was established in Elgin under Alexander III., but their original monastery appears to have fallen into decay. It was, however, revived under James I. (1424-37) for the order of Observantines introduced into Scotland by that king.

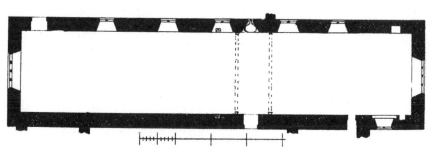

FIG. 1290.—Greyfriars' Church, Elgin. Plan.

Their first convent was in Edinburgh, where these friars were established in 1446. This convent was followed by one in St. Andrews, and a third house was settled at Aberdeen in 1450. The order then extended to Elgin, where it was introduced by John Innes, a member of a well-known Morayshire family, in 1479. The Franciscans, having no rentals to be taxed and no lands to alienate, probably fled when the

* Information regarding the history of this church is derived from a paper on the subject by the Rev. J. Cooper, M.A., in the *Transactions of the Aberdeen Ecclesiological Society, 1891.*

Reformation came. Their convent was plundered by Montrose, but the church was not demolished, and still stands with its four walls complete, though sadly damaged. The domestic buildings have been obliterated or converted to modern uses.

The church (Fig. 1290) is a simple oblong structure, 110 feet in length by 22 feet in width internally. It had an entrance door for the public in the north wall, near the west end. From the marks in the wall above it (Fig. 1291) there seems to have been a wooden porch or awning over the doorway.

The church has been well lighted with large traceried windows (see Fig. 1291) in the east and west end walls, and with six side windows in

FIG. 1291.—Greyfriars' Church, Elgin. View from North-West.

the north wall and one in the south wall. Each of the end windows had three mullions with intersecting tracery in the arch, and the side windows were all divided into two lights by a central mullion, with two curved divisions in the arch. Near the centre of the building, and on both sides, there occur two small windows, one over the other, the lower one being single with ogee head, and the upper one having a central mullion. These windows have evidently been for the purpose of lighting the rood screen and loft. The lower windows would light the space under the rood loft, where there was no doubt an altar, and the upper windows the gallery or space over the screen. The corbels which carried the loft can still be traced on both sides of the church. A piscina in each of the side walls, close to the screen, shows that there were altars placed against it. In the north window, adjoining the screen, there is a stone sink, probably used by the priests as a lavatory. At the east end of the church there is an ambry in each of the side walls, and a window in the south wall to light the sanctuary. Under it is a recess, probably used as a sedilia. The conventual buildings have evidently been built to the south of the church. The junctions of four walls forming buildings on two sides of a courtyard still remain, and in the south wall of the church, between the above, may be observed the corbels which carried the roof of the cloister walk. There are also two doors from this side into the church. The structure is of a plain and simple style, corresponding to the character of the mendicant friars who occupied it. It was doubtless erected soon after the Observantines were introduced in 1479, and bears the character of the architecture of the period.

After the Reformation the church was no longer used for service. Criminal Courts sat in it till the middle of the seventeenth century, and it also served as a place of meeting of the crafts or trades in Elgin. Afterwards it became a place for Episcopal services, and it is now the property of the Convent of St. Mary of Mercy.

GREYFRIARS' CHURCH, Aberdeen.

This structure, which took the place of an older one, was built by the well-known prelate Bishop Gavin Dunbar * at his own expense, between the years 1518 and 1532. Its architect was Alexander Galloway, parson

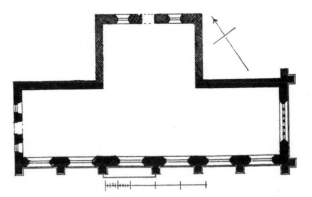

Fig. 1292.—Greyfriars' Church, Aberdeen. Plan.

of Kinkell, a well-known Churchman, who is specially referred to in the description of the later church. This church was dedicated to the Virgin.

* *View of the Diocese of Aberdeen*, p. 200.

At the Reformation it was bestowed on Marischal College, and was thereafter known as the College Kirk. It was at first an oblong structure (Fig.

FIG. 1293.—Greyfriars' Church, Aberdeen. View from South-West.

1292) * with massive buttresses, but in 1768 the north projection was
built, and the length of the church was reduced by 20 feet,† and probably

* We are indebted to A. Marshall Mackenzie, A.R.S.A., architect, Aberdeen, for
the plan and measured drawings of this church.

† *New History of Aberdeenshire*, Vol. I. p. 157.

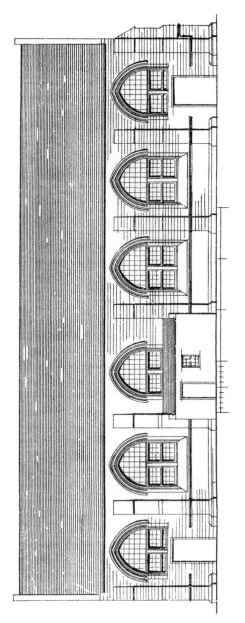

Fig. 1294.—Greyfriars' Church, Aberdeen. South Elevation.

the west end (shown in Fig. 1293) was then erected. There was formerly a spire or steeple, probably at the west end. The church now extends to six bays in the length (Fig. 1294), divided by buttresses, and having a pointed window in each bay. It is fitted up with galleries in the most incongruous style, but has several good examples of carved bench ends and other wood-work (Fig. 1295).

The chief feature of the building is the east end (Figs. 1296 and 1297), with its immense window, one of the largest examples of tracery now remaining in Scotland. It is divided into seven lights, and although it is of the simplest design, being merely a series of intersecting arches, an agreeable variety is obtained by stopping several of the bars near the top from running their full course, and thus obtaining larger openings, which contrast with the others of smaller size. A similar kind of design was very frequent in

FIG. 1295.—Greyfriars' Church, Aberdeen. Carved Bench End.

late work in Scotland, but none of the other examples possess the size and elegance of this one. The delicate detail of its slightly arched transome is noteworthy. The buttresses (see Fig. 1297) also are of a good form ; indeed, it is remarkable, considering its lateness, how pure and simple the details are.

In the process of extending the college, it was contemplated to

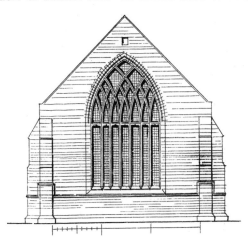

FIG. 1296.—Greyfriars' Church, Aberdeen. Window in East End.

demolish this church, but fortunately, we believe, that intention has been abandoned.

FIG. 1297.—Greyfriars' Church, Aberdeen.   East Wall and Window.

THE PRIORY CHURCH OF ST. CLEMENT, ROWDIL, HARRIS, INVERNESS-SHIRE.

Amongst the numerous remains of ancient ecclesiastical structures still surviving in the Western Isles, the Church of St. Clement, situated near the south point of Harris, holds a prominent place, being one of the very few ancient structures in that region which are not ruinous, and are still in use for public worship.

The origin of the church is uncertain, but it is supposed to have been originally founded by an emissary from Iona, and to have fallen into decay during the occupation of the Norsemen. It is thought that the necessities of the monastery, thus arising, were probably relieved by David I. " from the revenues of the newly instituted Abbey of Holyrood House," and that this may have given the monks of the latter the claim to St. Clement's, which they afterwards substantiated.*

It is agreed amongst writers on the subject † that the church was restored or rebuilt by Sir Alexander M'Leod, Rector of Harris, who seems to have used the materials of an older building in the restoration. This is evident from the random manner in which some carved figures are built into the walls of the west tower.

Mr. Ross points out that Alaster Crotach or Humpback had, in 1498, a charter from King James IV. for the hereditary lands of Ardmanich, &c., and that he was succeeded by his son William, who died in 1553.

The *Old Statistical Account* informs us that the church was repaired by the said Alexander M'Leod, who died (as the inscription on his tomb in the church bears) in 1527.

Of the domestic buildings of the priory not a stone now remains. The church was burnt and was repaired in " 1784 by the late patriotic Alex. M'Leod, Esq., of Harris. After the church was roofed and slated, and the materials for furnishing it within laid up in it to a considerable value, it unfortunately took fire at night through the carelessness of the carpenters, who had left a live coal in it among the timbers. So zealous, however, was this friend of religion and mankind in his design of repairing it, that by his orders and at his expense it was soon after this accident roofed, and it is now [1794], though left unfinished since the time of his death, used as one of the principal places in the parish for celebrating divine service."

The church was again repaired in 1787. About 1866 it had once more become dilapidated, and was repaired under the supervision of

* *Old Statistical Account*, Vol. x. p. 378.

† See paper by Alexander Ross, architect, Inverness; *Proceedings of the Society of Antiquaries of Scotland*, 1884-85, p. 118. See also Muir's *Characteristics*, p. 69.

Mr. Alexander Ross, architect, Inverness, to whose kindness we are indebted for permission to use the description and illustrations in his

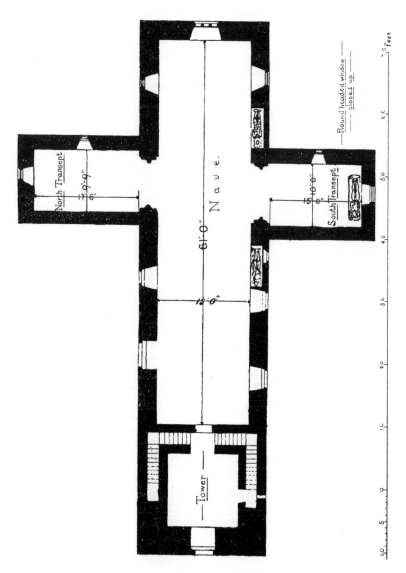

Fig. 1298.—Priory Church of St. Clement. Plan.

article on St. Clement's in the *Proceedings of the Society of Antiquaries of Scotland*, above referred to.

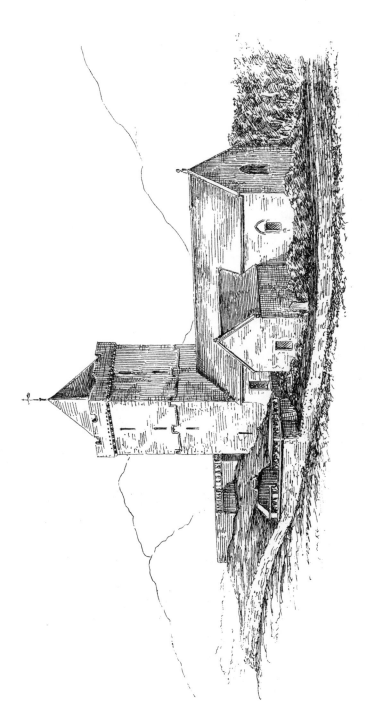

FIG. 1299.—Priory Church of St. Clement. View from South-East.

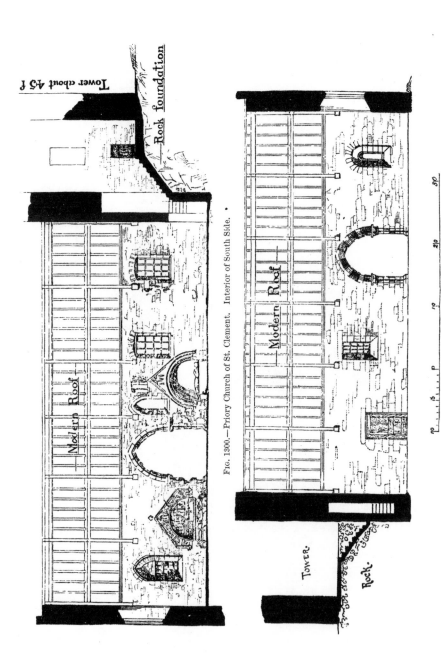

FIG. 1300.—Priory Church of St. Clement. Interior of South Side.

FIG. 1301.—Priory Church of St. Clement. Interior of North Side.

The building is chiefly remarkable from containing an elaborately sculptured monument to Alexander M'Leod of Dunvegan or Harris.

The structure (Fig. 1298) is small and is cruciform in plan. It has a square tower at the west end, the full width of the nave, which is founded on a rock at a higher level than the nave (Fig. 1299).

The choir is not architecturally distinguished from the nave, and the whole building is 61 feet in length (internally) by 15 feet in width.

It has a square east end, and is lighted by a large traceried east window, and by two small windows in the side walls. The former is

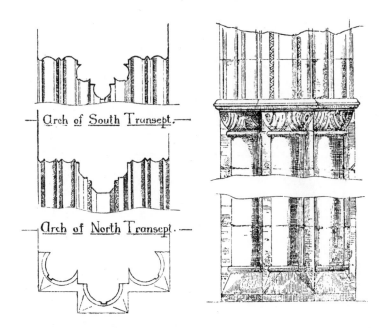

FIG. 1302.—Priory Church of St. Clement. Responds and Mouldings at Entrance to Transepts.

pointed, and is divided by two mullions into three lights. The tracery in the arch-head consists of a circle divided by six radiating bars.

The church (Fig. 1300) has two square-headed windows and two pointed windows in the south wall, and one square and one round-headed window in the north wall (Fig. 1301), and the entrance doorway, which is in the north wall, is also square lintelled.

The transept consists of a north and south chapel, which are not exactly opposite one another. They have square-headed windows in the north, south, and east walls. Each chapel is entered from the nave by a moulded and pointed arch (see Figs. 1300 and 1301) springing from responds. The latter have both in their section and caps (Fig. 1302) a certain resemblance to Norman work. As pointed out by Mr. Muir, the details indicate the second pointed period, "though, as in the mouldings at Iona, the adoption of forms resembling Norman and first pointed has given to it an appearance of greater antiquity."

FIG. 1303.—Priory Church of St. Clement. Monument in Choir (East of South Transept).

The monuments are the most remarkable features in the building. These are three in number, two of them being placed against the south wall, one in the choir and one in the nave (see Fig. 1300) on either side of the arch leading into the south transept. The third monument is at the south end of the south transept.

The monument in the choir is the most elaborate, being specially rich in sculpture. Its form (Fig. 1303) is peculiar, having, in addition to the usual recessed arch, a sloping gable-shaped moulding, which encloses the design on top, and is continued perpendicularly down each side. The space between the arch and the enclosing moulding is divided into nine panels, each containing a distinct carving of figures. That in the apex represents God the Father, holding between his knees a cross bearing a figure of the Crucifixion. Each of the panels at the sides contains one or two figures of angels waving censers, and saints holding scrolls. The wall

FIG. 1304.—Priory Church of St. Clement. Effigy of Alexander M'Leod of Harris.

at the back of the arch is also divided into panels, containing sculptures in three rows. In the upper row the panels comprise angels censing with a star in the centre, and at each side an angel holding a candle. In the central row the chief panel contains the Virgin and Child, supported by a bishop or abbot on each side, one of whom holds a skull. These figures are each enclosed in a Gothic canopy. The left panel shows the faint outline of a castle, and that on the right a galley (the M'Leod arms). The third row exhibits several panels. That on the left is a hunting scene, a knight with sword and spear, followed by attendants holding dogs in leash. The next panel contains three stags, well carved. To the right of this is a panel representing an angel holding up a pair of scales to weigh the

FIG. 1305.—Priory Church of St. Clement. Effigy in South Transept.

souls of the departed, in which process he is interfered with by a demon. A similar scene is carved on one of the pier caps in the choir of Iona Cathedral (see Fig. 985).

To the right is a long panel containing the following inscription in Gothic letters :—

HIC · LOCULUS · CŌPOSUIT · · · · ALLEXĀDER · FILIUS · VILM̄I · MAC · CLOD · DÑO · DE · DŪVEGAN · ANNO · DÑI · Mᵒ · CCCCCᵒ · XXVIIIᵒ

The meaning of this apparently is that Alexander, son of William MacLeod of Dunvegan, made this tomb A.D. 1528.

III.   2 A

On the pedestal under the arch lies the effigy of the said Alexander M'Leod of Dunvegan (Fig. 1304), clad in full armour, and holding a long sword with cross hilt. The effigy is unfortunately much decayed. The head rests on a pillow with an animal above, and the feet rest on a lion. At the side of the monument a lion encloses the tomb.

The style of the carving and the subjects represented recall the sculptures at Iona. The figures of the abbot and bishop are similar in style to that of the abbess at the Iona Nunnery, and the scene of the angel weighing souls with a demon interfering occurs on one of the caps in the Iona

FIG. 1306.—Priory Church of St. Clement. East Elevation.

choir. The division of the flat surfaces into panels, each containing a separate subject, is characteristic of Celtic decoration. The hunting scene and the ship are also common in Celtic work. The peculiar Celtic foliage of Iona is here wanting. Enough, however, exists to associate the style of the work with that of the rest of the Western Isles, while the Gothic influence is also very distinct.

The date is fixed by the inscription, and the introduction of the nail-head ornament shows the revival here, as at Iona, of earlier forms, as above pointed out by Mr. Muir.

The tomb in the recessed arch to the west of the south transept is of much simpler design than the corresponding one to the east above described. It consists (see Fig. 1300) of a semicircular moulded arch with a hood moulding stopped on carved corbels at each end. Over the upper part of the hood a triangular space is enclosed with a moulding, finished at the apex with a fleur-de-lys. This triangular space contains an oblong panel, much decayed, exhibiting the Crucifixion, with a figure on each side. The effigy "represents a man in armour with high peaked bassinet and camail over a habergeon reaching to the knee. The nature of the defences of the feet and legs is not indicated. He holds a long, straight, cross-hilted sword in front, the pommel reaching to the breast, and the point placed between the feet. A dagger hangs at his left side, but the military belt is wanting." *

Fig. 1307.—Priory Church of St. Clement. North-East Elevation.

The third tomb is at the end of the south transept. The effigy (Fig. 1305) is somewhat similar to the last described, but is much wasted by exposure.

A remarkable recessed tomb having some analogy with those at Rowdil is described and figured in a paper by Professor Norman Macpherson in the *Proceedings of the Society of Antiquaries of Scotland*, Vol. XII. p. 583. It consists of a plain round arch in the north wall of the ruined Church of St. Donan in the island of Eigg. In the wall at the back of the recess is a large square panel containing sculptures, which "afford an interesting example of Celtic notions of heraldry." These

* See Mr. Ross's Paper, p. 125.

sculptures appear to represent the Clanranald shield, having in the place of the first quarter a hand grasping a cross, in the second what appears to be a lion, in the third a galley, and in the fourth a castle. A tree, like a laurel, springs from the base and stretches to the top, with a bird on the highest branch.

FIG. 1308.—Priory Church of St. Clement. Figure, &c., in West Elevation.

The external appearance of St. Clement's is shown by Fig. 1299 and by the elevations (Figs. 1306 and 1307). The latter also show the tower and the peculiar carved heads and other figures, above alluded to, as probable insertions from an older structure. Fig. 1308 shows the small figure of a saint, inserted over the cabled string course on the west side of the tower, and the narrow cusped window above it. The north elevation (see Fig. 1307) and the sections (see Figs. 1300 and 1301) explain the mode in which the tower is built upon a higher level than the church.

ORONSAY PRIORY,* ARGYLLSHIRE.

Notwithstanding the very numerous small churches and chapels found in the Western Isles,† there are comparatively few remains of monasteries. The original Celtic religious establishments were, doubtless, monastic in their form and structure, but of convents in the later sense, corresponding with those so common on the mainland, few traces are now to be seen. Next to the great Abbey of the Isles at Iona and the nunnery on the same island, the largest monastic establishment in the Western Isles of which the structures survive is the Priory of Oronsay.

This island lies about ten miles west from Jura, and can be most conveniently reached from Portaskaig, in Islay. The isle is about

* We are indebted to Mr. William Galloway, architect, for the Plan of this priory and for most of the description of the buildings ; while our thanks are due to Mr. J. Harvey Brown for the photographs from which the views are copied.

† See Vol. I. p. 65.

two and three-quarter miles broad from east to west by about two miles from north to south. It stands at the south end of the larger island of Colonsay, from which it is separated by a narrow channel, dry at low tide.

It is traditionally narrated that St. Columba and his companion, St. Oran, landed on Oronsay after leaving Ireland; but finding that the latter country could still be seen from the highest point of the island, they forsook it and sailed to Iona. St. Oran, however, gave his name to the island, and, together with Colonsay, it seems, from the numerous remains of churches which once existed on these islands, to have been a sacred locality, the remains of nine old churches and the sites of three more—ten in Colonsay and two in Oronsay—being still traceable. The most important appears to have been the Monastery of Kiloran, in Colonsay, of which no remains now exist. Next to it was the Priory of Oronsay. This priory of Canons Regular of St. Augustine appears to have been founded in the fourteenth century by the Lord of the Isles as a cell of the Abbey of Holyrood at Edinburgh.

The priory is situated at the extreme west end of the island, on the lowermost slope of the *Beinn Oronsay*, just short of the point where its rugged cliffs front the Atlantic.

The general arrangement of the buildings (Fig. 1309) is peculiar. The ground slopes rapidly from north to south, necessarily carrying the drainage with it; yet, contrary to the usual custom, the cloisters and residential buildings were placed to the north of the church. Exclusive of projections at the north-east and south-west angles, and a mortuary chapel on the south, the structures occupy a parallelogram about 87 feet from north to south, by 65 feet from east to west. The latter length is also that of the church proper, which occupies the south side of the square, but has at the west end a narthex about 15 feet square internally, which projects beyond the general range of the buildings. The walls of the narthex are now level with those of the church, but as there are roughly hewn corbel stones for carrying a floor overhead, it is probable this is only the lower stage of a bell-tower, of which the upper part has been long since demolished. The greater thickness of the walls and two sadly injured freestone buttresses on its south face (Fig. 1310) favour this idea. Entrance is obtained by a doorway with a plain pointed freestone arch, having a hood moulding close to the westmost buttress (see Fig. 1310). The church is, internally, nearly 18 feet in width; and at the right hand, on entering, there remains the solid foundation of a stone stair leading to a tribune or organ gallery, recesses for the ends of massive beams to carry it being still visible, together with rough rubble corbelling on either side.

On the left is a narrow doorway, neatly formed with thin schist stones, leading to the cloisters. Internally the church is entirely devoid of architectural decoration, but an extensive range of stalls, of which traces still exist, and other wood-work, including an open roof, must have redeemed an otherwise bald interior, into which very little light can have been admitted. The principal source of light was a 5 feet wide window at the east end (Fig. 1311), divided by mullions into three lanciform lights,

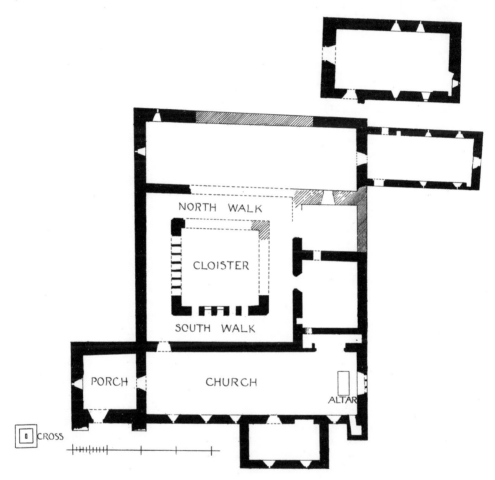

NORTH WALK

CLOISTER

SOUTH WALK

PORCH

CHURCH

ALTAR

CROSS

Fig. 1309.—Oronsay Priory. Plan.

the pointed arch-heads of which run up to the main arch. The other gable, seen on the right in Fig. 1311, is modern, and forms the entrance porch to what may have formerly been the chapter house, but which has been appropriated, in recent times, as a burial-place by the proprietor of the island. Apart from this there were only three windows in the nave, two very small, and another rather longer with a cusped head, all formed in freestone, and on the extreme east end of the south wall near the altar a square-headed window with slab lintel and sill. Between these windows a

Fig. 1310.—Oronsay Priory. Cross and South Side of Narthex and Church.

plain schist doorway gives access to the mortuary chapel of the M'Duffies or M'Fies, which is about 25 feet long by 12 feet wide over the walls. These are unbonded into the south wall of the church, and were covered with a plain lean-to roof, in which there was evidently a priest's apartment. The chapel is lit from the south by two small windows, and in a recess on the north side is the burial-place of Abbot M'Duffie, covered with a carved slab representing the abbot fully vested, with his right hand raised in benediction, and a pastoral staff in his left. Pennant says:—
" In the same place is a stone enriched with foliage, a stag surrounded with dogs, and a ship with full sail ; round which is inscribed ' Hic jacet

Fig. 1311.—Oronsay Priory. East End of Church.

Murchardus Macdufie de Collonsa An. Do. 1539 Mense Mart Ora me ille, Ammen.'"* Beyond this chapel, at the south-east angle of the church, is a singularly massive buttress, at the bottom of which, on the level of the floor and accessible by a narrow opening from the interior of the church, is a curious ambry about 3 feet cube, strongly lintelled overhead, and designed, no doubt, for the safe keeping of the church treasure, but is now desecrated as a "bone-hole." The altar still remains built of freestone, evidently reused from some previous building.

On the north side of the chancel the arrangement is very peculiar.

* Pennant, Vol. II. p. 271.

An opening about 8 feet wide, with a plain pointed freestone arch (Fig. 1312) resting on schist impost caps, gives access to a kind of trance or passage, having an ambry at the ground level on the left and a blocked up window on the right. It is formed between the north wall of the church and the south end of the chapter house, which is gabled independently of the church. Its only apparent use may have been as a sacristy. It is roofed in by large flat stones, with a rapid slope to the east. The east range of buildings is pretty complete, except on the north, where the gable fell some years ago. On the ground floor a large apartment, 19 feet 6 inches long by 15 feet 4 inches wide, with a doorway entering on the east cloister walk, was no doubt the chapter house.

The range of domestic buildings on the north has been sadly ruined, this having been the point where entry was obtained, in recent times, for the removal of materials, and thus of the north and south walls only fragments remain. A massive wall, still happily intact, encloses the cloister on the west. The internal area is rather over 41 feet square, with cloister walks about 7 feet broad, and the arcading presents some very singular features. The south arcade (Fig. 1313), which is evidently the most ancient, is composed of five low narrow arches with circular heads, very neatly turned with thin schist slabs, without any freestone or architectural dressing of any kind. The other three arcades were evidently part of a later restoration, and the peculiar form in which they were constructed is evidently due to the nature of the materials employed, viz., schist slabs of the same quality as that used for the sculptured slabs.

When Martin visited the island in the latter part of the seventeenth century, the three arcades and the enclosing walls were quite complete. A century later, in 1772, Pennant found the north arcade demolished with the exception of the end arches, while the east and west arcades remained intact. These subsequently disappeared also, and it was not until 1883 that Mr. Galloway found, scattered throughout the church and churchyard, sufficient materials to complete the restoration of one arcade. This was accordingly done on the west side (see Fig. 1313) in that year. Amongst the shafts and "pillars" found there were happily both of those mentioned by Martin as bearing inscriptions. The hewn work of these arcades was formed entirely of the peculiar kind of schist used in the sculptured crosses and memorial stones in the Western Highlands, and it may have been the facility of obtaining this material in the slab, rather than the cube form, which determined the special character of the arcading. Each arcade had openings or arches nearly 30 inches from centre to centre, there being seven in the east and west arcades, and probably one or two more in the north arcade. They were built with slab shafts, averaging 2 feet 10 inches high by 1 foot broad, and 2 or 3 inches thick, with neatly moulded and socketed caps and bases. On these

Fig. 1312.—Oronsay Priory. Arch on West Side of Church.

FIG. 1818.—Oronsay Priory. South and West Arcades of Cloister.

there rested the slabs, shaped at each end so as to meet exactly in the middle, thus forming a straight lined arch, and the haunches were filled up with rubble. With this both Martin's and Pennant's descriptions exactly agree.

The north range of the buildings, which no doubt contained the refectory and dormitories, has been too much dilapidated to admit of any intelligible description. In a line with it, however, and extending eastward beyond the priory square (see Plan), there is a small chapel of very early character, built entirely in rubble, without any freestone dressings. It is 17 feet over the walls and 33 feet in breadth ; but for no apparent reason the west gable is slewed round to the south, making an inequality of 2 feet in the length of the sides. There has been a wide window in the east gable, but owing to the demolition of the wall its character cannot be judged. There are two small windows in the north side and one in the south, mere slits with no provisions for frames or glazing. There is an entrance doorway on the south side at the west end and a priest's door at the east. On the north side there is a very small door nearly opposite that of the entrance on the south.

The foundations of the altar still remain, and a line of stones still indicates the position of the chancel rail. The base of the pulpit remains on the north side, and at the west end there has been a tribune or organ gallery, which has been accessible by a door in the east gable of the priory buildings. In this gable, on the ground floor, an archway has been formed 6 feet 8 inches in width, with a plain pointed rubble arch, which seems to have been subsequently filled in, and a square-headed doorway of much smaller size substituted.

Immediately to the north of this chapel, and separated from it by an 8 foot wide passage, is a most interesting example of a monastic barn and byre, 39 feet in length by 22 feet in breadth. It is an excellent specimen of rubble building with freestone dressings to the windows, &c., in the same style as the church, and may be coeval with the later restoration. The windows are small, and on the north side close to the ground are openings for the discharge of refuse from the byre. In the south-east angle a small chamber has been formed for the herd, with a little eyelet and ambry, and it would no doubt be cut off by partitioning from the other occupants. At the south-west angle there is a small door opening inwards, and some indications that a chamber had been formed between the building itself and the north wall of the priory. At the south wall head (internally) there has been inserted a 4 or 5 foot long schist slab, with a quaint human head carved in the centre. It serves no purpose where it is, and must evidently have been a relic of some older structure. There can be no doubt there was a doorway to the west, but, if so, the present entrance shows no traces of it. The building is still roofed, and in use.

Pennant states that the church "contains the tombs of numbers of the ancient islanders, two of warriors recumbent (7 feet long), a flattery perhaps of the sculptor to give to future ages exalted notions of their prowess. Besides, there are scattered over the floor lesser figures of heroes, priests, and females, the last seemingly of some order, and near them is a figure cut in stone of full size, apparently an abbess." *

These figures, as illustrated by Pennant, strongly recall the corresponding monuments at Iona and elsewhere throughout the West Highlands and Islands.

The slabs have now been set up against the walls of the church (see Fig. 1311), while others still exist in the burying-ground outside.

Close to the south-west angle of the narthex stands the celebrated Oronsay cross † (see Fig. 1310). It stands on mason work covered by a slab 3 feet by 3 feet 3 inches, perforated with a hole in which the cross is fixed. The shaft is 12 feet in height. On the west face there is a Crucifixion on the disc, and the shaft is carved on both sides with the usual Celtic ornament in round panels. The inscription near the base is now illegible.

ST. MAELRUBBA, LOCH EYNORT, Skye.

The site of the ancient Church of St. Maelrubba, at the head of Loch Eynort in the south of Skye, is now occupied by a more recent ruin.‡ A very interesting relic of the ancient church is, however, preserved in the remarkable font (Figs. 1314 and 1315), which, after some wandering and neglect, has at last found a suitable resting-place in the Museum of the Society of Antiquaries of Scotland in Edinburgh. An account of its transference from the shore of Loch Eynort to the Museum is given by Mr. J. Russell Walker, in a paper on "Scottish Baptismal Fonts" in the *Proceedings* of that Society, 1886-7, p. 412. The bowl is circular, both externally and internally, and the basin is 1 foot 6½ inches in diameter and 13 inches deep. The circumference is divided into four equal parts by four figures representing—(1) The Crucifixion, (2) The Blessed Virgin with the Child, (3) a mitred bishop in full canonicals with a crosier in his left hand, and (4) St. Michael slaying the dragon. The panels to the right and left of the Crucifixion are filled with interlaced work, and those to the right and left of the bishop with inscriptions not now legible. On the lower sloping parts between the figures are floral designs. The font is of hornblende gneiss, and the carving is remarkable in that hard material. There seem

* Pennant, Vol. II. p. 270.
† Figured by Pennant, and in Stuart's *Sculptured Stones of Scotland*, plates 38 and 39.
‡ T. S. Muir, *Ecclesiological Notes*, p. 34.

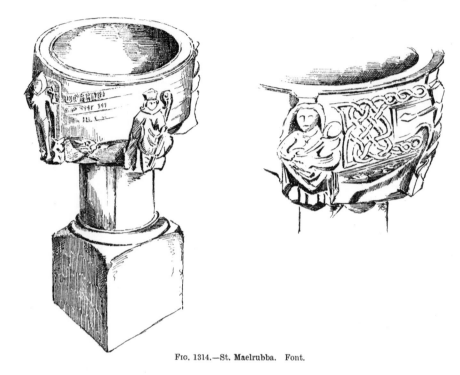

Fig. 1314.—St. Maelrubba. Font.

to be the remains of four caps, as if there had been four shafts to support the bowl.

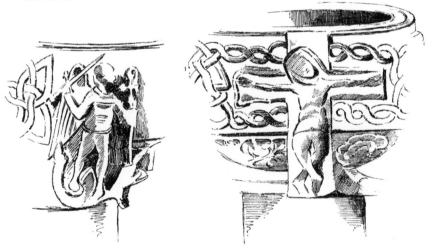

Fig. 1315.—St. Maelrubba. Font.

The carving of this font is a striking illustration of the peculiar mixture of Celtic and Gothic work, of which numerous specimens are above noticed in connection with the structures of the Western Highlands and Islands, as at Iona, Rowdil, &c.

The examples of the third or late pointed period of Gothic architecture given above sufficiently indicate the progress of the style during the period, and show its gradual decline.

The following examples of this period, being for the most part fragmentary, are arranged alphabetically by counties.

KINKELL CHURCH, ABERDEENSHIRE.

A ruinous building, very prettily situated on the left bank of the ·Don, about three miles north from Kintore. Kinkell was once, as its name signifies, the head church of the district, and had under it' six subordinate churches. In 1754 the Lords Commissioners for plantation of kirks annexed one third of the parish of Kinkell to that of Kintore, the remainder going to augment the parish of Keithhall. In 1771 the Church

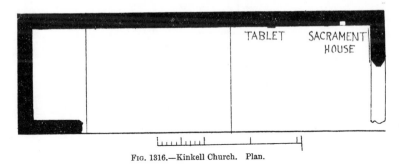

TABLET   SACRAMENT HOUSE

FIG. 1316.—Kinkell Church. Plan.

of Kinkell was unroofed in order to supply materials for use in the Church of Keithhall. The Church of Kinkell was remarkable for its fine design and workmanship, and contained several monuments and sculptures; but it is now sadly ruined, only the north wall and parts of the east and west walls remaining.

The edifice (Fig. 1316) was a simple oblong 73 feet in length by 18 feet 6 inches in width internally. There has been a large east window, only one jamb of which partially remains, and there are no other window or door openings preserved. The north wall seems to have been entirely without openings. A large modern burial vault has been erected in the centre of the church.

One or two features of the former fine ornamentation of the structure still remain *in situ,* but other portions have been removed, and are now to be found elsewhere, as will be pointed out.

In the north wall near the east end is a fine sacrament house (Fig. 1317). The design consists, as usual in these details, of a buttress on each side of the ambry, with crocketed finials, the carving of which is of a late style. Between the pinnacles is a panel which seems to have been

FIG. 1317.—Kinkell Church. Sacrament House.

ornamented with the usual monstrance supported by two angels, but the carving is nearly obliterated. Above this panel there runs a small crenelated parapet, supported by a double row of corbels. Immediately over the parapet is an oblong panel, which doubtless contained a Crucifixion or similar sculpture, but it is now empty.

To the right and left of the pinnacles are two panels, each containing a ribbon of different design. That on the left bears the inscription " Hic

EST SVATV," and that on the right the words "CORPS DE VIGIE NATUM," which may be read, "Hic est servatum corpus de Virgine Natum."

On the base of the ambry are the letters ANO. DNI. 1528, in the centre MEORARE, and on the right the initials A. and G. united by a cord. The letter G. also occurs at the end of the inscription in the right hand panel, and is probably a repetition of the last letter of the initials A. G.

The base is supported on a continuous corbel carved with foliage, and has in the centre a shield, bearing a lion rampant.

The initials A. G. twice repeated and the date, together with the late style of the work, point to the sacrament house having been designed by Alexander Galloway, who was rector of Kinkell in 1528, and who was also the architect of the first bridge of ten arches over the Dee at Aberdeen.

Another panel (Fig. 1318) is built into the north wall of the church a little to the west of the sacrament house. It contains a Crucifixion, with a figure of the Virgin Mary on one side and an angel on the other. The initials of Alexander Galloway occur three times on this sculpture, and the date 1525.

FIG. 1318.—Kinkell Church.
Panel in North Wall of Church.

The font which was removed from the Church of Kinkell long stood in a garden, but is now restored and placed in St. John's Episcopal Church, Aberdeen. Of the original font only the granite basin now exists. It is octagonal in form, and each face is illustrated with one or more sacred emblems, as shown in Fig. 1319, except one face, on which occur the initials of Alexander Galloway, parson of Kinkell. He was one of the best known ecclesiastics in Scotland before the Reformation, and gifted this font to the Church of Kinkell. Galloway appears to have been one of the most able public men of his time, of whom Boece says,* "He was so great a favourite

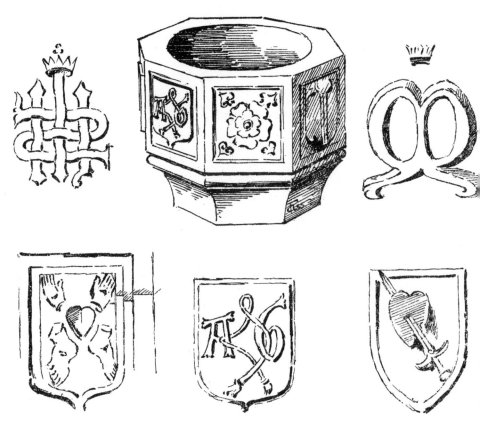

Fig. 1319.—Kinkell Church. Font.

with the Bishop (Elphinston) that none of his concerns of moment were transacted without him."

SACRAMENT HOUSE, KINTORE, Aberdeenshire.

Another piece of sculpture (Fig. 1320) said to have been removed from the Church of Kinkell is preserved at the Church of Kintore. It was at one time built into the outer wall of the Church of Kintore, but it has now been removed for better preservation into the interior. It

* "Life of Bishop Elphinston," *Orme's History,* p. 26.

originally consisted of two parts, the lower portion containing the ambry for the reception of the sacramental elements, and the upper portion being enriched with a beautifully carved bas-relief, representing a monstrance of elaborate tabernacle work, supported by two angels, and crowned with a sculptured crucifix. The ambry is now wanting, except the lintel, which bears the words Jesus Maria. Over the lintel is a panel which no doubt formerly contained sculpture, now removed. The whole design is surrounded with a frame composed of a series of baluster shaped shafts, covered with flat foliage of a Renaissance character.

Whether this decorated work came from Kinkell or not, it evidently belongs to the period when that church was built, being of the latest Gothic design, which prevailed immediately before the Reformation.

FIG. 1320.—Sacrament House, Kintore. Old Monument built into Wall.

ST. ADAMNAN'S CHAPEL, ABERDEENSHIRE.

A small chapel situated near Leask, some two or three miles inland from the old Castle of Slains. It is surrounded by what appears to have been a churchyard, but is now covered with stunted trees. The chapel (Fig. 1321) is filled with its own ruins and is utterly uncared for. The walls are fairly entire for a height of about 7 feet, while the east gable is nearly complete, and contains a pointed window about 7 feet wide, which was probably filled with tracery. The outside jambs are gone, but the inner splayed face of the arch is still entire. In the east wall are the remains of what may have been a piscina, and there is an ambry in the south wall adjoining. There are a window in the south wall and two openings of some kind in the north, with a narrow window high up in the west gable. The doorway is on the south side, but its jambs are gone, and only the bar hole remains to indicate that it was the doorway. The church measures, externally, 45 feet from east to west by 23 feet 3 inches from north to south.

Not much is recorded about this chapel. In the *View of the Diocese of Aberdeen* * it is referred to as the Parish Church of Fervie, "dedicated to St. Fidamnan, Abbot of Icolmkill."

From the charters preserved at Slains, we learn that "a letter of manrent by the Lard of Essilmont is dated 'at the Chapell of Laske' on

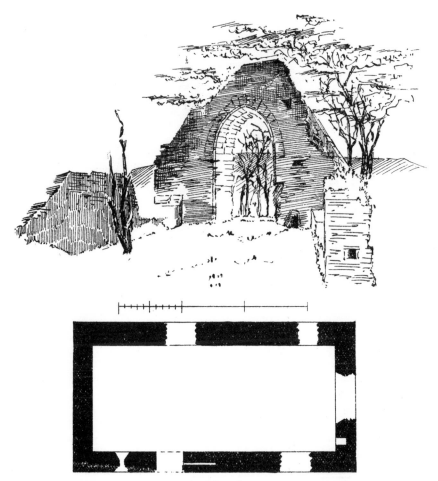

FIG. 1321.—St. Adamnan's Chapel. Plan and Interior View, looking East.

the 11th of September 1499." † Probably the church was erected during the foregoing century.

* Spalding Club, p. 388.
† *Antiquities of Aberdeen and Banff*, Vol. III. p. 147.

ARDCHATTAN CHURCH, Argyleshire.

Slight fragments of this ancient church are to be found on the north shore of Loch Etive, about four miles from Bonawe Ferry, near Taynuilt Station. This priory, dedicated to St. Modan, is said to have been founded in 1231 by Duncan Mackowle or MacDougal of Lorn, for monks of the order of Vallis Caulium. The remains (Fig. 1322) consist of the north, east, and west walls of what has been an oblong chamber, and apparently

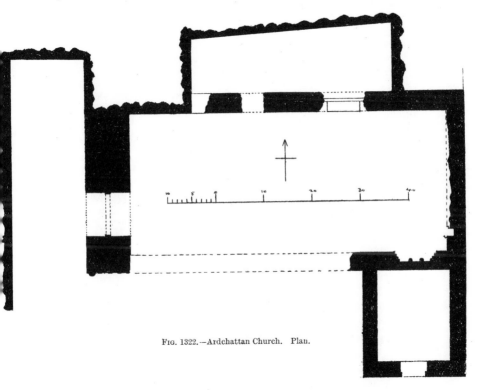

Fig. 1322.—Ardchattan Church. Plan.

the choir of a church. It measures 66 feet in length by 28 feet in width. In the small part of the south wall which survives there is a sedilia (Fig. 1323) with three seats. Each seat is marked by a sharply pointed arch, and the whole are enclosed in a deeply moulded semicircular arch. Some fragments, including a piscina, are now built into the back of the seats, but these are modern insertions. At the right hand termination of the large arch a small lion is sculptured, which recalls some of the carved work at Iona, and at the bases of the smaller arches carved leaves are introduced. There has also been an ambry in the east wall (see Plan).

At the west end of the building a double wall 9 feet in thickness has been erected. It is pierced with a round-headed archway, and has projecting jambs in the centre. This archway now leads into an open courtyard connected with a mansion. Its former use is difficult to determine.

To the north of the choir is preserved the outline of an irregular structure, which may have been a sacristy. It is 42 feet long by 14 feet wide at the east end, and 11 feet wide at the west end, and has been connected with the choir by a doorway and two windows. The exterior walls are now nearly demolished.

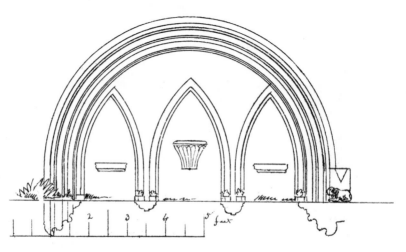

Fig. 1323.—Ardchattan Church. Sedilia.

To the south of the choir is an open space enclosed with a wall 18 feet long by 15 feet wide, evidently erected as a burial-place. It has an arched entrance gateway at the south end. On the keystone of the arch are the letters C. K. and the date 1614. Lying within the choir are several monuments, one being in the recess of the larger window opening into the sacristy. Two are monuments of priors of the Macdougal family, and bear the dates of 1500 and 1502. The inscriptions have given rise to much discussion.

In 1644 the Macdonalds, led by Colkitto, burnt and destroyed the priory.

KILMUN CHURCH, ARGYLESHIRE.

On the north shore of the Holy Loch, about one mile and a half from Strone, stand the small ruins of the ancient Collegiate establishment of

Kilmun. According to Dr. Skene a Columban establishment was here founded by St. Fintan Munnu of Teach in Munnu in Ireland. The district of Cowal, in which this establishment was situated, was long in the possession of the Lamont Clan, but was subsequently acquired by the Campbells. The church had, in the thirteenth century, passed into lay hands, " as, between 1230 and 1246, Duncan, son of Ferchan, and his nephew Laidman, son of Malcolm, grant to the monks of Paisley lands which they and their ancestors had at Kilmun, with the whole right of patronage in the church of Kilmun." *

In 1442 a collegiate establishment was founded by Duncan Campbell of Lochow, for a provost and six prebendaries. The founder was buried

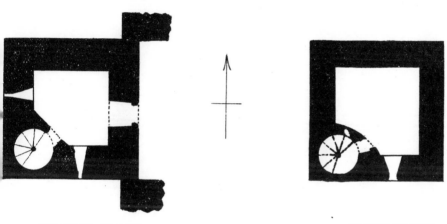

GROUND FLOOR.   FIRST FLOOR.

FIG. 1324.—Kilmun Church. Plans.

here in 1453, and Kilmun has since then continued to be the burial-place of the Argyll family. The great Marquis of Argyll was interred here in 1661, and the mausoleum of the family stands in the churchyard.

Of the College Church only a small portion remains, a modern church having been erected on the site of the old structure.

The remaining portion (Fig. 1324) consists of a tower about 20 feet square and about 40 feet in height. The basement floor is vaulted, and contains a doorway which entered from the west end of the church, and small loops in each of the south and west sides. That the church extended eastward from the tower is apparent from the fragments of the side walls

* *Celtic Scotland*, Vol. II. p. 411.

and the mark of the roof, which still exist on the east side of the tower (see Fig. 1325). A wheel stair is carried up in the south-west angle of the tower, which gave access to three stories on the upper floors. The first floor contained a small rectangular window to the south. The floor above had a fireplace and a south window with pointed and cusped arch-head

Fig. 1325.—Kilmun Church. View from South-East.

(Fig. 1325). Over this was an attic, now ruined. From the above fire-place and ornamental window, we may perhaps assume that the tower was the abode of the provost, and from the strength with which it is built, and general resemblance to a keep, the tower was doubtless designed to form a place of strength in case of need.

ALLOWAY KIRK, Ayrshire.

This old structure, made famous by the genius of Burns, stands in its churchyard, surrounded with ancient trees, on the banks of the Doon, about three miles southwards from Ayr. The burying-ground contains many strangely sculptured tombstones, and a plain slab marks the grave of the poet's father. Mention of Alloway occurs in 1236. In the beginning of the sixteenth century, when James VI. refounded and enlarged the Chapel Royal of Stirling, he annexed to it the Church of Alloway in Kyle, to form the prebend of one of the canons of that collegiate chapel. In 1690 the parish of Alloway was annexed to that of Ayr, and the church allowed to become ruinous.

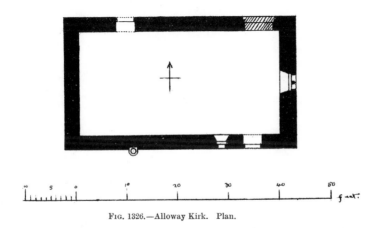

Fig. 1326.—Alloway Kirk. Plan.

The building (Fig. 1326) is 40 feet long by 20 feet broad internally. It is evident that the walls are ancient, but owing to alterations it is difficult to assign the building to any definite date. The principal feature is the two-light window (Fig. 1327), enclosed within one arch in the east gable, but this might be of almost any period before the seventeenth century. The belfry is massive and by no means without good effect, but it is clearly a post-Reformation structure.

On the outside of the south wall an old stoup or benitier has been let into the wall, but what purpose it can have served is far from clear. The church has evidently been used for worship in the seventeenth century, but is now a roofless ruin.

Part of the roof was standing when Captain Grose visited it in the end of last century.

FIG. 1327.—Alloway Kirk. View from North-East.

OLD DAILLY CHURCH, AYRSHIRE.

A ruin situated in the vale of the Girvan Water, about three miles east from Girvan. It stands in the centre of a spacious churchyard, planted with noble trees. Within its walls rest the remains of several of the Martyrs of the Covenant. The church was anciently called Dalmakervan, and was dedicated to St. Michael. It was granted by Duncan, first Earl of Carrick, to the monks of Paisley, and confirmed to them by Alexander II. in 1236. It was afterwards transferred to the monks of Crosraguel, and the name was changed to Dailly, possibly from the site of the church having been changed.

The structure (Fig. 1328) is very long and narrow, being 92 feet in length and 26 feet wide over the walls. There is a gable wall at each end, and each gable is crowned with a belfry (Fig. 1329). It is difficult to account for the presence of the two belfries. That on the east gable is the more

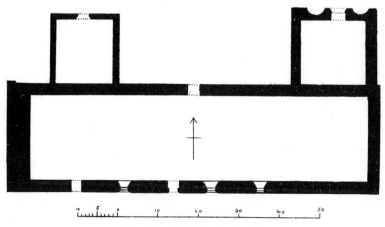

FIG. 1328.—Old Dailly Church. Plan.

ornamental of the two, but its ornament is obscured by ivy. The western belfry is plain and rather ruinous. The walls contain no doorways, and

FIG. 1329.—Old Dailly Church. View from North-East.

only part of one window. From the details of the latter, the work seems to be of the seventeenth century, but the walls may be older. A new church was erected at New Dailly, and divine service transferred to it in 1696, since which period the old church has fallen into ruin.

A burial vault has been constructed within the east part of the building, in connection with the Bargeny Estate, which adjoins. Another similar vault for the use of the Killochan Estate, situated on the opposite side of the Girvan Water, has been erected at the north-east angle of the church (see Fig. 1329). It is evidently a seventeenth century structure. The north front is peculiar, having a deep niche on each side of the doorway. The latter is now built up.

STRAITON CHURCH, AYRSHIRE.

The village of Straiton stands near the north base of the mountains which form the boundary between Ayrshire and Kirkcudbrightshire. It is situated in a pastoral district about seven miles south-east from Maybole, and near the right bank of the Girvan Water.

FIG. 1330.—Straiton Church. South Wing.

The existing church is plain and of post-Reformation date, except a wing (Fig. 1330) which extends like a transept to the south, and measures about 21 feet 3 inches each way. This wing has been built in Gothic times, and when first erected probably formed part of the church, having a large traceried window in the south end, and a piscina in the inside of the east wall. The wing is now divided into two stories by a floor which has been inserted about 6 feet from the ground level, so as to convert the upper story into a gallery, with a private room adjoining, for the use of the Blairquhan family, whose domain adjoins. This upper floor is entered by a stair which has been erected on the south side of the wing (but is omitted in the sketch).

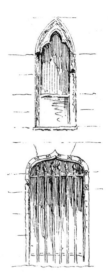

The south wing or transept contains, besides the large east window above referred to, a doorway (Fig. 1331) in the north-west angle, with an ogee shaped arch, surmounted by a panel having a pointed and trefoiled arch-head, and an enriched moulding surrounding the jambs and arch.

These features all indicate a late date. The large window in the south gable is of handsome form and construction, and the tracery is well designed and executed. It would naturally be assigned to the fourteenth century, but for the lower members, which are formed with straight lines, and certainly point to a later period, probably the sixteenth century. This window thus shows the tendency there was in Scotland to revert at the latter date to the forms of an earlier period.

FIG. 1331.
Straiton Church.
South Doorway and Panel over.

The mode of finishing the gable also indicates a late time. Large gabled crowsteps, such as are seen here, are rare features in ecclesiastical edifices in this country. We do not recall any example of such large crowsteps, except at Methven Church, Perthshire, which is undoubtedly a late example.

The Church of Straiton was dedicated to St. Cuthbert, and granted, by Alexander II. in 1236, to the monks of Paisley, but afterwards transferred to Crosraguel Abbey.*

* Statistical Account.

CULLEN CHURCH, Banffshire.

The ancient town of Cullen stood on the right bank of Cullen Water, at a little distance from the coast. It was greatly destroyed in the time of Montrose, and has been rebuilt on a new site nearer the sea. The old church, however, which is dedicated to St. Mary, still stands, surrounded

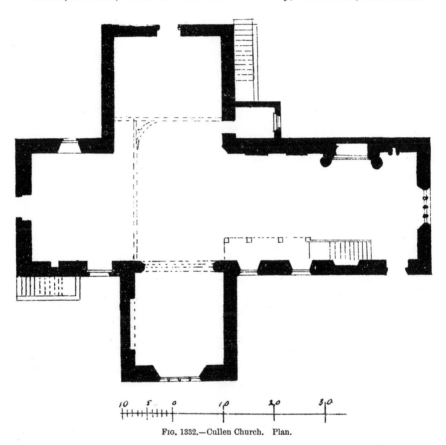

Fig. 1332.—Cullen Church. Plan.

by the churchyard, on the old site near Cullen House, and continues to be used as the Parish Church. Although it has been altered at different times it still retains part of the ancient work, the oldest portions being the east end and the south aisle. The edifice (Fig. 1332) is cruciform in plan, having nave, choir, and transepts, all without aisles. The choir would appear, from the coats of arms it bears on the outside, and from the splendid monument in the interior of the north wall, to have been erected by Alexander Ogilvie, who died in 1554, and his second wife, Elizabeth Gordon.

There was a chaplainry in the church dedicated to St. Ann. This foundation, with the name of the founder and other particulars, are recorded by inscriptions cut upon different parts of the south aisle or transept.* "The first quoted inscription is from the arch of a recess tomb on the west side of the aisle. It is carved in raised and prettily formed capitals, and accompanied by a craftsman's mark.

"IHON · HAY · LORD · OF · FORESTBON̄ · AZ̆E · & · TOLIBOVIL · GVDSIR · TO ELEN · HAY · Yᵗ · BIGIT · YIS · ILE · LEFT · A · CHAPLARI · HEIR · TO · SING PERSONALI · OF · HIS · LĀDIS · OF · ORDIHVF."

The places named in the above inscription were received by Alexander Seton of Gordon (first Earl of Huntly) through his marriage with the heiress of Sir John Hay of Tilibody. "It was probably John's son, David Hay, who, about 1390-1406, had a charter from Robert III. of the place of Cullen."

"The next quoted inscription not only presents the important and interesting facts of the name of the chaplainry, the extent of the gift, and the services required, but also the names of the founder of the chaplainry and the persons to be prayed for, together with those in whom the patronage of the living was to be vested after the decease of the heirs of the donor. It is carved round the arch of the large window of the south aisle, in the same style as the above inscription.

"SANT · ANIS · CHAPLAN · HEIR · DOTAT · Yᵗ · 35 (?) ACRE · GVD · CROFT LĀD · IN · CULĀ · & · TENEMENTIS · SAL · BE · A · GVDE · SINGAR · OF · HALI LIF · BVT · ODIR · SERVICE · & · DAELI · RESIDENT · TO · PRAIE · FOR · ELEN HAY · · HER · BARNIS' · HIS · FYIV · DŌRS · AT · GIFT · OF · ION · DUF · & HIS · ARIS · OF · MADAVAT · & · FALING · YAROF · AT · GIFT · OF · YE · BALZEIS AND COMUNITIE · OF · COLĀ."

The words PER · ELENA · HAY are carved upon the lower side of one of the stones of the arch of the south window. Upon the west side of the arch is this notice of the building of the aisle:—

". . . ELENGE · HAY · IŌN · DUFFIS · MODR. · OF · MALDAVAT · YAT · MAID YIS · ISLE · YE · CHAPLANRI. . . ."

The two inscriptions last quoted "show that Elen Hay was mother of John Hay of Muldavit, who died in 1404, to whom, until 1792, there was a recumbent effigy in the recess tomb in the south aisle at Cullen, also an inscribed slab with a rudely engraved figure in armour."

The entrance to St. Ann's Chapel from the main church is by an arch with pilasters and capitals, and below the caps of the west pilaster are the words ME · MĒTO · MORI, and on the east DISCE · MORI. Below the last

---

* For information regarding the inscriptions in this church, we are indebted to a paper by the late Mr. Andrew Jervise in the *Proceedings of the Society of Antiquaries of Scotland*, Vol. IX. p. 278.

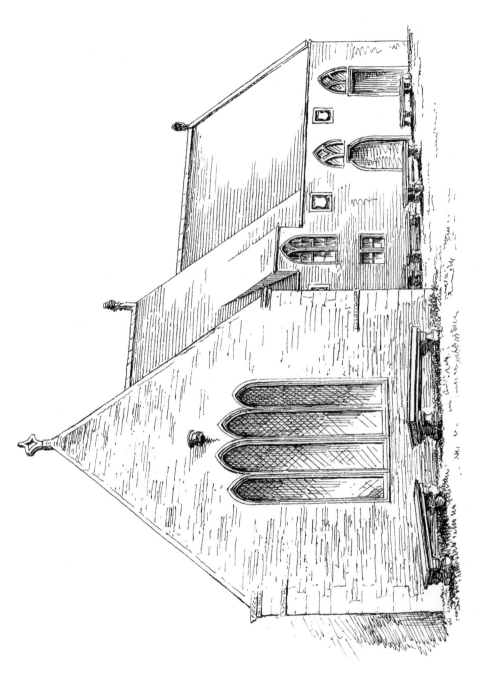

Fig. 1883. – Cullen Church.   South Aisle and Choir.

FIG. 1334.—Cullen Church. Monument of Alexander Ogilvie.

motto is the name of the mason who built the aisle, viz., ROBERT · MOIR MASON, and his mark, ‡. On the outside of the aisle (Fig. 1333) one corner stone bears PER ELENA · HAY, and another SOLI DEO · HONOR · ET · GLORIA.

Although Mr. Jervise attributes the above inscriptions and the erection of the chapel to 1404, the style of the lettering and the abundance

FIG. 1335.—Cullen House.
Sacrament House in Choir.

of it, together with the style of the mottoes, would rather tend to the conclusion that the work is of a considerably later date. The arch forming the entrance from the church to the chapel, with its pilasters, has certainly the character of sixteenth century work. The group of four pointed windows in the south end of the south aisle has not the appearance of decorated work, such as prevailed about 1404. On the contrary, these windows recall the revived and imitative work of the sixteenth and seventeenth centuries. This group of windows, with its four pointed lights (round the inside of which one of the above inscriptions occurs), is evidently a late design. Possibly an aisle was built in the beginning of the fifteenth century, when the bequest was made, but it seems to have been rebuilt in the following century, when the inscriptions, which are scattered very irregularly over the structure, were reinserted and added to. The edifice was probably rebuilt when, about 1543, the Church of Cullen was converted into a college by Alexander Ogilvie of Deskford and Findlater, for the accommodation and maintenance of a provost, six prebendaries, and two singing boys. A bead-house was also erected by the same individual, for the support of a number of decayed men and women.

The choir, which is a portion added at the east end, contains a richly decorated monument in the north wall, erected by Alexander Ogilvie at the date of the church being made collegiate. The monument (Fig. 1334) is large, and extends from the floor to the roof. It consists of an arched recess with a group of ornamental shafts at each side, and large spandrils above, containing two large round panels, each having in the centre a sculptured figure in bas-relief. Along the top runs a series of canopies

Fig. 1336.—Cullen Church. Interior of Choir.

and pinnacles of peculiar design. Within the arch lies an effigy of the founder clad in armour, supported on a basement, which is divided into eight panels, each containing a figure attired in a hood and long robe with book in hand. On a slab at the back of the arched recess is carved the following inscription :—

CORPUS · ALEX^r · OGILVY · DE · FINLATER · HĒROS

·.· AC · SPONSĒ · ELEZABETH · GORDON · BTRVMQ · EBBAT

PRESIDE · PVRIS · BISTER · PVERISQ · DVOBVS

·.· HAS · IACINT · EDES · IV̄CTVS · VTERQ · PIVS

MIGRAVIIT · ET · HAC · LVCE · HIC · DIE · 4 · MĒNS · IVLII

1554 · ILLA · DIE · · · · · · MĒSIS · · · · · · 155–

FIG. 1337.—Cullen Church.
Carved Wooden Pillar.

FIG. 1338.—Cullen Church.
Carved Wooden Pillar.

The inscription is accompanied by a variety of curious carvings, and by the Ogilvie and Gordon arms. The style of the monument corresponds with the date upon it, being one of the last attempts in the style of Gothic work executed just before the Reformation.

Mr Jervise mentions that in 1863, when alterations were made on the east portion of the church, a stone altar-piece and ambry, in fine preservation, were found. These were 5 to 6 feet in height, embellished with the representation of two angels raising the host and other ornaments, and the text (John vi. 54-56) below the cornice.

CARO · MEA · VERE · EST · CIB · ET · SANGVIS · ME · VERE · Ē · POT · Q MĀDVCAT · MEĀ · CARNĒ · Ṫ · BIBIT · MEV̄ · SĀGVINĒ · VIVET · Ī · ETERNV̄.

It is further stated that the ambry and altar-piece were unfortunately reconsigned from view. A sacrament house, answering somewhat to the above description of the ambry, is, however, now visible in the north wall of the choir, to the east of the monument (Fig. 1335). The design shows the two angels supporting a monstrance, and is very similar to, but much simpler than, the sacrament house at Deskford, "which bears to have been erected by Alexander Ogilvie, and his second wife, Elizabeth Gordon," of which an illustration is given below.

FIG. 1339.—Cullen Church. Carved Wooden Pillar.

The east end of the church has evidently been a good deal altered, as is apparent from the south wall (see Fig. 1333), where doorways are visible, which have been built up, and windows introduced above.

The coats of arms of the Gordons and Ogilvies on the exterior correspond with those in the interior. The choir contains a large east window divided by three mullions, which cross one another in curved branches, forming plain tracery in the arch-head (Fig. 1336).

On the south side of the choir is still preserved a fine example of a laird's pew (see Fig. 1336). It is in two stories, the upper story (which forms a gallery) being supported on four solid square wooden pillars (Figs. 1337, 1338, and 1339), which are well carved with numerous ornaments of Renaissance work, and bear the date of 1608. The upper portion or gallery is also old, and contains some good carved woodwork of the post-Reformation period. It is still used as the proprietor's pew, and is occupied by the Earl of Seafield, whose mansion of Cullen House is close to the church. The lower story is occupied by ordinary pews.

DESKFORD CHURCH, Banffshire.

The old church of Deskford is situated in its ancient churchyard, about four miles south from Cullen. The church is now a roofless ruin, a new church having been erected in the vicinity. The building is a plain parallelogram, and has no features of note, except the large sacrament house in the north wall near the east end. It seems to have been the fashion in the sixteenth century in this part of the country to make these features very ornamental. Such are the ambries or sacrament houses at Kinkell, Auchendoir, and Cullen. The last was erected by the same individual to whom that at Deskford is attributed, viz., Alexander Ogilvie of Deskford and Findlater, whose splendid monument exists in Cullen Church (see Fig. 1334).

The sacrament house at Deskford (Fig. 1340) is very large, being 8 feet in height by 3 feet 6 inches wide. The design is somewhat similar in all the above sacrament houses, consisting of two angels above the ambry supporting a monstrance, with a quasi-buttress on each side, and several inscriptions and enrichments. At Deskford the side buttresses are a good deal broken and their pinnacles removed. The whole design is surrounded with a scroll ornament of grapes, and there are several inscriptions on various parts of the design. The first is on two scrolls immediately over the ambry, "Os meum es et cara mea"—"Thou art my bone and my flesh;" and another occurs on the broad sill of the ambry, "Ego sum panis vivus qui de celo descendi quis manducaverit ex hoc pane vivet in æternum"—from sixth chapter of John's Gospel. Beneath the latter are two shields, the first containing the arms of Ogilvie of Deskford and Findlater, viz., 1st and 4th a lion passant gardant gules for Ogilvie, 2nd and 3rd argent a cross engrailed sable for Sinclair of Deskford, with motto Tout jour. The initials A. O. occur at the sides of this shield. The second shield contains, impaled with the above, the arms of Gordon, for Alexander Ogilvie's second wife, Elizabeth Gordon, and the motto Laus Deo.

Under the coats of arms there is a long inscription, which is remarkable as being the only one in English on any of the above sacrament houses. It also authorises the name of sacrament house for these ornamental ambries. It is as follows :—

THIS · P̄NT (present) LOVEBLE · VARK · OF · SACRAMĒT · HOVS · MAID · TO YE · HONOR ✠ LOVĪG · OF · GOD · BE · ANE · NOBLE · MAN · ALEXANDER OGILVY · OF · YAT · ILK ✠ ELEZABET · GORDON · HIS · SPOVS · THE · ZEIR OF · GOD · 1551.*

The date would lead one to expect the very debased Gothic work which is found here, the influence of the approaching Renaissance being very apparent in the style of the ornamentation.

* See *Aberdeen Ecclesiological Society's Transactions, 1893*, p. 95.

FIG. 1340.—Deskford Church. Sacrament House.

ST. MOLOC'S OR ST. MOLUOG'S CHURCH, MORTLACH, BANFFSHIRE.

It was formerly believed, on the evidence of Boece, that Malcolm II. in a battle with the Danes, looking up to the Chapel of St. Moloc at Mortlach, vowed that, if successful, he would there erect a cathedral and found a bishop's see. The record of the See of Aberdeen appeared to support this statement, and mentioned further that the see was afterwards transferred by David I. to Aberdeen. But Professor Cosmo Innes has

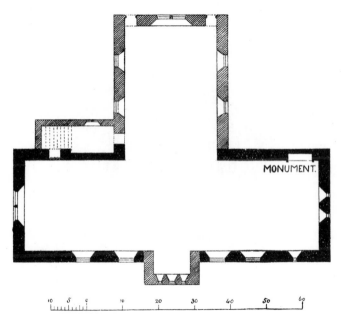

FIG. 1341.--St. Moloc's or St. Moluog's Church.   Plan.

proved that these stories are forgeries, and must be entirely rejected. It is, however, probable that there was an early religious settlement at Mortlach, which may have given some foundation for the above fables. At all events, in 1157, a Bull of Pope Adrian IV. mentions the monastery of Mortlach and the five churches belonging to it.

The existing structure (Fig. 1341) consists of an old building of simple oblong form, 83 feet in length internally by 24 feet in width, to which was added, in 1826, a large north wing or aisle. This wing was further extended in 1876, and now measures, internally, 36 feet long by 26 feet wide. A small wing or projection has also been added to the south to contain an organ, and the whole church has been reseated and fitted up for service in modern style. There are two lancet windows in the east end, which, together with some portions of the walls, may be ancient (perhaps of thirteenth century date), as it is understood that these windows were found built up, and were reopened during the late restoration, but the remainder of the church has been completely modernised.

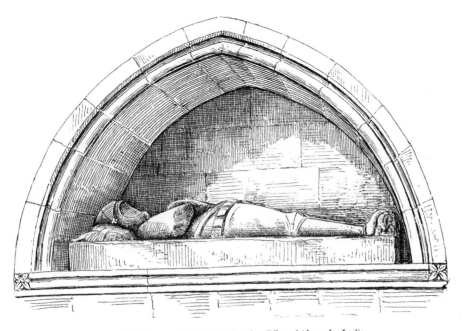

Fig. 1342.—St. Moloc's or St. Moluog's Church.   Effigy of Alexander Leslie.

Under a pointed arch in the thickness of the north wall, close to the east end, lies the recumbent effigy of a knight in armour (Fig. 1342), supposed to be the monument of Alexander Leslie, the first of Kininvie,* who died about 1549. The figure used to stand upright, but has now been placed in its proper position.

A remarkable sculptured stone † stands in the flat ground below the church, where the battle with the Danes is said to have taken place, and of which it is traditionally believed to be a memorial.

* See *The Castellated and Domestic Architecture of Scotland*, Vol. IV. p. 394.
† Illustrated in Dr. Stuart's work on the sculptured stones.

ABBEY ST. BATHANS, Berwickshire.*

The Abbey of St. Bothan was a convent for Cistercian nuns. Its scanty remains are situated about four miles south-west from Grant's House Railway Station, in a beautiful valley on the right bank of the Whitadder, which here flows a calm full stream, surrounded by gently swelling hills—an ideal situation for such a house. The modern parish church appears to occupy the site of the ancient church of the abbey, and probably the nunnery buildings were included within the existing church-yard, which lies on the south side of the church. The east wall of the

Fig. 1343.—Abbey St. Bathans. East Wall.

church only is old, and is entirely ivy clad, the east window (Fig. 1343) being just visible. It is round-arched and is of two lights, each 9 inches wide, with a quatrefoil above, having rather rudely formed cusping. The mullion is modern, and the tracery is recessed to about the middle of the thickness of the wall, being about 18 inches back from the outer face. There is a set-off on the gable, hidden by ivy. It is impossible to say how much of the other walls are old, but probably the modern church occupies the old foundations, in which case the ancient church was

* In connection with the Berwickshire churches, we are indebted to Mr. Ferguson and Mr. Fortune, Duns.

of small size, being about 45 feet
long by 24 feet wide.* There is
a sundial on the wall-head of the
south wall at the east end. At
the north corner of the east end
there are indications of a wall
with a splayed base having extended eastwards.

In the interior of the church
a modern arched recess (or what
appears on the face as modern)
contains the recumbent figure
of a prioress (Fig. 1344). It
measures 6 feet long, and is in
good preservation. There appears to have been a dog lying
at her feet, but it has been
knocked off.

About a quarter of a mile to
the south of the church, on the
slope of a hill, there are the
foundations of a chapel (Fig.
1345) measuring about 38 feet
long by 15 feet wide internally.
The end walls are each about
5 feet thick, and the side walls
about 3 feet. Nothing else belonging to the church remains,
except a few fragments of what
was probably a circular font,
and a window sill lying amongst
the ruins. It shows that the
window was eight inches wide.
A plain slab 6 feet long by
18 inches wide lies in the centre
of the building.

The Convent of St. Bothan's
was founded by Ada, daughter

* Mackenzie Walcott, in his notice
of "St. Bothan's," in *The Ancient
Church of Scotland*, p. 379, says,
"The chapel measured 58 feet by
84 feet," and he quotes the *Caledonia*,
where, however, nothing is said about
its dimensions.

Fig. 1344.—Abbey St. Bathans.
Figure of a Prioress.

of William the Lion, in 1184. She married Patrick, Earl of Dunbar, and they made adequate endowments to the convent.* According to Chalmers there was a previous church here, dedicated to St. Bothan,

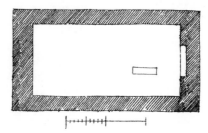

FIG. 1345.—Abbey St. Bathans. Plan of Chapel.

which was probably given to. the Countess Ada's nuns. It is just possible that the second church, noticed above, may be the church referred to.

BASSENDEAN CHURCH, BERWICKSHIRE.

The ancient parish of Bassendean is now incorporated with that of Westruther, both in the south-west part of Berwickshire, and the church has long been disused.

The remains of Bassendean Church, which was dedicated to St. Mary, lie five and a half miles west of Greenlaw. The walls are broken down,

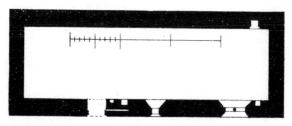

FIG. 1346.—Bassendean Church. Plan.

but the plan (Fig. 1346) can still be traced. The structure is a simple oblong, measuring 54 feet 6 inches in length by about 20 feet in width externally. The doorway is in the south side, and has been provided with a slot for a bolt. The remains of a stoup and ambry exist beside the door, and there is a recess for a piscina near the east end, and an ambry

* *Caledonia*, Vol. II. p. 344.

in the north wall opposite it. In the centre of the south wall there has been a single-light window, and towards the east end a larger two-

FIG. 1347.—Bassendean Church. (From *The Churches of Berwickshire*.)

light window with a central mullion, now built up (Fig. 1347). The plan of the jamb (Fig. 1348) shows that the structure has been of an advanced date. The grooves for the glass are in the centre of the wall. There is no window in either of the east, north, or west walls. Fragments of the font are lying amongst the rubbish in the inside.

The old church of Bassendean is still used as a burial-place by the Homes of Bassendean.

The church belonged to the priory of Coldstream, and appears to have been abandoned at the Reformation. It was again used for divine service from 1647 to 1649, when a new church was erected at Westruther, and St. Mary's was allowed to fall into ruin.

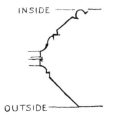

FIG. 1348.
Bassendean Church.
Window Jamb.

COCKBURNSPATH CHURCH, BERWICKSHIRE.

The village of Cockburnspath is situated about seven miles south-east of Dunbar. The church here is peculiar and unique, in having a round tower in the centre of the west wall. It is a long narrow building (Fig.

1349), measuring about 80 feet in length by 18 feet 3 inches in width. The structure has been much knocked about, having undergone at least two restorations at different times, the last being about twenty years ago. It is therefore not surprising to find that there is nothing left inside the building of any architectural interest. Four angle buttresses at the corners, however, remain intact, together with portions of an early base course near the east end, and the head of a window, containing geometrical tracery (Fig. 1350), has been preserved and built into the south wall over the door near the east end. Judging from these details and from the thickness of the walls (3 feet 2 inches) it seems probable that the church is not later than the sixteenth century.

The tower (Fig. 1351) is about 9 feet in external diameter, and its interior diameter is about 6 feet. It is about 30 feet high, and contains

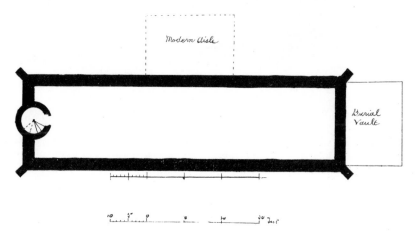

FIG. 1349.—Cockburnspath Church. Plan.

a circular stone stair. There is a string course above the level of the ridge of the church, above which the tower rises one story. In this there are several openings or loop holes of a roughly formed cross shape, similar to those sometimes found in the old castles. The tower is built of rubble work in quite a different style of masonry from that of the church. There is nothing to indicate that it is older than the church, except its position. Mr. T. S. Robertson* is probably correct when he states, "From its position, I am clearly of opinion that it existed before the church, and that the church walls were built up to it. I cannot believe that any one capable of building the round tower would have taken out the centre of a gable fully 3 feet thick to insert this tower," for it will be observed

* To whom we are indebted for the drawings and notes in connection with this church.

that the tower projects inside. "The most that would have been done, had the church been earlier than the tower, would have been to slap a door of communication through the wall of the church." The tower was probably erected independently as a belfry and for other occasional purposes. A circular stair beginning at the level of the church floor, and entering from the church by a square-headed door, is carried up as far as the upper story of the tower, which has been mended with brick work, otherwise the tower is all of one age. The walls are only 18 inches thick, but the

Fig. 1350.—Cockburnspath Church. Door and Window Head at East End.

stone steps of the stair bind them together, and make the building as strong as if it had been built of one solid mass of masonry.

The small building at the east end is probably a century later than the church. It has a pointed barrel-vaulted roof, and an original square-headed doorway in the centre of its east wall. It is now used as the heating chamber of the church.

On the apex of the south-west buttress there is a remarkable sundial, which has already been illustrated.*

* *The Castellated and Domestic Architecture of Scotland*, Vol. v. p. 382.

From Mr. Ferguson's remarks * it is evident that the history of this building has not been investigated. There were a chapel and a hospital at

FIG. 1351.—Cockburnspath Church. View from South-West.

Cockburnspath in early times. Robert, Chaplain of Colbrundspath, is mentioned in 1255, but Mr. Ferguson has doubts as to this being the site of the chapel referred to.

PRESTON CHURCH, BERWICKSHIRE.

A ruined church situated about two miles north from Duns. It is in a state of complete dilapidation, and is densely covered with ivy. The structure (Fig. 1352) consists of a nave and chancel of equal width, the whole internal length being about 70 feet by 14 feet 6 inches in width, and the chancel is about 18 feet 6 inches long. The round chancel arch is blocked, and it is doubtful if it is original. There are two narrow pointed windows in the east wall and one in the west wall, all widely splayed towards the interior, and finished with a segmental arch.

* The pre-Reformation Churches of Berwickshire, p. 18.

Another window in the south wall of the chancel (shown in Fig. 1353) is of the same character, only that it is lintelled on the inside instead

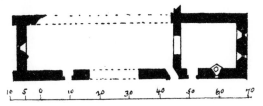

FIG. 1352.—Preston Church. Plan.

of being arched. Beneath this window there is a peculiar piscina (see Fig. 1353). It consists of a triangular shelf projecting about 17 inches from the wall (Fig. 1354) and having a shallow basin supported on a rounded base. Above the shelf there is a round-arched recess 2 feet 2 inches high by 18 inches wide. The back of this recess leans forward, so that while it is $8\frac{1}{2}$ inches deep at the base, it is only 3 inches at the crown of the arch.

There are two south doors with square lintels, one in the chancel and another in the nave near the west end. A later door has been made at the east end of the nave.

All the doors and windows are finished on the outside with a simple chamfer.

There has probably been a sacristy on the north side of the nave.

Mr. Ferguson* assigns this church to an early period. The small windows

FIG. 1353.—Preston Church. Piscina.

* *The pre-Reformation Churches of Berwickshire*, by J. Ferguson, Duns, to whom we are indebted for the Plan.

2 D

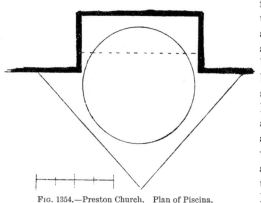

FIG. 1354.—Preston Church. Plan of Piscina.

in the end walls and the shallow buttresses at the west end have an early appearance, but the same cannot be said of the details shown in Fig. 1353. Mr. Muir * is doubtful as to its "just claim to antiquity." This church, with that of Bunkle, about two miles distant, belonged to the Bishopric of Dunkeld.

ST. MARY'S ABBEY, ROTHESAY, BUTESHIRE.

About half a mile westwards from the town of Rothesay, and approached by an avenue of fine old trees, there stands in the ancient burial-ground the choir of the Abbey Church of St. Mary. The west end has been built up with a wall containing a wide gateway, but otherwise the chancel remains in fair preservation, although roofless. A modern church has been erected beside it, but with an interval of a few inches between the new and old structures.

The ancient chancel (Fig. 1355) now measures 27 feet in length by 18 feet in width internally. The east wall, with its gable (Fig. 1356), still survives, and contains a large three-light window, of which the tracery has been of the simple intersecting kind. The east ends of the side walls had each a single pointed light with pointed rear arches. Near the west end of the north wall is a plain pointed doorway, and a small window with square lintel. The west end of the south wall contained a doorway, now built up.

Opposite one another, in the centre of the north and south walls, are erected two more than usually interesting monuments. Both are recessed in the wall, and are covered with an arched canopy, and in each the effigy of the person commemorated is preserved. The monument in the south wall (Fig. 1357) is the larger and finer of the two. It measures nearly 11 feet over the side buttresses. The ogee arch in which it is enclosed contains bold, but late, mouldings. The arch has been ornamented with large crockets, but they are now much wasted away. The monument has doubtless been erected in memory of one of the Stewarts of Bute, who buried here, but its heraldry is peculiar. At the apex there is a shield, which appears to contain the royal arms, but has two lions for supporters,

* *Characteristics of Old Church Architecture*, p. 57.

instead of the usual unicorns. There is also on the base or pedestal of
the monument a coat of arms, containing quarterly first and fourth the
Stewart arms, and second and third the royal arms. The shield is
supported by two angels. In a paper by Mr. John Mackinlay,* written
in 1825, these arms are fully described and illustrated. They were then
doubtless better preserved than they now are, but the arms can still be
deciphered. Mr. Mackinlay tries to explain the remarkable circumstance
of the Stewart arms having precedence in the lower shield over the royal
arms, by supposing that they are placed on the tomb of the chief of the

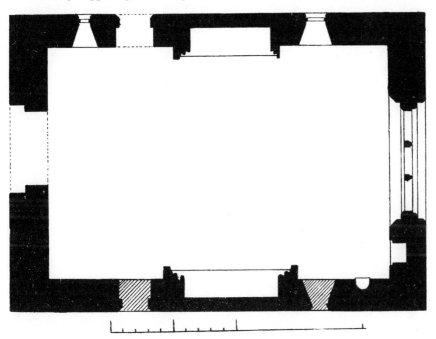

Fig. 1355.—St. Mary's Abbey, Rothesay. Plan.

Clan. But the name of the person whose monument this is has not been
discovered.† As the bearings in quartered shields are often reversed by
mistake, the same may have happened here.

The effigy is that of a knight in complete plate armour. The head
rests on a tilting helmet, with a dog's head for crest, which is attached to
a cap put on over the helmet. The round hollow visible to the spectator
represents the inside of the helmet. The feet rest upon a lion. The

* *Archæologica Scotica*, Vol. III. p. 1.

† There is also an interesting paper on this subject by Mr. James C. Roger in the
Proceedings of the Society of Antiquaries of Scotland, Vol. II. p. 446.

figure is considerably worn, but the plate armour and the gauntlets are still distinctly seen. The bottom of the shirt of mail worn under the cuirass and the jewelled sword belt and hilt of the sword are also clearly visible. A coat of arms, similar to that on the pedestal, is carved on the breast, being intended to represent the arms wrought in embroidery on the surcoat.

The lower part of the monument has been divided into panels, each containing a quatrefoil, and between the panels there were at one time small

Fig. 1356.—St. Mary's Abbey, Rothesay.   View from South-East.

figures of armed knights, each holding a spear. When Mr. Mackinlay wrote, one of these figures survived; now they are all gone, together with parts of the quatrefoils, and an irregular empty space is left where they once stood. Mr. Mackinlay mentions that some excavation was made, and an arched recess was found under the monument in which the coffins had been placed, and three skulls were discovered therein. In the upper part of the monument over the arch are two recesses, which probably at one time contained coats of arms.

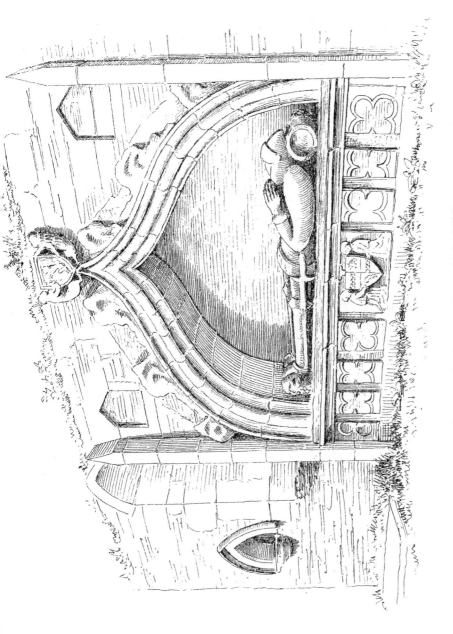

Fig. 1357.—St. Mary's Abbey, Rothesay. Monument in South Wall.

The other monument (Fig. 1358) in the north wall of the chancel has been erected in memory of a lady and child, whose effigies it contains. The

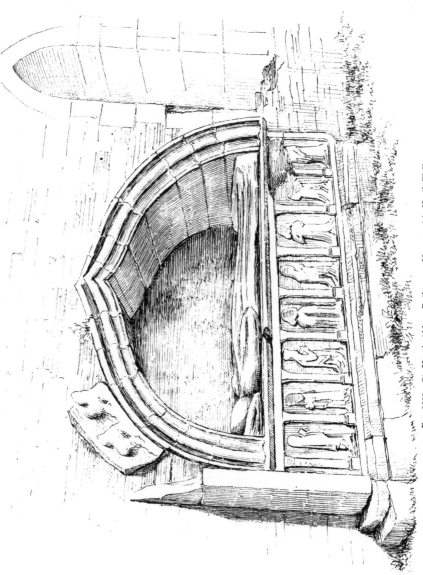

FIG. 1355.—St. Mary's Abbey, Rothesay. Monument in North Wall.

figures of the lady and child are cut in a thin slab of stone, and have not the bold effect of the knight in armour. There are no arms or inscription on this monument, and the name of the person commemorated is unknown. The arch over the figures is of the same description as that of the opposite monument, but it is lower and not so effective. The mouldings are also similar, and there have been crockets over the arch, which are now greatly decayed. The width of the monument over all is fully 8 feet.

The lower part of the monument on which the effigies rest is divided into eight panels by shafts, and each panel contains a sculptured figure. Mr. Mackinlay says that they represent saints, and that amongst them is the Virgin and Child. In their decayed condition the latter is not now recognisable. The figures seem rather to resemble persons in the dress of the fifteenth century, and some of them appear to be kneeling.

At the east end of the chancel there is a pointed piscina in the south wall (see Fig. 1357) and an ambry in the east wall.

The style of the structure and of the monuments is undoubtedly late, probably sixteenth century.

THE PARISH CHURCH AND THE COLLEGIATE CHURCH
OF ST. MARY, DUMBARTON, DUMBARTONSHIRE.

The town of Dumbarton is situated on the left bank of the river Leven, near its junction with the Clyde, and not far from the detached rock on which stands the Castle of Dumbarton. A church existed here from a very early time, and the parish church appears to have been rebuilt at least three times, and is now a modern edifice of 1811. Previously the parish church was represented by the quaint structure shown in Fig. 1359, which has entirely disappeared, along with the hospital or bead-house adjacent, which was erected in 1636 by Buchanan of Auchmore, and endowed by him with £1021. This view is copied from a pencil sketch made by Paul Sandby in 1747, which forms part of a valuable collection of sketches relating to Scotland, preserved in the Library of the Royal Scottish Academy, to the Council of which we are indebted for permission to reproduce it.

The parish church (see Fig. 1359) was probably intended to consist of a choir and nave with a central tower, but only the choir and tower would seem to have been built. As frequently happened, a north aisle or transept appears from the view to have existed. This contained what was known in later times as Mr. Campbell of Stonefield's gallery and the town council gallery, and it was entered by an outside stair. From the description of the interior in Glen's *History of Dumbarton*, p. 74, the church was evidently a typical specimen of those picturesque, though plain, interiors which have now almost disappeared. The pulpit stood on the south side, and there were various galleries for the trades and for the

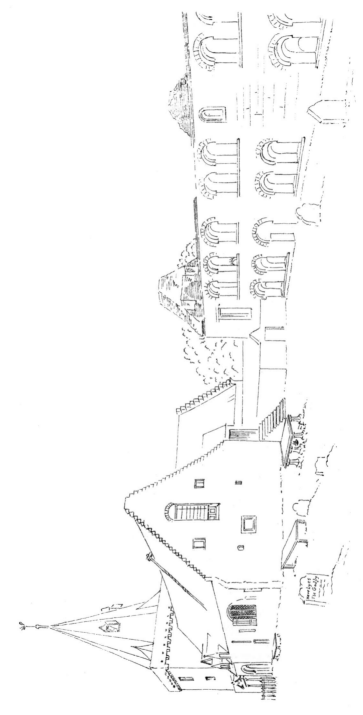

Fig. 1859.—Dumbarton Church and Hospital. (From a Drawing by Paul Sandby, 1747.)

garrison, while an upper end gallery called the hen-bauk was occupied by single ladies. In 1622 Dame Jean Hamiltone, Lady of Luss, having no convenient seat, was granted liberty by the kirk-session "to build ane seat for hirsel, upon ye top of the east gavil." The spire was of wood, and was presumably covered with lead. Shortly after this sketch was made the spire appears, from the Burgh Records, to have been ruinous, so that its leaning appearance may be quite correct. The tower was of the low squat form, with plain parapet, common at the time.

The hospital appears, from the view, to have been of considerable extent. It was evidently two stories in height, and was lighted by round-headed windows. This bead-house and the small chapel attached to it

FIG. 1360.—Portion of Tower of Collegiate Church, Dumbarton.

were ultimately dismantled and lay in a ruinous state till, in the year 1758, they were entirely demolished by the magistrates, and the stones used to build the East Bridge and for other purposes. The church appears to have been used as the parish church till about 1810, when it was taken down and a new church built on the site.

The Collegiate Church and Hospital of St. Mary were founded in 1450 by Lady Isabella, Duchess of Albany and Countess of Lennox. She was the widow of Murdoch, Duke of Albany, who was beheaded at Stirling in 1425. About the beginning of the sixteenth century, the Earl of Lennox gifted the church, with the temporality, to the Abbey of Kilwinning. The chapter consisted of a provost and six canons, and was endowed with the parish churches of Bonhill, Fintry, and Strathblane, and also held considerable lands in the neighbourhood of Dumbarton, which yielded to Kilwinning at the Reformation an annual revenue of £66, 13s. 4d. sterling.

The founder erected the college for the repose of the souls of "her dearest husband, her father, and her sons," who had been slain by their relative James I. of Scotland, under the belief that they had been to blame in connection with his long imprisonment in England.

After the Reformation the college was allowed to fall into ruin, and its materials were gradually carried off. In 1858, in order to make room for the railway station, the last remnants of the edifice, one of the pier arches and its piers (Fig. 1360) were removed from their position on a grassy knoll, from which a fine view of the Leven was visible, and re-erected as the gateway of a house.*

CHAPEL AT THE KIRKTON OF KILMAHEW,†
DUMBARTONSHIRE.

This structure is an interesting example of a private ecclesiastical foundation. The remains of the chapel stand in an ancient churchyard, on a knoll close to a small stream, about one and a half miles north-west from Cardross Railway Station. The building has attached to it the piece of land with which it was endowed, and is surrounded by the estate of Kilmahew, the property of John William Burns, Esq., to whom we are indebted for bringing the structure under our notice.

This chapel is believed to have been erected for the convenience of the inhabitants of the locality, owing to the great distance of their parish church at Roseneath, and also of the church of the neighbouring parish of Cardross. The Napiers were proprietors of Kilmahew from about 1300. John Napier was one of the defenders of Stirling Castle in 1304, along with Sir William Olyfard. In 1406 William Napier obtained a charter of the half lands of Kilmahew, "where the chapel is situated." ‡

A chapel existed here in 1370, when a charter was granted to Roger Cochran of the lands of Kilmahew, "with the chapel thereof." In 1467 a new chapel was erected by Duncan Napier, then proprietor of Kilmahew, who endowed it with an annual rent of 40s. and 10d. out of tenements in Dumbarton. In the above year the new chapel, dedicated to St. Mahew,

---

* Information regarding the history of the above structures has been kindly supplied by Mr. Donald M'Leod, author of *The God's Acres of Dumbarton*, and other works relating to the district.

† The particulars of the history of this chapel are taken from Irving's *Dumbartonshire*.

‡ The ancient castle of the Napiers at Kilmahew is illustrated in *The Castellated and Domestic Architecture of Scotland*, Vol. III. p. 443.

was consecrated by George, Bishop of Argyll, in mitre and full pontificals, with the permission of the Bishop of Glasgow, in whose diocese it was situated. Possibly the existing chancel is part of the structure then dedicated.

At the Reformation this chapel was used as a preaching station by a reader under the minister of Roseneath, but when the site of Cardross Church was altered so as to bring it into its present more convenient position as regards this locality, the chapel fell into disuse. The burying-ground attached to it, however, continued in use for interments till recent years. In 1640 a portion of the chapel was turned into a school, in terms of an agreement between Robert Napier of Kilmahew and the other heritors. Under this agreement Kilmahew bound himself—first, "to give the use of his chapel of Kilmahew bewest the quir thereof, for and in place of a school; second, to mortify to the schoolmaster annually five

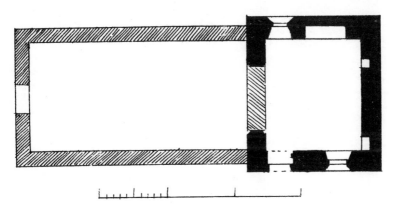

Fig. 1361.—Chapel at the Kirkton of Kilmahew. Plan.

bolls one firlot of tiend bear, and also a house and a piece of land layand thereto beside the chapel of Kilmahew, extending to about an acre or therby, together with ane piece of land for pasture, which was of old possest by the priest of Kilmahew, by order of the said Robert Napier of Kilmahew his predecessors in time of superstition and popery; and in case the annual value of these provisions should fall short of eighty merks to make it up to that sum; third, to entertain the school master present and to come, in meat, drink, and bedding, in household with himself within the house of Kilmahew, so long as he shall discharge the duty of family exercise and prayer within the said family." *

The acre of ground above referred to is now in the possession of the School Board, together with two acres excambed in 1795 for the priest's right of pasturing a cow on Kirkton farm.

* Irving's *Dumbartonshire*, p. 431.

The building is now unoccupied, but it is kept in good repair. It consists (Fig. 1361) of an eastern portion or choir, which is roofed, and of a western portion or nave, which is roofless. The former is ancient, but the latter appears to be comparatively modern. The choir is, internally, 13 feet 6 inches in length from west to east, by 16 feet 3 inches in width from north to south, and the walls are 3 feet in thickness. In the west wall there is a rounded and chamfered arch 9 feet 2 inches in width, now built up. The choir has two windows, one in the north

Fig. 1362.—Chapel at the Kirkton of Kilmahew.   View from South-East.

wall and one in the south wall (Fig. 1362), each of which is square-headed, and the outer jambs and lintel have a double splay. The door-way, which is in the south wall, has also a square lintel and a bold bead and hollow round the opening. In the interior of the north wall there is an arched recess 8 feet in length by 2 feet in depth, which may have contained a monument, or may have been an Easter sepulchre. The east wall has two recesses, one of which may have contained a piscina, while the other (Fig. 1363) is an ambry of an ornamental character, but evidently of very late date. There is also a window in this wall placed at a very high level, and out of the centre (see Fig. 1362). The gables are finished with crowsteps, and on the south skew putts there are shields (Fig. 1364), that at the south-west end containing the sacred monogram I. H. S., and that at the south-east end the initials M. C. In the east gable, which has a set-off above the wall-head, there is a window placed so as to light an upper room in the roof, which probably formerly existed.

The nave measures 34 feet 7 inches in length by 19 feet 8 inches in width over the walls, which are thinner than those of the choir. There is a doorway in the west end, and the enclosure contains some flat monuments lying on the

FIG. 1363.—Chapel at the Kirkton of Kilmahew.
Ambry in East Wall.

ground, which commemorate some of the Napiers of Kilmahew and Buchanans of Drum (1789-80). This enclosure probably occupies the site of the original nave, but the wall appears to have been rebuilt. There was apparently a nave in existence in 1640, as it was the chapel "bewest the quir" which Robert Napier then agreed to give as a school.

FIG. 1364.—Chapel at the Kirkton of Kilmahew.
South Skew Putts.

Fig. 1365.—Canonby Priory. Sedilia.

CANONBY PRIORY, Dumfriesshire.

"Some remains of this canonry were, until recently, visible at Hal-green. . . . A portion of the ancient church (the sedilia) may be seen in the churchyard."*

This priory was founded during the reign of David i. by Turgot de Rossendal, near the junction of the Esk and Liddel, and was destroyed by the English after the battle of Solway Moss in 1542. The annexed illustration (Fig. 1365) shows the only fragment that survives. It is probably of thirteenth century work (but was omitted in Vol. ii.)

The priory, as the residence of the canons, became known as Canonbie.

KIRKBRYDE CHURCH, Dumfriesshire.†

A ruin situated five or six miles south-east from Sanquhar.

The church (Fig. 1366) measures 42 feet 4 inches in length by 14 feet 6 inches wide inside.

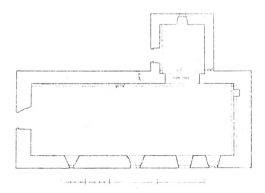

Fig. 1366.—Kirkbryde Church. Plan.

There is a north chapel, measuring about 10 feet by 9 feet 3 inches, opening into the church by a round arch.

The east wall (Fig. 1367), on which is the belfry, is almost entire, as is also the greater part of the west wall and the south wall (Fig. 1368).

* *History of Liddesdale and the Debateable Land,* by R. Bruce Armstrong, p. 119. We are indebted to Mr. Armstrong for the accompanying illustration.

† The plan and sketches of this structure are copied from drawings made and kindly lent by Mr. Robert Weir Schultz, architect, Gray's Inn Square, London.

The north wall is pretty well preserved at the east end, as well as the chapel and north archway (Fig. 1369). At the west end the north wall is very fragmentary.

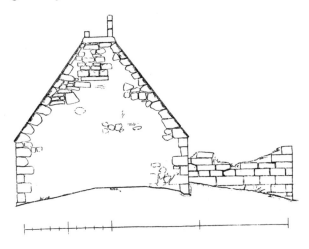

Fɪɢ. 1367.—Kirkbryde Church. East Elevation.

The doorway in the south wall has a pointed arch cut out of two stones (see Fig. 1368). There are three windows on the south side of

Fɪɢ. 1368.—Kirkbryde Church. South Elevation.

the church (see Fig. 1368). One of them is entire, and has a pointed arch cut out of two stones. A kind of shoulder is wrought on the

Fig. 1369.—Kirkbride Church. View from North-West.

Fig. 1370.—Kirkbride Church. Window in South Wall.

stone above the arch (Fig. 1370). The east window is square lintelled, and is provided with strong iron bars. There are no windows in the north wall.

The masonry of the north chapel is of a better kind than that of the main building. The opening arch is about 7 feet 2 inches wide, and is entirely plain, without even a splay on the edge.

ST. CUTHBERT'S, Moffat, Dumfriesshire.

On a hill on the opposite side of the River Annan from the town of Moffat stand the small remains of St. Cuthbert's Church.

The building is believed to have been originally erected by the Knights Templars, who had considerable possessions in this locality. All that now remains of the structure is a portion of what appears to have been the west wall, containing parts of a pointed window (Fig. 1371), which has been divided into three lights by two mullions, one of which, and one arch and half of another, only remain. The three lights had sharply pointed openings, and the principal arch had two splays on its ingoing. The design might belong to almost any period of Gothic, but the form adopted was common in late work.

The east wall of the church appears to have been made available as part of a farmhouse, and its features are quite obliterated. Considerable foundations of other structures are observable in the grassy mounds scattered around.

2 E

FIG. 1371.—St. Cuthbert's, Moffat.

SANQUHAR CHURCH, DUMFRIESSHIRE.

The old church of Sanquhar was demolished in 1827, and the present church was built partly on its site, as indicated by the dotted lines shown

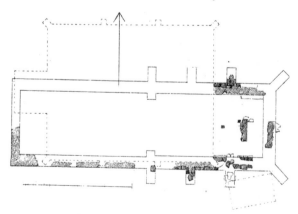

FIG. 1372.—Sanquhar Church. Plan.

on the Plan (Fig. 1372). In 1895 Lord Bute had excavations made, which partly revealed the Plan now submitted.*

The position of the east wall was thus determined, as likewise that of the east end of the north wall with one buttress, and considerable portions of the south wall throughout its whole length, with indications of three buttresses and the return of the west wall at the south-west corner. The dimensions of the building were ascertained to be about 96 feet from east to west by about 30 feet 6 inches from north to south over the walls. The angle buttresses shown at the east end are con-jectural, and are based on a tradition that the corners of the existing church were copied from the form of the east end of the old church.

FIG. 1373.—Sanquhar Church. Effigy.

Mr. Schultz states that an old burial list, of which the date is uncertain, but which may be of the seventeenth or early eighteenth century, alludes to certain graves which can still be recognised as so many feet from the "queer pillar" (buttress), *i.e.*, the buttress opposite which the chancel arch is represented. Mr. Schultz assumes from this that the choir or "queer" ex-tended as far as this buttress; and the fact that a splayed base was found all along the choir wall as far as this point, and that no such splay existed farther west, gives a certain sanction to the above view, as does also the circumstance that the nave or western part of the building had no but-tresses. It is frequently found that the eastern end was treated in a different manner from the west end. A foundation was found inside the building, at a distance of about 6 feet from the east wall, and it is conjectured that this may represent the seat of an altar. The windows, of which several stones were found, appear to have had single mullions with simple pointed arches.

Although only demolished in this century, there does not appear to be any view of the old church known. It is described by Symson, in his *Large Description of Galloway*, "as a considerable and large fabrick,

* This Plan has been kindly supplied by Mr. Robert Weir Schultz, architect, London, under whose directions the excavations were made.

consisting of a spacious church and stately quire, where are the tombs of the Lord Crichtons of Sanquhar, wrought in freestone, and before them some Lords of the name of Ross." *

The effigy of an ecclesiastic (Fig. 1373) was taken from Sanquhar to Friars Carse when the old church was demolished, but it has recently been brought back by Lord Bute.

CARNOCK CHURCH, Fifeshire.

A ruinous structure comprising some fragments of the ancient parish church which was remodelled soon after the Reformation. The church (Fig. 1374) now measures, internally, about 42 feet in length by 17 feet 6 inches in width. The east end contains one narrow, but complete, pointed window, with a simple jamb moulding, and the remains of another similar window, both having wide internal splays. Another narrow

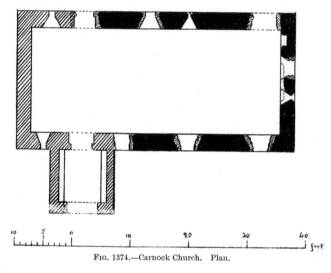

FIG. 1374.—Carnock Church. Plan.

pointed window yet exists in the north wall, but in the south wall the windows have been enlarged. The west wall (Fig. 1375) has been rebuilt or heightened, and a belfry of Renaissance style erected upon it. A round-headed doorway has been inserted in each of the north and south walls, and the round arch of the south door now stands detached. A south porch has also been added (see Fig. 1375) with a stone seat on each side, and having a round-headed entrance with large bead on jambs and arch. Two small windows near the ground at the west end seem to

* *History of Sanquhar*, by James Brown. Menzies & Co., 1891.

indicate that there has been a gallery above them at that end. The church is now disused, but still stands in the old churchyard, and is greatly covered with ivy.

FIG. 1375.—Carnock Church.   View from South-West.

John Row, the ecclesiastical historian, was minister of this parish from 1592 to 1646. It is situated about three miles west from Dunfermline.

DYSART CHURCH, Fifeshire.

This church has already been illustrated and described at length;[*] but as it is a building of considerable importance, it is introduced here in order to illustrate some points not formerly brought out. The edifice is a long parallelogram, with central avenue and north and south aisles, and is fairly entire along its whole length, except the outer wall of the north aisle. It has a lofty pele-like tower quite entire at the west end of the south aisle (Fig. 1376), which enters from the interior of the church by a doorway about 10 feet above the floor.

The tower is strong and quite capable of resisting a considerable

* *The Castellated and Domestic Architecture of Scotland*, Vol. v. p. 145.

attack. The main arcade is supported chiefly on round pillars, but at intervals the piers may be described as portions of the wall, as they

Fig. 1376.—Dysart Church. View from North-East.

extend to five feet and even 9 feet in length, and have rounded ends corresponding to the intermediate pillars. The pillars at the east end are gone, but there were probably seven bays in the whole internal length of 135 feet. The tower occupies one bay at the west end of the surviving bays. Only the bay adjoining the tower on the south

FIG. 1377.—Dysart Church. South and East Side of Tower.

side and the two bays opposite on the north side now remain (see Fig. 1376). The centre pillar on the north side is low, and supports lofty pointed arches. The second piers from the west are the large ones already described. Their caps are, as will be seen, at different levels, being higher on the east side than the west. The arcade to the eastwards may thus have been round arched, at all events the arches were not so acutely pointed as the western ones. The corbels for supporting the rafters of

FIG. 1378.—Dysart Church.
Niche on South Porch.

FIG. 1379.—Dysart Church.
Cap in North Aisle.

the roof are visible along the north face of the tower, and those for supporting the roof of the north aisle, with the drip moulding above, will be observed over the two arches at the west end, there being no stone vaulting used in the building. Fig. 1377 shows the east and south sides of the tower, and the large south porch with its stone covered roof and round arched doorway, over which is the canopied niche (Fig. 1378), and the bracket, ornamented with the pot of lilies, for supporting a statue. The figure was therefore probably one of the Virgin. The windows in the south aisle wall were (some of them at least) square headed.

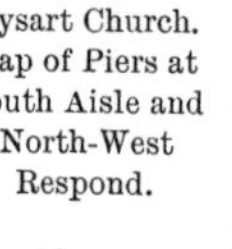

FIG. 1380.
Dysart Church.
Cap of Piers at
South Aisle and
North-West
Respond.

Fig. 1379 shows the capital of the pillar in the north aisle as far as it can be seen, on account of the modern wall, in which it is almost lost. It is formed to the shape of the double splayed arch moulding, and dies off into the round pillar below. The mouldings of the cap indicate very late work. Fig. 1380 is a still simpler cap from the south aisle and from the north-west respond.

KILCONQUHAR CHURCH, Fifeshire.

A small ruin consisting of three arches of an old church, which stood on the ancient site before the present modern structure was erected in the immediate vicinity. The village of Kilconquhar is situated on a large loch about one mile and a half north-west from Elie.

Fig. 1381.—Kilconquhar Church. View from South-West.

The name is derived from the ancient Saint Connacher. There is little of the history of the church preserved. It was granted in 1200 by Duncan, Earl of Fife, to the Convent of North Berwick, and in 1266, after a controversy between the Laird of Kilcomath and the prioress of North

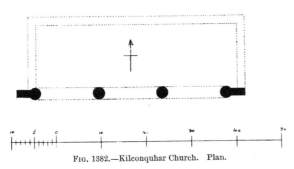

Fig. 1382.—Kilconquhar Church. Plan.

Berwick regarding the right of patronage, it was resigned into the hands of the Convent.*

The three arches (Fig. 1381) are all that now survive of the old church.

* *East Neuk of Fife,* p. 92.

They probably formed the arcade between the centre and side aisle, but there is nothing to show how the rest of the building was placed with reference to them. The north wall of the enclosure of a burying-place (shown by dotted lines in Fig. 1382) has an ancient look, and may be part of the old church.

The arches have plain splays. The round pillars have caps formed by a single hollow without any necking, and the bases are formed with a splay. Both caps and bases follow the curve of the pillars. They indicate a structure of very late date, probably about the time of the Reformation.

KILRENNY CHURCH, FIFESHIRE.

The village and church of Kilrenny stand about one mile inland from the coast at Anstruther. The only record before the Reformation is that in 1268 a pension was given to the vicar, who in 1336 was a certain "John." * The tower of the church (Fig. 1383) is old, and is attached to a modern edifice. It is of the form common in Fife about the time of the Reformation, being carried up (Fig. 1384) without buttresses or ornament,

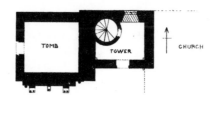

FIG. 1383.—Kilrenny Church. Plan of Tower, &c.

and having a parapet supported on corbels similar to those used in the castles of the period. There are traces of a large arch in the east wall of the tower, and another in the south wall, as if intended to open into a building, possibly the old church. The mark of the roof over the building on the south side still remains, and also a portion of a thick wall running southwards from the tower. In the internal angles of the tower there are square shafts with rude caps, apparently intended to support a vault, but there are now no traces of any vaulting. There are also the remains of a two-light window in the north wall of the tower. Attached to the west end of the tower is a stately monument erected by the family of Lumsdaine of Innergelly.

* *East Neuk of Fife,* p. 93.

In the churchyard of Kilrenny may still be seen the monument of
Cardinal Bethune or Beaton. It is an enclosure which stands to the east-

FIG. 1384.—Kilrenny Church. Tower, &c., from South-West.

ward of the church, built with ashlar and ornamented with Ionic pillars. The frieze and cornice are unfortunately wanting.

The entrance is in the east end, and in the opposite wall is a well-carved representation of the arms of Bethune of Balfour, viz., quarterly, 1st and 4th, azure a fesse between three mascles, or, for Bethune; 2nd and 3rd, argent on a chevron sable an otter's head erased of the first, for Balfour. Crest, an otter's head proper; motto, "Debonnaire."

ROSYTH CHURCH, FIFESHIRE.

A ruin situated on the shore of the Frith of Forth about five miles west from North Queensferry and about one mile east of Charleston.

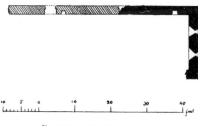

FIG. 1385.—Rosyth Church. Plan.

Part of the structure is ancient, but the western portion has been added in post-Reformation times. All that now remains of the building consists

FIG. 1386.—Rosyth Church. View from North-East.

(Fig. 1385) of the east wall and gable, and a considerable part of the north wall. The east end (Fig. 1386) contains two narrow pointed windows with a simple moulding on the outside, which is returned round the sill. The moulding (see Fig. 1386) is rebated on the exterior for a shutter. The ingoings are widely splayed and have pointed rear arches. The ancient part of the north wall is built with ashlar work, the stones being of a cubic form, resembling Norman work, and the mortar is well washed out of the joints. The remainder of the north wall is built with irregular courses, and the wall opening has a straight lintel. There is an ambry in the north wall near the east end, and a recess in the wall near the doorway. The church has been 15 feet wide internally, and probably about 50 feet in length.

THE CHURCH OF THE DOMINICANS OR BLACKFRIARS,
St. Andrews, Fifeshire.

Amongst the many remains of religious establishments still visible in this old ecclesiastical centre, the ruins of a small part of the Church of the Blackfriars are prominent from their situation, being an ivy clad fragment of the church which stands detached in the grounds of the Madras College, and forms a conspicuous object close to South Street, one of the leading thoroughfares of the town.

The Dominicans or Friars preachers were introduced into Scotland in 1231 by Bishop Clement of Dunblane, and they were encouraged by Alexander II., who founded eight houses of the order in the principal towns of Scotland. This order was brought to St. Andrews by Bishop William Wishart, well known from the great works carried out by him at the cathedral.

Bishop Elphinstone, the distinguished prelate of Aberdeen and founder of the University in that city, died in 1514, leaving a sum of £10,000, part of which Prior Hepburn of St. Andrews succeeded in obtaining from the executor, Sir Thomas Myrton, Archdeacon of Aberdeen, for the purpose of rebuilding the convent of the Friars preachers in St. Andrews. In connection with this arrangement, the provincial of the order, John Adamson, a great reformer, held a chapter at Stirling in 1519, in which the revenues of the convent at Cupar and part of those of St. Monans were transferred to St. Andrews, while these convents were suppressed.*

No record is preserved of the buildings erected at this time, but probably the church was rebuilt and a series of domestic structures erected round a quadrangle on the south side of the church. The monastery was attacked and pillaged by the mob in 1560. The possessions of the convent

* "The Dominican Friars at St. Andrews," *Transactions of the Aberdeen Ecclesiological Society,* by David Henry, F.S.A. Scot. 1893.

had been gradually disposed of in the beginning of the sixteenth century, and after the Reformation the monastery was abandoned, and the buildings gradually fell to pieces, the materials being carried off in the usual manner.

The only portion now surviving is an apsidal wing or chapel (Fig. 1387) which projected from the north side of the church. It is 26 feet long by 21 feet in width internally. The three-sided form of the north end is not uncommon in the sixteenth century in Scotland, but it is not usually adopted in side chapels or transepts, being generally reserved for the east end of the chancel. At Ladykirk, Berwickshire, however, we have an example of the three-sided apse introduced in the chancel, and also

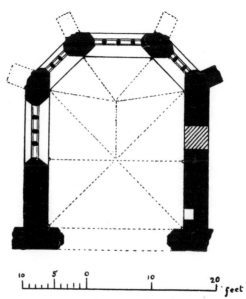

Fig. 1387.—Church of the Dominicans or Blackfriars, St. Andrews. Plan of North Chapel.

in the north and south transepts. There is a window in each of the three sides of the apse (Fig. 1388), the central one containing four lights and the diagonal windows three lights. A large window in the west wall has also four lights. The tracery in the windows has been renewed in modern times in a somewhat imperfect manner. The buttresses on the exterior angles have been almost entirely carried away. The altar probably stood on the east side, where there is an ambry, with the arch-head carved with a debased form of tracery. There seems to have been a doorway in the east wall, now built up.

The vaulting of the chapel (see Fig. 1388) is partly preserved. That over the square portion is a pointed barrel vault with ribs, arranged in sexpartite form. The ribs spring from corbels and small shafts. One of the corbels is carved with the Hepburn arms. The central boss of the vault bears the heart surrounded with two hands and feet,

FIG. 1388.—Church of the Dominicans or Blackfriars, St. Andrews. North Chapel.

emblems of the Passion. The vault of the apse is broken away, but it has been divided into three panels by ribs rising to a point at the apex. The vaulting of the main part of the chapel is of plain barrel form, and the cross ribs are introduced as ornaments on the surface, a common arrangement in late work. The ribs of the apse spring from two vaulting shafts rising from corbels, the caps of which have shields bearing the Hepburn arms (on a chevron a rose between two lions rampant). The chevron is still distinguishable. From the threefold repetition of these arms, it is supposed that this chapel was erected by Prior Hepburn, as a memorial and, perhaps, a burial chapel. The responds at the entrance, with their caps and other details, are of the third pointed period, and correspond with the date when the chapel was erected. A row of plain corbels, visible over the main arch, doubtless supported the roof of the principal nave of the church.

THE CHURCH OF ST. LEONARD'S COLLEGE,
St. Andrews, Fifeshire.

In the middle of the thirteenth century the Hospitium or Guest Hall of St. Leonard's was founded by Prior John White, for the reception of pilgrims and visitors to St. Andrews. Some remains of the Guest Hall

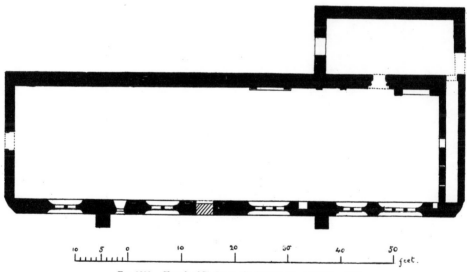

Fig. 1389.—Church of St. Leonard's College, St. Andrews. Plan.

have recently been excavated in the ground eastward from St. Leonard's Church, from which it appears that it was a hall with central nave and two side aisles. The building was afterwards converted into a nunnery. In 1512 it was appropriated for a college.

FIG. 1390.—Church of St. Leonard's College, St. Andrews. South Side.

This college was founded by John Hepburn, Prior of St. Andrews, in conjunction with Archbishop Alexander Stewart. It remained under the authority of the prior and chapter, and was designed for the education of twenty-four poor students. The college, however, soon became famed for its learning, and was attended by sons of the nobility. The students were specially instructed in music, and helped to spread a knowledge of sacred music throughout the country. George Buchanan, the well-known scholar, was at one time Principal.

The chapel (Fig. 1389) is a simple oblong chamber, being, internally, about 80 feet in length by 20 feet 6 inches in width, and has no division between chancel and nave. The design of the windows and buttresses (Fig. 1390) accords well with the date of erection in the sixteenth century, being in the perpendicular style, such as is common in the colleges in England. The windows are all square-headed, and the three-light ones have the heads of the lights cusped like quatrefoils. The church appears, from the marks in the walls, to have been extended 24 feet at the east end, probably at the time when it was converted into the college.

On the north side of the church is a room with a round barrel vault, probably the sacristy. From the door of the sacristy a narrow passage runs along the east end of the church in the thickness of the wall, and from it there are two loops into the church. Above this passage, and also in the thickness of the wall, another narrow passage is constructed in the east wall, which is continued round in the north wall as far as the vault of the sacristy extends. There is a shallow piscina in the east window sill. The west end has a door in the centre, and three remarkable niches above it. They have the appearance of having been placed there in recent times, when the west end was rebuilt. The arms of Prior Hepburn are inserted in this wall, and they are also carved on one of the south buttresses.

There are no windows in the north wall, but the interior contains several good Renaissance monuments. In the floor is the flat tombstone of John Wynram, Superintendent of Fife, who died in 1582; and against the north wall is the monument of Robert Stewart, Earl of March, who was commendator of the priory after the Regent Moray's death.

The church was for long used for public worship, but after the College of St. Leonards was united to that of St. Salvator in 1747, the former was abandoned in 1759.

A long range of buildings on the south side of the church was occupied as the students' lodgings, but these were also abandoned, and have now been converted into private residences.

Several alterations were likewise made on the church within recent times, the steeple being taken down, and the west end "set back," so as to give more room for access to one of the private houses.

CHURCH OF THE HOLY TRINITY,
St. Andrews, Fifeshire.

This church, usually called the Town Church, is of ancient foundation, but was almost entirely rebuilt at the end of last century. The church which was then demolished is believed to have been erected in 1412. The north-west tower (Fig. 1391) is the only part of the old structure which survives. Like the north-west tower at Cupar it rises from the north and west walls of the north aisle, without buttresses to mark its outline or break the upright form of the walls. The square outline, however, is partly relieved by a square projection at the north-west angle, which contains the staircase. The east and south walls are carried by arches, which formerly allowed the lower story of the tower to be included within the church, and the round pier at the south-east angle is made of extra thickness, so as to bear the weight of the tower. The tower is carried up square to the parapet with only a string course beneath the windows of the belfry story. In the latter trefoil-headed double windows are introduced, except on the north side, where a mullioned window is inserted between the stair turret and

Fig. 1391.—Church of the Holy Trinity, St. Andrews.
Tower, from North-East.

the east angle. The parapet is plain and rests on simple corbels. Above this rises an octagonal spire, with lucarnes. The spire is rather short and stunted, like most of the late Scottish examples.

Over the staircase a small turret with pointed roof is carried up within the parapet, and groups picturesquely with the main spire. The tower resembles that at Wester Crail, and, like it, is of fifteenth century date.

AIRLIE CHURCH, Forfarshire.

Two relics of the ancient church of St. Medan (demolished 1783) have been preserved, one being a mutilated figure of St. John the Baptist (Fig. 1392) built into the west gable of the existing church, and the other a sacrament house (Fig. 1393) inserted in the wall under

Fig. 1392.—Airlie Church.
Figure in Tower.

Fig. 1394.—Airlie Church.
Belfry.

the stair to the gallery. The sacrament house is of rude design and workmanship, and is evidently of very late date. The ambry has an opening $10\frac{1}{2}$ inches in width, and its size over all is 2 feet 5 inches in height by 21 inches in width. It has, as usual in such features, a broad base surmounted by the recess to contain the consecrated host. The opening is finished with an ogee arch-head having a cable-moulding on the jambs and arch, and a fleur-de-lys on top. As usual the ambry is

FIG. 1393.—Airlie Church. Sacrament House.
(From Sketch kindly supplied by Mr. Archibald M'Pherson, architect.)

flanked by small buttresses. In the panels at the spandrils there are carved on one side a cross with a crown of thorns, and on the other the heart, with hands and feet showing the five wounds of the Passion.

The back of the ambry is formed with a stone containing the initials W. F., and the arms of the Fentons of Baikie, which are turned upside down, probably by mistake, when rebuilt in the present position.

The belfry of the church (Fig. 1394) is a good example of a structure of that description of the date it bears (1783).

INVERGOWRIE CHURCH, Forfarshire.

A simple oblong ruin situated about three miles west from Dundee. The site is associated with the Celtic Church, and is one of the churches believed to have been founded by St. Boniface, in Angus, about the

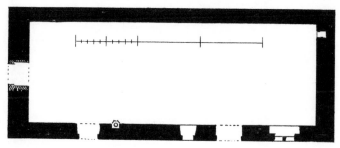

Fig. 1395.—Invergowrie Church. Plan.

beginning of the seventh century, Restennet being another.* Several fine sculptured stones of an early period are still preserved in the building.

Fig. 1396.—Invergowrie Church. View from South-East.

* *Celtic Scotland*, Vol. ii. p. 230.

Between 1153 and 1165 the Church of St. Peter, Invergowrie, was given to Scone by Malcolm IV. ; but of this early structure nothing whatever remains, and the existing building is probably not earlier than the first half of the sixteenth century. The walls of the structure (Fig. 1395) are entire, although the west gable hangs in a very tottering manner. The building measures inside about 46 feet in length by 15 feet 9 inches in width. There are two doorways in the south wall (Fig. 1396), the one towards the west end being round-arched, but not built on the arch principle, being cut out of two large stones. The other doorway is lintelled. There are two windows also in the south wall, the one being round-arched and cusped (Fig. 1397) and having the

FIG. 1397.
Invergowrie Church.
South Window.

arch cut out of a single stone. The other window is lintelled and had a central mullion. There is a high window in the west gable, and a west doorway, which probably dates from Presbyterian times. A stoup adjoins the western doorway in the interior of the south wall, and a locker recess occurs in the east gable. Lying inside the church there is the curious cross-like object (Fig. 1398). It is pierced in the centre, and appears to have had a shaft, which is broken, as shown.

FIG. 1398.
Invergowrie Church.
Cross-like Object.

MAINS CHURCH, FORFARSHIRE.

This fragment of a church is situated in the centre of its churchyard, on the margin of a romantic glen, on the opposite side of which stands the ruined Castle of Mains, in the region of Strath Dichty, about three miles north from Dundee. The remains consist of a small building which projected from the south side of the church, and which Mr. Muir * calls " the sacristy of the demolished church of Mains." The view (Fig. 1399) shows three lancet windows in the south gable, which are of very simple design, having merely a splay on their outer edge. The place is locked up, but Mr. Muir says that the windows have separate rear-arches.

Over the window there is a very beautiful sculptured fragment representing the Annunciation. It is sadly wasted, the head of the Virgin, and what may have been the descending dove, being an indistinct mass. The lower part of the figure, however, is well preserved, and is

* *Mainland Characteristics*, p. 47.

extremely graceful. The figure of the angel, although wasted, is in good preservation, while the scroll and pot of lilies are fairly distinct. Beneath the pot there is a shield on which are visible two piles issuing from a chief, with the remains of what may be mullets or annulets on the piles. There were probably three piles at first.

Fig. 1399.—Mains Church. Surviving Fragment.

The Church of Mains belonged to the Abbey of Arbroath.

There is a sundial, of more recent date than the building, carved on the south-west corner, similar to the sundials on the porch of Linlithgow Church and on the south transept of Melrose.

MARYTON CHURCH, Forfarshire.*

Maryton Church is situated about two miles south-west of Montrose.

The fine grave slab (Fig. 1400) was found by Mr. Robertson lying broken and uncared for; and at his suggestion the minister, Mr. Fraser,

* The annexed drawing is from a sketch by Mr. T. S. Robertson.

FIG 1400.—Maryton Church. Grave Slab.

had it removed and placed in the church vestry. The upper part is occupied with a finely incised figure of a knight in sixteenth century costume, and the lower portion is occupied with the arms, supporters, helmet, and mantling. The arms are, an oak tree growing out of a mount (for Wood of Bonyton), between two cross crosslets (for Tulloch of Bonyton). Walter or William Wood married Dorothy Tulloch, one of the co-heiresses of Bonyton, sometime before 4th January 1493, in which year they got a confirmation of a charter by James IV. An inscription can still be partly traced round the slab, and it is believed to date from 1530.

PERT CHURCH, FORFARSHIRE.*

An old church situated on the North Esk about midway between Montrose and Edzell. The building (Fig. 1401) is in a state of ruin and covered with ivy. It measures in the inside about 43 feet from east to west by about 18 feet in width.

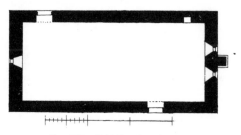

FIG. 1401.—Pert Church. Plan.

There is a door in each of the north and south walls near the opposite ends, which have square lintels with rounded shoulders, as shown in Fig. 1402; and three narrow lancet windows (Figs. 1402 and 1403), two in the east wall and one

FIG. 1402.—Pert Church
Doorway and Window.

FIG. 1403.—Pert Church.
Central Buttress.

* For the drawings of this church we are indebted to Mr. T. S. Robertson.

in the west wall. These windows are about 12 inches wide, and have the arches cut out of two stones, with wide splays towards the interior. Between the two, in the east gable, there is a central buttress with splayed base (see Fig. 1403).

These features appear to indicate that this was originally rather an early church, probably of about the close of the first pointed period, but it appears to have been almost rebuilt, probably in the fifteenth century.

The belfry on the west gable (Fig. 1404) is even later, and bears the date of 1676.

FIG. 1404.—Pert Church. Belfry.

ST. VIGEAN'S CHURCH, FORFARSHIRE.*

This church is pleasantly situated at the head of a little valley through which winds the stream of the Brothock, at a distance of between one and two miles north from Arbroath or Aberbrothock. Previous to the Reformation it was the parish church of Arbroath. The edifice stands on the top of a regularly shaped mound, and occupies nearly the whole of the summit. It has been the site of a religious settlement from a very remote period, far earlier than the erection of the great abbey at Arbroath. This is shown by several Norman wrought stones that have been found on the site, as well as a large and most important group of elaborately carved sculptured stones, relics of the Celtic church which once stood here. Vigianus has been recognised as the Latinised form of the name of St. Fechin of Fohbar, an Irish saint who died in 664. Dr. Joseph Anderson mentions that the twelfth century builders had utilised a large quantity of fragments of sculptured monuments as building materials.†

In 1871, under the direction of Dr. R. Rowand Anderson, architect, the church was restored and considerable additions were made to it. A large polygonal apse, with massive buttresses, was built at the east end, a second aisle was formed on the north side of the existing north aisle, and the tower was raised and finished with a saddle-back roof. At the same time a new roof and internal fittings were added, making the edifice one of the most seemly parish churches in Scotland.

Previous to this restoration, the structure consisted (as shown in Fig. 1405) of a central nave of eight bays, with north and south aisles, and a western tower. The original Norman church appears to have occupied the site of the north aisle, and to have extended in width to about the centre

* For a fuller notice of this church and its sculptured stones, see *Proceedings of the Society of Antiquaries of Scotland*, Session 1870-72, Vol. IX., by the Rev. Dr. Duke, to whom we are indebted for assistance; as also to Mr. Robertson for some notes and a sketch.

† *Scotland in Early Christian Times*, p. 49.

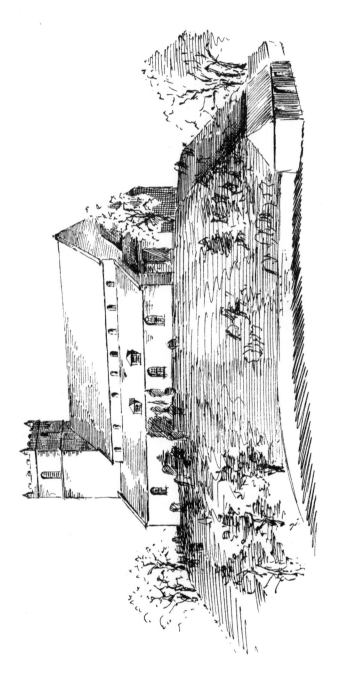

FIG. 1405.—St. Vigean's Church. View from South-East (before 1871).

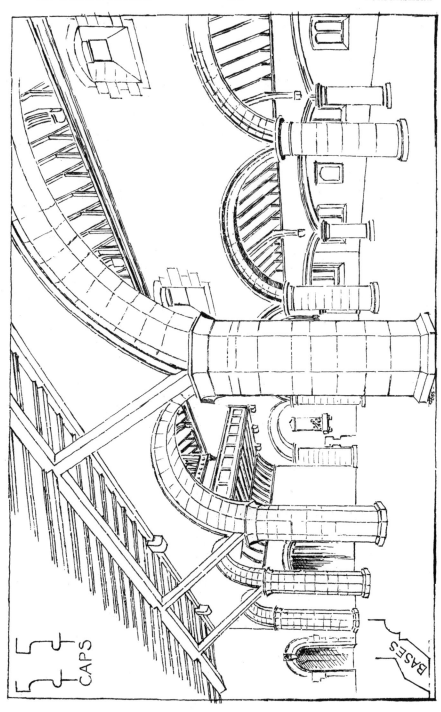

Fig. 1406.—St. Vigean's Church, looking West.

of the present nave. Parts of the east and west gable walls still remain. At a later period, probably about the middle of the fifteenth century, the church was extended to the south, and was converted into a building with a nave and a north aisle; and again at a still later period, in 1485, the south wall was taken down and a south aisle erected. The north and south aisles correspond in a general way with each other (Fig. 1406), and although the pillars on the north side are round and those on the south side are octagonal, both have very simple caps and bases, all of late form.

The arches of the arcade on both sides are round with broad notched splays. There are three clerestory windows on the north side, of a square shape. They formerly had oak lintels on the inside, but these, being decayed, were removed during the restoration, and the stone arches shown in Fig. 1406 were put in. On the south side there are eight clerestory windows, arched throughout.

The west tower is not in the centre, but occupies the space between the centre of the nave and the line of the south arcade. It appears to be an addition, but its lower plain vaulted story was probably erected before the addition of 1485, while the upper portion is of later construction. There is an entrance through the tower to the church, which, from the relative positions of the two, is not in the centre. The opening of a flat arched form is shown in Fig. 1406.

In 1242 Bishop de Bernham consecrated the Church of St. Vigean. It was again consecrated, along with two altars and the cemetery, in 1485 after the additions were built by Bishop George O'Brien, Bishop of Dromore, in Ireland,* acting probably, as Dr. Duke says, for the Bishop of St. Andrews.

MONASTERY OF RED OR TRINITY FRIARS, DUNBAR,
HADDINGTONSHIRE.

This fragment (Fig. 1407) is all that remains of the monastery of the Red Friars at Dunbar. The field in which it stands is still known as the Friars' Croft.

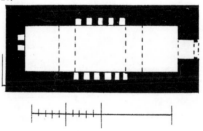

FIG. 1407.—Monastery of Red or Trinity Friars, Dunbar. Plan.

* For an account of this Bishop see *Antiquities and History of Ireland*, by the Right Honourable Sir James Wace, Knight; Dublin, 1705, p. 68 of Lists of Bishops.

It is generally supposed * that this building was originally a belfry of the monastery, and that it was, at a subsequent period, converted into a pigeon house ; but it is much more likely that, besides being the belfry, it was also the pigeon house of the monastery from the first. It appears to be still very much in its original state. The walls which support the central portion (Fig. 1408), which rise from arches in the interior (Fig. 1409) and give the structure its belfry-like aspect, are evidently as old as any other part of the structure, and the supporting arches with their corbels are not insertions.

Fig. 1408.—Monastery of Red or Trinity Friars, Dunbar.

It will be observed that in order to get solidity and strength in the walls under these arches, the nests or pigeon holes are almost entirely left out in those portions (see Fig. 1409). The cross beam and upright post seen in the sketch are old. The ladder, which is fixed, enabled a man to go up and search for the eggs.

This monastery was founded in 1218 by Patrick, sixth Earl of Dunbar,

* *History of Dunbar*, by James Miller, p. 184.

Fɪɢ. 1409.—Monastery of Red or Trinity Friars, Dunbar.

but these remains clearly belong to an age some two or three centuries later. From the history above referred to, the monastery appears to have been suppressed before the Reformation, about the year 1529, at which date the brethren were translated to Peebles.

KEITH CHURCH, HADDINGTONSHIRE.

On a knoll within the grounds of Keith House, situated about five miles east from Tynehead Station, and a similar distance south from Ormiston, stand the ruins of an ancient church. It is surrounded by an old churchyard, and has a number of monuments erected against the south wall. According to an inscription on a tablet fixed to the wall, this edifice was "erected as a private chapel in the reign of David i. (1224-53) by Hervie de Keith, King's Marischal; in the reign of Alexander ii. (1214-49) it became the church of the parish of Keith Marischal; in 1618 this parish was joined to that of Keith Hunderbey, now called Humby." *

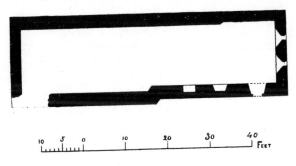

Fig. 1410.—Keith Church. Plan.

The church (Fig. 1410) is now a ruin and is covered with a thick growth of ivy. It measures, internally, 59 feet 8 inches in length by 14 feet in width at the east end, and 15 feet in width at the west end. The east end is apparently the oldest portion, the east wall and north wall, as far as the break shown in the Plan, and a corresponding portion of the south wall being faced with ashlar. The remainder of the structure, westwards from the above, is built with rubble, and is apparently of later date. The north wall is much broken down, but the other walls are in fair preservation. The east end, as viewed from the interior (Fig. 1411) (where the growth of ivy allows the features to be tolerably seen), is an unusual and rather striking design, consisting of two narrow lancet windows, widely splayed internally, and a large vesica-formed opening

* See *Caledonia*, Vol. ii. p. 332.

above them. These windows have a broad double splay on the exterior of
the jambs and arches.

One round-headed and cusped window survives in the south wall close
to the east end (Fig. 1412), and the Plan shows that there has been another
window adjoining, but it is now built up. The west end wall (Fig. 1413)

Fig. 1411.—Keith Church. Interior of East End.

contains a single small pointed window, evidently of a late date. So far
as can now be ascertained from the building the east end or chancel is
comparatively ancient, probably of the beginning of the sixteenth century,
and the remainder has been rebuilt not long after the Reformation.

A good seventeenth century monument is erected against the south
wall (see Fig. 1412).

FIG. 1412.—Keith Church. View from South-East.

FIG. 1413.—Keith Church. West Wall.

ST. PALLADIUS' CHURCH, FORDOUN, KINCARDINESHIRE.

The village of Fordoun lies in the picturesque glen of the Luther Water, about 2½ miles west from Fordoun Railway Station. The name of Saint Palladius, the early "apostle of the Scots," is attached to a small

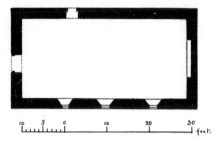

FIG. 1414.—St. Palladius' Church, Fordoun. Plan.

chapel which stands in the churchyard surrounding the parish church. Dr. Skene's opinion* is that Palladius was sent to Ireland (then the country of the Scots) and that Terrananus or Ternan, his disciple, brought

FIG. 1415.—St. Palladius' Church, Fordoun. View from South-West.

his relics either from Ireland or from Galloway (in one of which places he had been martyred) to his native district in the territories of the Southern

* *Celtic Scotland*, Vol. II. p. 27.

Picts, and as the founder of the church of Fordoun, in honour of Palladius, became to some extent identified with him. Be that as it may, the name of Palladius has been handed down from the fifth century in connection with a religious establishment in the place. A chapel, a well, and an annual fair are named after him. The small chapel which now bears the name of the Saint is a modern restoration. It is a plain oblong structure (Fig. 1414), 39 feet by 18 feet internally. The walls are low, and there is a pointed gable at each end (Fig. 1415). The east wall has a recess, which probably contained a monument, and the west wall a round-headed entrance doorway. There are three small square-headed windows in the south wall and a doorway in the north wall.

The east end is probably the oldest part. There is a burial-vault beneath it. An ambry with round head near the north door, and a plain pointed piscina at the south side of the eastern recess, are the only ancient appurtenances.

A chapel here is frequently mentioned in the records of the Priory of St. Andrews. It is not called a church till 1244.*

The Friars' Glen, which runs north-westward from Fordoun, was, in the fifteenth century, in the possession of the Carmelite Friars of Aberdeen.

OLD GIRTHON CHURCH, KIRKCUDBRIGHTSHIRE.†

A roofless ruin (Fig. 1416), about two miles south of Gatehouse, with walls fairly entire. It measures internally about 71 feet long by about 20 feet wide, and is lighted by windows in the south wall, and two high narrow windows in the east end, over which, in the apex, there is a shallow niche. There is only one small high window in the north wall.

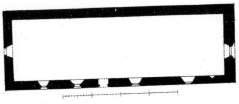

FIG. 1416.—Old Girthon Church. Plan.

The entrance door is in the south wall, not far from the centre of the church. In each end of the church there is a doorway, but these are probably modern. In the south wall, near the east end in the usual position of the piscina, there is what Mr. Coles calls an ambry, roughly

* A. Jervise in *The Proceedings of the Society of Antiquaries of Scotland, 1874,* p. 730.

† We are indebted to Mr. F. R. Coles for the drawings and notes of this church.

formed out of a single stone. It is surrounded with a large hollow moulding 4 inches wide, over which it measures 1 foot 8 inches wide by 2 feet 6 inches high, and 9 inches in depth.

Mr. Muir * classes Girthon with a number of other churches which may be either of the Norman or first pointed period.

BLANTYRE PRIORY, LANARKSHIRE.

The fragmentary ruins of this structure are situated on the left bank of the Clyde near Bothwell, at a point where the river forms a sudden bend from west to north, and where the priory is confronted on the opposite side by the great donjon of Bothwell Castle. The eastern walls of the priory stand on the very edge of a precipice, which rises perhaps 80 or 100 feet above the river. The buildings at this part are situated on fairly level ground, but immediately to the west the ground rises rapidly, so that the cloister garth (Fig. 1417) and the western enclosing walls are on a considerably higher level than the main buildings. The ruins cover a space of ground measuring about 150 feet from east to west by about 115 feet from north to south. The western enclosing wall is from 5 to 10 feet in height, and the northern wall stands to the height of about 10 feet. The southern wall is nearly all gone, except a part at the return of the buildings at the east and west ends.

At the north-east corner stands a two-storied structure, the walls of which, except the south one, are almost entire. This was probably the prior's house. It enters by a doorway at the west end of the south wall, and adjoining the door there appears to have been a stair to the upper floor (which is the floor shown on the Plan), but the place is in so confused a state with ruins and vegetation, that little regarding its arrangement can be made out. The house contained two rooms, one at each end, with the stair between. There are a fireplace and a window in each gable, and the eastern window looks straight across the river to the castle donjon. Along the north side of the house the ground is steep and inaccessible. On the south side of this house there was a courtyard with a building at the east end, the end wall of which still stands two stories high, in continuation of the gable of the prior's house.

Adjoining this to the south is an apartment said, by the local guide, to be the chapel. Of this, however, almost nothing remains, except a part of the west wall, in which there is a stoup (Fig. 1418) hollowed out of a stone wrought with all the appearance of a corbel, like those found in the castles. On the face of the corbel is an incised cross. It is this feature which has obtained for the apartment the name of the chapel. There is a window in the west wall above the stoup, but with nothing of

* *Characteristics*, p. 56.

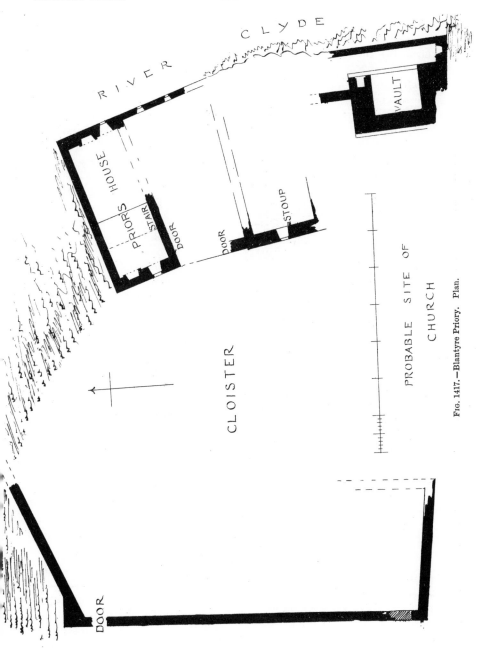

RIVER CLYDE

PRIORS HOUSE

STAIR

DOOR

DOOR

STOUP

VAULT

CLOISTER

PROBABLE SITE OF CHURCH

DOOR

Fig. 1417.—Blantyre Priory. Plan.

an ecclesiastic character about it. This building does not appear to have been the church. It is more likely that the latter was placed somewhere about the line of the south boundary wall. It could not have stood anywhere outside of what is shown in the Plan on the north side, as in all this locality the ground is inaccessible.

A ruined fragment stands at the south-east corner of the monastery. It is a vaulted apartment, commanding the long reach of the river before

it takes its northern bend. There is a narrow pathway in front of this apartment, giving access to it. The path is protected from the cliff by a parapet wall returned at the south end, where there is a shot hole. This parapet has gone on to join the buildings at the prior's house.

The parish church of Blantyre stood in a village of the same name, and belonged to the priory, which is said to have been founded for Austin canons, and endowed with the tithes and revenues of the parish church,

FIG. 1418.—Blantyre Priory.
Stoup.

by Alexander II. Spottiswoode asserts that Blantyre was a cell depending on Holyrood. In *Bagimond's Roll* (1275), it is valued at £66, 13s. 4d. Chalmers states that this small monastery was founded by Alexander II. for canons regular brought from Jedburgh, and that the monks of Jedburgh retired here during the war with England.

The barony belonged to the Dunbars as far back as 1368. Walter Stewart, son of the Laird of Minto, was made commendator by James VI., and the Barony of Blantyre was erected, in 1606, into a temporal lordship in his favour, with the title of Lord Blantyre.

COVINGTON CHURCH, LANARKSHIRE.

Covington is a hamlet in the Upper Ward, about four miles south from Carstairs Junction. A church existed here from the time of David I., and is frequently referred to in deeds. It stood near the Castle * of the Lindsays of Covington, who acquired the manor before 1442, and was no doubt in their gift and that of their predecessors in the property. The dedication seems to have been to St. Michael.†

    * *The Castellated and Domestic Architecture of Scotland*, Vol. III. p. 239.
    † *Upper Ward of Lanarkshire*, Vol. I. p. 462.

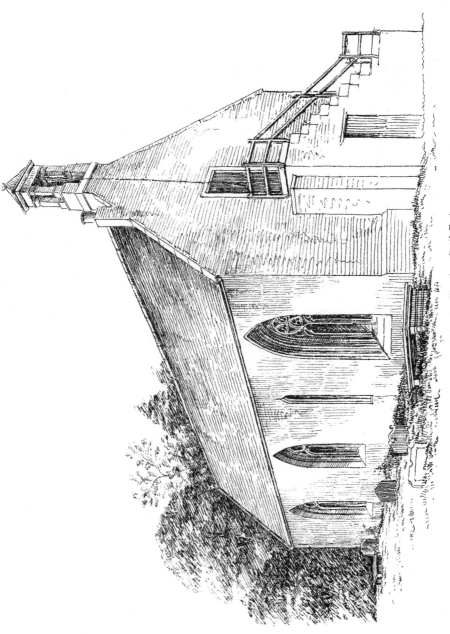

Fig. 1420.—Covington Church.   View from South-East.

The existing church (Fig. 1419) is of considerable age, but has been a good deal tampered with. It stands in the old churchyard, no doubt on the same site as the original edifice. The church is a simple oblong

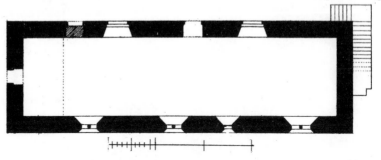

FIG. 1419.—Covington Church. Plan.

chamber 72 feet 3 inches in length and 22 feet 4 inches in breadth externally. The old pointed windows (Fig. 1420) still remain in the south wall, three of them having a mullion and simple tracery, that of the east-most being very good. The eastmost window has also good mouldings in the jambs and arch (Fig. 1421). The second window from the east is narrow and ogee headed, and probably marks the position of the rood screen.

An old doorway remains, though built up, near the north-west angle. In the arch there is inserted a shield (Fig. 1422) bearing the arms of the Lindsays, to whom the castle be-longed, and the letters W. L. and the date 1659.

FIG. 1421.
Covington Church.
Mouldings of
South-East Window.

FIG. 1422.
Covington Church.
Arms in
North Doorway.

The east end has been entirely altered, the east window having probably been built up, and an outside stair erected to give access to a gallery at that end.

AULDCATHIE CHURCH, LINLITHGOWSHIRE.

Before the Reformation Auldcathie formed a separate parish, but it is now included in the parish of Dalmeny, of which it forms a detached portion. The ruins of the old church (Fig. 1423) now stand neglected in the middle of a large field. The walls are much reduced, and are gradually crumbling away, but the plan is still quite entire. The structure measures, internally, about 30 feet in length by 15 feet in width. There has been a door near the west end, both in the north and south walls, two windows in the south wall, and none in either of the north, east, or west walls. There is a recess for a benitier, an ambry near the south door, and an ambry in the east wall. Some more ancient stones seem to have been

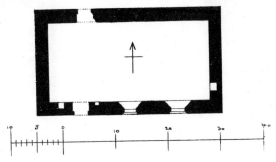

FIG. 1423.—Auldcathie Church. Plan.

used in building the latter. The features are all so simple that it is difficult to fix the date of the edifice, but it does not appear to be very old.

In the ancient *Taxatio* this church is valued at only 4 marks. As it is not taxed in *Bagimond's Roll*, it appears to have belonged in the thirteenth century to some religious house.

RESTALRIG COLLEGIATE CHURCH, MID-LOTHIAN.*

According to the legendary history of the Blessed Virgin Triduan, Lestalrig or Restalrig, a village to the east of Edinburgh, might claim a very great antiquity. Triduan is said to have died at Restalrig in the year 510.

A church can be traced here as early as the twelfth century, and it afterwards became the parish church of Leith. This edifice is frequently mentioned in connection with gifts bestowed upon it. The church of Restalrig was erected into a Collegiate establishment by James III., and was rebuilt by him, as stated in the Papal Bull of 1487. James IV. was also a benefactor to the foundation, and endowed an additional chaplain in 1512, and twelve years later another rectory was annexed to the church by James V.

The edifice has unfortunately been almost entirely destroyed. In 1560 it was resolved "that the Kirk of Restalrig, as a monument of Idolatrie be

* See preface to *Registrum of the Collegiate Churches of Mid-Lothian*, by D. Laing, p. xliii.

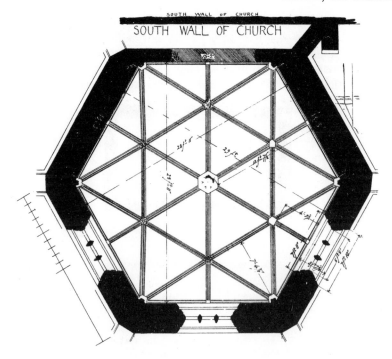

FIG. 1424.—Restalrig Collegiate Church. Plan of Chapter House.

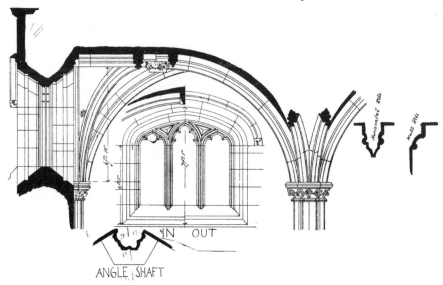

FIG. 1425.—Restalrig Collegiate Church. Section.

raysit and utterlie caste downe and destroyed." This was apparently done, as it is recorded that the ashlar work from the church was used by a certain citizen " to big his hous with."

In 1836 the church was restored, being practically rebuilt.

In the churchyard, however, there still exists a somewhat remarkable structure. Externally it is a mausoleum-like building, covered with turf. It is sometimes supposed to be "the crypt or family vault erected by Sir Robert Logan of Restalrig (who died

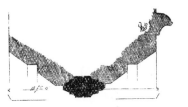

FIG. 1426.—Restalrig Collegiate Church. Jambs and Mouldings of Windows.

1440-41), by whom indeed it may have been built, while it has been used as such by successive proprietors." "It was undoubtedly

FIG. 1427.—Restalrig Collegiate Church. Vaulted Roof.

attached to the college, perhaps as the chapter house or St. Triduan's Chapel."

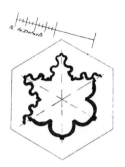

FIG. 1428.
Restalrig Collegiate Church.
Pier and Arch Ribs.

This building is a hexagon on plan (Fig. 1424), measuring 29 feet in internal diameter, and stands about 3 feet from the south wall of the church, against which the angle buttresses have impinged.

On each of the three sides facing towards the south there is a window, now built up, each of which has a very flat four-centred arch, and contains three cusped lights (Fig. 1425), divided by two mullions. The section of the jambs and mullions is shown in Fig. 1426. The roof is vaulted (Fig. 1427) with ribs springing from a central pier, which has a filleted roll towards each angle (Fig. 1428)

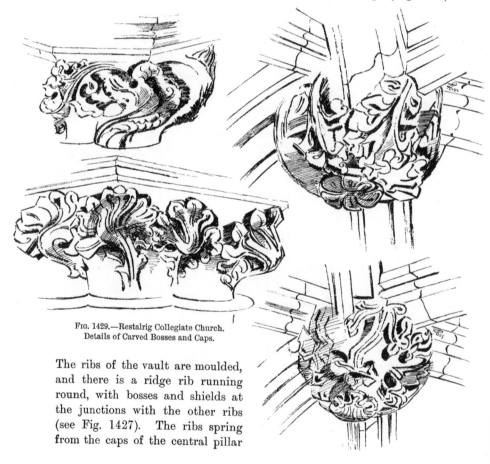

FIG. 1429.—Restalrig Collegiate Church.
Details of Carved Bosses and Caps.

The ribs of the vault are moulded, and there is a ridge rib running round, with bosses and shields at the junctions with the other ribs (see Fig. 1427). The ribs spring from the caps of the central pillar and the caps of shafts in the angles. The style of the carving of these caps and the foliage of the bosses is evidently of the third or late period (Fig. 1429). From its use as a sepulchral vault the floor has now been greatly filled up with earth, which rises almost to the caps of the central shaft and wall shafts.

It is not known when the turf was piled up over the roof, but it is very desirable that it should be removed, and the windows opened up, and the interior cleaned out. It would then be seen to be, as Mr Laing says, "a charming specimen of the architecture of the fifteenth century."

NEWLANDS CHURCH, Peeblesshire.

The ruined church of Newlands stands in the midst of the old church-yard, in the retired and quiet valley of the Lyne, which flows southwards towards the Tweed from near the foot of the Pentland Hills. It is about four miles from West Linton Station on the Dolphinton Railway.

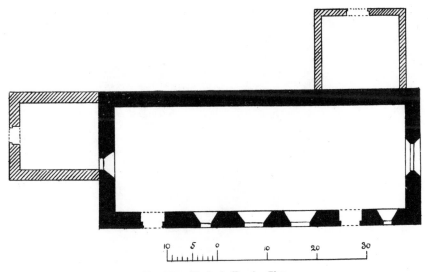

Fig. 1430.—Newlands Church. Plan.

The church (Fig. 1430), which is a simple oblong in plan, is evidently in some degree of ancient date; but it has been considerably altered in post-Reformation times, in order to make it suitable for Presbyterian service. For this purpose two large square-lintelled windows (Fig. 1431) have been inserted in the south wall, and one doorway near the east end of that wall (Fig. 1432) (the lintel of which bears the date of 1705). The ancient round-arched doorway near the west end (see Fig. 1431) has been

Fig. 1481.—Newlands Church. View from South-West.

FIG. 1482.—Newlands Church. View from South-East.

preserved, and has also been made available in later times. The later internal arrangements would thus be the usual Presbyterian ones, of having the pulpit placed in the centre of the south wall, with a large window on each side of it, and a central passage down the church, to which access was obtained by the two doorways near the east and west ends.

The church was doubtless originally lighted by several small windows in the south and west walls, and by a large pointed window in the east wall. The latter (see Fig. 1432) and the round-headed doorway near the west end of the south wall are the principal ancient features. The doorway has a bead on edge, and a plain hood moulding. It has all the appearance of being of early date. The east end is partly built with ashlar, and has a moulded string course near the ground running along part of it. The pointed window has double splays on the jambs and arch, both in the interior and exterior. It has doubtless had mullions at one time, but it is now impossible to find traces of them. The window is doubtless of third pointed date.

Various sepulchral enclosures have been added to the church, both internally and externally. That at the west end (see Fig. 1431) has probably had a coat of arms in the recess above the door, but it is now gone.

A number of quaintly carved tombstones of seventeenth and eighteenth century date are still crumbling away in the churchyard.

"The name of Newlands refers to the era when the lands lying around the Kirktown were first brought into cultivation by Scoto-Saxon bands." *   At the end of the thirteenth century Newlands belonged to the monks of Dunfermline. In *Bagimond's Roll* the *Rectoia de Newland*, in the Deanery of Peebles, is valued at £16.

CROSS CHURCH, PEEBLES.

The fragmentary ruins of the church of the monastery of the Redfriars stand in the middle of a fir plantation immediately to the west of the town of Peebles. All architectural interest connected with the edifice has been destroyed. The freestone work which Grose specially commends has been carried away, leaving only bare and ragged whinstone walls, and giving the structure a very desolate appearance. The monastic buildings were situated on the north side of the church; and the fir plantation, which seems to represent their extent, runs in that direction for about 100 feet, with an average length from east to west of about 250 feet, the whole extent of the plantation being a little less than an acre. It is probable, from these dimensions, that the monastic buildings were extensive, but, unfortunately, their destruction has been very complete. The ruins of the nave remain (Fig. 1433), and measure, within the walls, about 70 feet

* *Caledonia*, Vol. ii. p. 950.

6 inches from east to west by a width of 26 feet 9 inches. Grose gives the length of the church as 102 feet, and there are indications (see Plan) that it was longer at one time than it is now. There is a tower at the west end, which measures about 20 feet by 21 feet, and had an opening into the church, now built solidly up. From a view of the church in Grose's *Antiquities of Scotland*, the building was evidently in a much better condition in 1790 than now. It appears to have been then entire, wanting only the roof, and the tower was finished with a projecting parapet and two gables, after the manner of a pele tower.

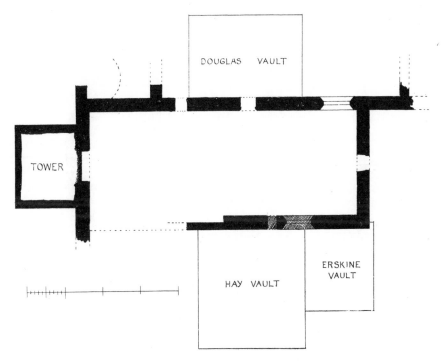

FIG. 1433.—Cross Church, Peebles. Plan.

So completely has the place been harried that little is left to describe. There were three pointed windows in the south wall and one in the east gable, the latter of which (Fig. 1434) still partly remains. Against the north wall of the church there is an erection called the Douglas vault, to which a door opens from the church. It is in a very dilapidated state, although the vaulted roof is complete. Immediately to the west of this vault, with a passage between of about 7 feet, there are indications of other vaulted buildings, and similar indications are found at the east end of the church, all in a very fragmentary condition.

In the historical books relating to the locality, a story is repeated of the finding, on this site, of a magnificent cross in 1261, of the miracles performed by it, and the ultimate founding of a church by the king, which was called the Cross Church. Such a church existed in 1296, for Frere Thomas, Mestre de la Maison de Seint Croce, de Pebblis, swore fealty to Edward I. at Berwick.*

At the Reformation the Cross Church became the church of the parish, and on the lintel of the door at the east end are cut the words "Feir God," with the date 1656. A portion to the west of this may have been

FIG. 1434.—Cross Church, Peebles.   View from South-West.

the part, about 30 feet in length, which Grose says was walled off to form a school, probably at the date just mentioned.

The monastic buildings were used for various purposes, such as a school and schoolmaster's house, and for persons suffering from the plague, but from about the beginning of the eighteenth century they gradually became ruinous, and have now reached their present lamentable condition.

* *Caledonia*, Vol. II. p. 942.

ST. ANDREW'S CHURCH, Peebles.

Rather less than a quarter of a mile west from the Cross Church there stands the tower of St. Andrew's Church. It has been so completely restored or transformed by the late Dr. Chambers, that it is now of no interest whatever as a specimen of the ancient architecture of Scotland. A view of the tower as it appeared at the end of the eighteenth century will be found in the *Antiquities of Scotland* by Captain Grose; and on the Ordnance Map there is a plan of the church, from which it may be gathered that the tower was a western one, in a similar position to that of the Cross Church. The plan shows a nave measuring about 75 feet long by 40 feet wide, and a choir about 50 feet long, having apparently a building of some kind, either an aisle or chapel, along the north side. The total length of the building was about 140 feet.

The Church of St. Andrew at Peebles was consecrated by Bishop Jocelin of Glasgow in 1195.* St. Andrew's was the parish church of Peebles.

In 1543 this church was made Collegiate. In 1548 it was burned down by the English, and never rebuilt. Captain Grose says that all the arches of the doors and windows were semicircular.

ABERUTHVEN CHURCH, Perthshire.

A ruined church situated near the village of the same name, about two and a half miles east from Auchterarder. The walls are almost entire, except part of the south one, which has been knocked down to give room

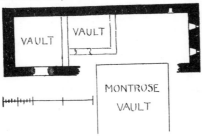

Fig. 1435.—Aberuthven Church. Plan.

for a mausoleum of the Montrose family, bearing the inscription "John Adam—fecet 1736."

The church (Fig. 1435) measures, externally, 65 feet 2 inches by 21 feet 9 inches. Its only architectural features are a seventeenth century

* *Caledonia*, Vol. II. p. 942.

belfry on the west end (Fig. 1436), and two small pointed windows (Fig. 1437) in the east end. The belfry, almost concealed with ivy, has long

narrow openings on the east and west sides, and small side openings. The east windows are between 2 and 3 feet above the floor, and are about 8 inches wide. The daylight of the northmost of these windows (Fig. 1438) is 2 feet $8\frac{1}{2}$ inches high, and for some inexplicable reason that of the south window is about 4 inches less. Both have an ogee arch-head, and are lintelled on the inside. There is an ambry in

FIG. 1436.—Aberuthven Church.
View from South-West.

the north wall near the east end. The usual set-off occurs on the east wall just above the windows.

The west end of the church is occupied by a modern burial vault and is not accessible, but it appears to be vaulted with a barrel vault. Another burial vault occupies

FIG. 1437.—Aberuthven Church.
Interior of East End.

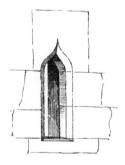

FIG. 1438.—Aberuthven Church.
North Window in East Wall.

the centre of the building. The church was a cell of Inchaffray, and was dedicated to St. Cathan. The existing structure is evidently of late date.

ST. MOLOC'S CHURCH, ALYTH, PERTHSHIRE.

Alyth is now a busy manufacturing town, and forms the terminus of a small branch line off the main railway between Perth and Forfar. It stands on the north side of Strathmore, at the point where the hills begin to rise, and the houses of the old part of the town are picturesquely terraced on the hillside. On one of these terraces may be seen the ruins of the ancient

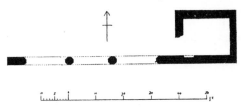

FIG. 1439.—St. Moloc's Church, Alyth. Plan.

church of St. Moloc or Malachi, according to the *Statistical Account*, but Mr. Muir calls it St. Ninian's. The original fair of the village is still called St. Mologue's and the date corresponds with the day of St. Moloc. Before the Reformation the benefice of Alyth was attached to one of the prebends of Dunkeld, and the patronage was exercised by the Bishop.

FIG. 1440.—St. Moloc's Church, Alyth. Arcade.

The old church was demolished about 1845, having been unroofed at that date when the last *Statistical Account* was written.

The portion which still survives (Fig. 1439) in the middle of the churchyard consists of the south arcade of the nave and part of the chancel. The arcade (Fig. 1440) has plain octagonal pillars and three round arches with broad splays. The caps and bases are moulded, and indicate a late date.

The chancel is surrounded with a plain wall 6 to 7 feet high, and has a piscina in the south wall.

AUCHTERARDER CHURCH, Perthshire.

This old church is situated a little to the north of the town, and is surrounded by an old churchyard. It is densely ivy clad and generally

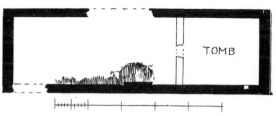

FIG. 1441.—Auchterarder Church. Plan.

concealed by vegetation, and thoroughly neglected. The church (Fig. 1441) measures about 81 feet long by about 24 feet 6 inches wide externally. There is almost no architectural feature now

FIG. 1442.
Auchterarder Church.
Piscina.

visible except a piscina (Fig. 1442) in the usual place in the south wall near the east end, which

FIG. 1443.—Auchterarder Church. View from South-West.

part of the building is walled off as a tomb house. The piscina is triangular headed, somewhat like the one in the choir of Paisley Abbey.

It is only visible through a chink in the door of the tomb. There has been some kind of projection in the south wall near the centre, but owing to vegetation and rubbish (Fig. 1443) it cannot be properly examined, nor for the same reason can anything be made out regarding any openings in the south wall. Both of the side walls are considerably ruined. There is a slightly projecting splayed base at the east wall, with the usual set-off just below the gable.

The edifice was dedicated to St. Mechessock, and in 1198 the church of Auchterarder was given by Gilbert, third Earl of Strathearn, to the Abbey of Inchaffray, but the existing ruin belongs to a much later age.

A well at a short distance south from the church still bears "St. M'Kessog's" name, and on his day (10th March) the principal fair of the town is held.* The church was served by a parochial curate appointed by the Abbot of Inchaffray.

CAMBUSMICHAEL CHURCH, Perthshire.

Finely situated on one of the most beautiful reaches of the Tay, a little below the Linn of Camsie and opposite the village of Stanley, this ruined church, with its churchyard, occupies the end of a plateau which slopes suddenly down to the river on the north side, and to a deep

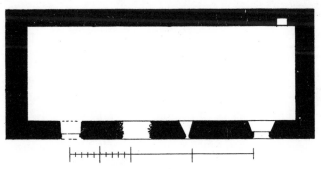

Fig. 1444.—Cambusmichael Church. Plan.

ravine on the east; so that, like most churches bearing the name of St. Michael, it stands on a height. The building, as will be seen from the Plan (Fig. 1444) and the view (Fig. 1445), is still in a fair state of preservation, although it is quite evident, on the spot, that the trees which crowd the inside (but which are not shown on the sketch) will soon work the destruction of the walls. One great trunk has half obtruded itself into the heart of the wall at the doorway, and has so burst the wall that the doorway and the whole of the south-west corner will probably soon

* A. G. Reid, *Notes and Queries*, 8th. s. January 1897, p. 45.

come to the ground. Another tree has toppled over the upper stone of the belfry, which lies not yet broken to pieces.

The church is finely built, and is well worth some little attention. It is of small dimensions, measuring on the outside 50 feet 5 inches by

FIG. 1445.—Cambusmichael Church.

20 feet 6 inches, and on the inside 43 feet 10 inches by 15 feet. The doorway, which is in the usual place on the south side near the west end, is round-arched with a wide splay, and is built with large stones. There

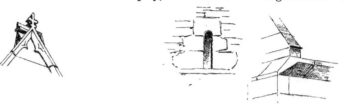

FIG. 1446.—Cambusmichael Church. Centre Window.

were probably three windows, all on the south side. One adjoining the doorway is lost where the wall is ruined, and another at the east end has only the sill remaining. The centre window (Fig. 1446) is complete; it is

5 inches wide with a slight chamfer on the edge, and with the opening on the inside splayed out to 3 feet 5 inches wide. An ambry occupies the usual position in the north wall. Both of the end walls have a set-off at the level of the eaves, as shown by Fig. 1445. The projecting eaves course and this set-off coincide, and their splays are very simply worked out (see Fig. 1446). The belfry on the west gable is a pre-Reformation example of a type which became very common in Presbyterian times. Below the belfry there is a small splayed slit with a segmental arched lintel. The east gable is terminated with a cross with a massive gableted base.

COUPAR ABBEY, Perthshire.*

Of this once great abbey almost nothing remains. The present parish church stands partly on the site of the monastic church, and the conventual buildings, with the cloister garth, occupied the ground which now forms the churchyard, at the south corner of which is the gateway with the angle buttress shown in Fig. 1447. This small fragment is the only piece of building, properly so called, which exists. It comprises a plain opening 6 feet wide by about 7 feet high, leading through a wall about 9 feet thick, and at the corner it is flanked by a massive angle buttress. The ruin rises to a height of about 25 to 30 feet, and stands about 70 yards south from the church.

The churchyard extends for a distance of about 400 feet from east to west, by about 280 feet from north to south, and these dimensions in all probability give an idea of the extent of ground formerly occupied by the monastery, and which is believed to have been the site of a Roman camp.

The monastery was founded by Malcolm IV. in 1164, and was the sixth in the order of construction of the thirteen Cistercian Abbeys in Scotland. William the Lion granted a site for the abbey of

Fig. 1447.—Coupar Abbey. Gateway.

* Information regarding this abbey has been obtained from the *Rental Book of the Cistercian Abbey of Coupar Angus*, edited by the Rev. Charles Rogers, LL.D. The Grampian Club, 1879.

about 50 acres of land, and also gifted it with the King's Chase and a portion of waste land. In 1233 the church was dedicated, under the invocation of the Blessed Virgin, during the time of Alexander, the eighth abbot. King Alexander II. was a generous benefactor to the abbey, and amongst the nobles the Hays of Errol and the Earls of Athole were conspicuous in their gifts, the latter presenting, amongst other things, timber for the construction of the buildings. At the Reformation the value of the estates of the abbey are estimated by Dr. Rogers "as equal to at least £8000 of present money."

The buildings, it is believed, were destroyed by the excited multitude who wrecked the religious houses at Perth and neighbourhood in 1559, and a portion of the buildings seems to have been occupied as a residence by Leonard Leslie, the first lay commendator, who died in 1605. In 1606 James VI., desirous to "suppress and extinguish the memorie of the abbacie," converted the lands and baronies into a temporal lordship in favour of James Elphinstone, second son of the first Lord Balmerino, with the title of Baron Coupar. This lord appears to have made the abbey his residence, as in 1645 it was assailed by 200 soldiers belonging to the army of Montrose, in revenge for the support given to the Covenanters by Elphinstone. Probably this was the finishing blow given to the buildings, as in 1682 the place is described as "nothing but rubbish."

In the Rental Book, from 1480 and onwards, there are several notices of the Porters, who, from their office, assumed that name as their family designation, the office having become hereditary. When the last of them demitted office it is stated in a charter that they had been hereditary porters from time immemorial, and in the Chamberlain's Accounts Robert Porter received a commuted allowance, consequent on the secularisation of the abbey.

At the west end of the present church there are the remains of some of the main piers of the nave. As shown by Fig. 1448 these indicate work of the first pointed period, probably of the thirteenth century.

A broken slab, measuring about 3 feet 3 inches high by 3 feet in breadth (Fig. 1449), is lying in the churchyard. In the Rental Book it is referred to as being built into the wall of the church which preceded the present one (erected about thirty years ago), and as bearing "the effigies of a priest," with the inscription on the margin—*Monachus de Cupro qui obiit anno dni. Millesimo quadringentesimo quqgesio.** From the present state of the fragment it is evident that little respect is paid in Coupar to the remains of the ancient abbey.

The two sculptured slabs (Figs. 1450 and 1451) which are at present lying in a tool-house in all likelihood adorned the base of a mural tomb. They are evidently works of the end of the fourteenth century or of the fifteenth century. They are supposed to be remains of a monument to

* *Rental Book of Coupar*, Vol. I. p. xxiii.

the Hays of Errol. Fig. 1451 appears to represent a pair who have been guilty, and are suffering under the prospect of finding themselves in the hands of the headsman.

On a house opposite the abbey occur the royal arms, shown by Fig. 1452, and throughout the village there are numerous carved and moulded stones to be seen, showing that the whole place has been built out of the ruins of the monastery.

In the Chamberlain's Accounts for 1563 he describes the chapel "as being so completely wrecked, that with a view to preserve the timber, he had built up both doors; also the undermost door of

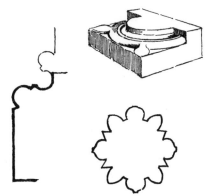

'FIG. 1448.—Coupar Abbey. Main Piers of Nave.

the steeple. In the cloister he had collected the slates which had been removed from the roof. He had also repaired the broken windows, providing them with iron framework. The abbot's apartments he had partially restored, and with proper fastenings made secure the granaries and store-houses. From having, in August 1562, accommodated the royal stud (during a passing visit of Queen Mary), the stables of the monastery are in the Account styled the 'quenes stables.'" *

We have already referred to the Earls of Errol as benefactors to the abbey, and amongst the Errol Papers † there occurs a "Copy of the Tabill Quhilk ves at Cowper of all the Erles of Erroll quhilk ver Buryd in the Abbey Kirk thair," from which it appears that sixteen Earls were buried in the monastery. Of these we suppose no memorial now remains; but we may take this opportunity of introducing a sketch (Fig. 1453) of a recumbent figure, now built into the churchyard wall of

FIG. 1449.—Coupar Abbey. Broken Slab.

* *Rental Book of Coupar*, Vol. II. p. xxxiv.
† *The Spalding Club Miscellany*, Vol. II. p. 348.

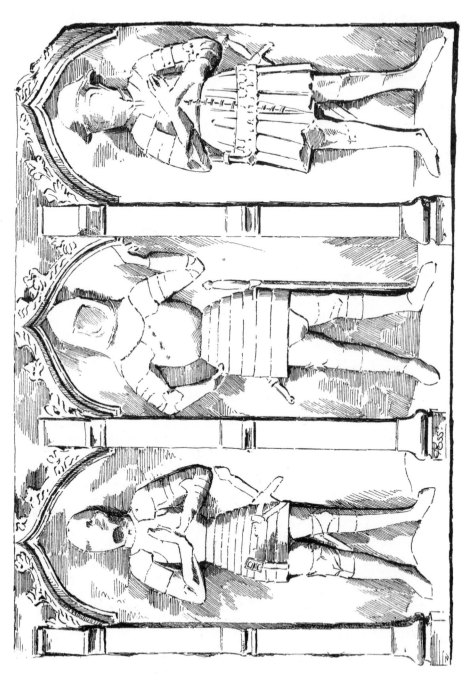

Fig. 1450.—Coupar Abbey. Sculptured Slab.

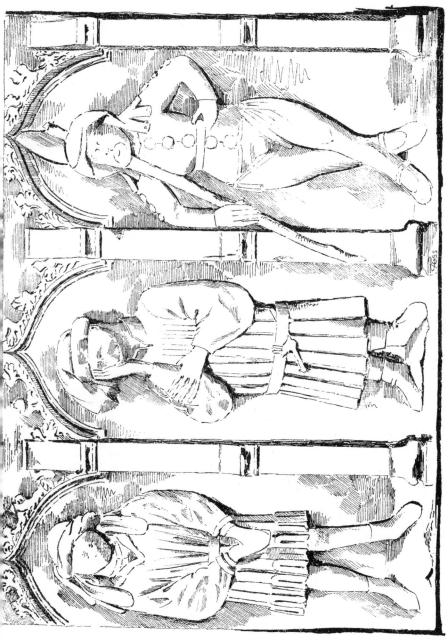

FIG. 1451.—Coupar Abbey. Sculptured Slab.

Errol (Carse of Gowrie), which, from the following inscription, probably represents the eighth Earl referred to in the above "tabill"—"Item penultimo die mensis Ianuarij, Anno Domini M.D.LX(X)III. obijt bone memorie Georgius comes De Errol. apud Pertham et sepultus est Errolie."

There are few notices of the buildings of the abbey. A plan of it was made about 1820 by William Mitchell, a mason, who corresponded with

FIG. 1452.—Coupar Abbey.
Royal Arms.

General Hutton regarding it; but they evidently could not come to terms, and it is not in his collection in the Advocates' Library. Mitchell calls it "a true and just plan of the outlines of that pile of building."

Dr. Marshall, in his *Historic Scenes in Forfarshire*, p. 144, had this plan before him when he wrote, and he characterises it as being unreliable. After a good deal of correspondence we obtained a sight of it, and have no hesitation in saying that it is a pure work of imagination, and is not a plan of the abbey at all; and, judging from the correspondence with General Hutton, we suspect the author intended to play a hoax on him, and yet was afraid to go the full length, and this is probably the reason why the General never got the plan.

In 1492 and following years there are references to Thomas Mowtray, mason. He was sworn to be "leyl and trew," during the term of his life, to the abbot and chapter, and he is obliged to "wyrk leilly and profitably the masonwerk of our forsaid abbay, and to be the master of the werk, in al thingis that langis hys craft of masonry in our abbay or in our qwarellis as it nedis." He was to have 6 "markis" yearly with his meat and drink, a house with $2\frac{1}{2}$ acres of land; further, the Lord Abbot "promised to give him yearly one of his old albs reaching to the ankles." He was to instruct the "prentys" in all "craft of masonry," *

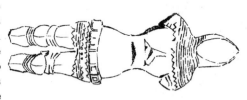

FIG. 1453.—Coupar Abbey. Recumbent Figure.

In 1485 John, the mason, and his son are continued in the service of the abbey. In 1468 Thomas Bel was hired "for the constant carpentry" of the abbey; he had workmen under him and apprentices. There are also agreements with smiths, as John Lutare, smith, who

* *Rental Book of Coupar*, Vol. I. pp. 304, 309.

"was hired (in 1484) for the common work of the monastery in the forge," and next year David Smyth is hired to succeed William Byning, who was formerly in the same service. John Duncanson, tiler, in 1492, was to labour in his trade and in every other work which he knew. Nine years earlier John Sclater was hired as apprentice to work at his trade of tiler (*tegulator*). Patrick Dog (in 1490) was the abbey sawyer, with three workmen under him, who each day were to turn out "fourteen draughts for each saw." *

DRON CHURCH, Perthshire.

A ruin situated on the braes of the Carse of Gowrie, in the parish of Longforgan, about two miles distant from Fowlis Church. It is in a very fragmentary condition (Fig. 1454), only the chancel arch remaining in anything like a perfect state, together with the foundations of the side

Fig. 1454.—Dron Church. View from South-West.

walls and part of the east wall. As shown in Fig. 1455, the chancel is about 28 feet long by 19 feet wide inside. The width of the chancel arch is about 11 feet, and from the ground to the top of the cap is about 7 feet 2 inches.

The jambs and arch mouldings (Fig. 1456) are of a simple character,

* *Rental Book of Coupar*, Vol. I. pp. 304, 309.

and they are separated by a moulded cap, shown in Fig. 1457. From the
form of the base of the jambs and the section of arch and jamb, it may be

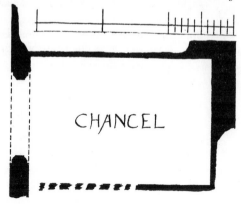

FIG. 1455.—Dron Church. Plan.

inferred that the building is not earlier than the end of the fifteenth or
beginning of the sixteenth century.

It will be seen from the Plan that the base of the east wall of the nave

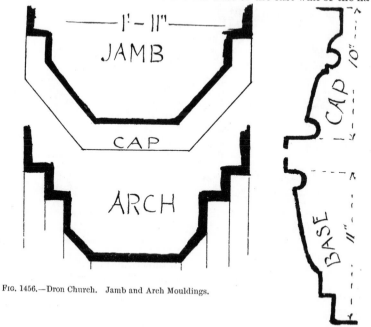

FIG. 1456.—Dron Church. Jamb and Arch Mouldings.

FIG. 1457.—Dron Church.
Base and Cap Mouldings.

extends a considerable distance northwards from the arch, which is suggestive of the idea that the church had a transept.

There appears to have been at one time a churchyard beside the church, which has now disappeared, having been absorbed into a neighbouring farm.

The Church of Dron belonged to the Abbey of Coupar, which was distant about six miles, in a north-westerly direction.

ECCLESIAMAGIRDLE OR EXMAGIRDLE CHAPEL,
PERTHSHIRE.

A small ruined chapel situated on the north side of the Ochil Hills, about three miles south-west from the Bridge of Earn. It is surrounded by an old burial-ground, and adjoins the picturesque seventeenth century mansion of Glenearn.

The building (Fig. 1458), which is roofless, is otherwise fairly entire, but it is densely covered with ivy and its features are not easily seen. It measures about 25 feet 7 inches long by about

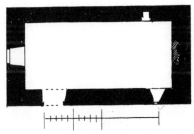

Fig. 1458.—Ecclesiamagirdle or Exmagirdle Chapel. Plan.

11 feet 5 inches wide inside the walls. The door in the south wall is lintelled and has a splay all round. There is a round-headed window (Fig. 1459) at the east end about 9 inches wide and about 2 feet high, having a stepped sill on the inside. A lintelled window in the west gable, now filled with a monument on the inside, measures about 29 inches wide. Both of these windows are splayed on the outside. The end window has been fitted with a smaller window at some later period.

In the centre of the east wall there appears to have been a recess about 4 feet 2 inches wide, and, as far as can be seen, it does not show on the outside. Its sill is about 4 feet up from the floor, and there has evidently been some kind of fixture against the end wall here, probably an

Fig. 1459.—Ecclesiamagirdle or Exmagirdle Chapel.   Round-headed Window at East End.

altar.   Adjoining this, on the north wall, is a small ambry, checked for a door flush with the inside wall.

FORGANDENNY CHURCH, Perthshire.*

The small fragment of ancient work left at Forgandenny, a few miles south of Perth, along with the more important remains in the district, point to the importance of Strathearn in early times.   That this has been originally a Norman church there can be no doubt, and it is suggestive and interesting to find such work here and at Dunning, each about two miles distant from Forteviot, the residence of the early Pictish kings.

The building is still in use as the parish church, but has been greatly altered at various times, and now it is only in some bits of detail that its antiquity can be detected.   It measures on the inside (Fig. 1460) 70 feet 7 inches long by 21 feet 7 inches wide.

The east wall is in the main of Norman masonry.   It has a splayed base, which returns at each corner, but is soon lost, as shown on Plan, by

* In connection with Forgandenny Church we are indebted for assistance to Mr. Collingwood Lindsay Wood of Freeland and Mr. T. T. Oliphant, St. Andrews, by the former of whom certain works were done to enable the building to be examined.

the rapid rising of the ground towards the west. From the east end the ground slopes downwards to a wooded dell which skirts the churchyard on that side.

Two widely splayed narrow windows are shown on the Plan in the east wall, but only the built centre mullion or pier now exists. It is of fine masonry, in four courses 2 feet 10 inches high, and is set at a height to the sill of about 8 or 9 feet above the floor. These windows have been built up, and all traces of them were lost till an examination of the wall for the purpose of preparing this Plan revealed their existence.

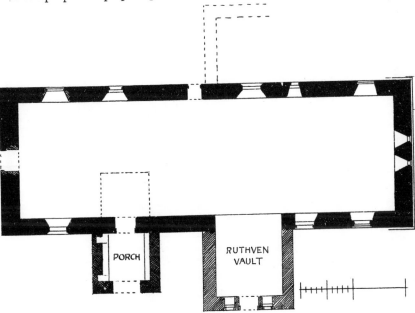

Fig. 1460.—Forgandenny Church. Plan.

Two or three windows in the side walls, with double splays on the exterior, probably belong to the fifteenth century. They are square-headed, and have been greatly knocked about. In the north wall there is a peculiar narrow door about 2 feet 3 inches wide, splayed on the exterior and lintelled like the windows just mentioned.

The doorway to the church, which is now built up, was in the south side near the west end. It appears to have been of Norman work, and a small piece of its enrichment still remains, consisting (Fig. 1461) of the trigonal moulding with a double notch enrichment, frequently found in the outer member of Norman arches. At some later time a porch has been added, as shown on the Plan, when probably the Norman door was dismembered, and the fragment now shown was built into the wall.

Sometime after the Reformation, a laird's seat (belonging to the Oliphants

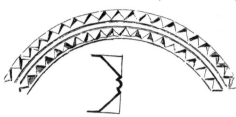

of Condie) was projected into the church, as shown by dotted lines on the Plan. It was on a high level, and the congregation gained access under it. This seat was done away with by giving the Oliphants of Condie the porch, which they converted into a burial vault,

FIG. 1461.—Forgandenny Church.
Enrichment of Norman Doorway.

enlarging it at the same time, and making their seat over it, with an opening into the church.

The Ruthven vault, situated further east, is probably a structure of the sixteenth or seventeenth century. Some closed up windows have features of that period. The seat belonging to Freeland House is situated over it.

The foundations of a building were recently discovered on the north side of the church, exactly opposite this vault (as shown by dotted lines on Plan), suggesting the idea that the simple Norman building had been converted into a cross church.

FIG. 1462.
Forgandenny Church.
Font.

The bowl of the font (Fig. 1462) still remains. It is octagonal, but

not equal sided, and is somewhat broken. It measures 2 feet $1\frac{1}{2}$ inches over all by about 15 inches high.

Fig. 1463 shows another font which exists at a chapel at Muckersey, a few miles distant. It likewise is octagonal and not equal sided, and has a coat of arms on one side, which we have not been able to identify. The chapel at Muckersey is now used as a family vault, and has no other ancient features.

FIG. 1463.—Font at Muckersey.

INCHAFFRAY ABBEY, PERTHSHIRE.

The ruins of the Abbey of Inchaffray, the ancient Insula Missarum, stand on a wooded mound not far from Madderty Station, about six miles east of Crieff.

The abbey was founded by Gilbert, Earl of Stratherne, who succeeded his father, Earl Ferteth, in 1171, and died in 1223, and his first wife, Matildis, the daughter of William de Aubegni. Their eldest son, Gilchrist, was buried in 1198 at Inchaffray, which had been founded before that date. In 1200, when the great charter of the abbey was granted, the Earl and Countess endowed it with various churches, including St. Mechesseok of Ochterardouer and St. Beanus of Kynkell (illustrated in this volume). They declared their affection for Inchaffray, affirming " so much do we love it that we have chosen a place of sepulture in it for us and our successors, and have already buried there our eldest born."

The abbey was dedicated to St. Mary the Virgin and St. John the Evangelist, and was a house of the canons regular of the order of St. Augustine. Although not reckoned as one of the great monasteries of

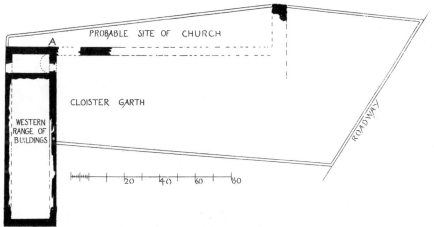

Fig. 1464.—Inchaffray Abbey. Plan.

Scotland, it was " endowed with many privileges and immunities by David and Alexander, Kings of Scotland," but its principal benefactors were the family of the Earls of Stratherne, Earl Robert, the son (1223 and 1231) of Gilbert being particularly liberal.

Only one of the abbots, Abbot Maurice, has obtained any popular recognition in history. He it was who blessed the Scottish army at Bannockburn in 1314. Five years afterwards he was promoted to the See of Dunblane, within which diocese Inchaffray is situated.

The first head of the house was Malis, a religious hermit, in whose piety and discretion Earl Gilbert and Matildis had full confidence. At the Reformation Inchaffray suffered the usual fate. Alexander Gordon, brother of George, fourth Earl of Huntly, was made commendator in 1553. Five years later he was promoted to the See of Galloway, and shortly afterwards he was accused, by the General Assembly, of neglecting his duties, and in particular, that he had resigned Inchaffray in favour of a young child, and set divers lands in feu in prejudice of the kirk. The young child was James Drummond, son of David, Lord Drummond of Innerpeffray, in whose favour the abbey was erected into a temporal lordship.

The ruins of the abbey are situated on ground which rises slightly above the surface of the valley. This valley in ancient times was a great

Fig. 1465.—Inchaffray Abbey. Exterior of North Gable.

marsh extending for many miles, and it was from this feature of its situation that the abbey received the name by which it was very generally known throughout the middle ages, of "Insula Missarum," or Isle of Masses. As early as the year 1218 the monks had reclaimed a portion of this marsh, and they doubtless continued their labours; but it was not till 1696 that an Act was obtained, under the authority of Parliament, for dealing effectively with it.*

* See *Liber Insula Missarum*, Bannatyne Club, 1847.

The fields around the abbey are now all cultivated, and the ruins are enclosed with stone dykes, as shown by double lines on the Plan (Fig. 1464); so that the few fragments which remain are now properly protected. Within the dykes almost nothing is visible but a dense mass of trees and brushwood, with mounds of ruins in the utmost confusion. A gable at the north-west corner stands

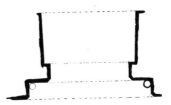

FIG. 1466.—Inchaffray Abbey. Plan of Doorway.

entire (Fig. 1465), with a round-arched vault adjoining, about 21 feet long by 10 feet 6 inches wide and 10 feet high. This is one of the

FIG. 1467.—Inchaffray Abbey. Interior of North Gable.

cellars of the western range of buildings. The walls of this range are fairly entire along their whole length for a height of 7 or 8 feet. The south end wall is also standing for about the same height. The length of this range from north to south is about 97 feet 7 inches. It is probable that the adjoining cellar to the south is entire, but the place is so covered with vegetation that little can be ascertained. The door-way entering from the cloister to the north-west cellar is undoubtedly of an early date. Not much of it remains, but enough to enable the Plan (Fig. 1466) to be made. The nook shaft, a fragment of the capital of which exists, is not later than the beginning of the thirteenth century.

The high gable adjoining (Fig. 1467) is certainly in part at least of a later date ; the upper part and the chimney, with its corbelled cope, being of the sixteenth or seventeenth century. On the first floor there has been a large fireplace, the flue of which is still partly visible (see Fig. 1467). A part of the north wall of the cloister stands near the gable. This was part of the south wall of the church (see Plan), and the greater portion of the church would thus be situated outside the present enclosing dyke on the north side.

There are indications at the north-east corner of the surviving gable (at A on Plan) of a wall having extended northwards, which was probably the west wall of the church. At the junction of the south wall of the church and the wall of the western range, and at the height of about 15 feet above the ground, there still exists the corner corbel for supporting the roof of the cloister walk. We can remember when there were other corbels along the church wall also, but they have now disappeared. The part of this wall now standing is in a very precarious state. It evidently extended eastwards for about 120 feet, when it met a cross wall, now represented by a mass of rough masonry about 7 or 8 feet square (see Plan). This mass may represent one of the great piers of a central tower. There are other pieces of masonry throughout the enclosure with numerous trenches and mounds, but, owing to the rank vegetation, it is impossible to make a more satisfactory Plan than the one now given. If the place were cleared out and a judicious search made, considerable remains would doubtless be found.

The average length of the enclosure as it now stands is about 210 feet.

INNERPEFFRAY CHURCH, Perthshire.

The structure of this church is still entire, although the building is now only used as a place of burial. It is situated on a high knoll over-looking the river Earn, about four miles south-east from Crieff. Near the church on the bank of the river stands the ruined Castle of Innerpeffray,

elsewhere described and illustrated.*   Close to the west end of the church
is the Library of Innerpeffray (shown in Fig. 1469), founded by David,
Lord Madderty, in 1691. It contains a fine collection of early printed
books, and is open to the public and is well worth visiting.

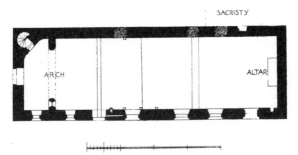

FIG. 1468.—Innerpeffray Church.   Plan.

The church (Fig. 1468) is divided, by modern walls, into three parts.
It is a long narrow building, measuring, internally, about 76 feet in length
by about 21 feet 4 inches in width. There was a sacristy on the north
side near the east end, its width and position being indicated by the

FIG. 1469.—Innerpeffray Church.   View from South-West.

absence of the moulded wall-head plinth (Fig. 1469), which runs round the
whole side walls except at this part. The door between the church and
sacristy still remains, but is built up. On the sacristy side it has a rough

* *The Castellated and Domestic Architecture of Scotland*, Vol. II. p. 193.

flat arch. To the east of this door there is, on the exterior, a splayed aperture about 2 feet 9 inches wide (see Plan) by about 2 feet high, and about the same height above the ground. There is no trace of it inside, the walls being plastered. This may have been what is called a squint,

Fig. 1470.—Innerpeffray Church. Arch near West End.

being situated in the same relative position as those at Seton and other churches.

The Church of Innerpeffray is peculiar, from having what resembles a chancel arch, situated at a distance of about 7 feet 6 inches from the west end. This arch (Fig. 1470) is round and about 14 feet 2 inches wide. It has a splayed squint about 2 feet wide on the south side, as shown on the sketch. It is difficult to give a satisfactory explanation of this arch, but it seems to have formed a vestibule in connection with the stair leading to an apartment on the upper floor. The archway appears to have been fitted with some kind of timber screen, which, if it was a close one, would help to explain the object of the squint.

There is a room on the first floor reached by the wheel stair in the north-west angle. This room, as it now exists, is of later construction than the church, and is not older than the seventeenth century. The stair, however, is part of the original construction, and is believed to have given access to a belfry on the west wall, as well as to the room which doubtless existed from the first over the vestibule, and which (see Fig. 1469) was provided with a fireplace and a window in the west gable.

Fig. 1471.—Innerpeffray Church.
Lintel of Eastmost Window.

The ceiling of the existing room (see Fig. 1470) cuts across the archway in an awkward manner. Doubtless the original room was at a slightly higher level, so as not to interfere with the arch. The ceiling and floor of the room are in a very ruinous state, the greater part having fallen. The ceiling is painted in bright colours. It has a figure of the sun in the centre with rolling clouds around, and till lately there was a complete figure of an angel on one side, of which only slight indications now remain. On the south side the ceiling has entirely fallen, and with it the figure of an angel corresponding to the one on the north side, and soon the whole thing will come to the ground.

Fig. 1472.
Innerpeffray
Church.
Jamb Moulding
of South Door.

The church, in its original state, had three doorways, one in the centre of the west end and one in the south wall, the latter being secured (see Plan) by a sliding bar. Both these doors have bead and hollow mouldings. The third door was in the north wall and is now built up. There are six windows in the south wall, the two westmost ones adjoining the great arch being markedly narrower than the others, and having evidently some connection with the west arch. These windows have all double splays on the exterior, except the eastmost one (Fig. 1471), which has a large quarter hollow moulding continued round the lintel, on which occurs a shield with the Drummond arms.

All the windows and doors have square lintels, with the mouldings or splays of the jambs continued round the lintels. The mode of securing the side door has already been referred to ; all the windows are likewise strongly secured with iron interlacing bars.

FIG. 1473.—Innerpeffray Church. South Doorway.

Fig. 1472 shows the jamb moulding of the south doorway. Over this doorway there is a small pointed opening (see Fig. 1469), probably intended to throw light on the rood screen which stood near it, as is evident from the corbels for carrying it, three of which still exist on the south side (see Plan) and one on the opposite side, the others having been removed to admit a monument. On the north side two of these corbels are placed (Fig. 1473), one on each side of one of the windows, which, as will be seen, has been converted into a doorway to give access to the central burial vault. Alongside the south door there is the stoup (see Figs. 1473 and 1474). It is of plain design, with a slightly projecting bracket. The piscina or small recess at the east end is quite plain, not even having a splay.

A very interesting feature of this church is the altar, which is still standing against the east wall (see Plan). It has been rough cast over, so that it cannot be examined thoroughly. It is needless to say that few ancient altars remain in Scotland, one of the best preserved ones being at

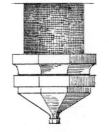

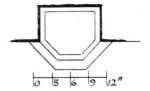

the Church of Stobhall, about twenty miles distant, a view of the exterior of which church is subjoined (Fig. 1475).* Stobhall and Inner-peffray churches were both built by the same family of the Drummonds, who adhered to the ancient faith, and successfully defied the power of the reformed Church to cast down their monuments of idolatry, as altars and other appendages of the ancient Church were termed.

The east gable at Innerpeffray is quite plain, with the exception of a small niche, which probably held a figure. Besides the painted ceiling already referred to, there are considerable traces of painting through-out the interior, particularly on the east wall. Several consecration crosses are also painted on various parts of the church.

FIG. 1474.
Innerpeffray Church.
Stoup.

From what has been said, it will be seen that this is a church of very considerable interest and some almost unique peculiarities, and it is unfortunate that it should be divided up with unseemly walls, and that no effort should be made to preserve the painted work, of which so little remains in Scotland. Were it put in the same condition as the Church of Stobhall and as well cared for, it would be a circumstance for which all who are interested in Scottish church architecture would be grateful.

This church, which was a Collegiate one, was dedicated to the Blessed Virgin, and was founded by Sir John Drummond, the first of Innerpeffray, in 1508. In the account which follows (kindly supplied by Mrs. Birnie, keeper of the Library) it appears that a church existed here in the previous

* For description of Stobhall Church, see *The Castellated and Domestic Architecture of Scotland*, Vol. II. p. 359.

century, and indeed it is stated * that it is mentioned as early as 1342.
The existing building, however, was doubtless erected at the period above
mentioned.

　"In 1483 the Church of Innerpeffray must have been in existence, as
the patronage is then conveyed by the Mercers to Lord Oliphant.

FIG. 1475.—Stobhall Church, from Courtyard.

　"One reason for considering the foundation of considerable antiquity is
the fact that the market held on the day of dedication (Lady-day) was one
of the great marts and one of the great holidays of Strathearn. (The
market was removed to Crieff about eighty years ago.) Institutions so
popular as this are generally found to have their origin in a remote
antiquity. . . . Its proximity also to the meeting point of the four

　* *Chronicles of Strathearn*, D. Philips, Crieff, 1896, p. 325.

Roman roads, from Ardoch and the south, from Comrie and Loch Earn on the west, from the Sma' Glen on the north, and from Perth on the east, made it a suitable centre. . . . Convenience of access and the popularity of Lady Fair appear to confirm the remote date of the church, &c.

"John Freebairn, minister and preacher of the Gospel at Madderty (1620-1657), who was connected with the Drummonds by marriage, in a genealogical history of the House of Drummond, leaves on record the following :—'John, first Lord Drummond, having re-edified the Chapel of Innerpeffray from the ground and erected it into a college for some few prebendaries to pray for requiems for him and his house, ordained it to be their burying-place for all time coming, and being near 80 years of age he framed one of the most material and perfyte testaments that ever I saw and syne closed his eyes and time togidder and was most honourably interred at Innerpeffray, in the year 1519.'

"On 4th June 1507 the King confirmed in Mortmain the charter of John, Lord Drummond, by which (for the souls of the King and Queen, for his own soul and that of Elizabeth Lindesay, his wife, and the umquhile Margaret Drummond, his daughter, &c.) he granted as a pure free almsgift to four chaplains, to celebrate the divine offices for ever at the four altars in the church, dedicated in honour of the Blessed Virgin, of Innerpeffray, an annual income of forty marks from his lands of Innerpeffray and Dunfallys, with houses, residences, and gardens to be marked off and built for each, with the right to each of them of obtaining necessary fuel in the Common Mure of Innerpeffray with four sums for grasses and for one horse. In 1508 occurs the name of Walter Drummond, the first Provost of Innerpeffray. Here was buried the second Master of Drummond, who died before his grandfather, and left an infant son, David, afterwards second Lord Drummond. . . .

"The King, on 20th October 1581, confirmed the charter of William Lindesay, provost or principal perpetual chaplain of the Church of the Blessed Virgin Mary of Innerpeffray, in which with consent of Patrick, Lord Drummond, patron of the said provostry, he demised to James Drummond of Innerpeffray six acres of land, the Smithlands, &c. &c., reserving to the said provost one chamber (camera) only when he should stay there.* . . . Four roundles or towers stood one at each corner of the churchyard, and tradition says that these formed the residences of the four chaplains."

KINFAUNS CHURCH, Perthshire.

This edifice is situated about four miles east from Perth, and continued to be the parish church till about forty years ago, when it was abandoned

* Possibly the chamber over the vestibule above described.

and allowed to fall into ruin. It is now roofless and the walls are very much reduced, except the south aisle, which contained the seats of the family of the Greys of Kinfauns and their burial-place. When the church was dismantled a painting was found on the plaster inside the west wall, but unfortunately no drawing was made of it, and it has now entirely disappeared.

The church (Fig. 1476) measures about 65 feet long by 18 feet 2 inches wide within the walls, and is probably a structure of the fifteenth century. It has been considerably altered during Presbyterian times, new windows and doors having been broken through the walls. The south doorway is original, and is round arched with a bead moulding towards the outside,

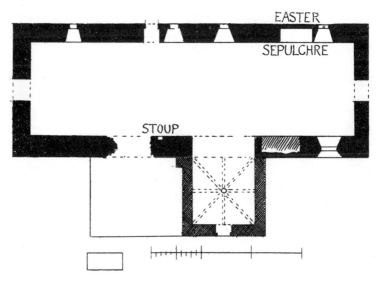

FIG. 1476.—Kinfauns Church. Plan.

and lintelled on the inside with a stone slab having a cross carved on it, evidently a companion stone to the one shown in Fig. 1477. This cross, which wants part of its length, measures 5 feet 11 inches long by 1 foot 7 inches in width at top, tapering to 1 foot 4 inches at lower end by 10 inches thick. It is well wrought with sloping sides, having the form of the cross completed, as seen by the rounded disc rising out of the slope on each side. There was probably a south doorway opposite the north doorway, adjoining the stoup shown in the south wall. The eastmost window on the south side is also original; it is square lintelled and has the usual wide splay all round.

The most interesting feature in the church is the arched recess in the north wall (see Fig. 1477), which was probably an Easter sepulchre. It was only discovered after the church became a ruin, having previously been covered over. It has thus been well preserved, except that the projecting crockets along the top of the hood moulding, as well as most of the hood itself, have been chipped away, so as to make an even surface at the wall. It measures about 6 feet 6 inches long by 3 feet in depth, and about 4 feet high. It has well wrought mouldings, which die against

FIG. 1477.—Kinfauns Church. Recess in North Wall.

a rounded jamb, supported on a short shaft having a very simple cap and base. The floor of the recess was slightly raised above the floor of the church. The details of the mouldings show that this is a late design, probably sixteenth century.

The "Gray Aisle" on the south side of the church is roofed with a late example of groined vaulting (Fig. 1478), and it is curious to observe how the tradition of this kind of work survived to a period when the style of art practised throughout the country was of the kind represented by the panels on the east and west walls. There are three panels on these

Fig. 1478.—Kinfauns Church. The "Grey Aisle," looking West.

walls. The central one on the west side (see Fig. 1478) contains the Lindsay arms, as shown. On the east side there are two coats (Fig. 1479) containing the Charteris arms. On one of the panels of that side is the following inscription, which gives the name of the founder of the aisle :—

Fig. 1479.—Kinfauns Church. Panels in East Side.*

"John Chartrvs and Jannat Chisolim In ovr tym buildit this," and on the other is the inscription, "George Chartus sonn and har to the sad John and deppartit. Bot $\frac{succe}{ssvn.}$" (without succession). The date over the entrance door is 1598.

MEIGLE CHURCH FONT, Perthshire.

The old country town of Meigle is situated in the middle of Strathmore, not far from Alyth Junction on the railway between Perth and Forfar. The church stood in the middle of the village, and was rebuilt about

* From a sketch by Mr. T. S. Robertson.

the beginning of this century. When the old building was demolished, a font was dug out of the rubbish and erected on a pedestal in the minister's garden. It remained there for a time, but when an Episcopal chapel was built, the font was removed into it, and is now in use there. It is one of the best specimens of an old font now remaining in Scotland,

and it evidently belongs to a late period, probably sixteenth century.

The font is octagonal and made of one stone. It is 2 feet 3 inches in diameter, and the basin measures 1 foot 9 inches across. Each of the sides of the octagon contains an arch with carved crockets, and the angles are marked by small buttresses and pinnacles. The carved

FIG. 1480.—Meigle Church Font.

work has been very spirited, but is now much damaged. In each arch is a bas-relief containing emblems and scenes connected with the Passion. Fig. 1480 shows three sides, which represent —(1) the Crucifixion, (2) the seamless coat and the scourges and dice, (3) the Resurrection. Fig. 1481 shows —(4) the Cross and crown of thorns, (5) the pierced hands, feet, and heart (showing the five wounds of the Passion), (6) the pillar with the rope twisted round it, and the cock on the

FIG. 1481.—Meigle Church Font.

top. The seventh side contains the ladder and the spear, reed, and sponge arranged saltierwise, and the eighth the three nails and the hammer.

These sculptures are all well preserved and well executed, but whether of native workmanship or not it is impossible to say.

METHVEN COLLEGIATE CHURCH, Perthshire.*

Of the Church of Methven, consecrated by Bishop David de Bernham of St. Andrews on 25th August 1247, nothing now remains.

The Collegiate Church or Provostry of Methven, as it is generally called, was founded in 1433 by Walter Stewart, the aged Earl of Athole. Before this time, King James I. had conferred the liferent of the Earldom of Strathearn upon the Earl of Athole, so that he was the great lord of the district, and was, besides, a son of Robert II. Three years after the founding of this church he suffered a terrible death, for his supposed connivance in the assassination of James I. in Perth.

What now remains of the church is the north transept, the north wall and gable of which are shown in Fig. 1482. In the *Edinburgh Architectural Association Sketch Book* † a plan of the church is given without any information as to how it was ascertained. Assuming it to be correct, it shows a cross church, having a chancel 40 feet long by 24 feet wide over the walls, with north and south transepts, and a nave of the same width as the chancel, extending for an indefinite length. The north transept extended from the north wall of the church 22 feet, and has a width over the walls of 21 feet, with walls 3 feet thick. The end window, which is the principal feature of the structure, is 6 feet 3 inches wide in the daylight; it has three lights, and the tracery, which is of a flowing pattern, is placed, as usual at this period, in the centre of the thickness of the wall. The mouldings of the jambs, which consist of a double splay, are stopped at the springing of the arch by a continuous impost moulding, and the arch mouldings are of a different section. On the east side of the window there is a bracket with a canopy over for a statue, possibly that of St. Marnoch, the patron saint of Methven.

In a panel on the west side of the window there are traceable the lion rampant of the royal arms, surmounted by a crown.

The gabled crowsteps with which the gable is coped form one of the best examples of that feature, which, however, is a rare one in the churches of this period. The cross on the apex is modern.

The collegiate church was in use as the parish church till 1783, and for long after the Reformation the Presbyterian minister was called " Provest of Methven, and Chaplin of Auldbar," the Church of Auldbar having been granted to Methven on its foundation in 1433.

* The history of this church and its provosts, *The Provostry of Methven*, was written by the late Rev. Thomas Morris, assistant Old Greyfriars', Edinburgh, and privately printed by the late William Smythe, Esq., Methven, 1875. See also *Memorials of Angus and Mearns*, by Andrew Jervise.

† Vol. II. New Series, 1887-1894.

Fig. 1482.—Methven Collegiate Church. North Transept.

MONCRIEFF CHAPEL, Perthshire.

A ruined chapel situated in the grounds adjoining the mansion house of Moncrieff, about three miles south-east of Perth. It is closely hemmed in with trees and is completely ivy clad, and measures in the inside about 34 feet 6 inches long by 13 feet wide. The building (Fig. 1483) is a pre-

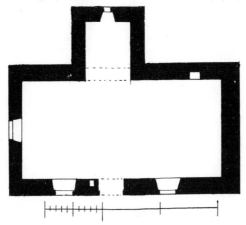

Fig. 1483.—Moncrieff Chapel. Plan.

Reformation church, but has evidently been used and altered in Presbyterian times, and within the last few years it has been enlarged with an apse and transepts, so as to form a burial-place. Most of the stones for this purpose were taken from the ruins of the splendid old bridge which crossed the Earn about a mile distant at Bridge of Earn.

There is a north aisle about 7 feet 8 inches wide by 7 feet 3 inches long, which is entered by a round arch, and is lighted by a window 14 inches wide, which has grooves for glass. The gable of this aisle has crow-steps. The doorway is in the south wall, and adjoining it on the west

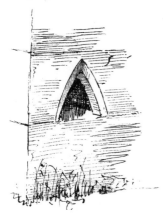

Fig. 1484.—Moncrieff Chapel. Stoup.

Fig. 1485.—Moncrieff Chapel. Apex Stone.

is a stoup (Fig. 1484) with a pointed arch cut out of a single stone, and in the north wall there is the usual ambry. There are two windows in the south wall and one in the west gable. This gable has the usual set-off at about 5 feet above the ground, and at the ground level in this wall there is a wide relieving arch, apparently intended to give scope for a tree root. The skews of this gable are finely wrought, and the apex stone, now lying inside (Fig. 1485), has the edge fillet continued as a saltier on the face of the ridge roll.

The belfry, entirely concealed by ivy, occupies an unusual position on the east gable. All the openings are lintelled, and appear to have been altered in Presbyterian times.

WAST-TOWN CHURCH, Perthshire.

A ruined structure situated in the centre of its churchyard, in the decayed hamlet of Wast-Town, at a distance of about two miles northwards from Errol Railway Station, and not far from the old Castle of Kinnaird. The church (Fig. 1486) has consisted of a nave and chancel, the former about 43 feet long by 15 feet 2 inches wide inside, having walls from 3 to 4 feet thick. The chancel was apparently of the same width as the nave,

NAVE

Fig. 1486.—Wast-Town Church. Plan.

but it has been entirely demolished, and the chancel arch has been built up. This was doubtless done to make the church suitable as a preaching station after the Reformation. There are a north and a south doorway, the former square-headed with a splay, the latter (Fig. 1488) round arched with a bead on edge all round. In the south side there are two windows with square tops and a bead moulding, and one window in the north side having a cusped and pointed top, as shown in Fig. 1487. This window has a moulding on the outside consisting of a hollow, wrought on a broad splay. All the windows are finished on the inside in a manner similar to the one shown, the width of their daylight being about 13 inches. There are three openings through the walls at the west end (see Fig. 1486) about 7 inches square and about 4 feet above the ground, the object of which is not very clear, and they are now considerably ruined. Possibly they are putlog holes.

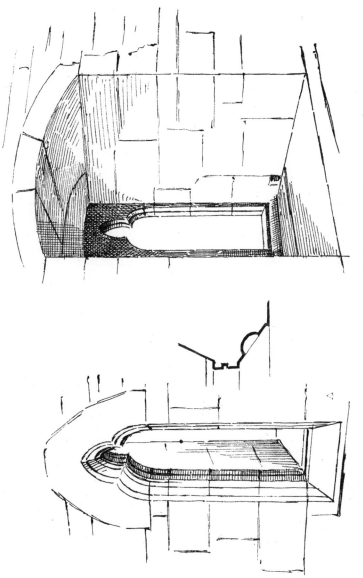

FIG. 1487.—Wast-Town Church. Window in North Side.

FIG. 1488.—Wast-Town Church. View from South-East.

The chancel arch, which is 9 feet 9 inches wide, is in two orders (Fig. 1489), each splayed on edge. The wall is 2 feet 4 inches thick, and the arch springs from wide spreading caps, which either rested on shafts, now removed, or only on corbels. This cannot at present be determined, owing to the building up of the archway. The detail of this cap or corbel is somewhat novel and peculiar in design.

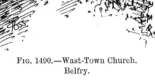

There is a plain belfry (Fig. 1490) on the west gable.

The date of this church is probably in the sixteenth century.

FIG. 1489.
Wast-Town Church.
Chancel Arch.

FIG. 1490.—Wast-Town Church.
Belfry.

MONUMENT IN RENFREW CHURCH.

This monument is placed in the modern parish church of Renfrew. It consists of a recumbent effigy resting on a sculptured tomb, and enclosed within an arched canopy. The inscription round the arch in Gothic raised letters is as follows:—"Hic iacet Johēs Ros miles quo(n)dam dominus de Hawkehede et Marioria uxor sua orate pro ipsis qui obit."

Crawford mentions in his *History of Renfrewshire*, p. 66, that Sir Josias (he means Sir John) Ross of Halkhead married "Marjory Mure, a daughter of Caldwel," and that their statues "as big as the life, with their coats of arms over them," are carved on the monument. The arms of the lady are not there now. Crawford states that this was "the first of the family who laid the foundation of that hereditary honour, which his successors have ever since enjoyed, who, being a favourite of King James IV., was by that prince created a baron of this realm, with the title of Lord Ross of Hawkhead and Melvil, about the year 1492."* It is to be observed, however, that the arms on the tomb are simply those of Ross, whereas the arms of Melville were quartered with those of Ross after the marriage of Sir John Ross with the heiress of Melville in the time of Robert II.

The monument (Fig. 1491) has been partly restored, the shafts at the sides with their bases and caps are modern, but they probably follow the original design. The mouldings of the arch, which are thickly coated with paint, appear to be original. The effigies, of which there are two, husband and wife, with the table on which they rest, remain untouched.

The tomb is 8 feet 6½ inches long by 2 feet 6 inches high, but the base is probably buried beneath the floor. The front is richly sculptured in a somewhat rude but vigorous manner, and is divided into eleven compartments. Each of the end compartments contains an angel playing on a musical instrument, namely, a violin and a viol. The other nine compartments contain shields supported by angels, with the following armorial bearings, as described by Mr. W. R. Macdonald :—

1. A chevron chequé between three hunting horns, for Semple.
2. A pale, for Erskine.
3. A griffin segreant, for Lauder of Hatton.
4. Quarterly, 1st and 4th—A lion rampant within a double tressure flory counterflory, for Scotland, as on No. 5 ; 2nd and 3rd—A fesse chequé (with four rows of panes), for Stewart, as on No. 6.
5. A lion rampant within a double tressure flory counterflory, for Scotland.
6. A fesse chequé (also with four rows of panes), for Stewart.
7. A bend, for ————.

* *Crawford's Renfrewshire*, p. 54.

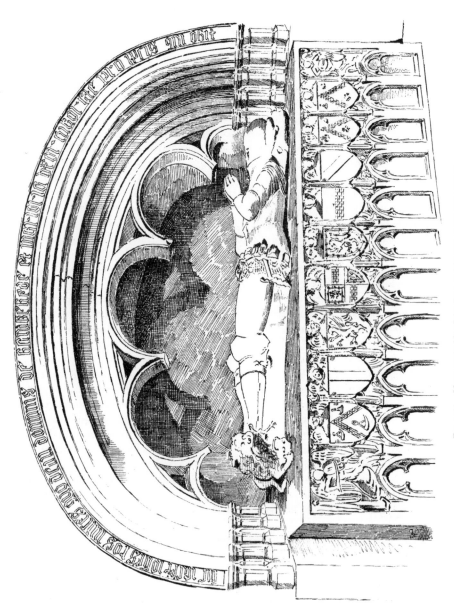

Fig. 1491.—Monument of Sir John Ross and Spouse in Renfrew Church.

8. A chevron chequé between three water budgets, for Ross of Halket.
9. A chevron chequé between a hunting horn in dexter chief, a water budget in sinister chief, and a demi hunting horn combined with a demi water budget in base, being the shields 1 and 8 dimidiated, but showing no dividing line.

On the knight's breast a chevron between three water budgets, for Ross of Halket, as in No. 8.

The Church of Renfrew was granted by David I. as a prebend of Glasgow, and is believed to have stood on the present site.

In 1557 mention is made of the chaplainry of St. Christopher in the Lord Ross's Aisle on the south side of the Church of Renfrew. The monument is situated on the south side of the present church. The Chapel of St. Christopher was probably connected with the ferry across the Clyde.

THE CHURCHES OF HOUSTON, ST. FILLAN'S, AND KILMALCOLM, RENFREWSHIRE.

These three churches lie to the north-west of Paisley, in a straight line, about four miles apart. The Church of HOUSTON is modern, and the only thing belonging to the ancient church which formerly stood there is shown in Fig. 1492, being the recumbent figures of one of the Houston family and his wife. The monument which contained these statues is entirely gone, and they now lie in a lighted closet, built for their reception, beside the new church. The Houston arms are carved on the knight's armour (a fesse chequé between three martlets). The figures probably date from the fifteenth century, and are believed to represent Sir Patrick Houston of that Ilk, who died in 1450, and his wife, Agnes Campbell, who died in 1456. Crawford states * that Sir Patrick, departing this life 1450, was buried in the Chapel of Houston, where there is a fair monument erected to the memory of him and his wife, with this inscription :—" Hic jacet Patricius Houstoun, de Eodem, miles, qui obiit anno MCCCCL ; et D. Maria Colquhoun sponsa dicti Domini Johannis quae obiit MCCCCLVI."

The parish of KILFILLAN or KILLALLAN was incorporated with Houston in 1760, and the church dedicated to St. Fillan has probably been in a state of ruin since about that time. It stands in a beautiful hollow in an elevated situation overlooking the valley of Strathgryfe, midway between Houston and Kilmalcolm. The walls are fairly entire, but without the gables, and are densely covered with ivy. The masonry shows that they are of considerable age, if indeed they are not of the Norman period. While this may be so, all the openings are of seventeenth century work, and the doorway at the west end of the south wall is dated 1635. About that

* *Crawford's Renfrewshire*, p. 100.

time the openings were probably changed into their present forms, and the pre-Reformation character of the building was altered to suit Presbyterian

Fig. 1492.—Houston Church. Effigies of Sir Patrick Houston and his Wife.

ideas. The old plan (Fig. 1493), however, resembles many of the ancient churches in its long proportions, and in having the north and south doors

FIG. 1493.—St. Fillan's Church, Killallan, Renfrewshire. Plan.

opposite each other. Adjoining the church and churchyard there still exists a quaint old Scottish mansion house of seventeenth century style, which may probably have been the residence of the clergymen.

KILMALCOLM.—The church here was dedicated to King Malcolm III., who along with his wife, Queen Margaret, were commemorated as saints. A fragment of the east wall of a pre-Reformation church remains, with three plain lancet windows, which may possibly belong to the thirteenth century. It forms a part of the parish church. The above three churches, along with all the others in Strathgryfe (except Inchinnon), were comprehended in the grant which Walter, the son of Alan, made to the Abbey of Paisley in 1164.

PARISH CHURCH, SELKIRK.

Of the important churches which existed here in the twelfth century no trace now remains. The parish church was in a state of ruin at the beginning of the sixteenth century, when a new one was built, which in turn followed its predecessors, and in the year 1747 another church was erected, the ruins of which still exist.

The following description of the church taken down in 1747 occurs in *Our Journall into Scotland*, p. 15.* "They have a very pretty church where the hammermen and other tradesmen have several seats mounted above the rest, the gentlemen below the tradesmen in the ground seats; the women sit in the high end of the church, with us the choir, there is one neat vaulted porch in it, my Lord Bucplewgh's (Buccleuch) seat is the highest in the church, and he hath a proper (private) passage into it in at the outside of the vaulted porch. On a corner of the outside of the choir is fastened an iron chain with a thing they call the Jogges," &c. "The form of it is a cross house, the steeple fair, handsomely tiled as the Royal Exchange at London, it having at each corner four pyramidal turrets, they call them pricks; my Lord Maxfield's house at Langham being of the form of the steeple. The church was tiled upon close joined boards and not lats" (laths).

* *Our Journall into Scotland*, A.D. 1629, by C. Lother. Edinburgh: David Douglas, 1894.

FIG. 1494.—Selkirk Parish Church. Slab in Wall of Church.

The grave slab shown in Fig. 1494 is built into one of the walls of the existing ruins. It is of red sandstone, and measures 6 feet 4 inches high by 2 feet 5 inches wide. It is very much mutilated, and from its exposed situation and the friableness of the stone, it is rapidly decaying, and unless some proper means are taken to preserve it, will at no distant date be obliterated. The figure represents that of a stout yeoman with hands folded on the breast, having a belt round his waist. On a shield at his feet is a bend, any other charges which may have been on it being obliterated. The inscription in raised letters is more than half gone, but from the first syllable of the place of Aikwood being still legible, and in

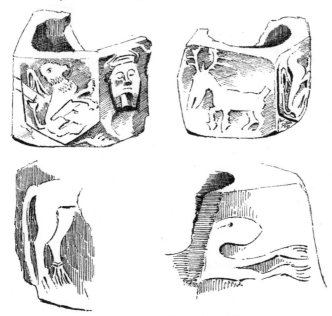

Fig. 1495.—Selkirk Parish Church. Stoup.

conjunction with the arms, it is supposed by Mr. T. Craig Brown * to commemorate one of the Scots of Harden, who lived at Aikwood or Oakwood, a tower still standing not far from Selkirk. The stone probably dates from about the early part of the sixteenth century.

The following figures represent three stoups in the possession of Mr. Craig Brown, Selkirk. Fig. 1495 shows the five sides of one of these. On one face is a lion rampant, and on the adjoining space to the right is a human face, the mouth of which forms an opening for emptying the basin. On the space to the left is carved the figure of a buck or hart. The other two faces are broken. On one is the hind quarters of an ox

* *History of Selkirkshire*, by T. Craig Brown.

having a long tail and cloven feet, and on the other the forequarters and head of a hare in full flight.

The lion may be heraldic or it may have a symbolic meaning. The hart is probably an allusion to the beginning of the xlii. psalm—"As the hart panteth after the water brooks." This verse is inscribed on a font of the eleventh century, at Potterne, Wilts,* and the figure of a hart is of frequent occurrence on Celtic and Norman work, where, as is now generally

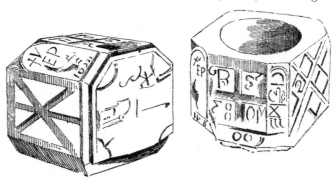

FIG. 1496.—Selkirk Parish Church. Stoup.

believed, it has a symbolic meaning. The ox and hare, being also animals referred to in Scripture, are probably to be considered in the same category. This example is from Peebles, and was given to Mr. Brown by a gentleman who believes it was found at some ruined building there. It measures about 13 inches across on top by $9\frac{3}{4}$ inches high, and the bowl is 4 inches deep.

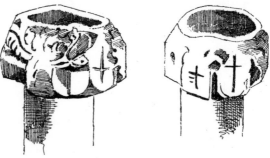

FIG. 1497.—Selkirk Parish Church. Stoup.

Fig. 1496 shows two views of a stoup, which is square, with the angles cut off, converting it into an unequal-sided octagon. It is decorated in a very curious manner with signs and letters of which we can give no explanation. It was found built into an old house at Selkirk when it was

* *Early Christian Symbolism*, by Romilly Allen, p. 374.

taken down many years ago. A mason took possession of it and used it for a flower pot, and chiselled a hole in the bottom. The fragment measures about 14⅝ by 16 inches. The basin is 11 inches over by 10 inches deep.

Both of these specimens are cut out of red sandstone.

The third stoup (Fig. 1497) is cut out of hard blue whinstone, and has an unfinished appearance. It is decorated with shields, some having an incised cross, and with foliage of a Gothic character. The plan on the under side is in the form of a Greek cross. It measures about 18 inches in diameter by 10½ inches high, with a basin 11 inches wide by 9 inches deep.

WIGTON CHURCH, WIGTONSHIRE.*

An ivy clad ruin standing in the old churchyard of Wigton. Only the east end (Fig. 1498) with a considerable portion of the south wall and a small portion of the north wall remain. The first measures 21 feet 2 inches wide on the inside, and the south wall extends for a length of about 55 feet.

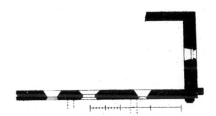

Fig. 1498.—Wigton Church. Plan.

Mr. Muir writes of this church as follows: †—" By the remains of a string course and other bits of minor detail at the east end, it would appear that the building has been originally of first pointed date, though perhaps still earlier features were destroyed at the various repairs which it underwent in modern times. One or two objects—The stump of a cross, and a small baptismal font of tapering form " (which seems to have now disappeared) " were to all appearance Norman, and very likely, therefore, the earlier portion of the primitive structure was of twelfth century date." The church was dedicated to St. Machutus, and belonged to the Priory of Whithorn.

A ruined building of late date, with walls about 7 feet high, projects about 17 feet out from the south wall by about 23 feet in width outside measure.

* We are indebted for the Plan of this church to Mr. F. R. Coles.
† *Ecclesiological Notes on some of the Islands of Scotland, &c.* p. 245.

CHURCHES OF THE SIXTEENTH AND SEVENTEENTH CENTURIES.

The ecclesiastical architecture of the mediæval period terminated at the introduction of the Reformation in 1560, but during the latter half of the sixteenth and the greater part of the seventeenth century a number of churches were erected which show some attempt to maintain or revive the style of earlier times. This tendency was doubtless encouraged by the strenuous effort which was made, under James I. and Charles I. and II., to establish the Episcopal forms of Church government and service in Scotland. These forms being contrary to the desire of the Presbyterians, who comprised the great body of the people, gave rise to two opposing parties. The party favourable to the Episcopal form of religion supported the erection of churches and the maintenance of the worship as nearly as possible after the old model, while the Presbyterians and Puritans discouraged everything which savoured of the ancient faith, whether in buildings or services. The result was that during the century which followed the Reformation there were two styles of ecclesiastical structures erected in the country, one style showing some reverence for the house of God in its form and decoration, and in the appropriateness of the divine service; while the other seemed to be designed, both in its buildings and forms of worship, to be as far removed as possible from any outward or visible sign of inward sweetness or grace.

It is proposed to conclude this work with some examples of the different styles of churches erected during the above period.

A number of specimens have already been given in a former work.*

These churches were introduced into a work on the domestic architecture of the country, in order to illustrate the influence of the domestic style on the ecclesiastical architecture of this period. Many of these edifices were, therefore, only partially illustrated, and it has been thought desirable to treat some of them more fully in this book, so as to complete the illustration and description of their architecture.

The examples which are now given will amply illustrate the remaining specimens which still survive of this somewhat heterogeneous epoch.

Most of the churches of the seventeenth century are either very poor imitations of Gothic work or tasteless examples of plain walls, while a few contain the germs of what might have been wrought into a picturesque style, founded on the domestic architecture of the period. Such, for example, are the churches of Stirling (west end), Anstruther Easter, and Pittenweem.

Several of the monuments of the period are also given.

The following examples are arranged in alphabetical order.

* *The Castellated and Domestic Architecture of Scotland*, Vol. v. p. 130.

ABERDOUR, ABERDEENSHIRE.

A village about eight miles west of Fraserburgh. In the *Book of Deer* it is written, "Columcille and Drostan son of Cosgrach his pupil came

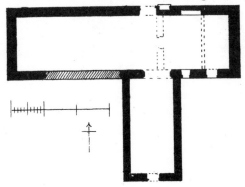

FIG. 1499.—Aberdour. Plan.

from I as God had shown to them unto Abbordo-boir and Bede the Pict was mormaer of Buchan before them, and it was he that gave them that

FIG. 1500.—Aberdour. View from South-West.

town in freedom for ever from Mormaer and tosech." In these words a scribe, writing in the eleventh or twelfth century, tells of the planting of Christianity in the North about A.D. 580. It is probable that the clerics tarried at Aberdour for a time, and founded a monastery on the land which had been granted to them.* In later times the parish church was dedicated to St. Drostan, and in 1178 and 1318 there are notices of its erection into a prebend of St. Machar's Cathedral.† In 1557 there is a mandate

FIG. 1501.
Aberdour.
Jamb of Arch
to Aisle.

* *Book of Deer*, preface, p. iv.
† *Shires of Aberdeen and Banff*, Vol. II. p. 373.

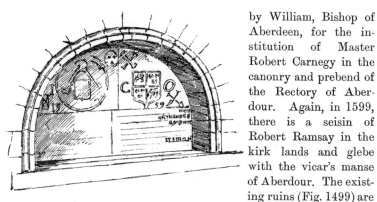

FIG. 1502.—Aberdour. Tomb in North Wall.

by William, Bishop of Aberdeen, for the institution of Master Robert Carnegy in the canonry and prebend of the Rectory of Aberdour. Again, in 1599, there is a seisin of Robert Ramsay in the kirk lands and glebe with the vicar's manse of Aberdour. The existing ruins (Fig. 1499) are not earlier than the sixteenth century, and consist of a nave 70 feet long by 21 feet 3 inches wide, and a south aisle 30 feet 4 inches long by 17 feet 4 inches wide, all outside measure. The walls (Fig. 1500) are still tolerably entire, but are fast crumbling away. The west end of the nave has been partitioned off into two burial vaults, as also is the aisle. The arch between the nave and aisle is round, with an impost moulding (Fig. 1501) at the springing of the arch. The arch and jambs are chamfered, the chamfer terminating on a splayed base. In the north wall of the nave is the round arched mural tomb shown in Fig. 1502.

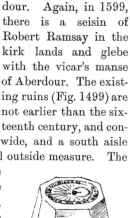

FIG. 1503.—Aberdour. Font.

The font is still in existence. It is quite plain and octagonal, being 2 feet in diameter by about 2 feet 2 inches high. After the abandonment of the church the font appears to have been built into the wall, and to have had a sundial carved on its lower end (Fig. 1503).

ANSTRUTHER, EASTER AND WESTER, FIFESHIRE.

These adjacent towns form one of the very interesting group of ancient seaports and places of commerce on the northern shore of the Frith of Forth. Anstruther is divided into two portions by the little river Dreel, which formed the harbour of Anstruther Wester, while Easter Anstruther extends in a wide crescent along the coast, and has a larger harbour of its own.

Anstruther Wester belonged to the Priory of Pittenweem, and the parish church was dedicated to St. Nicolas. The town obtained a charter from the monastery in 1549, and another in 1554.* The church is now modernised, but the old tower (Fig. 1504) is a fair specimen of the keep-like structures so often erected in connection with Scottish churches in the sixteenth century.

Anstruther Easter was, before the Reformation, in the parish of Kilrenny, and was disjoined from it by the General Assembly, with the consent of the bailies and council of the town, in 1639. In 1640 Anstruther Easter was erected into a separate parish, and the reason assigned in the Act was "the Burgh being a part of the parish of Kilrenny a mile distant of deep evil way in winter and rainy times." †

A proposal to build a church at Anstruther Easter had thus been in contemplation for some time, and in 1636 an agreement was come to regarding it between Mr. Colin Adams, the first minister of the parish, and the bailies and council. The new church was erected, and "ten years later a steeple was added after a Dutch model." ‡

Fig. 1504.—Anstruther Wester.

* *East Neuk of Fife*, p. 343.   † *Ibid.* p. 361.   ‡ *Ibid.* p. 632.

The arrangement of the Plan (Fig. 1505) and the design of the tower seem, however, to contradict the latter statement. The debased but picturesque architecture of the tower (Fig. 1506) so strongly resembles the other Scottish church towers of the period as to render its origin beyond dispute. It combines the ornamental treatment of the upper part with the plain features of the lower portion, so usual in the castles of the time; and the classic balustrade and the gabled termination of the staircase recall similar domestic features of Scottish castellated architecture very common in the seventeenth century, both in churches and houses.

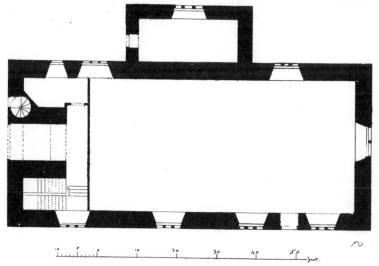

FIG. 1505.—Anstruther Easter. Plan.

The church measures, externally, 92 feet in length by 41 feet in breadth. The entrance doorway leads into a simple barrel-vaulted passage 9 feet wide. This originally opened directly into the body of the church, having a staircase to the gallery on the south side and a small room or vestry on the north side. The body of the church is of the usual oblong form (Fig. 1507) and is lighted with windows, which, from their mullions and round arches, retain a slightly ecclesiastical appearance. This is chiefly striking in the large east window. There were originally two doorways in the south wall, but one has been built up.

Altogether, this church, the date of which is known, forms a complete and characteristic example of the Scottish ecclesiastical architecture of the earlier part of the seventeenth century.*

* A number of examples of this style have been illustrated and described in *The Castellated and Domestic Architecture of Scotland.* See "Churches and Monuments," Vol. v. p. 130.

FIG. 1506.—Anstruther Easter. West End and Tower.

FIG. 1507.—Anstruther Easter. View from South-East.

FIG. 1508.—St. Mary's, Auchterhouse.
Chancel Arch.

FIG. 1510.—St. Mary's, Auchterhouse.
South Doorway in Chancel.

ST. MARY'S PARISH CHURCH,
AUCHTERHOUSE, FORFARSHIRE.

The village of Kirkton or Auchterhouse is situated about five miles north of Dundee.

FIG. 1509.—St. Mary's, Auchterhouse.
Section of Chancel Arch Mouldings.

The old church consists of a nave and chancel, with a square west tower. The nave is about 56 feet long by 33 feet wide, and the chancel is about 27 feet long by 21 feet 6 inches wide. The date (1630)

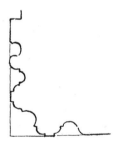

FIG. 1511.—St. Mary's, Auchterhouse.
Jamb of Doorway in Chancel.

is carved on the east gable, but the building undoubtedly is, in part at least, of older date. There are a great many stones, pieces of window tracery, and other carved work lying about the churchyard, which show that there was a former building, probably of fifteenth century work, here, which was doubtless in part taken down and rebuilt in the seventeenth century. The chancel arch (Fig. 1508) belongs to this earlier church. It is 12 feet 3 inches wide and is acutely pointed; the wall is about 3 feet 2 inches thick. The mouldings of the arch consist of double hollows, as shown on section (Fig. 1509), with a cap moulding of the form shown on the same figure.

FIG. 1512.—St. Mary's, Auchterhouse. South Doorway.

The south doorway in the chancel (Fig. 1510) also belongs to the earlier church. The moulded jambs (Fig. 1511) abut against a square lintel, somewhat in the same manner as occurs in one of the windows in the tower at South Queensferry. The jambs rise at the base from a splay sloping inwards. The doorway to the nave (Fig. 1512) is more classic in design, and is of the seventeenth century. No other features of the church, except its sundials (see *The Castellated and Domestic Architecture of Scotland*, Vol. v.), call for special notice.

AYTOUN CHURCH, BERWICKSHIRE.

The town of Aytoun (formerly written Eytun) stands on the river Eye, about seven miles north from Berwick-on-Tweed, and half a mile from the railway station.

The old church is situated in an open burial-ground, in connection with which a new church was erected some years ago. The old building appears, from the remains of its ivy-covered walls, to have been of considerable extent, but no details can now be made out. The only portion which remains in a tolerable state of preservation appears to have formed a south aisle or wing.

Fig. 1513.—Aytoun Church.

There is a plain segmental headed doorway in the east side, and a large circular headed window in the south end (Fig. 1513). The latter is divided by two mullions into three lights, each finished at the top with a round-arched head. The window has a transom in the centre. It is evident from the nature of the design and the form of the mouldings that the window is of late date, probably of the end of the sixteenth century.

Aytoun was granted by the Scottish Edgar to St. Cuthbert's Monks, and thus became the property of the Priory of Coldingham, and shared its fate.

BALLINGRY CHURCH, FIFESHIRE.

The present church of Ballingry is a modern structure built in 1831. It stands on the site of a pre-Reformation edifice, which has entirely disappeared. The window shown in Fig. 1514 clearly belongs to the seventeenth century, being part of a north aisle, which was evidently built about that time. The window is the only feature of interest in the

FIG. 1514.—Ballingry Church. Window in North Aisle.

building, and it is a good example of the Renaissance style, modified by the grafting on to it of Gothic features.

BLAIR CHURCH,* BLAIR-ATHOLL, PERTHSHIRE.

The walls of this old church (Fig. 1515) still stand within the grounds of Blair Castle, the seat of the Duke of Atholl, and about five minutes' walk from the Castle. The building is roofless and the walls are almost complete, but they have been much slapped and altered to make the place suitable for Presbyterian worship.

The masonry is rubble work, built with stones gathered off the hills. The doors and windows have hewn jambs and lintels of freestone, all square-headed and splayed. A gravestone, dated 1579, has been built in the inside of the north wall. The chief interest of the ruin arises from its containing the vault in which Claverhouse is buried. A tablet on the inner face of the south wall of the church, west of the aisle which contains the vault, bears the following inscription :—

* We have to thank Mr. T. S. Robertson, architect, Dundee, for the Plan and description of this church.

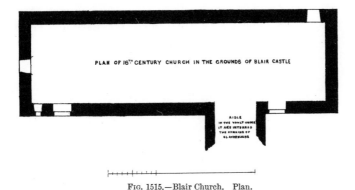

PLAN OF 16ᵀᴴ CENTURY CHURCH IN THE GROUNDS OF BLAIR CASTLE

AISLE
IN THE VAULT UNDER
IT ARE INTERRED
THE REMAINS OF
CLAVERHOUSE

FIG. 1515.—Blair Church. Plan.

Within this vault beneath
Are interred the remains of
JOHN GRAHAM OF CLAVERHOUSE
Viscount Dundee
Who fell at the Battle of Killiecrankie
27 July 1689, aged 46
This memorial is placed here by
John, 7th Duke of Atholl, K.T.
1889

ST. BRANDAN'S, BOYNDIE, BANFFSHIRE.

The ruined Church of Boyndie or Inverboyndie stands on a slight elevation near the mouth of the small river of the same name, about two miles west from the town of Banff. The parish was formerly conjoined with Banff till 1634, when it was erected into a separate parish. The church is of ancient foundation, and was granted in 1211-14, along with that of Banff, to the monks of Arbroath.

The old church stands in the churchyard, which is still used. It was abandoned in 1773, when a new church was built. Since that time it has fallen into complete decay, so much so that the plan cannot now be properly distinguished. The only portions still preserved in tolerable condition are the west wall and belfry (Fig. 1516). These do not appear to be of great age. The wall contains the entrance doorway of the church. It has a round arch and jambs with a small splay, such as was common in the sixteenth and seventeenth centuries. The top of the gable has a small belfry, which has latterly occupied the position of a former one, which was much larger. The older belfry must have been of considerable size, as is apparent from the large corbels which carried it, and which project

III.   2 M

boldly from both sides of the wall.   These were arranged so as to carry
an octagonal erection, which must have had a very picturesque effect.

Fig. 1516.—St. Brandan's, Boyndie.

They are evidently copied from the domestic architecture of the period.
This structure seems to belong to the seventeenth century.

ST. MICHAEL'S CHURCH, Cupar, Fifeshire.

The old Church of Cupar having become decayed, the Prior of St. Andrews, in 1415, erected a new church on a new site in the town. But in 1785 this church was also found to be in a decayed condition, and was rebuilt on the same site as that of the fifteenth century. Part of the old structure at the north-west angle was, however, not destroyed, and still survives. This portion (Fig. 1517) comprises three arches of the main or central nave and the tower at the north-west angle. The latter (Fig. 1518) is quadrilateral, and its north and west walls are raised upon the outer walls of the church at the north-west angle, portions of which walls still exist, together with the jamb of a large west window. The tower is unrelieved by buttresses. On the east and south the walls are carried on arches, the lower story being thus included in the interior of the church.

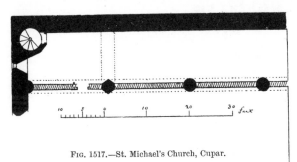

Fig. 1517.—St. Michael's Church, Cupar.

The pier at the south-east angle which supports these arches is hexagonal in form, while the remaining piers of the church are round. The caps and bases are of the usual late form. The tower is oblong in plan, being 22 feet from east to west, and 18 feet from north to south. This inequality produces a peculiar effect in the broached spire which surmounts it, and which was erected in 1620 by the Rev. William Scott, the minister of the parish, at his own expense. The balustrade forming the parapet and the other features of the spire are quite in the character of the Scottish seventeenth century steeples, common in Fifeshire, such as those at Anstruther and Pittenweem.

The tower itself is plain with simple pointed lights, those of the upper story being double, so as to be suitable for the belfry. In the west wall there occurs a small window with peculiarly shaped head, and below it the string course is studded with square shaped flowers.

In the present church is preserved a good recumbent effigy (Fig. 1519) of one of the Fernies of Fernie, but it is without date. The arms over

FIG. 1518.—St. Michael's Church, Cupar. Tower.

the monument—a fesse between 3 lions' heads erased—are those of Fernie of that Ilk. Several members of this family were Constables of Cupar in

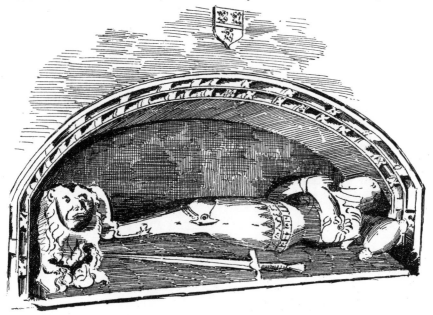

FIG. 1519.—St. Michael's Church, Cupar.   Monument of one of the Fernies of Fernie.

ancient times. The lands of Fernie lie a few miles to the west of the town.

ST. BRIDGET'S CHURCH, DALGETY, FIFESHIRE.

A remarkable structure, which stands near the Forth at the head of a small bay about two miles south-west from Aberdour, the road to it passing through the beautiful grounds of St. Colm House.

The old church (Fig. 1520) forms the eastern part of the structure, while to the west has been erected a two-story building, containing on the ground floor a burial vault, and on the upper floor a "laird's loft" or room for the Lord of the Manor, from which access was obtained to a gallery in the church.

The ancient church was dedicated to St. Bridget in 1244. It retains a simple pointed doorway at the south-west angle, a number of altered and square-headed windows in the south wall, and a piscina at the east end of the same wall, but there are scarcely any of the old details preserved to indicate the date of the building. It has evidently been greatly altered, to make it suitable for Presbyterian worship after the Reformation. There are two projecting buildings on the north side and one on the south

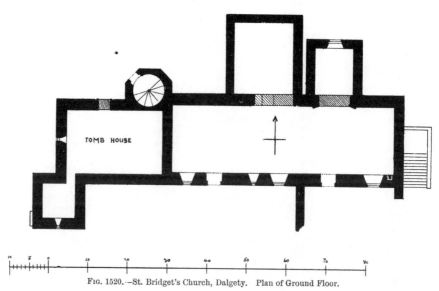

TOMB HOUSE

FIG. 1520.—St. Bridget's Church, Dalgety. Plan of Ground Floor.

side, all much ruined, but the mouldings of the jambs of the northern projections at the openings into the church are preserved and indicate Renaissance work. These outside structures were probably burial vaults.

FIG. 1521.—St. Bridget's Church, Dalgety. View from South-West.

The house at the west end is undoubtedly post-Reformation. In the vault is buried the celebrated Chancellor Seaton, and the building, to judge from its style (Fig. 1521), was probably erected by him about the beginning of the seventeenth century. The upper floor is reached by a projecting octagonal stair turret on the north side. The interior of the walls of the principal room on the first floor (Fig. 1522) is built with ashlar work, and the walls are divided into moulded panels in stone work and a stone cornice runs round the room.

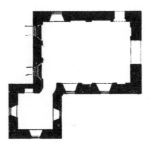

FIG. 1522.—St. Bridget's Church, Dalgety. Plan of First Floor.

A wide aperture in the east wall of the room opens into the church at a high level, and no doubt gave access to a gallery at the west end. The belfry is placed on the west gable of this room and still contains a small bell, the chain for ringing which has cut a deep groove in the wall outside. The small room at the south-west angle contains a fireplace. There has been another gallery at the east end of the church. The outside staircase for access to it still remains. A good monumental slab is built into the north wall of the church, bearing date 1540.

ST. JOHN'S CHURCH, DALRY, KIRKCUDBRIGHTSHIRE.*

The village of Dalry or St. John's Town stands on the east bank of the ·Dee, in the northern or Glenkens district of Kirkcudbrightshire, and is about ten miles north from Parton Railway Station. The old parish church was removed in 1829-31, when a new church was erected on the old site.

An old burial vault formerly attached to the church, and known as the Kenmure burial aisle, has, however, been preserved, which (Fig. 1523), with its crow-stepped gable and large antiquely grilled window and panelled coat of arms, forms an interesting relic of the seventeenth century.

This adjunct to the old church formed a projection on its south side, and measures internally 17 feet in length by 14 feet 2 inches in width (Fig. 1524). The entrance from the church, which was about 7 feet wide, was by a plain rubble archway, which is now built up. The doorway in the west wall is square-lintelled, and 2 feet 8 inches wide. The window in the south wall is also square-lintelled, and the iron grill

* We have to thank Mr. William Galloway, Whithorn, for the drawings and particulars of this structure.

appears to have been built in along with the wall. The coat of arms in the panel over the window is divided in pale, having the three boars' heads of the Gordons on the dexter side, and a lion rampant on the sinister side. These, Mr. Galloway suggests, may be the arms of John Gordon of Kenmure, who was Justiciar of the Stewartry in 1555, and died in 1604, and who here combines the provincial with the family arms—the lion rampant being the heraldic emblem of the province of Galloway.

There is an ambry in the south-west angle 1 foot 7 inches wide by 1 foot 9 inches high, and 1 foot 3 inches deep.

Fig. 1523.—St. John's Church, Dalry.   View from South-West.

On the outside of the north-east angle there is an interesting relic of the south wall of the old church, a portion of one rybat of a window having been preserved. Three courses of freestone yet remain, having a bold splay externally, a groove for glass, and a splayed ingoing. This shows that the chancel of the old church must have extended some distance to the eastward.

Some of the dressed granite stones of the old church have been reused in the modern building.

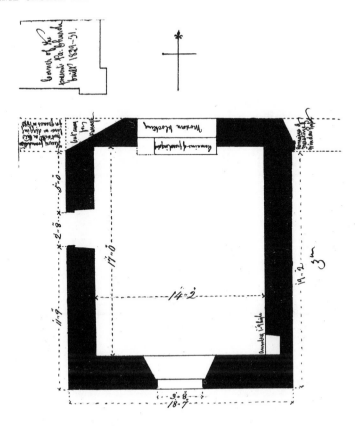

Fig. 1524.—St. John's Church, Dalry. Plan.

DRAINIE CHURCH AND MICHAEL KIRK, MORAYSHIRE.

These two churches are examples of the revived Gothic architecture of post-Reformation times. The parish of Drainie was formed by the union of the two old parishes of Kineddar and Ogstown. They both lie on the Morayshire coast, about five to six miles north of Elgin, and fully two miles from Lossiemouth. The country is low lying, and used in former times to be marshy. Kineddar was a seat of the Bishopric of Moray before it was moved to Spynie, and ultimately to Elgin. There too stood a large fortified castle (of the first period), consisting of a great wall of enceinte surrounded by a deep ditch, but it has now been taken down, and the plough passes over the site. This castle formed the residence of some of the Bishops of Moray before Spynie Palace was erected.

The Church of Drainie was built in 1666, and is a good example of the period. It has evidently been designed to meet the requirements of the Presbyterian service of the time (Fig. 1525). The pulpit would be in the centre of the south wall, with a window placed on each side of it. Beyond these, on either hand, are two doors, each admitting to a short passage, which would give access to a central one. The main body of the church is 62 feet in length by 24 feet in width, and in the centre of the north side is a wing 24 feet by 18 feet. This wing or "aisle" is spanned by a stone arch, which may have carried a gallery above, to light which a small window is introduced in the north gable. The ground floor of the north wing would be seated in the usual manner, and is provided with an entrance door and two windows. Similar arrangements of plan are common in the Scottish churches of post-Reformation times.

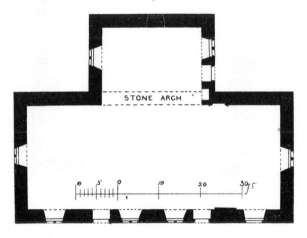

Fig. 1525.—Drainie Church. Plan.

The windows and doors (Fig. 1526) have pointed arches, and the windows are each divided by one mullion, which branches into two in the arch-head. These door and window dressings are all chamfered on the edges. The cornice is of classic form, and the gables are crow-stepped. The west gable is finished on top with an ornamental belfry in the Renaissance style of the period, in which some revival of Gothic features was attempted.

MICHAEL KIRK.—About half a mile west from Drainie stood the ancient church of Ogstown, the site of which is now occupied by the remarkable specimen of revived Gothic shown in Fig. 1527. This edifice was erected as a mausoleum for his family by Lodvic Gordon of Gordonston, an estate in the vicinity. Mr. Gordon belonged to a branch of the

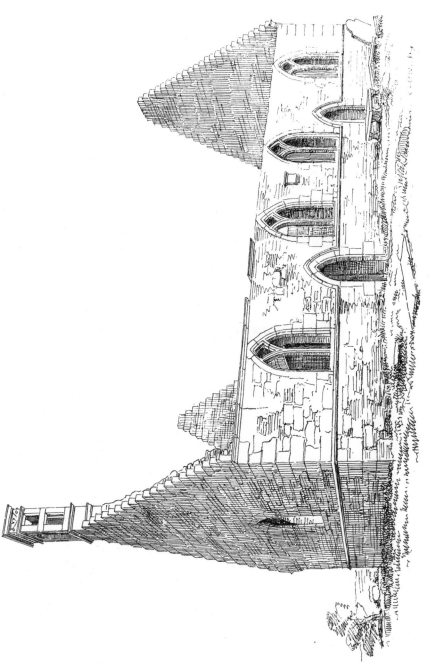

Fig. 1526.—Drainie Church.   View from South-West.

Sutherland family, the first baronet being Sir Robert Gordon, the author of the *History of Sutherland.*

FIG. 1527.—Michael Kirk.
Ornaments in East Window.

The edifice (Fig. 1528) is 45 feet in length by 20 feet in width externally. It has large pointed and traceried windows in the east and west gables, and the south wall contains a central door and a two-light window at each side of it. The openings are all pointed, and the windows have a kind of tracery. The north wall has no openings, being apparently designed to receive monuments, of which it already contains several. This structure bears the date of 1703, and is a remarkable product of that period. The forms of the tracery (Fig. 1530) indicate a very slight acquaintance with Gothic, and the mouldings have all more of a

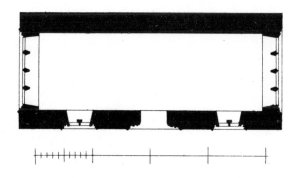

FIG. 1528.—Michael Kirk. Plan.

classic than a Gothic character. The ornaments introduced in the transoms are peculiar. Those in the east window consist of a series of Cupids' heads (Fig. 1527), while those of the west window show a variety of flower patterns (Fig. 1529) carved with considerable spirit. The urns which act as finials on the gables betray the Renaissance feeling of the period. In the architrave-like moulding which surrounds the door and windows are introduced a series of alternating stars and roses.

FIG. 1529.—Michael Kirk.
Ornaments in
West Window.

It may be thought astonishing to find a revival of Gothic so prominent in this northern region ; but it must be borne in mind that the Episcopal form of Church government encouraged by royalty in the seventeenth century found considerable favour in this part of Scotland.

FIG. 1530.—Michael Kirk. View from South-West

DURNESS CHURCH, SUTHERLANDSHIRE.*

It is interesting to find in the neighbourhood of Cape Wrath a specimen of ecclesiastical architecture, even though of the seventeenth century. The old parish church, which is now a ruin, occupies the site of a cell of Dornoch monastery. It was built in 1619. The Plan (Fig. 1531) is somewhat irregular, but not unlike, in general form, to many of the churches of Scotland at the same period, having the pulpit placed in the centre of the long side wall, and facing the wing.

* The Plan is drawn from a sketch kindly supplied by the Rev. Alex. Miller of Buckie.

In a recess is the grave of Duncan MacMorroch, a relation of the chief of the clan, believed to have been very serviceable in getting rid quietly of

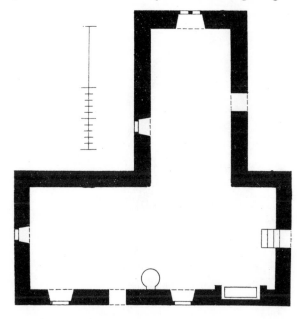

Fig. 1531.—Durness Church. Plan.

troublesome hindrances. This gentleman was desirous to be buried in the sacred edifice, but as some doubts existed as to his sanctity, it was resolved

Fig. 1532.—Durness Church. View from South-West.

not to admit his body quite into the church, so he was buried under the wall. His tomb is dated 1619, and his epitaph hands down his name to posterity in the following words :—

> " Duncan MacMorroch here lies low
> Was ill to his friend, waur to his foe
> True to his master in weird and wo."

The adjoining gable has crowsteps and is topped with a belfry (Fig. 1532). The lintel of the doorway in the wing bears the letters and figures 16 · HMK · A. In the gable of the wing there is a two-light window with a pointed arch, a central mullion dividing into two small arches at the head (the space between being left solid), and a transom.

An old font lies in the main part of the church.

EAST CALDER CHURCH, Mid-Lothian.

This edifice was the parish church of East Calder till 1750, when a new church was erected at Kirknewton, and East Calder was united with that parish. These two parishes lie about ten miles west from Edinburgh.

The Church of East Calder was dedicated to St. Cuthbert. At the accession of William the Lion the church was granted to the monks of Kelso. This parish was formerly called Calder-Clere, to distinguish it from

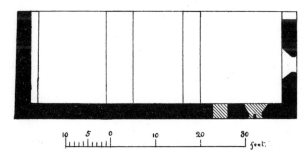

FIG. 1533.—East Calder Church. Plan.

Mid-Calder, which lies about one mile west of it, on the opposite side of the river Almond. The church, which is now a ruin, stands in its old churchyard. It is a simple oblong (Fig. 1533), internally 56 feet in length by 17 feet in width. The north wall has been removed, and the interior divided into burial-places, separated by walls and railings. The doorways and windows have been built up, and few of the wall openings can now be seen. One window is still partly preserved in the east end (Fig. 1534). It has evidently been divided into two lights by a mullion, which is removed, and each light has had a round-arched head. Another window in the south wall, near the east end, is of similar form.   The mullion and round heads of the opening have been preserved by being built up.   A doorway, also built up, adjoins the window in the south wall on the west.

FIG. 1534.—East Calder Church.   View from South-East.

There may be other built up openings, but the wall is so thickly covered with ivy that they cannot be identified.   The belfry on the west gable is plain, and evidently late in date.   The few details which survive indicate a post-Reformation style, probably of about 1600.

EASSIE AND NEVAY, FORFARSHIRE.

Two ruined parish churches, each in its churchyard, situated within two miles of each other and about nine miles south-west of Forfar. They are small buildings, measuring respectively 56 feet 6 inches by 15 feet 6 inches, and 53 feet 6 inches by 18 feet 6 inches within the walls (Fig. 1535).   Neither church has any openings in the north wall.   At Eassie (Fig. 1536) all the doors and windows are square-headed, and at Nevay they are the same, except that the west doorway is round-headed, but not arched, being cut out of one stone.   At Eassie the westmost doorway on the south side is of eighteenth century work, but the eastmost one is original.   An ivy-mantled belfry crowns the west end of each edifice.

On the lintel of the south door at Nevay there is the date 1695, with the initials D. N. between the first two and last two figures. These are

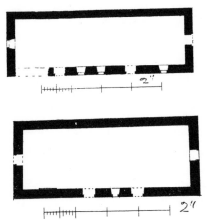

FIG. 1535.—Eassie and Nevay Churches. Plans.

doubtless the initials of David of Nevay, whose father, a Senator of the College of Justice, died shortly before this date. The church, however,

FIG. 1536.—Eassie Church.

appears to be of earlier date, as a tombstone of 1597 is built into its walls.

These churches were in the diocese of St. Andrews, and in 1309

"Robert I. gave the advocation and donation of the Kirk of Eassie to the Monks of Newbottle.* "

St. Neveth, martyr, to whom the church was dedicated, and from whom it received its name, was a bishop "in the north," who was slain by the Saxons and the Picts, and Bishop Forbes † suggests that the martyr was buried at Nevay.

Eassie was dedicated to St. Brandon.

At Eassie Church there is one of the finest of the Scottish sculptured stones.

PULPIT FROM ST. CUTHBERT'S CHURCH, EDINBURGH.

The annexed sketch (Fig. 1537) shows the old pulpit of St. Cuthbert's Church as it stood in St. Cuthbert's Poorhouse, Lothian Road, Edinburgh, before that building was removed in 1868. It appears ‡ that when St. Cuthbert's Church was demolished in 1773, the pulpit was transferred to the Poorhouse. Its date can be pretty well ascertained. From a minute of the kirk-session of 15th August 1651, we find that Cromwell's soldiers had so completely sacked the church that there was "nayther pulpit, loft, nor seat left therein," all doors and windows having been broken, and the roof by cannon shot completely ruined. Steps were immediately taken to repair the damage, and in April 1652 the church was reopened for public worship. This pulpit was doubtless made between the above dates, and its style is characteristic of the time. It is of oak, and probably in the old church it stood on a loftier base than is shown in the sketch.

FETTERESSO CHURCH, KINCARDINESHIRE.

The parish of Fetteresso included a considerable part of the town of Stonehaven on the east coast of Kincardineshire. The old church, the ruins of which stand in a large churchyard, is situated near the Carron Water, about one mile and a half south-west from Stonehaven. The structure probably occupies the site of a very ancient church, dedicated to St. Cavan, which stood at the Hamlet of Fetteresso. It is beautifully situated amongst fine old trees.

* *Angus or Forfarshire*, by Alexander J. Warden, Vol. III. p. 205.

† *Kalendars of the Saints.*

‡ "The Old Pulpit of St. Cuthbert's," by Rev. Cumberland Hill ; *Edinburgh Daily Review*, November 1868.

Fig. 1537.—Pulpit from St. Cuthbert's Church, Edinburgh.

The existing edifice, which is roofless, appears, from the style of its architecture, to be chiefly post-Reformation. The walls and gables are well preserved and much covered with ivy.

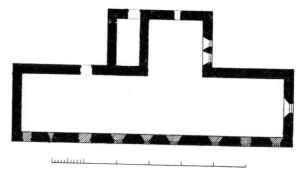

Fig. 1538.—Fetteresso Church. Plan.

The church (Fig. 1538) is, internally, 81 feet in length from east to west by 17 feet 6 inches in width from north to south. It has a wing

Fig. 1539.—Fetteresso Church. View from North-West.

thrown out to the north, which is about 17 feet square, and bears the date of 1720. A small adjunct to the west of the wing carries the date of 1857.

The wall openings are almost entirely in the south wall, in which there are three doorways and six windows. There is one window in the east end and one pointed doorway in the north wall. The north wing contains a north doorway and two windows in the east wall. This wing, doubtless, contained a gallery. The openings in the south wall are all built up, and the interior is converted into a private burial-ground. The details have all the character of eighteenth century work. The belfry (Fig. 1539) stands on the top of the west gable and still retains its bell, which is used on the occasion of funerals. The church and its surroundings are very picturesque.

FORDEL CHAPEL, Fifeshire.

This is a private chapel in the beautiful grounds of Fordel Castle,* about two miles north from Inverkeithing. It bears the date of 1650, and tradition has it that the works were interrupted by Cromwell's soldiers.

The edifice is now used as a mortuary chapel by the proprietors of Fordel House.

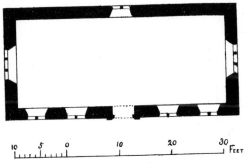

Fig. 1540.—Fordel Chapel. Plan.

The structure bears the mark of the period when it was erected in the mixed style of its architecture, being partly an imitation of Gothic and partly Renaissance. It measures (Fig. 1540) about 40 feet in length by 16 feet in width internally, and is a simple oblong in plan, with a doorway in the centre of the south side. It is lighted (Fig. 1541) by four symmetrically arranged windows in the south side, one in the centre of the north side, and a large three-light window at each end. The windows are divided by mullions, and have a species of tracery in the round arch-heads.

The west gable is crowned with a belfry having a small spire. The stone cresting on the ridge has the small ornaments common at the period.

* Described and illustrated in *The Castellated and Domestic Architecture of Scotland*, Vol. II. p. 237.

Fig. 1541.—Fordel Chapel.

Over the doorway (Fig. 1542) are the quaintly carved arms of J. Henderson and his wife, M. Monteath (the Hendersons being the ancient

Fig. 1542.—Fordel Chapel.   Arms over Doorway.

proprietors of the domain), with their initials and the date 1650. The same initials are repeated on tablets both on the exterior and interior of the chapel.

GARVALD CHURCH, HADDINGTONSHIRE.

Situated about five miles south-east from Haddington, in the secluded valley of the Papana Water, stands the rebuilt Church of Garvald. Only a very few fragments remain (Fig. 1543) of the ornament of the ancient

FIG. 1543.—Garvald Church. String Course.

Norman structure which formerly existed. These are built into the walls of the church, which was restored and enlarged in 1829.

GAMRIE CHURCH, BANFFSHIRE.

This church, dedicated to St. John the Evangelist, has a splendid situation, standing high above the cliffs overlooking the sea, and having a small fishing village on the beach immediately below. The building is now a ruin, only the walls remaining. It is a curious looking structure and

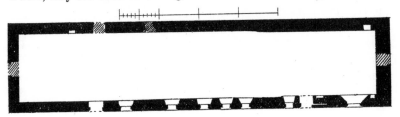

FIG. 1544.—Gamrie Church. Plan.

has been built at two periods. The east end is the earliest part. The total length of the church internally (Fig. 1544) is about 94 feet 4 inches by 15 feet 6 inches wide. The later part of the structure is about 10 inches wider than the earlier, the walls being thinner. The external dimensions are 96 feet long by 21 feet 8 inches wide. The chancel or east end was probably heightened at the time when the west end was built. The east gable has a sett-off at the level of what was apparently the original height (Fig. 1545). There are two doors on the south side, that in the chancel being lintelled and having a hole for a sliding bar, while the other in the nave is round arched, as is also a door in the opposite wall. These doors have all beaded mouldings. There is only one window on the north side. On the south side the windows are of various sizes, and are scattered about in an irregular way. Two of them, which are placed high in the wall, are checked for outside shutters; the others have all simple splays.

Fig. 1545.—Gamrie Church. View from South-East.

There is a plain ambry in the east wall at a high level, and adjoining it in the north wall there is a recess, probably a *credence*, as suggested by the Rev. Dr. Pratt.* This part of the building is in a neglected condition, being fitted up as a toolhouse for the gravedigger's implements. There is built into the interior of the east gable a memorial tablet, with very quaintly carved letters and mouldings, to the memory of Patricius Barclay dominus de Tolly, and his wife, Joneta Ogilvy, who died in 1547.† There were other interesting memorials connected with the church which are referred to by Dr. Pratt, but of these only mutilated fragments remain. The indignant remonstrance of the Rev. Dr. against the condition of the building, written thirty years ago, backed up by a poem by Principal Geddes, has not availed to secure any respect for the old walls.

The Church of Gamrie is frequently referred to in the twelfth and following centuries. It was granted by William the Lion to Arbroath between 1189 and 1198,‡ and in 1513 Mr. Henry Preston was presented

* *Guide to Buchan.*
† *Shires of Aberdeen and Banff*, Spalding Club, Vol. IV. p. 580.
‡ *Ibid.* Vol. II p. 363.

to the Church of Gamrie by the Abbot of Arbroath. Probably the existing walls were erected about the latter date, but the details indicate that great alterations have been made on the building, which convert it into a seventeenth century structure.

GLADSMUIR CHURCH, HADDINGTONSHIRE.

A ruin near the village of Longniddry.

The parish of Gladsmuir was formed out of several other parishes in 1695, at which time this church (Fig. 1546), now in ruins, was erected.

FIG. 1546.—Gladsmuir Church.

It was an oblong structure, and measures about 71 feet long by 25 feet 6 inches wide outside. There was, as frequently happens, an aisle on the north side about 24 feet square, opening into the church by the wide and lofty arch seen in the view. This arch, which is simply splayed on both faces, has two of its voussoirs projected about 6 inches beyond the others. These may have been rests for diagonal pieces to carry the continuation of the roof at the arch. A sundial (Fig. 1547), bearing the date 1700, stands in the usual place at the south-west corner.

FIG. 1547.
Gladsmuir Church.
Sundial.

The district was formerly served by a chapel which stood a mile or so to the south of Gladsmuir, of which all traces having been recently removed, only its site can be pointed out.

FIG. 1548. —The Tron Steeple, Glasgow.

THE TRON STEEPLE, Glasgow.

This tower, with its spire, stands in the Trongate, the most crowded thoroughfare of the city of Glasgow, and, as will be seen (Fig. 1548), it projects on to the street. It is believed that it is in contemplation to remove it; and as the old college buildings were got rid of a few years ago without much regret being expressed, the removal of a small steeple like this will, doubtless, be regarded as a very simple matter. Yet its destruction will deprive us of a very interesting example of a genuine seventeenth century spire, of which few were erected or now survive in Scotland. This steeple was erected in 1637. It has clearly been built in imitation of that of the cathedral, having similar features translated into the style of its time, and with rather a happy effect.

The steeple was attached to a church of older date, which was burned down in 1793. This was the Collegiate Church of St. Thenaw, which was erected in 1525, with the consent of the archbishop, Gavin Dunbar.

From the proximity of the public weighing machine or Tron to the church, it gradually came to be known as the Tron Church, and latterly the instrument itself stood in the ground floor of the steeple, which was then enclosed with solid walls. About forty years ago the Tron was removed, and the ground floor of the building was opened up to form an open passage along the street pavement. The wide arches on the street floor are thus modern.

GRANDTULLY CHAPEL, Perthshire.*

This chapel stands a little to the east of Grandtully Castle at a place called Pitcairn (anciently Petquharne), about three miles from Aberfeldy. It is situated at a considerable height above the valley of Strathtay, and commands an extensive view of mountain scenery. Any one seeing the chapel for the first time, and unacquainted with its existence, might easily mistake it for part of the adjoining farm buildings, it is so plain and humble in appearance. Only the presence of the churchyard surrounding it, and a very small cross on the east gable, serve to call attention to the fact that it is a sacred edifice, which on inspection is found to possess features of considerable interest.

The building (Fig. 1549) may be said to be entire in walls and roof. It measures on the outside about 79 feet long by about 23 feet 3 inches wide, and is at present divided into two parts by a stone partition.

There are two doors and several small windows on the south side. These openings are all straight lintelled and quite unadorned. A door on

* See *Red Book of Grandtully*, Sir William Fraser. Privately printed.

the north side is probably modern. There is a small locker, 14 or 15 inches square, in the usual position in the north wall near the east end. This ambry, which is about four feet from the floor, is of great interest, as it is quite entire, having a wooden door and hinges, an almost unknown condition in Scotland. There is another small recess about 17 inches square and about 3 feet from the ground in the east wall. But the principal feature of the chapel, and what renders it almost unique, is the

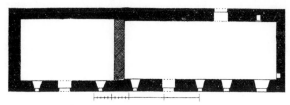

FIG. 1549.—Grandtully Chapel. Plan.

painted ceiling at the east end. This ceiling is constructed, as shown on the sketch (Fig. 1550), at the west end of the eastern division. The roof consists of rafters and ties, on which, at the east end, boards are fixed so as to present a circular form, in the same way as in several of the other painted ceilings of Scottish castles and mansions, such as Pinkie, Culross, and Earl's Hall. It is not known whether this painted roof extended the whole length of the chapel or was confined, as it now is, to the east end. The painting presents four rows of circular discs, each containing six circles, which are variously ornamented. Four of them are occupied with the four Evangelists, and others with coats of arms, including the royal arms—1st and 4th, Scotland ; 2nd, England ; 3rd, Ireland, with an inner-escutcheon. The arms of England and Scotland also occur on separate shields, as well as those of the Earls of Athole and of the Laird of Grandtully and his wife, Dame Agnes Moncrieff. The paintings were rather exposed for some years to damp, and in many places the sub-jects and inscriptions, which are numerous, are considerably effaced ; but further decay is arrested by the roof having recently been put in good order. Amongst the paintings there are complicated monograms, and a large panel in the centre contains an elaborate composition show-ing buildings with quaint figures.

This chapel is first noticed in a "Notarial instrument, recording sasine given by Alexander Steuart of Garntulye, from devotion and with the view of promoting divine worship" of certain lands, "in terms of a charter to be made, to Alexander Young, sub-prior of St. Andrews, as representing the curate who is to officiate at the chapel built near the manor-place of Petquharne, and to be consecrated to God, the Virgin Mary, St. Andrew the Apostle, St. Adamnanus and St. Beanus. Dated 9th May 1533."

Following this, in the 3rd June of the same year, is the charter referred to conveying the land and privileges to the church and to a chaplain, " who was to be a suitable curate, personally residing and celebrating divine worship and the sacraments irreproachably in the Church of St. Mary of Grantulye." The church was "to be held for prayers to be made by the

Fig. 1550.—Grandtully Chapel. Interior.

said chaplain for the universal church, the prosperity of King James v. and his kingdom, the granter's own soul, and the souls of certain of his relatives," &c.

This gives us the period of the erection of the church, but the painting is later, being shown by the style and by the arms to have been done by

Sir William Steuart about the year 1636. Sir William was an intimate friend from childhood of King James VI., and was by him greatly beloved. He married Agnes Moncrieff, daughter of Sir John of that Ilk, and, as already mentioned, their arms are on the ceiling, and their initials are also carved over a small window in the east gable.

GREENLAW CHURCH, BERWICKSHIRE.

This church, with its venerable tower, overlooks, in a very prominent manner, the small county town of Greenlaw. The present building occupies the site of an early church, and probably dates from the

FIG. 1551.—Greenlaw Church.

beginning of last century. It is a very simple structure, and harmonises well with the ancient tower. The latter (Fig. 1551), which is a part of an earlier church, is an interesting example of a Scottish church tower. It is quite plain in its lower stages, and has a corbelled out parapet at the top, which is reached by a stair in the projecting turret, seen in the sketch. The tower is a place of considerable strength, being vaulted on the ground floor, and is probably a building of the fifteenth century.

The manor of Greenlaw belonged to the Earls of Dunbar and Gospatrick, and the third Earl granted the church, in 1159, to the Abbey of Kelso. Greenlaw was one of the churches dedicated by Bishop David de Bernham.

INSCH CHURCH, ABERDEENSHIRE.

The town of Insch is a station on the Great North of Scotland Railway between Aberdeen and Huntly. The old parish church, which is

FIG. 1552.—Insch Church. Front and Side View of Belfry.

abandoned, stands in the churchyard.   The west wall, crowned with its belfry, is almost all that now survives.   The belfry (Fig. 1552) is ornate, and is a good specimen of the Scottish Renaissance designs erected in the beginning of the seventeenth century.   It bears the date of 1613, when it is believed the church was erected.   On the south side the tympanum carries a shield with the Leslie arms and the initials M. I. L.

KEMBACK CHURCH, Fifeshire.*

Situated at the entrance to Duraden, near Dairsie Railway Station, are the ivy-covered ruins of the sixteenth century church of Kemback, surrounded with its ancient burial-ground.   The building (Fig. 1553)

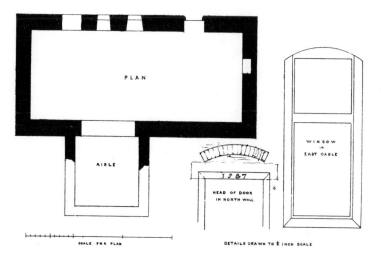

PLAN

AIBLE

1 5 87

HEAD OF DOOR
IN NORTH WALL

WINDOW
IN
EAST GABLE

SCALE FOR PLAN

DETAILS DRAWN TO ¼ INCH SCALE

FIG. 1553.—Kemback Church.   Plan.

retains the Gothic feeling in the external splays on the square-headed doors and windows, but the Renaissance influence is apparent in the east window.   Contrary to the usual practice, the door and windows are in the north wall.

About half a mile distant the site of an older church is pointed out, but all that remains of it is the late headless effigy of a lady.

* We are indebted to Mr. T. S. Robertson, architect, for the Plan and description of this church.

THE GLENCAIRN MONUMENT, KILMAURS, AYRSHIRE.

The Church of Kilmaurs, situated near the village of that name about two and a half miles north-west from Kilmarnock, was formerly collegiate, having a provost and six prebendaries. It has been rebuilt, and the

FIG. 1554.—The Glencairn Monument, Kilmaurs.

burial aisle of the Earls of Glencairn, which no doubt was formerly attached to it, now stands apart. The aisle was erected by the seventh Earl in 1600, and contains the fine monument (Fig. 1554) of William, ninth Earl, who was Lord High Chancellor of Scotland. He died in 1664, and was buried in St. Giles', Edinburgh.

The monument is of a classic design, somewhat resembling some others in the south of Scotland, such as that of the Kennedies at Ballantrae and

M'Lellan at Kirkcudbright,* having shafts at each side, and an entablature crowned with a panel containing the family arms.

Within the frame formed by the pillars and entablature are half-length figures of the Earl and his lady, with open books in front of them, and a panel between which contained a long inscription, now illegible. A row of small figures beneath doubtless represents the family of the deceased.

KINNEIL CHURCH, LINLITHGOWSHIRE.

The ruins of this old parish church are situated a few yards to the west of the ancient mansion house of Kinneil, near Bo'ness. The church

FIG. 1555.—Kinneil Church.

* *The Castellated and Domestic Architecture of Scotland,* Vol. II. p. 155, and Vol. III. p. 304.

was abandoned about 1636, at which time a new one was built at Bo'ness, about one mile distant. What remains of the old church is the west wall, crowned with a double belfry (Fig. 1555), and the returns of the side walls. The end wall measures 26 feet wide outside, and is 3 feet 9 inches thick. The length of the church cannot now be traced, but there are indications of buildings at a distance eastwards of about 64 feet.* From indications on the north side of the church, there appear to have been some attached buildings. The ruins are quite overgrown with ivy, and nothing definite can be said further regarding them.

ST. BEAN'S CHURCH, KINKELL, PERTHSHIRE.

Situated on the right bank of the Earn about two miles south from Auchterarder, this church, which is a post-Reformation one, stands in the centre of a small churchyard on a hillock overlooking the river, and

FIG. 1556.—St. Bean's Church, Kinkell.

is entire, but roofless (Fig. 1556). It is now divided by cross walls into three burial-places. The building (Fig. 1557) measures about 65 feet 2 inches in length by 23 feet wide externally. Like most of the early

* Since this description was written the foundations of the side walls have been excavated by the Duke of Hamilton, and from these operations it has been discovered that the church was originally of Norman construction. The foundations of a south-west doorway have been laid bare, and show that it has had nook-shafts with Norman bases. A north door, opposite the above, has also been discovered.

Presbyterian churches it has a considerable resemblance, in plan, to those of the Gothic period, being long and narrow, with a south door near the west end, south windows, and an end window high up in each gable. All the openings are lintelled and splayed. There was a belfry on the west gable.

FIG. 1557.—St. Bean's Church, Kinkell. Plan.

The church was probably built about the end of the sixteenth century. It was repaired about the year 1680 at the instigation of the Bishop and Synod of Dunblane, and shortly afterwards the parish of Kinkell was absorbed into that of Trinity Gask, when the building was allowed to fall into ruin.

The Church of Kinkell was dedicated to St. Bean, and was a cell of Inchaffray.

MONUMENT IN KINNOULL CHURCH, PERTHSHIRE.

The old church of Kinnoull stood on the east side of the Tay opposite Perth. It may be said to have entirely disappeared with the exception of an aisle which was attached to the church, and now contains a seventeenth century monument to the Earl of Kinnoull (Fig. 1558). The moument is of a pompous kind, and inspires none of those feelings of reverence begotten by the monuments of the Middle Ages. It occupies the full width and height of the aisle, and has a high dado richly sculptured on the pedestals and sides with arms and insignia of power, and contains an ornate central panel. From the dado there rise three columns resting on pedestals. The columns themselves are twisted and carved. The capitals, which are in imitation of Corinthian, are very debased. The two end columns are backed by projecting pilasters at the wall. Above the columns there runs a carved entablature with cornice, supporting, by way of finish, a heraldic slab in the centre, with various separate figures on each side of it.

The principal feature of the monument, to which all the above are accessories, is the life-sized statue of George, first Earl of Kinnoull and Chancellor of Scotland. His history will be found in Crawford's *Lives of the Officers of State*. The monument was erected in 1635.

FIG. 1558.—Monument in Kinnoull Church.

KIRKOSWALD CHURCH, Ayrshire.

Kirkoswald is a village on the road between Girvan and Maybole in Carrick, containing an old church and churchyard. The church (Fig. 1559) is a simple oblong measuring about 93 feet 6 inches in length by 28 feet 4 inches in width over the walls. It seems originally to have consisted of plain walls without buttresses, but within modern times the

Fig. 1559.—Kirkoswald Church.

structure has been converted into a mausoleum by building up all the windows, and by adding buttresses along the south side. The pointed blank windows and the large pointed doorway in the south wall are also modern additions. The modern applied buttress at the south-west angle is now falling away.

At first sight the building presents an ancient appearance, but closer examination shows that it has been modernised beyond recognition.

LAUDER CHURCH, Berwickshire.

The small town of Lauder stands in the wide and fertile vale of the Leader Water, about six miles (over a high hill) from the nearest railway station at Stow. The ancient parish church of Lauder was bestowed, in the reign of David i., on Sir Hugh Morville, Constable of Scotland. It was afterwards given by Devorgilla, wife of John Baliol, to Dryburgh

Abbey, to which it remained attached till the Reformation. It appears that there were two chapels connected with the parish church in different parts of the parish.

The existing parish church (Fig. 1560) stands in the ancient church-yard. It has apparently been entirely rebuilt in 1673, which date is carved on the north gable. Chalmers, however, says that the ancient church was relinquished in 1617, when a new church was erected. The present structure, although very late, shows some reminiscences of Gothic forms, both in its plan and elevations.

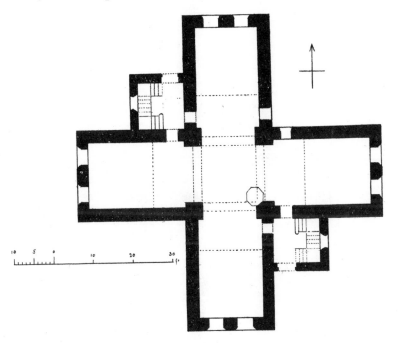

Fig. 1560.—Lauder Church. Plan.

The plan is a Greek cross having four equal arms extending from a central crossing. The latter is 14 feet square, and each arm is 28 feet 6 inches in length by 16 feet in width internally. The crossing is surmounted by four pointed arches, which spring from a massive pier at each angle, and carry the central tower. In the north-west and south-east angles of the arms there are introduced two entrance lobbies, giving access to the four arms and to staircases, leading to a gallery in each arm. The space on the ground floor below the galleries is low, and is lighted by two square windows in the end wall of each arm (Fig. 1561), with moulded jambs and lintel, while each upper floor or gallery is lighted by means of a large pointed window in the gable, filled with plain intersecting tracery, with mullions and transoms.

The entrance doorways have round arches with hood moulding, and the side windows of the staircases are pointed. The external angles of the building and the outline of the windows are all finished with a broad fillet, projected so as to receive rough casting. The skews of the gables are plain and do not project, and the joints are horizontal. Each skew has a large projecting stone at bottom. These appear to have carried small pyramidal ornaments, two of which are still preserved.

Fig. 1561.—Lauder Church. View from North-West.

The central tower is square till it reaches the ridge of the main roofs, above which point it becomes octagonal, and is finished with a slated roof. A small round-headed window of a late style is inserted in four sides of the octagonal part or belfry.

The staircase buildings in the two angles do not appear to be parts of the original structure, or at least would seem to have been a good deal altered.

In the neighbourhood of Lauder is Thirlestane Castle,* the residence

* See *The Castellated and Domestic Architecture of Scotland*, Vol. IV. p. 339.

of the Duke of Lauder, well known in connection with the attempted introduction in the seventeenth century of Episcopacy into Scotland. It seems not unlikely that the quasi-Gothic character of the church may have been the result of his influence.

LESWALT CHURCH,* WIGTONSHIRE.

A ruined church, the predecessor of the present one, which was built early in this century. It stands about four miles west from Stranraer. All the dressed stones of the wall openings have been taken out, so that nothing remains to tell the date of the structure. In the seventeenth century a wing (Fig. 1562) has been erected against the north wall, which probably contained a gallery above and a burial-place below, as was frequently the case in similar erections about that time. The wall between the wing and the church is still standing several feet high.

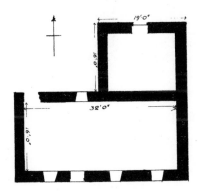

Fig. 1562.—Leswalt Church.

The wing has been entered by a plain flat lintelled door in the north wall (Fig. 1563), over which is a window divided into four compartments by a moulded mullion and transom. This window would light the private room or gallery on the upper floor. A panel (Fig. 1564) below the window shows that the place was used as a burial vault, as it contains an inscription and two coats of arms. The inscription states that it is in memory of Patritus Agnew of Lochnaw, Earl of Wigton, and Margaret Kennedy, his spouse; A.D. 1644. The arms on the shields beneath are those of Agnew and Kennedy.

* We have to thank Mr. T. S. Robertson, architect, for the drawings of this church.

FIG. 1563.—Leswalt Church.   North Gallery.

FIG. 1564.—Leswalt Church.
Panel over Door.

After the new church was erected the old one was used as the parish school, which accounts for a fireplace still visible in the east wall of the church.

Fig. 1565 shows its present ruined condition.

Before the Reformation the Church of Leswalt belonged to the Monks of Tungland, and in Episcopal times to the Bishop of Galloway.

FIG. 1565.—Leswalt Church.

ST. COLM'S CHURCH, Lonmay, Aberdeenshire.

Only the merest fragment of this church now remains. Its dimensions can be determined as having been 62 feet in length by 15 feet 3 inches wide inside. Part of the west gable survives for a height of about 10 or 12 feet, with a small square-headed window. Nothing else is left but grass-covered ruins and fallen pieces of masonry.

LOUDOUN CHURCH, Galston, Ayrshire.[*]

This was originally a structure of the first pointed period, but it is now in a state of complete ruin, except the choir, which has been fitted up in the seventeenth century as a burial vault.

The west gable stands nearly entire, but the side walls are completely demolished, except at the choir (Fig. 1566). The building is externally

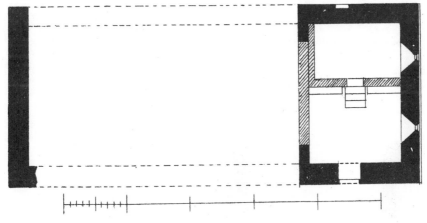

Fig. 1566.—Loudoun Church. Plan.

64 feet long by 27 feet wide. The choir is about 14 feet 9 inches long, and is separated from the nave by a plain round arch 15 feet 6 inches wide (Fig. 1567). In the east wall (Fig. 1568) there are two pointed windows about 10 inches wide, with slight splays on the outside, and widely splayed inside (Fig. 1569), where they are finished with round

* For the illustrations of this church we are indebted to Mr. R. Weir Schultz, architect, London.

arches. There are two set-offs on the east wall, and the same occur on the west wall. The structure has been greatly modified in the seventeenth century. The south doorway into the choir and the window, with

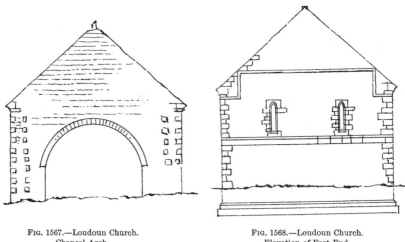

FIG. 1567.—Loudoun Church.
Chancel Arch.

FIG. 1568.—Loudoun Church.
Elevation of East End.

panels and arms (Fig. 1570), are probably all insertions of that period, as also is the vault seen in the drawings. The ground has accumulated

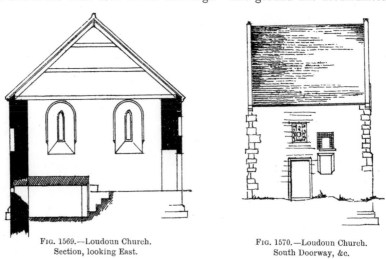

FIG. 1569.—Loudoun Church.
Section, looking East.

FIG. 1570.—Loudoun Church.
South Doorway, &c.

round the church so that the splayed base seen in Mr. Schultz's drawings is now buried to the extent of about 2 feet.

The masonry of the ruin is of fine ashlar, in regular courses.

LYNE CHURCH, Peeblesshire.

This building, which is still used as the parish church, is situated on the Lyne Water, near the Tweed, about three miles above Peebles. It stands on the summit of a mound, which is occupied as the churchyard.

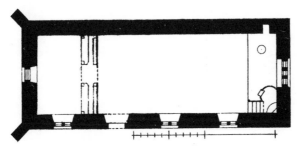

Fig. 1571.—Lyne Church. Plan.

The building (Fig. 1571) is a tiny one, measuring internally only about 34 feet by 11 feet. The windows and doorway are on the

Fig. 1572.—Lyne Church. View from South-East.

south side (Fig. 1572) and in each gable, there being no opening in the north wall. The windows have simple tracery of a late type, and the

jambs have backfillets (a late feature) round the openings. There are
angle buttresses at the west end, and a modern belfry on the apex of the
west gable.

Fig. 1573.—Lyne Church. Pulpit.

Some good fragments of old woodwork survive in the church, particularly a pulpit (Fig. 1573), which, it is usually stated, was made in Holland. Lyne is distant from the sea and must have been difficult of access; for which reason, amongst others, we doubt whether there is any truth in the tradition. The pulpit, which is circular in plan, is quite simple in design, and its construction would not present a formidable task to a Scottish country wright, judging by other examples of woodwork made in Scotland about this time. Some of the other woodwork bears the date 1644, and one of the pews, now removed, was dated 1606.* The church has been frequently repaired, which accounts for the loss of such examples.

"The district was, in the twelfth century, a chapelry dependent on Stobo." † Robert, the chaplain of Lyne, is a witness to a charter in the Register of Glasgow, between 1208 and 1213; but of the early church then existing nothing now remains, the present structure probably dating from the beginning of the seventeenth century.

MORHAM CHURCH, Haddingtonshire.

A retired parish church about four miles east from Haddington. It is stated to have been built in 1724, but some portions of ornamental carving built into the south wall (Fig. 1574) would seem to indicate that they had formed part of an earlier structure.

Fig. 1574.—Morham Church. Fragment built into South Wall.

The only architectural feature connected with the church is the elevation of the north wing or aisle (Fig. 1575), which, although it corresponds well with the date of the building, is in a somewhat unusual style for a Scottish church of the period.

* *Origines Parochiales.* † *Ibid.*

FIG. 1575.—Morham Church.   North Aisle.

CHURCH OF ST. FIACRE OR FITTACK, NIGG, KINCARDINESHIRE.

A ruined church standing in the centre of an ancient churchyard, situated about three miles south-east from Aberdeen. The church is probably one of those built during the short period of Episcopal government in the seventeenth century. It consists (Fig. 1576) of a single chamber, but there are indications of an arch across from side to side, where shown by dotted lines on the Plan, which may have marked a chancel. The building is 48 feet 6 inches in length by 20 feet 6 inches in width internally, and has been roofless for more than half a century.

FIG. 1577.—Church of St. Fiacre or Fittack, Nigg.   View from South-West.

The lintelled door is on the south side, and there are two other doors on the north side, one of them being in the supposed chancel.

The belfry (Fig. 1577) appears to have been rebuilt in 1703. A row of projecting corbels, which probably supported a previous belfry, are left projecting under the new one.

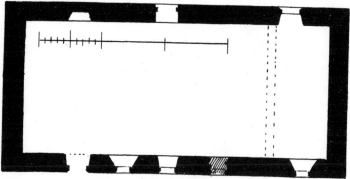

FIG. 1576.—Church of St. Fiacre or Fittack, Nigg. Plan.

Immediately adjoining the ruin there is a stately seventeenth century house, formerly the manse, now occupied by an agricultural tenant and farm labourers.

The building is on the site of an early church, which was granted by William the Lion to his favourite Abbey of Arbroath, and it remained as one of its dependaries till the Reformation.

OLDHAMSTOCKS CHURCH, Berwickshire.

The main portion of this church, although its walls may in part be old, is not of much architectural merit, but the chancel (Fig. 1578) is not without interest as a specimen of late Gothic work. It is now used as a burial vault, and is completely ivy clad. It measures about 18 or 20 feet square, and is of modest height, being some 10 or 12 feet to the eaves.

The chief feature is the east window, with its rude tracery. The latter, which is of a different stone from the jambs and sills, is probably a restoration of late in the sixteenth century, while the chancel itself may be a little earlier. The building is vaulted with a barrel vault, and is covered on the exterior with overlapping stone slabs. It is impossible to say whether it contains any features of pre-Reformation times. The door seen on the south side of the choir is dated 1701.

Of the panels half concealed in the ivy, the one on the right contains the arms of Thomas Hepburn, incumbent of Oldhamstocks, and of his wife, Margaret Sinclair, who died in 1581. This Thomas Hepburn was admitted Master of Requests to Queen Mary two days after her marriage with Bothwell, and he was tried and convicted for aiding the Queen in her escape from Lochleven.*

FIG. 1578.—Oldhamstocks Church.

This church is of an old foundation. In 1127 Aldulph, the presbyter of Aldehamstoc, witnessed a charter of Robert, the Bishop of St. Andrews, and the church is rated in the ancient *Taxatio* and in *Bagimond's Roll.* It is also recorded as an existing rectory in the Archbishop's Roll of 1547.

* See *Caledonia*, Vol. II. pp. 479 and 550.

There is a peculiar sundial on the south-west corner of the church, which is illustrated.* It may be mentioned that in the centre of the west end of the church there is a tower which is finished at the top with a modern belfry. This tower or turret is probably of pre-Reformation date.

ORMISTON CHURCH, HADDINGTONSHIRE.

Only a small portion of the old church of Ormiston, in which Wishart and Knox more than once officiated, has been preserved. It stands close to the mansion house of Ormiston Hall, about one mile south from the village of Ormiston. A new church having been erected about a quarter of a mile distant, the old church has been allowed to go to decay. The surviving fragment of the latter appears to have been the east end. There are several stones built into the walls which must have belonged to a Norman church, being carved with the chevron ornament.

The Church of Ormiston was dedicated to St. Giles. It was granted to the Hospital of Soltre, founded by Malcolm IV., which was confirmed by the Bishop of St. Andrews in the thirteenth century.

This church was subsequently made a prebend of the Church of the Holy Trinity at Edinburgh, founded by Mary of Gueldres.

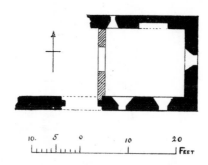

FIG. 1579.—Ormiston Church. Plan.

The building (Fig. 1579) has been enclosed at the west end with a modern wall, and measures, within the enclosure, 16 feet 6 inches in length by 13 feet 6 inches in width. It contains in the south wall the outlines of two windows, now built up, and of one window in the north wall. These have apparently been altered at some time and made square-headed. An archway of considerable height (Fig. 1580) stands in the continuation of the south wall westwards. It is in two orders, the outer order square

* *The Castellated and Domestic Architecture of Scotland*, Vol. v.

and the inner order splayed. This doorway has apparently entered into the church, which, judging from the height of the archway, must have had side walls of considerable height. They are now reduced as shown, and a roof was put upon the east portion during this century, which renders the interior very dark.

In the north wall of the chancel there is a monument of some importance (Fig. 1581), as it contains one of the few brasses which exist in Scotland. The brass consists of an engraved plate containing an inscription to the memory of Alexander Cockburn, one of the members of the family to whom the adjoining mansion house belonged. He died, as the inscription tells, at an early age. The upper part of the inscription is metrical, and was composed by the learned George Buchanan, and

Fig. 1580.—Ormiston Church. South Side.

appears in his published works. Alexander Cockburn was a pupil of John Knox, and in 1547 sought refuge in the Castle of St. Andrews. On the dexter base of the brass are engraved the Cockburn arms, and on the sinister base the arms of Sandilands, for the mother of a Cockburn, who was of the family of Sandilands of Calder. These arms are quartered with the arms of Douglas, and show the ancient relationship between that family and the Sandilands.*

The barony of Ormiston was the property of the Cockburns from the middle of the fourteenth century, when they acquired it by marriage.

The monument was no doubt erected not long after the death of the person commemorated, or towards the end of the sixteenth century. It corresponds in style with that of the Regent Murray, in St. Giles' Cathedral,

* See Mid-Calder Church.

FIG. 1581.—Ormiston Church. Monument to Alexander Cockburn.

Edinburgh * (1570), the inscription on which was also composed by George Buchanan.   That at Ormiston is as follows :—

Omnia quæ longa indulget mortalibus ætas
    Haec tibi Alexander prima juventa dedit
Cum genere et forma generoso sanguine digna
    Ingenium velox, ingenuumque animum
Excolint virtus animum ingeniumque Camenae
    Successu studio consilioque pari
His ducibus primum Peragrata Britannia deinde
    Gallia ad armiferos qua patet Helvetios
Doctus ibi linguas quas Roma Sionet Athenae
    Quas cum Germano Gallia docta sonat
Te licet in prima rapuerunt fata juventa
    Nonimmaturo funera raptus obis
Omnibus officiis vitae qui functus obivit
    Non fas nunc vitae est de brevitate queri
        Hic conditur Mr. Alexander Cokburn
        primogenitus Joannis domini Ormiston
        et Alisonae Sandilands ex preclara
        familia Calder, qui natus 13 Januarii 1535
        post insignem linguarum professionem
        Obiit anno ætatis suae 28 Calen. Septe.†

PITTENWEEM PRIORY, Fifeshire.

Of the old monastery of Pittenweem, which was connected with that on the Isle of May in the Frith of Forth, only some altered fragments survive.   The priory seems to have derived its name from its being built close to a cave or "weem" on the shore of the Frith of Forth, with which it had communication by a vaulted chamber in the garden and a long straight staircase.   The monastic buildings surrounded a courtyard.   On the south side was the prior's mansion (now restored and occupied by the Episcopal clergyman of the place).   On the west side was the refectory, now converted into the Town Hall, and to the north of it the dormitories.

Some of the walls of these structures still exist, with two square projecting windows overlooking the courtyard.   On the east side is the gatehouse, a battlemented structure with a round archway passing through it, now greatly decayed and covered with ivy.   Beyond the courtyard to the north lay some outer grounds and a chapel.‡

---

* See Vol. II. p. 453.

† See description by Rev. John Struthers, *The Proceedings of the Society of Antiquaries of Scotland*, Vol. IV. p. 225.

‡ See paper by the late Walter F. Lyon, in *The Proceedings of the Society of Antiquaries of Scotland*, 1892-3, p. 79.

Fig. 1583.—Pittenweem Priory.   Tower, from North-East.

After the Reformation the buildings passed into the hands of laymen, and the monastery became the "manor place of Pittenweem." In 1588 a portion of the grounds was granted to the burgh, in order that a suitable church might be erected, which was carried out soon thereafter (Fig. 1582). Possibly some portions of the church of the priory are included in this building, but it has in recent years been restored and extended.

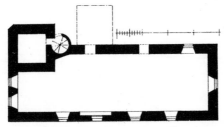

FIG. 1582.—Pittenweem Priory. Plan.

The quaint tower (Fig. 1583), with its mixture of Gothic and classic features, is the only part which has not been interfered with. The tower, which stands at the north-west angle of the church, is about 18 feet square externally. It rises with a plain square outline for a considerable way without buttresses or anything to distinguish it from a castle keep. There are even shot-holes under the windows, as in the domestic structures of the time. The stair turret in the north-east angle has the outline and corbelled gablet similar to the cape-house of the stair turrets of the Scotch castles of the period. The spire, with its remarkable lucarnes, helps to give the erection a little more of an ecclesiastical character, but the balustrade again recalls the attention to the domestic and Renaissance style of the design.*

POLWARTH CHURCH, BERWICKSHIRE.†

This church (Fig. 1584) was reconstructed in 1703, and is believed to rest on the foundations of an older structure, dedicated by Bishop Bernham in 1242. The building measures 55 feet by 24 feet over the walls. Although of such a late date, it is of pleasing form, and has fine large mouldings round the doors and panels above them. A stone on the east gable contains the Polwarth arms, three piles engrailed.

The font of the old church stands outside the building. It is of a round form 28 inches in diameter. The basin, which is 22 inches in diameter,

* See *The Castellated and Domestic Architecture of Scotland*, Vol. v. p. 149.
† For further information see *Pre-Reformation Churches of Berwickshire*.

FIG. 1584.—Polwarth Church.

is 11½ inches deep, with a central aperture. The height of the fragment is 21 inches.

HERALDIC PANEL FROM PRESTONPANS CHURCH, HADDINGTONSHIRE.*

This panel (Fig. 1585) was discovered in 1891 during some alterations of the seating of the church. It then formed the back of a seat in the gallery, and was concealed by a green cloth. Doubtless, from its heraldic decorations, it must originally have occupied a more prominent position. The arms and initials show that it belonged to the Hamiltons of Preston. The date on the panel (1604) connects it with an earlier church, the present church having been erected later. The panel is of oak and in good preservation, except where cut away to make it fit its new position, and the colours are still rich and fresh. The panel is in two pieces, each 2 feet 3 inches high. The whole is divided into eight compartments, of which only four bear arms. They are all arched, and are separated by

* This church is illustrated in *The Castellated and Domestic Architecture of Scotland*, Vol. v. p. 171. See Paper by the late J. Fowler Hislop in *The Proceedings of the Society of Antiquaries of Scotland*, 1892, p. 241.

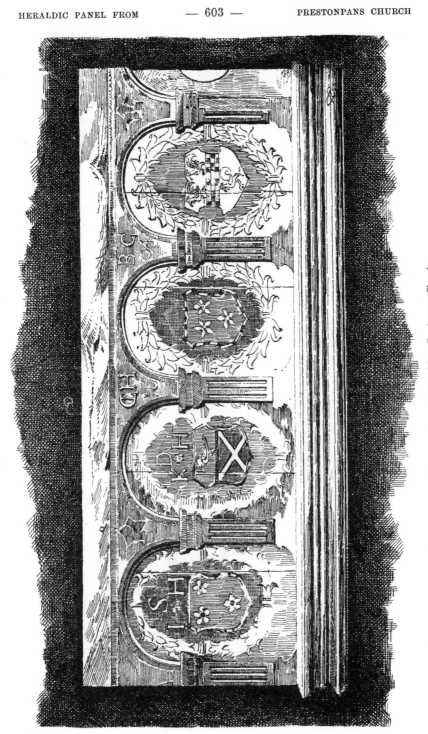

FIG. 1585.—Heraldic Panel from Prestonpans Church.

pilasters. On the four compartments arms, surrounded by laurel wreaths, are blazoned in colour, together with initials. The initials G. H. and B. C., which refer to George Hamilton, Laird of Preston, and Barbara Cockburn, his wife, are carved in relief in the spandrils. The letters painted within the arches, viz., $_\text{J.}^\text{S.}{}_\text{H.}$ and $_\text{K.}^\text{D.}{}_\text{H.}$ stand for Sir John Hamilton, the son of the above, and Dame Katherine Howieson, his second wife, married 1620. The lady died 1629. The shields beneath these initials contain the Hamilton arms twice, and the Cockburn and Howieson arms for the wives of the father and son. The initials of the son and his wife were carved over the windows of the tower, while over the centre window they appear in a monogram with the date 1626.

This panel, which is one of the very few early coloured decorations which survive in Scotland, is now in the possession of General Sir William Stirling Hamilton of Preston.

RATHAN CHURCH, Aberdeenshire.

A ruinous building situated about three miles south from Fraserburgh, and standing in an old churchyard. The east end has entirely disappeared, and only a small part of the north wall remains (Fig. 1586). What

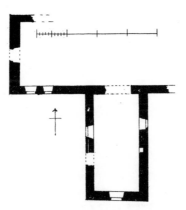

Fig. 1586.—Rathan Church. Plan.

survives of the south wall of the nave is 49 feet long, but it doubtless considerably exceeded that length; the interior width is 21 feet. A south aisle is entire, but roofless. It enters from the nave by a plain round-arched opening (Fig. 1587) 8 feet 8 inches wide, and the outside dimensions of the aisle are 35 feet long by 20 feet 8 inches wide.

The nave (see Fig. 1587) has a door in the west end, with a window

FIG. 1587.—Rathan Church. Interior of South and West Sides.

above and a belfry on the apex of the gable, dated 1782, which probably superseded an earlier one.

The aisle has a round-arched doorway (Fig. 1588) with a bar hole in the west wall, and over it a panel with an inscription in raised letters, "ALEXANDER FRASER OF PHILORTH, PATRON," a coat of arms, and part of a broken stone with an inscription. It is possible that these stones are not original, but have been inserted; they are so covered with ivy that it is not easy to determine. In the south gable (Fig. 1589), which is crow-stepped, there is a well-moulded window with a straight lintel, and a

FIG. 1588.—Rathan Church. Doorway of Aisle.

sundial over. In the east wall there is an ambry (Fig. 1590) with an ogee arch, and alongside it what was probably a piscina is now filled with an old memorial inscription.

FIG. 1589.—Rathan Church. Window in South Gable.

The Church of Rathan was dedicated to St. Ethernan or Eddran, from whom the place is said to take its name. This saint lived towards the end of the sixth century. "He consecrated several churches, and particularly Rethin, which was afterwards dedicated to his own memory." *

Richard, parson of Rathen, is a witness to charters by Adam, Bishop of Aberdeen, between 1207 and 1228, and the benefice of Rathyn was given to the Chapter and College of Canons of St. Machar's Cathedral by Robert I. in 1328; and in 1520 Rathyne was let in lease for the yearly rent of £212.†

Of the early church nothing remains. On the south aisle of the existing structure, according to the Rev. Mr. Pratt, there is the date 1646. It may be that part of the church is somewhat older than this date. Ten years earlier there appear to have been building and repairs going on; and an action was brought before the Privy Council to restrain Alexander Fraser of Philorth from putting up his arms on the newly built kirk stile.‡ What was the result of the case we do not know, but Fraser evidently succeeded in getting his name carved on the church, as we see, together with his arms and his title of patron.

FIG. 1590.—Rathan Church. Ambry.

* *View of the Diocese of Aberdeen*, Spalding Club, p. 133.
† *Shires of Aberdeen and Banff*, Vol. II. p. 392.
‡ *Ibid.* Vol. IV. p. 126.

SOUTHANNAN CHAPEL AND CASTLE, West Kilbride, Ayrshire.

About one mile south from the railway station of Fairlie, on the level ground facing the sea, and with its back close to the railway, stands the ruin of Southannan Castle. It has been an extensive structure (Fig. 1591), having had a high enclosing wall, with a courtyard and an arched entrance porch to the west, defended with shot-holes (Fig. 1592). There

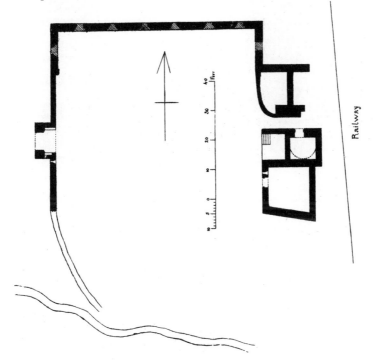

Fig. 1591.—Southannan Chapel and Castle. Plan.

has been a considerable range of dwelling-house accommodation, two stories in height, along the north side, and smaller buildings on the east side, leaving a large courtyard in the centre, now forming the garden of the adjoining farmhouse (Fig. 1593). The situation is fine, and the edifice is backed by the high range of thickly wooded hills which extends between Largs and Kilbride.

The lands of Southannan were granted to Lord Semple in 1504. Chalmers says * that John, Lord Semple, in the reign of James IV., built

* *Caledonia*, Vol. III. p. 561.

a chapel, which was dedicated to St. Annan or St. Ennan, and granted for the support of the chaplain in it an annual rent of 10 merks from certain lands, "with two sowmes of pasture grass in the mains of South-

FIG. 1592.—Southannan Chapel and Castle. View from West.

ennan, and an acre of land on the north side of the cemetery belonging to the said chapel for the chaplain's manse. This grant was confirmed by the king in June 1509. The ruins of the chapel are still extant in the

FIG. 1593.—Southannan Chapel and Castle. North-West Angle of Courtyard.

front of the fine mansion of Southennan, which is also in ruins." "Saint Inan or Innan is said to have been a confessor at Irvine, and to have died in 839."

The castle was much enlarged by Robert, fourth Lord Sempill, ambassador to the Court of Spain in 1596 ; but some of the existing remains have the appearance of being still more modern. The old mansion was dismantled towards the end of last century, and the materials used in the erection of farm-buildings and dykes. "What remains are chiefly the outer walls to the left (north) of the courtyard and some more ancient-looking remnants at the back (east), attached to which are remains of what may have been the chapel of the saint." * This may be the case, as some of the walls are old and have been altered ; but the vaulted chamber to the east has the appearance of being much more modern.

On the whole, we fear that the chapel has entirely disappeared, and that this account of Southannan should rather have appeared amongst the castles than the churches of Scotland.

STENTON CHURCH, Haddingtonshire.

The village of Stenton is situated about three and a-half miles south-east from East Linton Railway Station. The church (Fig. 1594), which, with the exception of the tower and the entrance doorway, is a total ruin (Fig. 1595), extends for a length of about 65 feet, but as the east end is

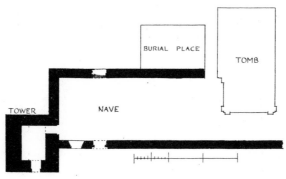

Fig. 1594.—Stenton Church. Plan.

entirely gone, it is impossible to say how much longer it was. The width of the building within the walls is about 18 feet. The doorway (Fig. 1596), which is on the south side near the west end, is arched with a flat segment of a circle, with the mouldings of the jambs (Fig. 1597) continued round the arch, and with a splayed impost separating the arch and jambs. The arch is finished with a hood moulding. The small flat-

* Pont's Cunningham, by Dobie, p. 325.

headed window seen alongside the doorway (see Fig. 1595) is an insertion probably of the seventeenth century, and no other feature of the church is now in existence, except indications of a north door (see Plan).

The tower, however, stands complete and entire at the south-west corner of the structure. It measures about 16 feet 6 inches by 15 feet

FIG. 1595.—Stenton Church. Tower, &c., from South-East.

9 inches over the walls, and is two stories in height. It is entered by a narrow flat lintelled door on the south side. The space inside is about 10 feet by 7 feet, but it has been narrowed by masonry at the ground level, as shown on the Plan, to a width of about 5 feet. The tower communicated with the church by a doorway, now built up.

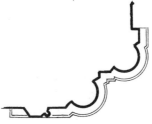

FIG. 1597.—Stenton Church.
Moulding of Doorway.

FIG. 1596.—Stenton Church. Doorway.

The upper story, which has a timber floor, has been reached by a ladder. It is lighted by a window on each face, round arched and widely splayed, and the arches are cut out of single stones. The tower finishes with a saddle-backed roof and crow-stepped gables, the whole being of the original construction.

From indications remaining against the north wall of the tower, there has doubtless been a high window in the west gable of the church.

FIG. 1598.—Font and Top Stone of Gable.

The whole structure appears to be of the sixteenth century. The top stone of the east gable and a simple circular font (Fig. 1598) are lying near the ruin.

STOW CHURCH, MID-LOTHIAN.

The village of Stow is situated on the Gala Water, in the southern part of Mid-Lothian, near the borders of Roxburghshire and Peeblesshire.

The parish was originally called Wedale, and the church belonged to the Bishop of St. Andrews, who had a residence there. Hence the village was known as the Stow of Wedale.

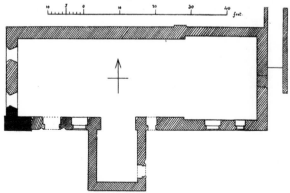

FIG. 1599.—Stow Church. Plan.

The original Church of St. Mary was at a distance from the village, but the existing ruin, which is partly of some antiquity, stands in the ancient churchyard close to the village.

FIG. 1600.—Stow Church. View from South-West.

The structure is for the most part of seventeenth century date, but a portion at the south-west angle is much older, and has been incorporated with the newer building. The plan of the church, as it now stands (Fig. 1599), consists of an oblong 67 feet in length by 21 feet in width internally, with a wing on the south side 14 feet long by 11 feet wide within the walls.

The principal oblong chamber appears to have been constructed at two different times, there being a break in the interior of the wall at 20 feet from the east end. There is also a slight exterior projection on the outside of the north wall at the same point. The eastern addition has evidently been made so as to provide a gallery, probably a private one, at this end. The gallery was entered by a long slope or ramp on the exterior of the east wall, beneath which was a door giving access to the space below the gallery. The gallery and space below were lighted by square-headed windows in the south wall. On the jamb of the east doorway is carved the date 1799.

The arrangements at the west end have been similar to those at the east end. There was a gallery, lighted by a large traceried window (Fig. 1600) in the west wall of seventeenth century design, and the space below the gallery had two square-headed windows in the same wall, divided with mullions. A round-headed doorway in the south wall gave

access to the space under the gallery, the mouldings of which (Fig. 1601) clearly indicate a late date. Adjoining this doorway is the portion of the structure above alluded to as being of ancient date. This consists of a plain buttress built with freestone ashlar, and a small part of the south and west walls connected with it, including a base splay on the south side. These walls are built with the same kind of materials as the buttress, while the greater part of the walls are constructed with rubble work. The buttress has the broad form with small projection, and the simple water table of Norman or transition work.

FIG. 1601.
Stow Church.
Mouldings of
South Doorway.

The projection or "aisle" on the south side of the church has also contained a private gallery, with a fireplace in the south wall. The mouldings of the doorway indicate seventeenth or eighteenth century work.

There are no windows in the north wall, but some portions of the masonry are of ashlar work and may be of the period of the south-west angle.

The belfry, the vane of which bears the date of 1794, is a comparatively late addition. It is supported on corbels projecting from the inside of the wall.

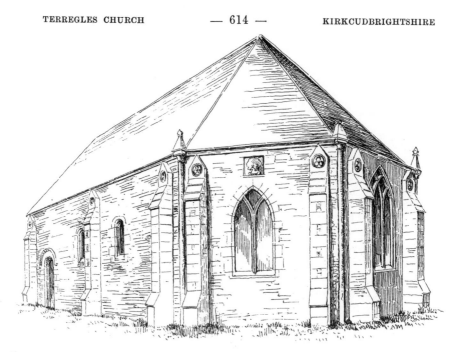

FIG. 1602.—Terregles Church after Restoration.

FIG. 1603.—Terregles Church before Restoration.

TERREGLES CHURCH, Kirkcudbrightshire.

This curious structure (Fig. 1602) is situated about two and a-half miles north-west from Dumfries. It was erected by the fourth Lord Herries shortly before his death in 1583.

A few years ago this "queir" or choir was completely restored, and the buttresses were then added. Omitting these it may be regarded as a fair example of the quaint architecture of James vi.'s time, when the revival of Gothic was attempted, along with the revival of Episcopacy.

FINIALS ON CORNERS OF CHANCEL

AGNES LADY HERRIES

Fig. 1604.—Terregles Church. Details of Finials and Coat of Arms of Agnes, Lady Herries.

We are fortunate in being able to show a drawing (Fig. 1603) of the church made by the late Mr. W. F. Lyon, architect, in 1872, before it was restored. Fig. 1604 shows details of the finials and the arms of Agnes, Lady Herries, which are carved on the church. The date 1585 is cut in the cornice over the east window.

Before the Reformation this church belonged to the nunnery of Lincluden, and the collegiate church which succeeded it.

TURRIFF CHURCH, Aberdeenshire.

This ancient church, which was dedicated to St. Congan, is a very old foundation, having probably been established, in the seventh century, by a follower of St. Columba. It received donations at various early dates, amongst others one by King Robert the Bruce. In 1272 it was attached by the Earl of Buchan to an almshouse for thirteen poor husbandmen. The church was 120 feet long by 18 feet wide, but is now reduced to the fragment of the choir, crowned with the picturesque belfry shown by the sketches. The belfry (Fig. 1605) is interesting as an example of the application to an ecclesiastical edifice of the Scottish style so general in the domestic architecture of the seventeenth century. There is a strong dash of Renaissance taste in the design; but the cornice with its small corbels, and the string course with its moulded supports, might be details from any old Scottish castle. The bell bears the date 1557. A curious relic of the older structure has, however, been discovered in the choir, in the form of an antique wall-painting of St. Ninian.

The interior of the choir contains

FIG. 1605.—Turriff Church. Belfry.

FIG. 1606.—Turriff Church. Gateway to Courtyard.

a very interesting and remarkably picturesque series of monumental slabs, with a quantity of well-executed lettering. One of these tablets is to the memory of a member of the family of Barclay of Towie, of date 1636, with a Latin inscription still legible.

The churchyard contains a number of interesting monuments of the same date as the belfry.

The gateway to the churchyard (Fig. 1606) is a simple but pleasing specimen of the early Scottish Renaissance, similar in style to the belfry.

WALSTON CHURCH, Lanarkshire.

The parish church of Walston stands on a height overlooking the vale of the river Medwin, about two miles west from Dolphinton. Till near the end of the thirteenth century the Church of Walston was a lay rectory in the gift of the Lord of the Manor. It is specially referred to in an award of 1293.* The edifice stands in an ancient churchyard, and not far from what was formerly a mansion known as the "Place of Walston."

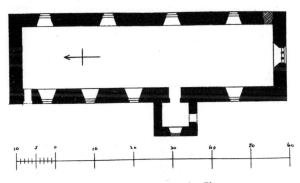

Fig. 1607.—Walston Church. Plan.

The existing church (Fig. 1607) stands north and south, and is a long single chamber 64 feet 6 inches in length and 16 feet in width internally. A portion has been cut off the north end to form a vestry. The original church is believed to have stood east and west. At the south end a portion of the existing structure is evidently, from its workmanship, of a different period from the remainder. The ashlar work of which it is built is seen to stop beyond the first window from the south (Fig. 1608). This was doubtless the wing or transept erected by Robert Baillie of Walston, in 1650, as a burial-place for his family. The remainder of the church was rebuilt in its new position in continuation of the south wing

* *The Upper Ward of Lanarkshire*, Vol. I. p. 385.

by the Rev. Patrick Molleson, minister (born 1746, died 1825), who has placed the letters M. P. M. and the date 1789 on the north gable.

Fig. 1608.—Walston Church. View from South-West.

The south wing is the only part worthy of notice. The window shows the feeling for the Gothic revival of the seventeenth century. In the panel over it is the inscription "Give God the onlie honour and glory."

Fig. 1609.—Walston Church, showing Dormer.

Anno 1656." The entrance doorway to the wing, which contained a tomb below and a gallery above, is in the east side. Over the flat lintelled door is the quotation, "Keep thy foot when thou goest to the House of God, and be more ready to hear than to give the sacrifice of fools.—Ecclesiastes, chapter v., verse 1." The tomb and gallery are now removed, and the space thrown into the church. In the pavement on the site is inscribed "In memory of John Allain, Esq., of Elsrickle." The quaint dormer window, shown in Fig. 1609, was taken down during the repairs made on the church a few years ago.

WEEM CHURCH, Perthshire.*

The ruined church of Weem stands in the village of that name, near the entrance to Castle Menzies, at a short distance from Aberfeldy. It is still in a fair state of preservation, the walls being entire, although greatly overgrown with ivy, and the roof being still intact, with the belfry on the west gable. The building has been abandoned for many years. According to Mr. A. H. Millar * the Church of Weem is mentioned about 1296 in the oldest charter at Castle Menzies, and references in charters are continuous till, in 1510, the Barony of Menzies was erected by charter from James IV., when "the patronage of the Kirk of Weem was specially included in the gift."

Fig. 1610.—Weem Church. Inscription over East Doorway.

The existing building, however, appears to be of a later date, since over the eastmost doorway there are the impaled arms of Sir Alexander Menzies and his wife, Margaret Campbell, with their initials, and the date 1600, together with the inscription shown in Fig. 1610.†

The church (Fig. 1611) is an oblong building, measuring internally about 62 feet 5 inches from east to west by about 19 feet wide, and has a north transept projecting 21 feet by 17 feet in width. It is ceiled and plastered at the roof ties. There are two doors and three windows on the south side, all of which are square headed. In each gable, high up near the ceiling, there is a window of a pointed form. All the windows and doors have large bead mouldings. In the inside of the south wall there

* The Historical Castles and Mansions of Scotland, p. 60.
† We are indebted for this sketch to Mr. A. H. Millar.

are two ambries, one of which contains the initials of Duncan Menzies and his wife, Jean Leslie, sister of the Earl of Rothes, who were married in 1623. And on the other occur the initials D. M.

There are several interesting grave slabs in the church, but the most remarkable feature is the monument shown in Fig. 1612, which stands against the north wall near the east end, as indicated on the Plan. It is an important example of Scottish Renaissance work, and contains a great amount of detail, much of it very elaborate.

The sixteenth or seventeenth century monuments in Scotland may be divided into two classes, viz. :—First, the class represented by the Montgomery monument at Largs,* and the seventeenth century monument in Seton Church, which are almost pure Italian, with very little of the previous Gothic manner, and almost nothing of local or Scottish feeling. Monuments of this class may probably be the design, if not the work, of foreign hands. In the second class are the monuments which seem to

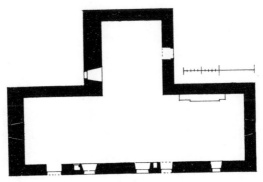

Fig. 1611.—Weem Church. Plan.

owe their design and execution to native skill, and amongst these may be included this monument at Weem. The structure measures about 13 feet in length at the base, and has a projection from the wall of about 2 feet.

The general scheme of the design is of an ordinary form, consisting of an arched recess above a dado or pedestal, which is divided into three panels separated from each other by delicate tapering shafts. At each side rises a half round engaged shaft to carry the moulded arch above. These shafts have capitals, rudely carved with oak leaves, supporting square abaci. Above the arch there is a level cornice slightly broken at intervals over figures beneath. At each side of the monument a large figure stands on a finely designed pedestal, the one representing Faith and the other Charity. The former holds a book with the inscription, *Quidquid fit sine Fide est peccatum*, while the figure of Charity is represented in the usual typical manner. The figures are surmounted with very beautiful

* See *The Castellated and Domestic Architecture of Scotland*, Vol. v. p. 193.

canopies reaching nearly up to the cornice. Above the cornice a rudimentary pediment contains the Menzies and Campbell arms and monograms, over which, and leaning forward, is a panel having a figure with

Fig. 1612.—Monument in Weem Church.

outstretched arms, supposed to symbolise the Creator. At each end of the cornice is a kneeling figure placed before a small pedestal shaped like a prie-dieu.

This monument having been erected not to the memory of one individual, but of several, was probably not intended to contain any recumbent figure, although the space for one is provided. Such a figure would have in a great measure concealed the descriptive tablet and its accompanying heraldry, which occupy the background of the recess. The monument bears the date of the 24th January 1616, and was erected by the Sir Alexander Menzies already referred to, to perpetuate the memory of his two wives and of his maternal ancestors, beginning with his great-great-grandmother. The names of all these ladies, with the arms of their respective houses, adorn the monument, and need not be repeated here, as full information regarding them will be found in Mr. Millar's work, already cited.

YESTER CHURCH, HADDINGTONSHIRE.

The parish church of Yester stands at the north end of the village of Gifford, about four and a half miles south of Haddington. The

FIG. 1613.—Gifford Tower, from South-West.

ancient church of Yester has already been described. It was super-seded last century by the present structure, which is a plain oblong chamber of the usual style of the period, but with a tower on the south side (Fig. 1613), which is a good example of that class of erection at the period.

NOTE.

The illustration or tailpiece on the following page shows a remarkable specimen of early Scottish sculpture, preserved in the Museum of the Society of Antiquaries of Scotland in Edinburgh.

The stone, which is about 6 feet in length, was found in the River May, Perthshire, and is supposed to have come from an ancient church which formerly occupied a site within a rath or stronghold which stood on the Holy Hill, on the bank of the river, near Forteviot, about two miles from Forgandenny.* The last traces of the rath and church were swept away by a flood which occurred in the beginning of this century.

This early church is probably that referred to in the legend of St. Andrew given in the *Pictish Chronicle* as the church built at Forteviot by Hungus, the Pictish king (731–761), in the last year of his reign, after the arrival of the relics of St. Andrew in Scotland.† Although the character of the sculpture seems rather to suggest a date not quite so early, it may, nevertheless, be surmised that the figures depicted on the stone are those of King Hungus and his three sons, seated in the usual royal attitude, with the sword across the knees.

From the arched form of the stone it seems most likely to have been a chancel arch, a feature which would scarcely be expected in Scotland in the eighth century. The primitive church may, however, have been rebuilt, possibly in the tenth century, when a church with a chancel would more probably be erected, having the stone in question for its chancel arch. The small upright animal in the centre of the arch, having a cross in front of it, seems to represent the Paschal lamb; while the other nondescript animal at the feet of the king may be an early example of the practice usual in mediæval monuments of resting the feet of the effigy on an animal.‡ On the Ruthwell Cross the figure of the Saviour appears standing on the heads of two animals.

* See *ante*, p. 500.

† *Chronicle of the Picts and Scots*, p. 183.

‡ *Sculptured Stones of Scotland*, Vol. II. p. 58; *Celtic Scotland*, Vol. I. p. 297 and Vol. II. p. 265; *Early Christian Symbolism*, by J. Romilly Allen, p. 239.

Sculptured Stone from Ruins of Ancient Church at Forteviot, Perthshire.

APPENDIX.

The following is a statement by Mr. W. Galloway in defence of his views regarding the date of the walls of St. Blane's Church, Bute : *—

"Objections are taken in the notice of St. Blane's Chapel, Bute (Vol. I. p. 297), to the views advanced by me in the *Archæologia Scotica* (Vol. v. p. 217) as to the priority in date and construction of the rubble part of the chancel, over the Romanesque structure conjoined with it. These are specially summarised under three heads, in the first of which exception is taken to the fact of there being a base, topped with a small splayed freestone course, with rubble above and below, which is supposed to contravene the ideas ordinarily entertained as to Celtic practice. This practice, however, was strictly dependent upon and fixed by the nature of the building materials that happened to be available in any particular locality. In out of the way districts and far-off islands, where freestone was unknown or not procurable, the builder had to be content with the stone that came most readily to hand, necessity, not choice, compelling his selection. This is proven by the avidity with which the Celt took to freestone whenever it could be got.

"No better illustration can be selected than Oransay Priory (Vol. III. pp. 372-381). There the south cloister arcade, the door to the church adjoining it, with the chapel projecting at the north-east angle (and to these may be added the *Teampul na ghlinne*, on the Colonsay side of the strand), are examples of rubble building, in the local schist, where arches are turned and openings formed without a trace of freestone or any material that could be hewn. The portion of a mullion of transitional date found in the ruins proves that freestone had been imported to the island by the close of the twelfth century, and was in constant use thereafter.

"It would be a serious mistake, however, to place in the same category the Island of Bute, where freestone (red) occurs locally, and the best qualities of rock on the adjoining mainland.. Freestone was in common use with the Romans both for monumental work and building, and it is precisely this simple splayed form of base which is most frequently to be found. As to its use in Celtic work there may be cited Cruggleton Chapel (Vol. I. pp. 212-215), about three miles from Whitherne Priory, which by every criterion is extremely primitive, much earlier than the priory, and also Celtic, founded most probably by the Carrols or M'Kerlies, who wrested the castle from the Norse jarls. There the base, which has been laid on the grass level, has a base course precisely similar to that of St. Blane's, with rubble above and below. In fact, the entire building is rubble, except the dressed work and the chancel arch. It is not freestone, but silurian grit, from the Stewartry shores. It is no doubt later in date than

* Since this proof was revised by Mr. Galloway, a month ago, we regret to be informed of his death.

St. Blane's, but Bute is much more favourably situated for freestone than Wigtonshire, where it is locally non-existent, and the combination of rubble and hewn work at Cruggleton is a striking testimony to the difficulty even of obtaining grit.

"The second head refers to the mode in which the strings and base courses would be stopped against the rubble. According to my drawings there has been a string on the north side of the nave, which dropped nearly two feet, has also run along the ashlar work of the chancel, but only two feet or so of it remains. On the south side this feature is entirely destroyed. The base, both on north and south sides of the nave, returns round the chancel gable and *there terminates*. Whether they were dropped also I cannot tell, as these drawings were made previous to the later reduction of the soil to the original level.* An important point in this junction of rubble and ashlar walls must be noted, viz., that while the ashlar walls are 2 feet 7 inches thick, the rubble wall on the south side is only 2 feet 5 inches, and that on the north 2 feet 3 inches. The walls meet flush on the outside, and on the inside the ashlar corner is splayed off in accommodation to the thinner rubble, and those who managed thus would find no difficulty in such trivialities as a string or a base.

"Under the third head it is queried whether the '*Norman* builders' were likely to show such tender mercy to a rubble fragment? I presume 'Norman here means *Anglo*-Norman, the conquering race, who looked with contempt on all that pertained to those they held in thrall. Civil changes notwithstanding, in Bute it was otherwise. There the same traditions were handed down from Celt to Scot, and the name of St. Blaan was reverenced, not merely on local grounds, but as being still more intimately associated with a northern see. The very curious *melange* at the east end of the chapel is attributed to one of those 'accidents' which, from a variety of sources, often befel buildings in ancient times. The late Mr John Baird, at a meeting of the Architectural Institute of Scotland held in Glasgow a good many years ago, suggested that the original termination had been an apse, but the chancel being found too small, this feature was demolished and the building extended to its present limits. Notwithstanding all that has been said, I consider both the apse and the accident theories to be at once untenable and unnecessary, and will, as briefly as possible, give three *criteria* on which I regard the proof of antecedency in date and construction of the rubble work ultimately to depend, and to be incontrovertible. First, in a rubble wall of any posterior date, built to conjoin with a previous ashlar one, it is only reasonable to suppose it would have been gauged to the same thickness, so that the respective wall faces might be flush, both externally and internally, so as to avoid the very awkward junction which there really has been. Second, this rubble wall must necessarily have been carried to the same height and level, in the wall-head, as the ashlar built portion, instead of being dropped nearly three feet below it, as the present rubble work really is. Third, the existing Romanesque structure shows that freestone, both red and white, was readily to be had by importation or otherwise in Bute, during the twelfth century, and ever afterwards, and it is beyond all reason and experience, that in the chancel especially rubble of some local rock should have been adopted when the superior quality previously in use could be so easily obtained.

* Since Mr. Galloway's drawings were made the ground round the chancel has been excavated, and the Norman base is seen to extend along the Norman part of the chancel, as mentioned in the text.

"These three *criteria* combined, the thinness (relatively) of the rubble walling, the lower level of the wall-head, and the extreme improbability of any subsequent builders being reduced to the necessity of falling back on rubble, lead irresistibly to the conviction that on this site there existed a much smaller and more ancient chapel, of which the *sacrarium*, carefully respected by all subsequent builders, now alone remains."

At the special request of Mr. P. Macgregor Chalmers, author of the work *A Scots Mediæval Architect*, we insert in this Volume extracts, revised and approved by him, from his reply to our criticism contained in Vol. II. pp. 378-382, in the hope that they may be found to throw additional light on the late period of Scottish architecture. It must, however, be understood that we are not to be held as concurring in all Mr. Chalmers' views. Our notice of his work was written after our second volume was to a large extent in type, and we should not have quoted Mr. Pinches' reference to church building in Galloway in 1508 (p. 378), as Mr. Chalmers had already shown in his work that this was a mistake; and on the same page we should have acknowledged his labours on the Melrose inscriptions. Mr. Chalmers says :—

"You tabulate four formal objections to my work (p. 380). The first appears to be that I have adopted a certain opinion, which differs from yours ; and you think my work is therefore a 'fiction,' a 'romance,' a 'dream.' The second objection, based on your *inference* that a man who had a Scots name was a Frenchman by extraction, because he was born in Paris at a time when Scotsmen were rife in France, need not be taken seriously. The answer to your third and fourth objections is that I have *proved*, from original documents quoted, that 'Morow' is 'Murray,' and that the variation in spelling, indicated in the Melrose inscriptions, is the variation for Murray. When you have grasped the importance and significance of my deduction from the evident choice of Melrose for the memorial inscriptions, I feel certain you will find more than 'fiction' in my work.

"I stated that the rood screen at Glasgow was erected by Archbishop Blacader, and that it was probably begun about the year 1492. The charter evidence is that the archbishop founded the two altars in their present position in the base of the screen, and that he founded the altar *for which the screen was erected*, the altar of Holy Cross. As the screen encroaches considerably on the original length of the choir, being of great depth from west to east, it is natural to suppose that its erection would entail the remodelling of the choir fittings. It was in the archbishop's time, then, that the new choir stalls were constructed. From the measurements given in the contract for this work, between 'the dene and cheptour of Glasgw on the tapairt, and Mychell Waghorn, wrycht, on the toder pairt,' it is evident that the carved canopy work was carried as a cornice across the east or choir side of the screen. Rejecting my work, you state that the screen at Glasgow was probably built by Bishop Cameron, who died in 1446. You have no charter evidence to support you. You have only the mouldings and the sculpture of the two periods to found your opinion upon. In the illustration I send you (Fig. 1) I show the earlier mouldings at A and the later mouldings of the screen at B. Students can now estimate the value of your opinion. The only moulding in the aisle of Car Fergus, of Blacader's time, is the vaulting rib which I show at C. This, you say, is a 'coarse' moulding. But the coarseness is not apparent when you compare it with the rib in the

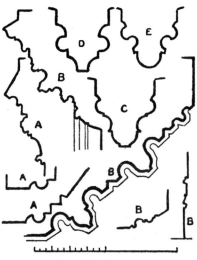

sacristy (D), of date about 1446; the rib in the chapter house (E), of date about 1425; or the same rib in the lower church, of date about 1240. You frequently give expression to your opinion that the work executed in Scotland about the year 1500 was 'inferior.' Sweeping generalisations of this kind are of no value in our work. I send you a process block (Fig. 2). It illustrates the carved boss in the vaulting of the aisle of Car Fergus, of Blacader's time, being the very first seen on entering, and so close to the eye that it may almost be touched by the hand. No work of any period—certainly not of Bishop Cameron's time — can excel it in beauty, and it is only one of many equally beautiful. You state that the work in the screen 'is considerably superior to that of the adjoining

FIG. 1.
Mouldings of Rood Screen at St. Mungo's.

altars, which are *certainly* by that bishop' (*Archbishop* Blacader). It is a fact that you are here comparing work, which is as sharp as when it left the carver's hand, with work at the floor level which is now so worn and defaced as almost to be obliterated. The altars are of different design, and that now on the north side is of *earlier date*, and was rebuilt and repaired only by the archbishop. If this single altar stood originally in the centre, as the one of the same name did at Durham, and if, as is not impossible, it was originally built by Bishop Cameron, then you condemn as 'inferior' what, if you had only known, you ought to praise as 'superior.'

"Mr. Honeyman, whose early opinion you quote, writing to me, for my use here, says, in reference to the Glasgow rood screen—'I must say that circumstances which you have brought to my notice have considerably changed my opinion regarding this. I quite recognise the close affinity of the south transept door at Melrose and the rood screen at Lincluden, and I am quite prepared to believe that the man who designed these, also designed the rood screen here. If it can be proved that the work at Melrose and Lincluden was not executed till about 1480, or later, then I shall feel bound to agree with you as to the age of our screen.' The proof as to the age of the Melrose door has been given in my book.

"Your reliance on your unwise generalisation regarding the 'inferior' quality of *all* work at the end of the fifteenth century has blinded you to the facts at Melrose, as elsewhere. The magnificent panel carved with the royal arms, of which I gave an enlarged photograph (p. 55), is dated 1505. There is nothing finer of its kind in the country, and the carved bosses in the presbytery vault are remarkable for their rare beauty, and yet one of them bears the arms of Margaret, wife of James IV. You state that 'the building or restoration of the eastern part of the edifice seems, from its style, to have been carried out towards the middle of the fifteenth century' (p. 372). The further statement is made that 'the design of the choir appears to have been borrowed from that of the transept' (p. 370). These statements are contradictory. The south transept was not erected until after the middle of the fifteenth century, by Abbot Andrew Hunter. His arms are to be found carved on it, and also in the nave chapel, where the work is unmistakeably from the hand of the same designer. It is indubitable that the 'perpendicular' work was inserted in the older transept. It has never occurred to you to endeavour to explain the presence in Scotland

Fɪɢ. 2.—Carved Boss in Vaulting of Aisle of Car Fergus.

of so marked a type of English art *in the middle of the fifteenth century*, and you have thought it wise to ignore my interpretation that this style was adopted as an expression of the international good feeling arising from the marriage of James ɪᴠ. with Margaret of England. Perpendicular work is also present at Linlithgow and Stirling, and there also it is associated with Queen Margaret.

"I described the statues at the apex of the east gable at Melrose as those of James ɪᴠ. and Margaret (p. 53). You say 'this is an entire assumption' (p. 381), and then you immediately *assume* that they illustrate the coronation of the Blessed Virgin. If your interpretation is correct, the act of coronation must be indicated, and the two figures must be correlated, Christ being turned towards the Blessed

Virgin, either to crown her by His own hand, or to indicate His interest in the ceremony, whilst Mary is turned towards Christ in an attitude of tenderness and adoration. These are obvious requirements. The figures are so disposed in the examples you cited and illustrated, and it is true of all the examples I have studied on the Continent and in the cathedrals of England. At Melrose the figures are not in any way related to each other. They look straight forward, and, as I proved by the aid of a telescope before writing my description, no act of crowning is indicated. The male figure corresponds exactly with that on the seal of James IV. to which I referred, and the group does not differ from that shown in a MS. of the middle of the fifteenth century, which represents a king and queen and their court. I understand and appreciate the fact that you see no significance in the angels in the niches below the central group of the king and queen, and that it is of no importance to you that the figures which were ranged on either side were not those of saints and martyrs, but of Churchmen, evidently contemporaries of King James. As the statue of an archbishop graces the apex of the east gable of York Minster, there is nothing ridiculous, as you would wish to make it appear, in a king and queen occupying a similar place at Melrose. The circumstances and temper of the moment made it appear appropriate. There is no sarcasm in the concluding paragraph of my work, although you profess to be able to detect it. It was not unpleasant to me to find that the point made by the author of *The Stones of Venice*, from exactly similar exhibitions of vainglory, could be made from the stones of Scotland.

P. MACGREGOR CHALMERS."

TOPOGRAPHICAL INDEX

OF BUILDINGS DESCRIBED IN THE WHOLE WORK.

ABERDEENSHIRE.

Aberdeen, King's College Chapel
—— Greyfriars' Church
—— St. Nicholas'
Aberdour, St. Drostan's
Auchendoir Church
Deer Abbey

Deer Parish Church
Ellon Monument
Insch Church
Kinkell Church
Kintore Church
Leask, St. Adamnan's
Lonmay, St. Colm's

Monymusk Church
Old Aberdeen, St. Machar's Cathedral
Peterhead, St. Peter's
Rattray, St. Mary's
Rathan Church
Turriff Church

ARGYLESHIRE.

Ardchattan Priory
Dunstaffnage Castle Chapel
Eilean Munde, Lochleven
Eilean Naomh
Faslane Church
Islay, Kilchieran Church
—— Kildalton Church
—— Kilnaughton Church
—— Kilneave Church
Iona Cathedral and Priory
—— Nunnery

Iona, St. Oran's
Inchkenneth, Ulva
Kilmun Collegiate Church
Kintyre, Cara Church
—— Gigha, St. Catan's
—— Kiels, St. Columba's
—— Kilchenzie Church
—— Kilchieven Church
—— Kilchouslan Church
—— Killean Church
—— Sanda, St. Ninian's

Knapdale, Eilean Mor
—— Kilbride Church
—— Kilmory Church
—— St. Carmaig's, Keil
Lismore Cathedral
Mull, Laggan Church
—— Pennygowan Church
—— Inch Kenneth
Oronsay Priory
Tiree, Kilchenzie Church
—— Kirkapoll Church

AYRSHIRE.

Alloway Kirk
Crosraguel Abbey
Kilmaurs, Monument
Kilwinning Abbey
Kirkoswald Church

Loudoun Church
Maybole Collegiate Church
Monkton, St. Cuthbert's
Old Dailly Church

Prestwick, St. Nicholas'
Southannan Castle and Church
Straiton Church

BANFFSHIRE.

Boyndie, St. Brandon's
Cullen Collegiate Church

Deskford, Sacrament House

Gamrie, St. John's
Mortlach, St. Moloc's

BERWICKSHIRE.

Abbey St. Bathans'
Ayton Church

Bassendean Church
Bunkle Church

Chirnside Church
Cockburnspath Church

BERWICKSHIRE—*continued.*

Coldingham Priory
Dryburgh Abbey
Duns Church
Edrom Church

Greenlaw Church
Ladykirk Church
Lauder Church
Legerwood Church

Oldhamstocks Church
Polwarth Church
Preston Church
St. Helen's, Cockburnspath

BUTESHIRE.

Rothesay, St. Mary's Abbey

Rothesay Castle Chapel

St. Blane's Church

CAITHNESS-SHIRE.

Lybster, St. Mary's

Olrig Church

DUMBARTONSHIRE.

Dumbarton Collegiate Church

Dumbarton Parish Church

Kirkton of Kilmahew

DUMFRIESSHIRE.

Canonby Priory
Kirkbride Church

Moffat, St. Cuthbert's

Sanquhar Church

ELGIN OR MORAYSHIRE.

Altyre Church
Birnie, St. Brandon's
Drainie Church

Elgin Cathedral
—— Greyfriars' Church
Kinloss Abbey

Michael Kirk
Pluscardine Priory

FIFESHIRE.

Abdie Church
Anstruther, Easter and Wester, Churches of
Ballingry Church
Balmerino Abbey
Burntisland, St. Adamnan's
Carnock Church
Crail, St. Macrubha's Collegiate Church
Creich, St. Devenic's
Cupar, St. Michael's
Dalgety, St. Bridget's

Dunfermline Abbey
Dysart, St. Serf's
Fordel Chapel
Inchcolm Abbey
Inverkeithing, St. Peter's
Kemback Church
Kilconquhar Church
Kilrenny Church
Leuchars Church
Lindores Abbey
Markinch Church
Pittenweem Priory

Rosyth Church
St. Andrews Cathedral and Priory
—— Dominican Church
—— Holy Trinity
—— St. Mary's, Kirkheugh
—— St. Leonard's
—— St. Regulus' or St. Rule's
—— St. Salvator's
St. Monans Church

FORFARSHIRE.

Airlie Church
Arbroath Abbey
—— Abbot's House
Auchterhouse, St. Mary's
Brechin Cathedral
—— Maison Dieu

Dundee Church
Eassie Church
Invergowrie Church
Lundie, St. Lawrence
Mains Church

Maryton Church
Nevay Church
Pert Church
Restennet Priory
St. Vigean's Church

HADDINGTONSHIRE.

Dunbar, Redfriars'
Dunglass, St. Mary's
Garvald Church
Gladsmuir Church
Gullane, St. Andrew's
Haddington, St. Martin's
—— St. Mary's

Herdmanston, Font
Keith, St. Maelrubba's
Luffness, Redfriars'
Morham Church
Ormiston, St. Giles'
Pencaitland Church
Prestonkirk, St. Baldred's

Prestonpans Church
Seton Collegiate Church
Stenton Parish Church
Tynninghame Church
Whitekirk Church
Yester Parish Church
—— St. Bothan's

INVERNESS-SHIRE.

Barra, St. Michael's,
Borve
—— Kilbar
Beauly Priory
Benbecula, Nuntown
—— St. Columba's, Bali-
vanich

Harris, Sound of Pabba
—— Toehead
Raasay, St. Moluac's
Rowdil, St. Clement's
Priory
Skye, Kilmuir

Skye, St. Maelrubba's Font
—— Mugstot
—— Skeabost
—— Trumpan
Uist, North, Carinish
—— South, Howmore

KINCARDINESHIRE.

Arbuthnott Collegiate
Church

Cowie Church
Feteresso, St. Cavan's

Fordoun, St. Palladius'
Nigg, St. Fiacre's

KIRKCUDBRIGHTSHIRE.

Buittle, St. Colmonel's
Dalry, St. John's
Dundrennan Abbey

Lincluden College
New Abbey or Sweet-
heart Abbey

Old Girthon Church
Terregles Church
Tungland Abbey

LANARKSHIRE.

Biggar Church
Bothwell, St. Bride's
Blantyre Priory
Carnwath Collegiate
Church

Covington, St. Michael's
Douglas, St. Bride's
Glasgow, St Mungo's
Cathedral
—— Tron Spire

Lamington Church
Lanark, St. Kentigern's
Rutherglen, St. Mary's
Walston Church

LINLITHGOWSHIRE.

Abercorn Church
Auldcathie Church
Bathgate Church
Dalmeny Church

Kinneil Church
Kirkliston Church
Linlithgow, St. Michael's
Strathbroc, St. Nicholas'

Queensferry, South, Car-
melites' Church
Torphichen Church
Uphall, St. Nicholas'

MID-LOTHIAN.

Borthwick, St. Mungo's
Calder, East, St. Cuth-
bert's
Cockpen Church

Corstorphine, St. John
Baptist
Crichton, St. Mary's
Dalkeith, St. Nicholas'

Duddingston Church
Edinburgh Castle, St.
Margaret's Chapel
—— St. Anthony's Chapel

MID-LOTHIAN—*continued.*

Edinburgh, St. Cuthbert's Pulpit
—— St. Giles' Collegiate Church
—— Trinity College Church
Gogar, Font
Holyrood Abbey
Lasswade Church
Mid-Calder Church
Newbattle Abbey
Ratho, St. Mary's
Restalrig, St. Triduan's
Rosslyn, St. Matthew's Collegiate Church
Stow Church
Temple Church

ORKNEY.

Birsay, Brough of
Deerness, Brough of
Egilsey Church
Enhallow Church
Head of Holland Chapel
Halcro Chapel, South Ronaldshay
Linton Chapel, Shapinsay
Orphir Church
St. Ola, Kirkwall
St. Magnus, Kirkwall
St. Tredwell's Chapel
Swendro Church, Rousay
Westray Chapel
Wyre Church

PEEBLESSHIRE.

Lyne Church
Newlands Church
Peebles, Holy Cross
Peebles, St. Andrew's
Stobo Church

PERTHSHIRE.

Aberdalgie, Monument
Abernethy Round Tower
Aberuthven, St. Cathan's
Alyth, St. Moloc's
Auchterarder Church
Blair Church
Cambusmichael Church
Coupar Abbey
Culross Abbey
—— Parish Church
Dron Church
Dunblane Cathedral
Dunkeld Cathedral
Dunning, St. Serf's
Ecclesiamagirdle Church
Forgandenny Church
Forteviot Church
Foulis Easter, St. Marnan's
Grandtully, St. Mary's
Inchaffray Abbey
Innerpeffray Collegiate Church
Kinfauns Church
Kinkell, St. Bean's
Kinnoull Church
Meigle Church
Methven Collegiate Church
Moncrieff Chapel
Muckersey Font
Muthill Church
Perth, St. John Baptist
Stobhall Church
Tullibardine Collegiate Church
Wast-town Church
Weem Church

RENFREWSHIRE.

Castle Semple Collegiate Church
Houston Church
Kilmalcolm Church
Paisley Abbey
Renfrew Church
St. Fillan's Church

ROSS-SHIRE.

Dun Othail, Lewis
Eorrapidh, Lewis
Fearn Abbey
Flannain Isles, or Seven Hunters
Fortrose Cathedral
Holy Cross, South Galston, Lewis
St. Aula, Gress, Lewis
St. Columba's, Ey, Lewis
—— Isle, Lewis
St. John Baptist, South Bragair, Lewis
St. Ronan, North Rona
Tain, St. Duthus'
Teampull, Beannachadh
—— Pheadair, Lewis
—— Sula Sgeir
Tigh Beannachadh, Lewis

ROXBURGHSHIRE.

Jedburgh Abbey
Kelso Abbey

Linton Church
Melrose Abbey

St. Boswell's Church
Smailholm Church

SELKIRKSHIRE.

Selkirk Church

SHETLAND.

Culbinsbrough, Bressay
Kirkaby, Westing, Unst
Meal, Colvidale, Unst

Ness Kirk, North Yell
Noss Chapel, Bressay

St. John's Kirk, Norwick,
Unst
Uya, Church at

STIRLINGSHIRE.

Airth Church
Cambuskenneth Abbey

Inchmahome Priory

Stirling Parish Church

SUTHERLANDSHIRE.

Durness, Church of

WIGTONSHIRE.

Cruggleton Church
Glenluce Abbey
Kirkmaiden Church

Leswalt Church
St. Ninian's, the Isle

Wigton, St. Machutus'
Whithorn Priory

GENERAL INDEX

TO THE WHOLE WORK.

ABAILARD, II. 1.

Abb's, St., Chapel, I. 437.

Abbey St. Bathans, description, III. 410.

Abdie, II. 218.

—— St. Magridin's Church, II. 293.

Abercorn Church, I. 318, description, 346.

Aberdalgie, Monument at, II. 551.

Aberdeen Cathedral, I. 47, III. 6, 40, 117, 408 ; description, 75.

—— Carmelites, III. 469.

—— King's College, II. 285, 445, 504, III. 234.

—— Greyfriars' Church, description, III. 358.

—— St. Nicholas, description, I. 426.

Aberdour, Aberdeenshire, III., description, 535.

Aberdour Church, Fifeshire, III. 40, 318.

Abernethy Tower, I. 11, 15, 26, description, 175 ; II. 86, 209.

Aberuthven Church, description, III. 485.

Adamnan, I. 11.

—— St., Church of, Aberdeenshire, description, III. 387.

Aidan, St., I. 11.

Airlie Church, description, III. 452.

Airth Church, description, I. 465.

—— Castle, I. 465, 469.

Aldcamus Church, I. 325.

Alexander I., I. 29.

—— II. and III., I. 50.

Allen, J. Romilly, I. 2, 306.

Alloway Kirk, description, III. 393.

Alnwick, I. 47.

Altyre Church, II. 290.

Alyth Church, description, III. 487.

Amiens Cathedral, II. 65.

Anchorites, I. 1.

Ancient details revived, III. 52.

Anderson, Dr. Joseph, I. 2, 3, 66 ; II. 209, 210 ; III. 459.

Anderson, R. Rowand, architect, II. 92 ; III. 459.

Anstruther, Easter and Wester, description, III. 536-547.

Anthony, St., Chapel, description, III. 145.

Antiquaries of Scotland, I. 101 ; III. 623.

—— Society of, III. 381.

Apses and square east ends, II. 4 ; III. 2, 3.

Arbroath Abbey, I. 38, 47, 48, 49 ; II. 2, 3, 4, 218, 332, description, 30 ; III. 456, 459.

—— Abbot's House, II. 49.

—— Regality Court House, II. 48.

Arbuthnott Church, II. 92 ; description, III. 235.

Arched Style of Building, I. 32.

Architecture, new development of, II. 1.

—— Scottish, of Fourteenth to Sixteenth centuries, I. 50.

—— division of, I. 53.

—— ceases to be like English, I. 52.

—— connection with French, I. 52.

—— gap in, II. 331.

Ardchattan Priory, II. 146, 245 ; description, III. 389.

Ardoilean, I. 8.

Armstrong, R. Bruce, I. 465 ; III. 431.

Aroise Abbey, Artois, France, II. 230.

Auchindoir Church, description, II. 281 ; III. 406.

Auchterarder Church, description, III. 488.

Auchterhouse, St. Mary's, description, III. 541.

Augustine, St., I. 12.
Aula, St., Gress, Lewis, I. 83.
Auldcathie Church, description, III. 474.
Aytoun Church, description, III. 543.

BABERTON HOUSE, III. 251.
Bairhum, Andrew, painter, I. 417.
Ballingry Church, description, III. 543.
Balmerino Abbey, II. 345, description, 505.
Bangor Monastery, I. 5.
Barrel vaults, II. 333 ; III. 2.
Bassendean Church, description, III. 412.
Bathgate Church, description, I. 474.
Batten, E. Chisholm, II. 147, 245, 395, 399, 402, 543.
Bays, design of, II. 4.
Beauly Priory, I. 289, 416, 417 ; II. 2, 146, 544, description, 245.
Bede, I. 12.
Beehive cells, I. 7, 24, 68.
Benedict Biscop, I. 12.
Beverley Minster, I. 54 ; II. 362.
Biggar Collegiate Church, description, III. 343.
Billings, R. W., II. 122, 389 ; III. 23, 43, 247.
Birnie, St. Brandon's, description, I. 218 ; II. 121.
Birsay, Brough of, I. 135.
Black's Brechin, II. 204, 215.
Blackadder's Aisle, Glasgow, II. 165, 170 ; III. 4, 628.
Blair Church, Blair-Atholl, description, III. 544.
Blane's, St., Bute, description, I. 292.
Blantyre Priory, description, III. 470.
Boniface, St., I. 14.
Border monasteries destroyed, II. 331.
Borthwick Church, III. 173, description, 214.
—— Castle, III. 173, 305.
Boswell's, St., description, I. 377.
Bothwell Church (St. Bride's), II. 333, description, 531 ; III. 173, 174.
—— Castle, III. 470.
Boyndie, St. Brandan's, description, III. 545.

Brandon's, St., Birnie, I. 218.
Brechin Cathedral, I. 49, 57 ; II. 3, 86, 223, description, 203.
—— Tower, I. 26, 48 ; II. 209.
—— Maison Dieu, I. 48 ; description, II. 215.
Brendan, St., I. 67.
Brook, J. S., III. 203.
Brown, J. Harvey, III. 372.
—— T. Craig, III. 531.
Brude, King, I. 10.
Buchanan, George, III. 450, 597.
Buckler, Messrs., architects, III. 61.
Buittle Church, Kirkcudbrightshire, II. 334, description, 300.
Bunkle Church, description, I. 314.
Burgundy, I. 35.
Burntisland Church, description, II. 269.
Bute, Marquis of, II. xiii, 6, 19, 23, 482,
—— St Blane's, I. 292.
Buttresses introduced, I. 34.

CAITHNESS CATHEDRAL, I. 47 ; II. 3.
Cambuskenneth Abbey, I. 30 ; II. 3, 515, description, 225.
—— Abbot of, III. 29.
Cambusmichael Church, III. description, 489.
Campbell, Rev. Dr., Balmerino, II. 505.
Candida Casa, I. 3, 5 ; II. 479.
Canmore, Malcolm, I. 15, 29.
Canonby Priory, description, III. 430.
Canterbury Cathedral, I. 12, 30.
Cara, Gigha, Kintyre, I. 82.
Cardonnell's Views, I. 446.
Carinish, North Uist, I. 81.
Carmaig, St., Eilean Mor, I. 89.
—— Knapdale, I. 84.
Carnock Church, description, III. 436.
Carnwath Collegiate Church, description, III. 349.
Carving, third pointed, III. 6.
Cashels, Irish, I. 7.
Castle Semple Church, description, III. 351.
Castletown Church, I. 378.
Catan's, St., Kintyre, I. 95.
Cathedrals, Scottish, I. 49.
—— chiefly thirteenth century, II. 2.

Caves, I. 5.
Cellach, I. 15.
Celtic art, I. 1.
—— carving, I. 426 ; III. 52, 370, 383.
—— Church, I. 65.
—— churches standing alone, I. 78.
———— built with chancel and nave, I. 93.
———— with pointed or late features, I. 95.
—— structures in Scotland, I. 65.
Chalmers, P. Macgregor, architect, II. 196, 199, 378, 379, 380, 381, 382, 393, 483 ; III. 9, 627.
Chambers, Dr. Wm., II. 443, 455.
Chancel architecturally distinguished, I. 79.
—— added to nave, I. 79.
Chapel on "The Isle," Wigtonshire, description, II. 297.
Chirnside Church, description, I. 322, 314.
Choir and nave, relative length of, II. 5.
Churches, dry-built, I. 80.
—— oblong, modified, I. 82.
—— with nave or chancel added, I. 88.
—— on islands, I. 105.
—— in Orkney, I. 100.
—— in Shetland, I. 101, 145.
Clackmannan Church, II. 231.
Claverhouse's Grave, Blair-Atholl, III. 544.
Clement's, St., Rowdil, description, III. 363.
Clonmacnoise, I. 10.
Cluny Loch, III. 40.
Coalisport Loch, I. 10.
Cockburnspath Church, I. 323 ; description, III. 413.
Cockpen Church, II. 303.
Coldingham Priory, I. 30, 48, 318, 379, 387, description, 437 ; II. 345 ; III. 543.
Coldstream Priory, III. 413.
Coles, Fred. R., III. 148, 469, 533.
Collegiate Churches, I. 51, 60 ; II. 334 ; III. 2, 7.
Collie, J., II. 163, 186.
Columba, St., I. 5, 10, 67, 69.

Columba Church, St., Balivanich, I. 88.
—— Ey, Lewis, I. 91.
—— Kiels, Kintyre, I. 92.
—— Isle, Lewis, I. 97.
Columban Church, I. 11, 12, 13.
—— Churches, I. 25.
Comgall, St., I. 5.
Cooper, Rev. J., III. 356.
Cordiner, II. 152, 157.
Cormac's Chapel, I. 28.
Corstorphine Church, I. 371 ; III. 1, 3, 173, description, 250.
Coupar Abbey, II. 345 ; III. 445, 499, description, 491.
Covington Church, description, III. 472.
Cowie Church, Kincardineshire, II. 273.
Craigmillar Castle, III. 4.
Crail Church, III. 452, description, 263.
Crailing, Upper Church, I. 378.
Cramond, III. 40.
Creich Church, II. 554.
Crichton Church, III. 173, 218, description, 243.
Crosraguel Abbey, I. 57, 58 ; II. 76 332, 342, 478, description, 402 ; III 138, 338, 394, 397.
Cross, St., Church, I. 36.
Cross Church, Peebles, description, III. 482.
Crosses, I. 9, 10, 17, 20.
Cruggleton Church, description, I. 212.
Culbinsbrough Church, Bressay, I. 157.
Culdees, I. 14, 15, 30.
Cullen Church, description, III. 398, 406.
Culross Abbey, I. 48 ; II, 2, 3, description, 231.
—— Palace, III. 572.
—— Old Parish Church, II. 243.
Cupar-Fife, St. Michael's, description, III. 547.
Cuthbert, St., I. 5, 12.

DALGETY, ST. BRIDGET'S, III. 549.
Dalkeith Church, III. 174, description, 205.
Dalmeny Church, I. 38, 309, 378, description, 298.
—— Early Sculpture at, I. 302.
Dalriada, I. 10.

Dalry, Kirkcudbrightshire, description, III. 551.

David I., I. 29, 30, 38.

Decorated style, I. 52, 53 ; II. 331.

—— examples rare in Scotland, II. 332.

—— Churches in England, III. 1.

Deer Abbey, II. 345, description, 274.

—— Church, description, II. 278.

Deerness, Brough of, I. 68, 101.

Denis, St., I. 8.

Deskford Church, description, III. 406.

Details, late, III. 5.

Devenish, Round Tower, I. 27.

Dioceses, Scottish, I. 29.

Donoughmore, County Meath, II. 210.

Doorways, I. 55.

Dore Abbey, Hertfordshire, II. 186, 381 ; III. 172.

Dornoch Cathedral, II. 3.

Douglas Church, description, II. 520.

Drainie Church, description, III. 553.

Dron Church, description, III. 497.

Drummond, James, R.S.A., I. 2, 323, 426 ; III. 49, 91.

Dryburgh Abbey, I. 38, 47, 48, 49, 57, description, 448 ; tailpiece, 478 ; II. 4, 267, 332, 345, 346, 349, 365.

Dryden, Sir Henry, I. 3, 68, 101, 172, 273, 282, 288, 290, 292.

Duddingston Church, I. 39, 382, description, 333.

Dumbarton Parish and Collegiate Churches, description, III. 423.

Dunbar, Redfriars, description, III. 462.

Dunblane Cathedral, I. 38, 48, 49, 50 ; II. 2, 3, 4, 116, description, 86 ; III. 121, 123, 331.

—— Celtic Cross at, II. 102.

Dundee Church, II. 218, 235 ; III. 116, description, 123.

Dundrennan Abbey, I. 30, 47, 48, 387, description, 388 ; II. 2, 3, 335, 342.

Dunfermline Abbey, I. 38, 309, 439, description, 230 ; II. 3, 92, 147, 486 ; III. 105.

Dunglass Church, III. 1, 3, 167, 173, description, 179.

Dunkeld Cathedral, I. 47, 49, 62 ; II. 3 ; III. 12, 21, 23, 121, 123, 318, 418, 487, description, 23.

Dunning, St. Serf's, description, I. 204 ; III. 500.

Dun Othail, Lewis, I. 81.

Duns Church, description, I. 381.

Dunstaffnage Castle, I. 48.

—— Chapel, description, II. 299.

Durham Cathedral, I. 37 ; II. 92, 345, 471.

Durness Church, description, III. 557.

Dysart Church, II. 235 ; III. 308, 318, description, 437.

Earl's Hall, III. 527.

Eassie Church, description, III. 560.

East Calder Church, description, III. 559.

Ecclesiamagirdle, description, III. 499.

Edinburgh Castle Chapel, I. 29, description, 224.

Edinburgh, St. Giles', description, II. 419.

Edrom Church, I. 314, 316 ; II. 162.

Edward I., I. 51.

Egilsay, Orkney, Church on, I. 26, 27 ; II. 209.

—— Choir, I. 100.

Eilean, Naomh, I. 66.

—— Mor, I. 77, 89.

—— Munde, I. 83.

Elgin Cathedral, I. 47, 48, 49, 387 ; II. 2, 3, 4, 146, 147, 152, 154, 196, 372, 331, description, 121.

—— Greyfriars' Church description, III. 356.

—— St. Giles', II. 157.

Ellon Monument, III. 85.

Ely, II. 92.

England, Church in, I. 12.

English Cathedrals, I. 40, 43.

—— influence, III. 5, 6.

Enhallow, Orkney, I. 116.

Eorrapidh, Lewis, I. 99.

Errol, Earl of, III. 493.

Eyre, Archbishop, II. 195.

Fail Abbey, II. 76.

Falaise, Normandy, II. 30.

Farne Island, I. 12.

Faslane Church, II. 557.

Fearn Abbey, Ross-shire, II. 542.

Ferguson, Mr. J., Duns, I. 382 ; III. 410, 416, 417.

Ferguson, Rev. John, III. 112.

Fernie, Cupar-Fife, III. 547.

Ferrerius, John, I. 416 ; II. 246.

Fetteresso Church, III. 562.

Fillans, St., Church, III. 527.

Finnian, St., School of, I. 5.

First pointed style, I. 39 ; II. 1, 2.

—— Introduced from England, II. 3.

—— in Scotland, I. 46.

—— Details of, II. 4.

Flamboyant style, I. 2, 57, 58.

—— tracery, III. 6.

Flannain Isles, I. 77.

Font at Birnie, St. Brandon's, I. 219.

—— Forgandenny, III. 502.

—— Fortrose, II. 401.

—— Foulis Easter, III. 196.

—— Gogar, II. 306.

—— Herdmanston, I. 384.

—— Inverkeithing, II. 549.

—— Isle, the, II. 298.

—— Kinkell, III. 385.

—— Meigle, III. 517.

—— Muckersey, III. 502.

—— Newbottle, II. 258.

—— Restennet, I. 185.

—— Selkirk, III. 529.

—— Stenton, III. 611.

—— Strathbroc, I. 345.

—— Whithorn, II. 485.

Fordel Church, description, III. 565.

Fordoun, St. Palladius, description, III. 468.

Forgandenny Church, description, III. 500.

Fortrose Cathedral, I. 57 ; II. 331, description, 394.

Fortune, Mr. G., architect, III. 410.

Foulis, Easter Church, description, III. 189.

France, architecture in, I. 40, 42, 43, 492.

Franciscans, Haddington, II. 492.

French influence, III. 5, 6.

Fullar, John, III. 111.

GALLOWAY, CATHEDRAL OF, II. 3.

—— A church in, II. 378.

—— William, architect, I. 178, 185, 213, 297, 383 ; II. 76, 80, 81, 297, 482, 486 ; III. 356, 372, 377, 551, 625.

Galloway, Alex., III. 358, 385, 386.

Gallowhead, I. 80.

Gamrie Church, description, III. 567.

Garvald Church, description, III. 567.

Germany, I. 35.

Gibbs, Wm., architect, I. 426.

Giles', St., Edinburgh, I. 49, 51, 57, 60, 62 ; II. 331, 457, 460, 466, 504, description, 419 ; III. 130, 295, 324.

Giric, King, I. 15.

Gladsmuir Church, description, III. 569.

Glasgow, Bishop of, I. 29.

—— Tron Steeple, description, III. 571.

—— Cathedral, I. 47, 48, 49, 50, 57, 58 ; II. 2, 3, 4, 125, 186, 324, 331, 379, 382, 520, description, 160 ; III. 4, 6, 21, 159, 172, 174, 175, 179.

—— High Kirk, II. 378.

—— College, III. 206.

—— Tolbooth, III. 295.

Glenluce Abbey, II. 379, description, III. 132.

Gloucester Cathedral, I. 401.

Gogar Church Font, description, II. 306.

Gothic architecture in Scotland, I. 2.

Grandtully Church, description, III. 571.

Greenlaw Church, description, III. 574.

Grose, Capt., I. 444, 446 ; II. 76, 80, 171, 204, 391, 393 ; III. 223, 343, 393, 482, 485.

Gullane, St. Andrews, I. 339.

HADDINGTON, ST. MARTIN'S, description, I. 362.

—— Priory, III. 264.

—— Nunnery, II. 492.

—— St. Mary's Parish Church, II. 445 description, 491 ; III. 1, 234.

Haddow's Hole Church (St. Giles') II. 454.

Hagnaston Church, Derbyshire, I. 306.

Halcro Chapel, South Ronaldshay, I. 105.

Halkerston, John, III. 121.

Hassendean, I. 378.

Hay, Rev. R. A., III. 151.

Head of Holland, Church at, I. 105.
Helen's, St., Church, I. 314, 366, description, 323.
Henry VII.'s Chapel, III. 6, 175.
Heraldic Panel, Prestonpans Church, description, III. 602.
Herdmanston Font, description, I. 384.
Heriot Parish, III. 218.
Hermiston House, III. 251.
Hermits' cells, I. 73.
Hexham, I. 12 ; II. 6, 345.
Holy Cross Church, Lewis, I. 83.
Holyrood Abbey, I. 30, 38, 47, 48, 371, 416 ; II. 2, 3, 4, 330, 332, description, 53 ; III. 251, 269, 363, 373.
Honeyman, John, architect, II. 160, 161, 165, 168, 169, 171, 198.
Horndene, III. 218.
Houston Church, description, III. 527.
Howmore, South Uist, I. 70.
Hunter, Blair, F. C., II. 402.
Hutton Collection, I. 180 ; III. 180, 188, 205, 496.

Iffley Church, I. 317.
Inchaffray Abbey, III. 486, 489, description, 502.
Inchcolm Abbey, I. 29, 48 ; II. 2, 92, description, 307 ; III. 29.
—— Oratory, I. 24 ; II. 310.
Inchkenneth, Ulva, I. 98, 165.
—— Mull, I. 165.
Inchmahome, I. 48 ; II. 3, description, 112.
Innerpeffray Collegiate Church, description, III. 506.
Insch Church, description, III. 575.
Inverboyndie Church, III. 545.
Invergowrie Church, description, III. 454.
Inverkeithing Church, II. 507 ; description, 547.
Inverness Fort, I. 417.
Iona, I. 10, 11, 14.
—— Cathedral, I. 49, 62 ; III. 29, 130, 363, 370, 381, 389, description, 47.
—— Carved Slabs, I. 23.
—— St. Oran's Chapel, I. 220.
—— the Nunnery, description, I. 421.
Irish influence, I. 2, 9.

Irish style of building, I. 8, 9.
—— Round Towers, I. 26, 27, 28.
Islands, Churches on, I. 8.
—— Western, Architecture of, I. 65, 80.
Isle, the, Chapel on, description, II. 297.

Jarrow, I. 12, 13.
Jedburgh Abbey, I. 38, 49, 309, 387, description, 398 ; II. 2, 75, 162, 332, 345.
Jervise, Andrew, II. 282, 283 ; III. 399, 404, 469.
John Baptist, Church of, Lewis, I. 95.
John, St., Kirk of, Unst, I. 148.

Keith Church, description, III. 465.
Kelso Abbey, I. 38, 39, 387, description, 347 ; II. 2, 75, 345, 520.
Kemback Church, description, III. 576.
Kenmore Aisle, III. 551.
Kentigern, St., I. 11.
Kerr, Henry F., architect, II. 492.
Kevin, St., cell of, I. 9.
Kiels, Knapdale, I. 84.
Kilallan (see St. Fillans).
Kilbar, Barra, I. 71, 72.
Kilbride, Knapdale, I. 98.
Kilchenich, Tiree, I. 88.
Kilchenzie, Kintyre, I. 93.
Kilchieran, Islay, I. 96.
Kilchoman Cross, I. 22.
Kilchouslan, Kintyre, I. 92.
Kilconquhar Church, description, III. 441.
Kildalton, Islay, I. 96.
Kilfillan (see St. Fillans).
Killean, Kintyre, I. 98.
Kilmahew, Kirkton of, description, III. 426.
Kilmalcolm Church, description, III. 527, 529.
Kilmaurs, Monument at, III. 577.
Kilmory, Knapdale, I. 85.
Kilmuir, Skye, I. 84.
Kilmun Collegiate Church, description, III. 390.
Kilnaughton, Islay, I. 96.
Kilneave, Islay, I. 96.
Kilrenny Church, description, III. 442.

Kilrimont, I. 11.
Kilwinning Abbey, II. 2, 3, 4, 332, description, 73 ; III. 425.
Kineddar Church, II. 121 ; III. 553.
Kinfauns Church, description, III. 513.
King's College, Aberdeen, I. 62 ; II. 285, 445, 504 ; description, III. 287.
—— Cambridge, II. 393.
Kinkell Church, Aberdeenshire, description, III. 383, 386, 406.
—— St. Bean's, description, III. 579.
Kinloss Abbey, I. 30, 289, description, 416 ; II. 121, 232, 246, 345, 402.
—— Abbot's House, II. 417, 421.
Kinneil Church, description, III. 578.
Kinnoul Church, description, III. 580.
Kinross, J., architect, II. 6, 23 ; III. 300.
Kintore, Sacrament House, III. 386.
Kintyre, I. 3, 10, 82.
Kirkaby, Westray, Shetland, I. 147.
Kirkapoll, Tiree, I. 87.
Kirkbryde Church, description, III. 431.
Kirkham Priory, I. 317.
Kirkheugh, St. Mary's, II. 29.
Kirkliston Church, description, I. 366.
Kirkmadrine, Crosses at, I. 4.
Kirkmaiden, description, I. 383.
Kirkoswald Church, description, III. 582.
Kirkton of Kilmahew, description, III. 426.
Kirkwall, St. Magnus' Cathedral, I. 38, 48, 50, 417, description, 259 ; II. 3, 4.
—— St. Ola, I. 109.

LADYKIRK, III. 3, 5, 173, 208, 310, 349, 446, description, 218.
Laggan, Mull, I. 98.
Laing, Alexander, II. 218, 219, 220.
—— Dr. David, II. 429 ; III. 7, 103, 188, 251, 253, 258, 475.
Lamington Church, description, I. 376 ; II. 37.
Lanark Church, I. 50 ; description, II. 266.
Lancet windows, II. 4.
Lasswade Church, description, I. 471 ; III. 214.

Late or third pointed style, I. 58.
—— in Scotland, I. 60 ; III. 1, 2.
Lauder Church, description, III. 582.
Lees, Very Rev. Dr. J. Cameron, III. 7, 23, 25.
Leeswalt Church, description, III. 585.
Legerwood Church, I. 314, 382, description, 320.
Leonard's, St., St. Andrews, description, III. 448.
Lerida Cathedral, Spain, II. 37.
Leuchars Church, I. 38, 378, description, 309.
Lewis, Butt of, I. 75.
Lincluden College, I. 57 ; II. 120, 333, 379, 381, 535, description, 383 ; III. 1, 6, 174.
Lincoln Cathedral, I. 45, 47 ; II. 3, 121.
Lindisfarne, I. 11 ; II. 354.
Lindores Abbey, II. 4, 294, description, 217 ; III. 123.
Linlithgow Church, I. 57 ; II. 445, 504, description, 455 ; III. 3, 82, 116, 117, 121, 174, 208, 315, 324, 456.
—— Palace, III. 121.
Linton Church, Roxburghshire, I. 318, description, 378.
Linton Chapel, Shapinsay, I. 122.
Lismore Cathedral, description, II. 263.
Loch Tay Monastery, III. 29.
Logierait Cross, I. 18.
Lombardy, I. 35.
Lonmay Church, description, III. 587.
Loudoun Church, description, III. 587.
Luffness Monastery, description, II. 288.
Lundie, St. Lawrence, description, I. 382.
Lybster, Caithness, I. 162.
Lyne Church, description, III. 589.

MACALPINE, KENNETH, I. 14.
Macdonald, W. Rae, III. 45, 198, 261, 525.
Maces of Universities, III. 203.
Mackenzie, A. M., architect, III. 236, 359.
Mackison, William, architect, II. 227.
M'Lean's Cross, Iona, I. 21.
Macpherson, Dr. Norman, III. 289, 371.

Macpherson, Archibald, architect, III. 453.

Madoe's Cross, I. 17.

Maelrubba, St., Skye, Font, description, III. 381.

Magnus', St., Cathedral, Kirkwall (*see* Kirkwall).

Mains Church, description, III. 455.

Maison Dieu, Brechin, description, II. 215.

Margaret, Queen, I. 15, 28, 29.

Marischal College, Aberdeen, III. 359.

Markinch Church, description, I. 193.

Martin, III. 377.

Martin's, St., Haddington, description, I. 362.

—— St., Cross, Iona, I. 21.

Martine's *Reliquiæ Divi Andreæ*, II. 19, 23, 24, 27, 29.

Mary's, St., Lybster, I. 93, 94.

—— Ratho, description, I. 371.

—— Rutherglen, description, I. 372.

Maryton Church, description, III. 456.

Mason's contract, St. Giles', II. 420.

Matheson, Robert, architect, I. 262.

Mavisbank House, II. 258.

May, Isle of, III. 599.

Maybole Collegiate Church, description, III. 338.

Meal, Colvidale, Unst, I. 148.

Medan's, St., Cave, I. 5.

Meigle Font, III. 517.

Melrose Abbey, I. 30, 47, 49, 51, 52, 55, 58, 62, 451 ; II. 19, 160, 251, 277, 331, 332, 342, 438, description, 344.

—— Resemblance of details to York, II. 333 ; III. 1, 3, 6, 167, 174, 456, 627.

—— Old, I. 11.

Merlioun, Walter, III. 106, 121.

Methven Church, III. 397, description, 519.

Michael's, St., Barra, I. 95.

Michael Kirk, description, III. 553.

Mid-Calder Church, description, III. 279.

—— Bond concerning, III. 279.

Middle Ages, art of, I. 2.

Middleton Church, I. 317.

Middle pointed style, characteristics, I. 53.

Middle pointed style in Scotland I. 55 ; II. 331 ; III. 1.

Miller, Rev. Alex., III. 557.

—— A. H., III. 619.

Mirin's, St., Chapel, III 3, 9 ; description, 23.

Moffat, St. Cuthbert's, description, III. 433.

Moluac, St., Raasay, I. 98.

—— Teampull, Lewis, I. 99.

—— Mortlach, description, III. 408.

—— Alyth, description, III. 487.

Monans, St., III. 10, 445.

Monasteries established, I. 31.

—— in Scotland, proportions, I. 49.

Moncrieff Chapel, description, III. 521.

Monkton Church, description, II. 285.

Monkwearmouth, I. 12, 13.

Monuments—

Abbey St. Bathans, III. 411.

Abdie, II. 296.

Abercorn Church, I. 346.

Aberdalgie, II. 551.

Aberdeen, St. Machar's, III. 83, 84, 85, 86, 88.

—— St. Nicholas', I. 431.

Aberdour, III. 536.

Airth, I. 469.

Ardchattan, III. 390.

Balmerino, II. 517.

Bathgate, I. 475.

Beauly, II. 249.

Borthwick Church, III. 216.

Bothwell, II. 536.

Cambuskenneth, II. 231.

Carnwath Church, III. 349.

Castle Semple Church, III. 354.

Coldingham, I. 446.

Corstorphine Church, III. 261.

Coupar Abbey, III. 496.

Creich, II. 556.

Crichton Church, III. 247.

Cullen Church, III. 401.

Culross Parish Church, II. 245.

Cupar, III. 549.

Dalgety, III. 549.

Dalkeith, III. 209.

Deer Church, II. 278.

Douglas, II. 520.

Dunblane, II. 112.

Monuments—*continued*.
Dundrennan Abbey, I. 395, 398.
Dunfermline Abbey, I. 258.
Dunkeld Cathedral, III. 32, 43, 45.
Durness Church, III. 559.
Edinburgh, St. Giles', II. 449.
Elgin Cathedral, II. 142.
Ellon, III. 85.
Errol, Earl of, III. 493.
Fearn, II. 546.
Fortrose Cathedral, II. 399.
Glasgow Cathedral, II. 203.
Glencairn, Kilmaurs, III. 577.
Haddington, II. 498.

Holyrood, II. 54.
Houston Church, III. 527.
Inchkenneth, I. 171.
Inchmahome, II. 119.
Iona, I. 426 ; III. 74.
Keith Church, III. 466.
Kennedy, Ballantrae, III. 577.
Kilmaurs, III. 577.
Kilrenny Church, III. 442.
Kinfauns, III. 513.
Kinnoul, III. 580.
Kirkwall Cathedral, I. 290.
Lasswade Church, I. 474.
Leswalt, III. 585.
Lindores, II. 225.
Maryton, III. 456.
Maybole, III. 341.
M'Lellan, Kirkcudbright, III. 578.
Montgomerie, Largs, III. 620.
Mortlach, III. 409.
Newbottle, II. 251.
Oransay, III. 376.
Ormiston, III. 596.
Paisley Abbey, III. 25.
Renfrew Church, III. 525.
Rosslyn, III. 179.
Rothesay Abbey, III. 418.
Rowdil, III. 367.
St. Andrews, St. Leonard's, III. 450.
—— St. Salvator's, III. 203.
St. Giles', Edinburgh, II. 441 ; III. 597.
St. Mirren's Chapel, III. 25.
Sanquhar Church, III. 436.
Selkirk, III. 530.

Monuments—*continued*.
Seton Church, III. 228, 234, 620.
Stirling Church, III. 324, 328.
Weem, III. 620.
Yester Church, III. 312.
Monymusk, I. 30 ; description, 215.
Morham Church, description, III. 591.
Morris, James A., II. 405.
Mortlach, III. 75, 238; description, 408.
Muckersey Font, III. 502.
Mugstot, Skye, I. 69.
Muir, T. S., I. 2, 26, 65, 195, 214, 316, 323 ; II. 215, 247, 283, 299, 395, 396, 449, 479 ; III. 247, 263, 368, 370, 381, 418, 455, 470, 487, 533.
Murray, Regent, Monument, III. 597.
Muthill Church, description, I. 196.

NATTES, J. CLAUDE, I. 196.
Neal's *Ecclesiological Notes*, II. 538, 540.
Ness, North Yell, I. 151.
Netherlands, I. 2 ; III. 264.
Nevay Church, description, III. 560.
New Abbey, I. 50 ; II. 332, description, 334.
Newbattle Abbey, I. 30 ; II. 75, 332, 345, 346, description, 251.
Newlands Church, description, III. 479.
Newtown, Benbecula, I. 83.
Nicholas', St., Aberdeen, I. 39 ; description, 426.
Nicholas', St., Strathbroc, description, I. 342.
Niddisdale, II. 378.
Nigg Church, description, III. 592.
Ninian, St., I. 3.
—— Sanda, I. 97.
Norham Castle, III. 218.
Norman architecture, I. 1, 28.
—— in Scotland, I. 191.
Norman immigrants, I. 30.
—— influence, I. 79, 84.
—— piers, II. 4.
—— style, I. 35.
—— —— in Scotland, I. 38, 314.
Norsemen, I. 14.
North Berwick, Convent, III. 441.
Northumbria, Church in, I. 11, 12.
Noss, Kirk of Bressay, I. 146.
Nunnery, Iona, description, I. 421.

OLA'S, ST., KIRKWALL, I. 109.
Old Dailly Church, description, III. 394.
Old Girthon Church, description, III. 469.
Oldhamstocks Church, description, III. 594.
Olrig Castle, Caithness, I. 99.
Oran's, St., Iona, I. 220.
Oransay Cross, I. 22.
—— Priory, description, III. 372.
Oratories, Irish, I. 8.
"Orders" in architecture, I. 33.
Orkney, I. 3.
—— Cathedral, II. 3.
Orkney and Shetland, churches in, I. 101.
—— characteristics, I. 159.
—— dates, I. 162.
—— monuments, I. 160.
—— proportions, I. 161.
Ormiston Church, III. 596.
Ornament, I. 35.
Orphir, Church, Orkney, I. 141.
Oswald's, St., Oxtall, I. 47.
Oudenarde, Belgium, I. 447.
Oxenham Church, I. 378.
Oxford Cathedral, I. 403.
Oxtall, St. Oswald's, I. 47.

PABBA, HARRIS, I. 84.
Painting in churches, I. 417 ; II. 123 ; III. 196, 217, 509, 511.
Paisley Abbey, I. 47, 62 ; II. 75, 286, 332, 378, 379, 393, 402, 501 ; III. 1, 40, 43, 47, 130, 328, 394, 397, 488, description, 7.
Palladius, St., I. 5.
—— Church, Fordoun, description, III. 468.
Papa, Westray, I. 106.
Parish churches, II. 5.
Parochial divisions, I. 31.
Parwick Church, Derbyshire, I. 306.
Patrick, St., I. 5.
Peebles, Cross Church, description, III. 482.
—— St. Andrew's, description, III. 485.
Pencaitland Church, description, II. 304.
Pennant's Tours, II. 392, 394 ; III. 376, 377, 380, 381.
Pennygowan, Mull, I. 98.

Periods of architecture, I. 2.
Perpendicular style, I. 2, 57, 58 ; III. 350, 450.
Pert Church, description, III. 458.
Perth, Blackfriars, III. 46, 104, 105.
—— St. John the Baptist's, description, III. 105.
—— Carmelites, III. 104, 105.
—— Carthusians, III. 104, 123.
—— Greyfriars, III. 104.
Peterhead, St. Peter's, I. 371.
Petrie, Dr., I. 3, 26.
Pictish Church, III. 29.
Piers, I. 55.
—— first-pointed, II. 4.
Pillar stones, I. 9.
Pinches, Frederick, II. 378.
Pinkie House, III. 572.
Pittenweem Priory, III. 547 ; description, 599.
Pluscardine Priory, I. 58 ; II. 2, 3, 4, 153, 349, description, 146.
Pointed arch, I. 79.
—— in Scotland, II. 2.
—— style, I. 40 ; II. 2, 3.
Polwarth Church, III. 601.
Porches, III. 6.
Pratt, Rev. Dr., III. 568.
Pre-Norman Churches, I. 13, 186.
Preston Church, Berwickshire, description, III. 416.
Prestonkirk Church, description, II. 271.
Prestonpans Church, III. 602.
Prestwick Church, II. 286.
—— de Burgo, II. 286.
—— Monachorum, II. 286.
—— St. Nicholas', description, II. 285.
Provence, III. 4.

QUEEN MARY OF GUELDRES, III. 89, 104, 121.
Queensferry, Carmelites' Church, III. 3, 147, 173, 310, 542 ; description, 296.

RAMSAY, JOHN, II. 253, 255.
Rathan Church, description, III. 604.
Ratho, St. Mary's, description, I. 371.
"Raths," Irish, I. 6.
Rattray, St. Mary's, II. 292.

Redfriars' Monastery, Luffness, II. 288.
Reeves, Dr., I. 3.
Reformation, architecture after, III. 534.
Regulus', St., St Andrews, I. 13, 28 ; description, 185.
Reilig Oran, I. 28.
Renfrew Church, description, III. 525.
Restalrig Collegiate Church, I. 471 ; description, III. 475.
Restennet Priory, I. 13, 48, description, 178 ; III. 454.
Restoration of churches in fifteenth century, II. 331.
Ribs, ornamented, III. 3.
Richard II., I. 51, 57.
Rievalle, II. 345.
Rievaux Abbey, I. 47.
Ripon, I. 12.
Robb's *Guide to Haddington*, II. 492, 504.
Robert I., I. 51, 55, 57.
Roberts, David, R.A., III. 165.
Robertson, T. S., architect, I. 181, 382 ; II. 42, 48, 49, 50, 51, 273, 517 ; III. 11, 21, 189, 191, 193, 236, 414, 456, 458, 459, 517, 544, 576, 585.
—— Dr. Joseph, I. 185.
Roman Church, I. 12, 14, 15, 65.
—— Masonry, I. 32.
Romanesque architecture, I. 1, 28, 32, 35.
—— abandoned, II. 1.
Romsey Abbey, I. 401 ; III. 172.
Ronan's, St., I. 73, 426.
Rosemarkie, II. 394, 395.
Ross, Alexander, architect, III. 363.
Ross, Cathedral of, II. 331.
Rossie, Priory Cross at, I. 19.
Rosslyn Church, II. 186, 199 ; III. 5, 6, 208 ; description, 149.
Rosyth Church, description, III. 444.
Rothesay Castle Chapel, II. 517.
—— St. Mary's Abbey, description, III. 418.
Round arch in Scotland, II. 2.
—— churches, I. 145.
Rowdil, St. Clement's, description, III. 363.
Royal Domain, France, I. 40.

Royal Scottish Academy, III. 413.
Rutherglen, St. Mary's, description, I. 372.
Ruthwell Cross, III. 623.

SACRAMENT HOUSES—
Airlie Church, III. 452.
Auchindoir Church, II. 283.
Cullen Church, III. 402.
Deskford Church, III. 406.
Kinfauns Church, III. 514.
Kinkell Church, III. 384.
Kintore Church, III. 386.
Lundie, I. 383.
Pluscardine Priory, II. 156.
Temple Church, II. 489.
Salisbury Cathedral, I. 41, 44 ; II. 3, 186.
Salvator's, St., St. Andrews, I. 471.
Sanquhar Church, description, III. 434.
Saxon influence, I. 1.
Schultz, R. Weir, architect, III. 431, 435, 587.
Scone Abbey, I. 29, 47 ; III. 29, 105, 106.
Scott, Sir Walter's, grave, I. 464.
—— Sir G. Gilbert, II. 172.
Sculptured stones, I. 3, 15, 16.
—— from Forteviot, III. 623.
Sculptures, symbolic, I. 10.
Selkirk Church, description, III. 529.
Semple, David, III. 9, 26.
Seton Church, II. 501 ; III. 3, 173, 174, 208, description, 223.
Seton, Chancellor, tomb of, III. 551.
Seven Hunters, I. 77.
Sharp's *Cistercian Architecture*, II. 241, 242.
Shetland, I. 3.
—— Churches in, I. 101, 145.
Sixteenth and seventeenth century churches, III. 534.
Skeabost, Skye, I. 68.
Skellig, Mhichel, I. 7.
Skipness, St. Columba, I. 48 ; II. 300.
Slabs, cross-bearing, I. 9, 15, 17.
Slezer (Culross), II. 233, 234, 235.
Small, J. W., architect, III. 326.
Smailholm Church, description, I. 378.
Smith, Dr. John, II. 378.

Southannan Castle and Church, description, III. 607.
Spires, with open work, I. 62.
Spottiswoode, Archbishop, II. 19, 29, 107.
Spynie Church, II. 121, 140 ; III. 553.
Stirling Parish Church, III. 3, 116, 208 ; description, 315.
—— Castle, III. 6, 121, 318.
Stobo Church, I. 39 ; description, 329.
Stenton Church, description, III. 609.
Stobhall, III. 511.
Stokes, Miss, I. 3 ; II. 209.
Stoney, Oxfordshire, I. 317.
Stone roofs, II. 333 ; III. 3, 4.
Stow Church, III. 218 ; description, 611.
Strathbroc, St. Nicholas', description, I. 342.
Straiton Church, description, III. 396.
Subordination of arches, &c., I. 35.
Suger, Abbé, I. 40.
Sweetheart Abbey, I. 49, 57, 395 ; II. 300, 332, description, 334.
Swendro, Rousay, I. 108.
Symbols, I. 16.
St. Abb's Chapel, I. 437.
St. Adamnan, I. 11 ; III. 387.
—— Burntisland, II. 269.
St. Aidan, I. 11.
St. Alban's Abbey, II. 73, 92.
St. Andrews, Blackfriars', III. 445.
—— Cathedral and Priory, I. 15, 30, 38, 47, 49 ; II. xiii, 2, 3, 4, 53, 86, 125, 256, 331, 342, 378, 379, description, 5 ; III. 72, 114, 469.
—— Franciscans, III. 199.
—— Holy Trinity, description, III. 451.
—— St. Leonard's, description, III. 448.
—— St. Mary's, Kirkheugh, II. 29.
—— Towers, II. 3.
St. Andrew's, Peebles, III. 485.
—— Gullane, I. 339.
St. Anthony's Chapel, description, III. 145.
St. Augustine, I. 12.
St. Aula, Gress, Lewis, I. 83.
St. Bathans, Abbey, description, III. 410.
St. Bean's, II. 86.
St. Blane's, Bute, I. 292 ; II. 86 ; III. 625.

St. Bothan's, Yester, description, III. 309.
St. Brandan, Boyndie, description, III. 545.
St. Brandon's, Birnie, I. 218.
St. Brendan, I. 67.
St. Bride's Collegiate Church, Bothwell, description, II. 531.
St. Bridget's or St. Bride's, Douglas, description, II. 520.
—— Dalgety, III. 549.
St. Carmaig, Eilean Mor, I. 90.
—— Knapdale, I. 84.
St. Catan's, Kintyre, I. 95.
St. Cavan's, Fetteresso, description, III. 562.
St. Clement's, Rowdil, description, III. 363.
St. Colmanel of Butyle, description, II. 300 ; 344.
St. Columba (see Columba).
St. Comgall, I. 5.
St. Cuthbert, I. 5, 12.
St. Cuthbert's, East Calder, III. 559.
—— Edinburgh, Pulpit in, III. 562.
—— Monkton, II. 285.
St. Denis, I. 40.
St. Duthus' Church, Tain, description, II. 537.
St. Fillan's, III. 527.
St. Giles', Edinburgh, I. 49, 51, 57, 60, 62 ; II. 331, 457, 460, 466, 504 ; description, 419 ; III. 130, 295, 324.
—— Divisions of, II. 454.
—— mason's contract at, II. 420.
—— Elgin, II. 157.
St. Helen's Church, I. 314, 366 ; description, 323.
St. John's, Gamrie, III. 567.
—— Dalry, description, III. 551.
St. John Baptist, Lewis, I. 95.
St. John, Unst, I. 148.
—— Baptist, Perth, description, III. 104.
St. Kentigern, I. 11.
—— Lanark, description, II. 266.
St. Kevin, Cell of, I. 9.
St. Leonard's, St. Andrews, II. 23 ; description, III. 448.
St. Machar's Cathedral, Aberdeen, III. 535 ; description, 75.

St. Madoe's Cross, I. 17.
St. Maelrubba, Skye, III. 381.
St. Magnus' Cathedral, Kirkwall, I. 17 ; description, 259 ; II. 3.
St. Magridin's, Abdie, description, II. 293.
St. Mahutus, Wigton, III. 533.
St. Martin's, Haddington, description, I. 362 ; II. 491.
—— Cross, Iona, I. 21.
St. Mary's, Kirkheugh, St. Andrews, II. 29.
—— Auchterhouse, III. 541.
—— Grantully, III. 571.
—— Haddington, II. 445 ; description, 491.
—— Lybster, I. 93, 94.
—— Ratho, description, I. 371.
—— Rattray, II. 292.
—— Rothesay, description, III. 418.
—— Rutherglen, description, I. 372.
—— Whitekirk, III. 3, 6, 173, description, 269.
St. Medan's Cave, I. 5.
St. Michael's Church, Linlithgow, description, II. 455, 445, 504.
St. Michael's, Barra, I. 95.
—— Cupar-Fife, description, III. 547.
St. Mirren's, Paisley, description, III. 25.
St. Moloc, Alyth, description III. 487.
—— Mortlach, description, III. 408.
St. Moluac, Raasay, I. 98.
St. Moluach, Lewis, I. 99.
St. Monan's, description, II. 471 ; III. 10.
St. Mungo's Cathedral, Glasgow, I. 47, 48, 49, 50, 57, 58 ; II. 2, 3, 4, 125, 186, 324, 331, 379, 382, 520 ; description, 160 ; III. 4, 6, 21, 159, 172, 174, 175, 179.
—— Borthwick, III. 214.
—— Church, Culross, II. 232.
St. Nicholas', Aberdeen, I. 39 ; description, 426.
—— Newcastle, II. 445.
—— Prestwick, description, II. 285.
—— Strathbroc, description, I. 342.
St. Ninian, I. 3.
—— Sanda, I. 97.

St. Ninian's on "The Isle," II. 297.
St. Ola, Kirkwall, I. 109.
St. Oran, Iona, I. 220.
St. Oswald, Oxstall, I. 47.
St. Palladius', I. 5 ; III. 468.
St. Peter's, Peterhead, I. 371.
St. Regulus', St. Andrews, I. 13, 28 ; description, 185.
St. Ronan, I. 73.
St. Salvator's, St. Andrews, I. 471 ; III. 175 ; description, 199.
St. Serf's, Dunning, description, I. 204.
St. Stephen's, St. Albans, II. 73.
St. Thenaw's, Glasgow, III. 571.
St. Tredwell's, I. 106.
St. Vigean's, Cross of, I. 20.
—— Church, III. 459.

TAIN, ST. DUTHUS', description, II. 537.
Talla Castle, II. 113, 119.
Tapestry, III. 333.
Teampull, Chalumchille, I. 89.
—— Pheadair, Lewis, I. 83.
—— Rona, I. 73, 74.
—— Sula Sgeir, I. 75, 76.
—— Na-Trianaide, I. 81.
Temple Church, II. 486.
Terregles Church, description, III. 615.
Third or late pointed style, II. 332.
Thirlstane Castle, III. 584.
Thomas, Capt., I. 82.
Throndhjeim Cathedral, I. 273, 280.
Tigh Beannachadh, I. 76, 77, 78, 80.
Tiles, encaustic, II. 262.
Toehead, Harris, I. 83.
Tolbooth Church, St. Giles', Edinburgh, II. 454.
Torphichen Church, II. 235 ; III. 147, 308, 318 ; description, 139.
Towers, Central, II. 3.
—— late, III. 6.
Transition style, I. 387 ; II. 2.
—— from Celtic to Norman, I. 174.
Tredwell's, St., Chapel, I. 106.
Triforium omitted, II. 4.
Trinity College Church, Edinburgh, I. 57, 60 ; II. 426, 478 ; III. 2, 4, 6, 175 ; description, 89, 596.
Trinity, Holy, St. Andrews, description, III. 451.

Trinity Hospital, III. 89, 100, 121.
Tron Steeple, Glasgow, III. 571.
Trophime, St., Arles, I. 33.
Trumpan, Skye, I. 84.
Tudor buildings, III. 175.
Tullibardine Church, description, III. 330.
Tungland Abbey, description, II. 301.
Turgot, I. 29 ; II. 6.
Turriff Church, description, III. 615.
Tynninghame Church, I. 325, description, 326 ; II. 234 ; III. 269.

UPHALL CHURCH, I. 39 ; description, 342.
Upsalla Cathedral, I. 273, 280.
Upsetlington Church, III. 218.
Urquhart Priory, I. 30 ; II. 121, 146.
Uya Church, Shetland, I. 149.

VAULTS, BARREL, I. 33 ; II. 333 ; III. 2.
—— groined, I. 34 ; III. 4.
—— late, I. 58.
—— pointed, I. 40 ; II. 2.
—— in England, III. 3.
—— in Scottish Castles, III. 5.
Vigean's, St., Church, description, III. 459.
—— Cross of, I. 20.

WALKER, J. Russell, architect, III. 381.
Walker, R. C., III. 127, 236.
Walston Church, III. 617.
Wast-town Church, description, III. 522.

Watson, Robt., architect, II. 172, 173, 184.
Watt, J. C., architect, III. 295.
Wattle construction, I. 6.
Wedale Church, III. 612.
Weem Church, description, III. 619.
Wenlock Abbey, I. 47 ; III. 7.
Westness Chapel, I. 108.
Westray, Orkney, I. 124.
Whitekirk, St. Mary's, I. 326 ; III. 3, 6, 173 ; description, 269.
—— Tithe Barn, III. 275.
Whithorn, crosses at, I. 4.
—— Priory, I. 213, 306 ; II. 379, 542 ; description, 479.
Wigton Church, description, III. 533.
Wilfred, St., I. 12.
William the Lion, I. 38.
Wilson, Sir Daniel, I. 2.
Winchester Cathedral, I. 61 ; II. 373 ; III. 3.
Windows, late, III. 2, 3.
—— elliptical, III. 5.
Wooden roofs, I. 60 ; II. 2.
Wyntoun House, II. 306.
Wyntown's *Chronykill*, II. 8, 19, 27.
Wyre, Orkney, I. 113.

YESTER, ST. BOTHAN'S, description, III. 309.
—— Monument in, III. 312.
—— Parish Church, description, III. 622.
York Cathedral, II. 3, 333, 363, 381.

F I N I S.